Thunder Go North

The Hunt for Sir Francis Drake's Fair and Good Bay

MELISSA DARBY

THE UNIVERSITY OF UTAH PRESS
Salt Lake City

The Defiance House Man colophon is a registered trademark
of The University of Utah Press. It is based on a four-foot-tall
Ancient Puebloan pictograph (late PIII) near Glen Canyon, Utah.

LIBRARY OF CONGRESS CATALOGING-IN-PUBLICATION DATA

Names: Darby, Melissa C., author.
Title: Thunder go north : the hunt for Drake's fair and good bay / Melissa C.
   Darby.
Description: Salt Lake City : The University of Utah Press, [2019] | Includes
   bibliographical references and index. |
Identifiers: LCCN 2019008129 (print) | LCCN 2019010503 (ebook) | ISBN
   9781607817260 () | ISBN 9781607817253 (pbk. : alk. paper)
Subjects: LCSH: Drake, Francis, approximately 1540–1596—Travel—Northwest
   Coast of North America. | Northwest Coast of North America—Discovery and
   exploration—British.
Classification: LCC F851.5 (ebook) | LCC F851.5 .D35 2019 (print) | DDC
   942.05/5092—dc23
LC record available at https://lccn.loc.gov/2019008129

Errata and further information on this and other titles available online
at UofUpress.com

Printed and bound in the United States of America.

Cover photo: Earliest known portrait of Francis Drake, ca. 1576. This portrait,
identified by art historian Angus Haldane in 2014 as Drake, was painted shortly
before the voyage of circumnavigation. Courtesy Angus Haldane Fine Art.

For Denny and Kathleen

Contents

List of Figures   ix

A Note on the Text   xi

Acknowledgments   xiii

1. The Problem   1

2. The Historiography of the Vexed Question   10

3. Mind the Gap   18

4. The Beginnings   32

5. Afar the Seas Were Blue and White   39

6. Either Here or There   70

7. The Great Discoveries   79

8. The California Juggernaut   87

9. Henry Wagner Huffs and Puffs and the British
   Blow Him Down   107

10. The Historian on the Hill   115

11. Behind the Scenes   132

12. The Authentication of the Plate of Brass   140

13. Investigations and Resolutions   148

14. The Commission and the Commemoration of
    Drake's Voyage   169

15. The People at the Landing   182

16. An Ethnographic Assessment for an Oregon Landing   192

17. Linguistic Analysis   214

18. Thunder and Lightning: Cosmological Correspondences   230

Epilogue   239

Notes   241

Bibliography   293

Index   305

Figures

3.1.   Photograph of the first page of BL Harley Manuscript 280, folio 83, recto.   19

3.2.   The west coast of the United States and the latitudes in question, showing "The Gap" of territory.   28

5.1.   *Golden Hind at Sea*, etching by Harold Wyllie.   42

5.2.   The *Golden Hind Capturing the Nuestra Señora de la Concepción*.   52

5.3.   Drake's track from Guatulco to the Northwest coast.   60

5.4.   Drake's route on the circumnavigation of the world, 1577–1580.   66

6.1.   Detail vignette from the Drake Broadside map, Jodocus Hondius, ca. 1595.   72

6.2.   Detail from Robert Dudley's manuscript chart of the west coast of America, ca. 1636.   73

6.3.   Topographic map of Whale Cove.   74

7.1.   Zelia Nuttall portrait, 1897.   80

8.1.   Detail of the Van Sype world map brought to light by Zelia Nuttall.   96

10.1.   Herbert E. Bolton and Beryle Shinn holding the Plate of Brass.   116

10.2.   Signature comparisons between L. E. Hammond and George Hammond's signatures.   128

13.1.   Postcard from ca. 1930 showing Drake's Prayer Book Cross, Golden Gate Park, San Francisco.   167

14.1.   Map showing the conjectured locations for Drake's "Bad Bay" on the Oregon coast, and the "Fair Bay" in the San Francisco Bay area.   170

16.1.   Cultural area map of the Oregon coast.   193

16.2.   Native Tolowa men's house, southwest Oregon or northwest California.   201

16.3.   Native Coos basket with beads and shells.   203
16.4.   Depoe Charlie in Native dress.   208
16.5.   Depoe Charlie with a collection of regalia.   209
16.6.   Photograph of Old Blind Kate.   210

Table

17.1.   Word Lists and Translations   215

A Note on the Text

The punctuation and spelling found in original documents and manuscripts have been silently corrected in places to clarify meaning for modern readers. All dates given are Old Style (O.S.), a synonym for the Julian
calendar, corresponding to dates ten days later in the modern calendar
(unless noted).

Acknowledgments

This book was written primarily for the general reader, unacquainted with the Drake landing controversy. But it contains considerable detail, including new historical and ethnographic material that will be of interest to the student and specialist.

I would be remiss if I did not acknowledge at the start my particular debt to archaeologists Christopher Knutson, Jeff La Lande, and R. Lee Lyman for their technical insights, corrections, and suggestions. In particular, the fine proofreading by Chris was invaluable. I owe a debt of gratitude to those who read early drafts, including the sharp-eyed Norm Berberick, and the thoughtful Michael Boeder. I am especially grateful to the three peer reviewers whose comments were important and as a result made this work better.

I would also like to thank United States Senator Jeff Merkley of Oregon who took time out of his busy schedule to read the manuscript. Many thanks to Ralph Falkiner-Nuttall, who graciously provided a photograph of his great aunt, Zelia Nuttall. I am deeply indebted also to Diana Dane Dajani and her niece Elizabeth Baker for providing access to the private papers of George Ezra Dane, Diana's father. The title of chapter five was inspired by the poem "California" by Joaquin Miller.

I appreciate the courtesy and advice of maritime historian Harry Kelsey and the assistance of early modern European historian J. Sears McGee. I appreciate the forthright help with the Harley Manuscript from Heather Wolfe of the Folger Shakespeare Library. I am indebted to my colleagues at Portland State University, including Michele Gamburd and Virginia Butler. My gratitude goes out to John Lyon, University of British Columbia, for his strong work and in-depth analysis of the linguistic material.

I am especially indebted to Mark Campion for sleuthing obscure but important information that added to several lines of inquiry. You are the best. If it were not for Garry Gitzen's works I would not have learned about the twelve-year-old girl who witnessed her father and other men discussing the Plate of Brass hoax. Finally, it was the research and writings of Bob Ward and later Samuel Bawlf that stirred my interest in the theory that Drake was on the Northwest coast.

I appreciate the staff help given me while I was doing research at the British Library, London; the Bayerische Staatsbibliothek, Munich; the Henry E. Huntington Library, San Marino; the Bancroft Library, Berkeley; California Academy of Sciences, San Francisco; the University of Oregon Special Collections and University Archives, Eugene; the North Baker Research Library of the California Historical Society, San Francisco; the Oregon Historical Society, Portland; and the Coos County Museum, Coos Bay, Oregon.

I appreciate the comments and suggestions from Kassandra Ripee, Tribal Historic Preservation Officer of the Coquille Indian Tribe; Jesse Beers, Cultural Director of the Confederated Tribes of Coos, Lower Umpqua, and Siuslaw; and Robert Kentta, Tribal Cultural Resources Director, Confederated Tribes of the Siletz Indians.

Thanks go out to the intrepid crew for their work during the archaeological testing and remote sensing operation at Whale Cove: Jacqueline Cheung, John Craig, Eric Gleason, William E. Kirk, Daniel Martin, Samantha Nemecek, Toyin Quichocho, Doug Scott, Tom Wilson, and Mark Belda. Special thanks to Richard Johnson and Bryce Buchannan for their hospitality.

CHAPTER ONE

The Problem

THE *GOLDEN HIND* was taking on water on a summer's day in 1579. Stormy seas off the Northwest coast of America had opened her seams and widened the leak she'd had in her hull since she was off the coast of Panama. The pump was well plied with seawater, and Francis Drake (who became Sir Francis after the voyage) and his crew were searching the rough coast for a well-protected cove with a sandy beach so they could carefully heel the ship over onto the sand in order to get to the leak. Complicating her predicament, the ship was loaded down to her marks, heavy with captured supplies and bullion—in fact, she was ballasted with Peruvian silver.

Imperiled on the far side of the world, the crew was in the best hands. Drake had no equal in seamanship and navigation, and many of his handpicked crew of able seamen had sailed with him for years. They were a tight, well-knit community. If by luck or providence they made it back to England, their fortunes would all be made on account of the treasure they bore in the now-soggy hold.

On a lee shore with the wind against them, they were forced to run in to what they called a "bad bay, it was the best road we could for the present meet with."[1] This was not a fit harbor to conduct the careening maneuvers they needed, and soon they were under sail again. Within a day or two, probably on or about June 17, "it pleased God to send us into a faire and good bay, with a good winde to enter the same."[2]

About eighty men and a pregnant Black woman named Maria made landfall in this lucky haven. This bay was described by one contemporary cartographer—who may have had his information from Drake

himself—as "porto bonissimo" (the best of harbors).[3] The treasure they
unloaded on this sandy shore was astonishing. One inventory of the bullion described 650 ingots of silver weighing nearly 23,000 pounds (over
eleven tons), and 36 parcels of gold ingots and cakes, weighing just over
100 pounds. Another source reported that there were five boxes of gold,
each a foot and a half in length.[4] There were Peruvian emeralds, and a
huge quantity of pearls—some of great value—as well as four crates of
Chinese porcelains, a quantity of fine clothing, and bolts of linen, taffeta, velvet, and silk. One source mentions that hundreds of the "lovely
pearls" were given to Queen Elizabeth, who adorned one of her gowns
with them.[5]

They rested and refreshed in this fair bay for a number of weeks.
The contemporary accounts are inconsistent on this point; the length
of their stay was at least five weeks, but it may have been as long as ten
weeks.[6] Once the leak was fixed and the ship floated and readied, the
crew packed and stowed their ballast of treasure, filled the water barrels,
loaded firewood for the galley stoves, and prepared to embark on the
first leg of the return voyage, which would take them across the Pacific
Ocean.

Just before they sailed, Drake ceremoniously erected a firm post to
which he attached a metal plaque engraved with a formal land claim in
the name of Queen Elizabeth for the territory they named Nova Albion.
By the rules of the time, this was a symbolic act of sovereignty.[7] Drake
chose the name Nova Albion (New England in Latin) because the white
sea cliffs he found there bore a resemblance to the white cliffs of Dover.
As the *Golden Hind* departed, the Native people became distraught, and
lit bonfires to burn tobacco and other items as sacrifices to be carried in
smoke as gifts to the English, because, as the English interpreted these
actions, they believed them to be gods.

Fifteen months later on November 3, 1580, the company arrived back
in Plymouth harbor, the place of their beginning, having circumnavigated the globe. Drake's voyage was the second expedition to circumnavi-
gate the earth, after Magellan's voyage in 1522, and the first to return with
its commander. In total their journey took them two years, ten months,
and a few days.

However, before Drake could even disembark the *Golden Hind*, a messenger rowed out to the ship and informed him he was in "Queen Elizabeth's bad graces on account of the robberies he committed" on the voyage, and the Spanish ambassador was asking for restitution.[8] Subsequently the crew was made to swear an oath of secrecy not to reveal where they had traveled on "pain of death." Drake was disavowed, called pirate in public, and the Privy Council initiated a professed official investigation into the voyage. Drawn-out discussions ensued with the ambassador from Spain about restoring the treasure, and perhaps relinquishing "Francis Drake the pirate" to the King of Spain to face the Inquisition.[9]

This was a cover story; a *ruse de guerre*. Francis Drake was a hero. He had met the unprepared Spaniards with such zeal and pertinacity "that Drake's name—El Draque or El Draco [the dragon]—became terrible to them."[10] Within a week of Drake's return to England, Queen Elizabeth quietly summoned him to court, and told him to "take her some samples of his labours and that he was to fear nothing."[11] In his audience with Her Majesty at Whitehall Palace, Drake presented her with his illustrated journal, and a very large gilded map of the world marked with a bold line that traced the path of the *Golden Hind* around the world. One of the samples he presented her was a coconut from the South Sea. (The Queen made it into a cup mounted in silver gilt and gave it back to Drake as a New Year's gift). Drake's journal contained his navigation records, detailed drawings of coastlines, sketch maps of islands, illustrations of particular episodes from the voyage, and natural history drawings of botanical and faunal specimens.[12]

Drake spent more than six hours in the Queen's audience going over the details of the voyage. Queen Elizabeth kept Drake's map, journal, and records under her own lock and key, and from that day on a cloak of secrecy was thrown over the voyage. Though there was no official public recognition of the circumnavigation, five months after he returned, Queen Elizabeth rewarded Francis Drake with a knighthood on the deck of the *Golden Hind*, and the ship was made into a monument. News of the voyage was suppressed, but ballads about the voyage were sung in the West Country of England, and students tacked poems to the main mast of the *Golden Hind* where she was berthed.[13]

In 1582 one author commented about the odd circumstance of the records being held by Queen Elizabeth:

> [Her Majesty] kept to herself the memorials of his voyage, in order that they should not be published. I don't doubt that many counseled her to hold back this information, so that it not be made known to strangers, or even to her subjects. But I don't know if there is good reason for this counsel: for making it known could not be but to the honor of her nation, if the information is such that other people might find benefit or convenience from it.[14]

The geographer Gerard Mercator also complained that information about the voyage was being suppressed, and questioned what the reasons were for "so carefully concealing the course followed during this voyage, [and] for putting out differing accounts of the route taken and the areas visited."[15] In spite of the secrecy oaths, disinformation, and an information blackout, soon whispers confirmed that Drake and his crew had, in fact, circumnavigated the whole globe and had hauled back a vast amount of treasure that was stacked up in a basement in the Tower of London.

Seven years after Drake's return, Raphael Holinshed challenged the information blackout on the voyage and wrote a short description of it in the second edition of his *Chronicles*. Holinshed's publication immediately caught the attention of the Privy Council, and it had been out only a month when they ordered a "stay of further sales and uttering" of the book. It was revoked and Holinshed's paragraphs pertaining to Drake and the voyage were completely removed.[16] A surviving copy has the five paragraphs that were cancelled. The narratives hardly seem dangerous or subversive. They sing Drake's praises, calling him "a man of rare knowledge in navigation," and describe how he surprised the unsuspecting Spanish who became terrified at the sight of "sack and spoil" and "fire and sword," and that the voyage "was of great adventure and prosperous success."[17]

Not only was Drake's original logbook of the voyage suppressed, by design and spycraft, contemporary accounts of this part of the voyage are contradictory. For many years Drake's gilded and colored map hung in a gallery at Whitehall Palace. The map was the only record of the voyage anyone was allowed to see, and only if you visited the Queen. Tragically, the gilded map and Drake's illustrated log or journal of the voyage were likely lost in one of the fires that burned Whitehall Palace, either in 1691 or 1698, though derivatives of the gilded map survived.

What was the secret being concealed? Presented here is the case that Drake's land claim included a vast amount of territory he did not see, and therefore could not have legitimately claimed by the tenants of the time. The present writer argues here that the latitudes he reached on the west coast of America were not the ones reported in the official record of the claim.

The Northwest coast theory of Drake's landing is at present unimaginable to many scholars, and uncritical acceptance of the dominant paradigm of a California landing is, understandably, the norm. The northern limits of Drake's voyage in the Pacific and, in particular, the location of Drake's purported fair and good bay, are questions that have vexed scholars for more than four hundred years.

The dominant paradigm has favored the lower latitudes (42° north as his northern limit and within a few degrees either side of 38° north for his anchorage). However, the major original maps and several manuscripts and narratives indicate the northern limit of his voyage was 48° north, in the vicinity of Cape Flattery on the Washington coast, and his anchorage was in the vicinity of 44° north, on the central coast of Oregon.

The artifacts that once underpinned the California landing theory include the Drake Plate of Brass, and seventy-seven porcelain sherds from Chinese wares dating from the Ming period that were recovered from midden sites at Drakes Bay. Drake's Plate of Brass (the purported land claim plaque found in 1936 and brought to light in 1937) was declared to be a hoax in 1977. It has only been since 2011 that a thorough scientific analysis led archaeologists to conclude that the porcelain sherds were all from a later shipwreck, and not from Drake's cargo.[18]

The theory that Drake landed in California was not always universally accepted. In the early twentieth century, new clues to Drake's movements in the Pacific came to light with the findings of anthropologist Zelia Nuttall. In February 1908, while working in the old colonial archives in Mexico City, Nuttall found a trove of contemporary documents about Drake's voyage and his actions and depredations in New Spain.

Further research in European archives led her to the conclusion that Drake landed on the Northwest coast of America, rather than the oft-cited California shore. This was a turnabout, and California historians tried to play it down because, by then, Drake was a hero to Californians. Nevertheless, the evidence mounted. Over the next two decades, British historians found more documents that added to the emerging narrative that Drake was on a mission for Queen Elizabeth; and one of his goals was to search for the western entrance of the Strait of Anian, a legendary northern water passage between the Pacific and Atlantic oceans (i.e., the Northwest Passage).[19]

Nuttall and the British historians asserted that the voyage was state sponsored, which meant that the voyage was not a piratical venture. (The California historians preferred Drake to be a pirate). In 1929 Nuttall's contention was proven correct when the manuscript with the plans or "plott" of the voyage was found in the British archives. For most historians it proved beyond a doubt that Drake was on a mission directed by Queen Elizabeth and the Privy Council.[20] Previous researchers had overlooked this tattered manuscript; its edges are burnt, and much of it is illegible, but it still retains most of the detailed instructions for the voyage. The instructions called for Drake to pass through the Strait of Magellan, find unknown shores not in the possession of any "Christian Prince," and to reconnoiter for minerals and special commodities such as spices, medicines, and scarlet dye.[21] It is no small point that the voyage was conducted with Elizabeth's knowledge and full support and that it was launched as a covert operation under the guise of piracy. The voyage was a manifestation of a new policy of exploration and expansion.

The difficulty Nuttall and the British historians who followed her faced was that Francis Drake and the story of the *Golden Hind* had become integral to California's historical identity. The early twentieth-century California historians who published and disseminated patriotic Golden State history found the Northwest coast landing theory dangerous to the received wisdom—and the cherished belief—that Drake the pirate had made landfall on the California coast and met the Coast Miwok or Pomo people.

In the 1930s, the theory that Drake was on the Northwest coast was gaining traction in America, only to be dramatically eclipsed when the alleged plate made by Drake to mark his land claim was found on a hillside above San Francisco Bay. In February 1937, the Drake Plate of Brass was shown to a popular and influential historian who immediately announced that the plate was almost certainly a true artifact of Drake, and it was cited as physical proof Drake landed on the California shore. The true identity of the hoaxer and his motives have heretofore remained unknown. Importantly, by the time the plate was found to be fraudulent (1977), the Northwest coast landing hypothesis had all but been forgotten.

The exact location of Drake's anchorage has been California's most prolonged historical discussion, and became especially acrimonious during the years the plate was considered authentic.[22] The location of the anchorage has been controversial because there is no clear, unequivocal information about the geographical location of the bay, and there is no "fair and good bay" or safe harbor that is suitable for careening a wooden vessel within a degree or two of 38° north latitude (the latitude recorded in the official account).

This debate is what Warren Hanna called, "the great-grandfather of all questions [in California history]. Unique, baffling, and highly absorbing, it presents an enigma which concerns the welfare of no one, yet challenges the imagination of everybody."[23] This polemic was described by Australian historian Oskar H. K. Spate as "almost a minor industry in the Bay Area."[24] Historian Donald Pike described the controversy over the landing as "a carbuncle on the corpus of California history for nearly two centuries—painful to contemplate and impossible to ignore."[25]

Since the 1970s the vexed question has been, for the most part, a tug-of-war among nonacademic proponents who assert that their favored bay is the one. These proponents are principally in California where there are three active groups, but there are two bays in Oregon that have their supporters, one in Washington state, and on Vancouver Island another group contends that Gonzales Bay (near Victoria) is the location of the fair and good bay.

This study is a necessary reckoning. Because the vexed question has largely been in the domain of rancorous proponents of one bay or the other, the question has become a quagmire that professional historians and archaeologists have largely avoided. What is missing is a critical analysis of the larger context of the question, and a discussion of the social and cultural importance of the voyage. There are significant Native American and Black stories associated with this voyage. Drake's crew (which included four Black crewmembers whom Drake had freed from the Spanish by taking them onboard), met the Native Americans of the rich Northwest coast cultural area, and the chroniclers of the voyage recorded the first ethnographic details of the lifeways of these people.

In unraveling this mystery I have inadvertently and almost certainly discovered the identity of the man who created the Plate of Brass hoax: Herbert E. Bolton, a popular and famous historian and professor. Significant evidence presented here also points to Bolton's involvement in the Chowan River Dare Stone, which, if my conjecture is correct, can now be declared a hoax as well. The Dare Stone was allegedly found on the bank of the Chowan River and brought to a professor of history at Emory University in Atlanta. Like the Plate of Brass, it was brought to the world's attention in 1937, and, like the Plate of Brass, was allegedly engraved in the late sixteenth century. The message on the Dare Stone was from Eleanor White Dare, one of the lost colonists of Sir Walter Raleigh's colony of Roanoke, and it described sickness and war with the "savages" resulting in the deaths of most of their group.

It is likely that the plate hoax was designed as a ploy to obstruct the Northwest coast landing theory, but Bolton may have had an additional motive: Drake's Plate of Brass served to promote an English hero and stressed a white national identity of America, as did the Dare stone and its alleged association with Eleanor Dare. The plate and the stone became potent symbols of America's English heritage and the founding of America, and underscored the ideology of white manifest destiny—the conviction that God destined whites to populate North America. These alleged artifacts were used by Bolton and the other historians involved in these hoaxes to promote much of the fabled narrative that fostered and furthered their racist ethos, and that of their white supporters.

In view of the important and deeply interesting problems involved, the vexed question of where Drake and company landed and repaired the *Golden Hind* in summer 1579 deserves a new analysis. Drake's famous voyage is likely the first European maritime expedition to explore the Northwest coast, and the first to attempt to find the Northwest Passage from its western (windward) entrance. This is all the more significant when one considers that this voyage occurred in Elizabethan times. Drake's circumnavigation of the world began five years before the establishment of Sir Walter Raleigh's ill-fated colony of Roanoke, thirty years before Jamestown was settled, and more than four decades before the Pilgrims came to America in the *Mayflower*.

Drake's ship was steered by a whipstaff tiller, not a wheel. These were the days before brass-buttoned sea coats. In Drake's day, sea captains and gentlemen wore finely embroidered doublets with lace-trimmed ruffs. In battle they wore armor, gauntlets, and chain mail. Superstitions informed their decisions; they believed there might be dragons in the sea, giants on the land, and they took precautions against them. Of the five ships that set out from Plymouth on the famous voyage, Drake's flagship, the *Pelican* (renamed the *Golden Hind* during the voyage), was the only one that made it to the north Pacific and back to England.

Shakespearean scholars suggest that the circumnavigations by Drake, and later by Cavendish, were such triumphs for England that Shakespeare commemorated these voyages when he named his theater The Globe.[26] Additionally the narrative of events at the "fair and good bay" may have provided the playwright with inspiration for *The Tempest*, which began with a storm and a shipwreck, and featured a Native who worshipped the new arrivals as "brave gods" bearing celestial gifts.[27]

CHAPTER TWO

The Historiography
of the Vexed Question

In order to understand how vexed this question has been, it is important to understand the origin of the idea that Drake landed on the California coast. The latitudes reported in the first official account of the circumnavigation indicated Drake and company sailed northwest from Mexico, far out into the Pacific on a bowline, and came east into the coast at about 42° north, then sailed south from the very southern coast of what is now Oregon to the central coast of California where they anchored in the vicinity of 38° north. This account is titled "The Famous Voyage of Sir Francis Drake into the South Sea, and There Hence about the Whole Globe of the Earth." This narrative was printed by Queen Elizabeth's official printer, dedicated to Sir Francis Walsingham (the Queen's secretary of state), and published in 1589 as a chapter in Richard Hakluyt's *The Principall Navigations, Voiages, Traffiques and Discoveries of the English Nation*.[1] In his second edition printed in ca. 1598, Hakluyt changed the highest latitude to 43° north. Drake and Fletcher's 1628 account kept the lower anchorage latitude but gave the northern most point as 48° north.

Drake's biographer and maritime scholar Harry Kelsey contends the various latitudes given in the contemporary accounts of the Drake voyage are of little or no value in determining Drake's anchorage on the west coast. Further, Kelsey dismisses the theory that some of the Chinese porcelain sherds found at Drakes Bay are evidence of Drake's cargo.[2] He wryly states, "As luck would have it these sherds are found in the exact same place where a Spanish ship wrecked in 1595."[3]

Luck may have had very little to do with it, and Drake may have had some inadvertent agency in the shipwreck. The ship wrecked at what is now called Drakes Bay in California was the *San Agustín*, sailing from Manila with a cargo of silk and several crates of Chinese porcelains.[4] Captain Sebastian Rodriguez Cermeño had instructions to explore the coast to search for the bay where Drake had reported his careenage site. An exact knowledge of this bay would be beneficial to the Spanish. Good careenage stations were scarce, and knowledge of their whereabouts was of incalculable value for those dependent on wooden ships. It is worth noting the *Golden Hind* was careened five or six times during this voyage, which became known as The Famous Voyage.

Cermeño wrote he complied "in every respect with the orders and instructions from His Majesty which I carried for the purpose."[5] They traveled somewhat further north than was typical of the route Manila galleons took, and sighted land at about 42° north. They then ran south along the coast, which the captain found "very rough and dangerous, as there was a heavy surf breaking on numerous small islands and reefs near the shore."[6] Cermeño may have believed he was in the same latitudes Drake had sailed, and perhaps he was the first of many to be misled by deliberately planted disinformation that described a fair and good bay where a ship could be careened and watered at about latitude 38° north.[7]

During one evening when Captain Cermeño judged they were close to their goal of finding a safe anchorage, they followed the coast "with all sails set so as by daylight to see if a port could be discovered and reached in which to enter."[8] At daylight they entered a bay, but almost immediately discovered it was quite rocky, and they turned back. Once in deep water, the pilot, master, and boatswain confronted the captain in the presence of Alonso Gomez, the *escribano* of the voyage, and on the formal record, insisted the ship continue on straight to Acapulco because "it was impossible to make a reconnaissance of the coast on account of the ship's being in such bad condition. The captain refused."[9] They entered the next bay, now called Drakes Bay, and anchored in seven fathoms of water.

Cermeño and his men disembarked and lined up on the beach in martial fashion and marched to a village. Cermeño reported, "There were fifty adult Indians looking on with much wonderment in seeing people never before seen by them."[10] The Natives of the country gave no indication they had ever seen Europeans before, and Cermeño made particular note in his report the people there had no articles of European manufacture. Drake had given cloth, clothing, and glass beads to the Natives, and perhaps iron, but there was no trace of Europeans having previously been there. Cermeño described the dwellings as "pits made in the sand and covered with grass, in the manner of the Chichimecos Indians [of central Mexico]."[11] The grass-covered huts the people lived in were not the plank-roofed, semi-subterranean houses Drake's men described. The official account by Richard Hakluyt (1552–1616) also mentioned canoes, but the people here had small boats "made of grass which looks like the bullrushes of the lake of Mexico."[12]

Within a few days the wind came up and their ship was wrecked on shoals. According to the pilot, it was more the fault of the captain than the weather.[13] A few men drowned, and the survivors, including Cermeño, worked to refit a pinnace for the long journey to Mexico in an open boat.

Drake, as it happened, was at that moment in the Caribbean on his final voyage with a fleet of twenty ships preparing to capture Panama. This expedition was a failure, and Drake, sick with dysentery, died at sea off the coast of Panama in late January 1596, exactly when Cermeño and his crew were making their way south in their open boat. Drake died before he could have learned of the wreck of the *San Agustín*, but if he had known about it he might have had a hearty laugh at the folly. The latitude of Drake's fair bay, which Cermeño was in search of, was likely falsified in the Hakluyt account as a piece of diplomatic deception in order to baffle Spain and claim a wide swath of land Drake did not actually see.

Subterfuge in official accounts like this was not limited to the English. When Drake's fleet was off the coast of Chile, he suspected the Spanish maps were falsified: "Maps of the Spaniards were utterly deceived for of a Malicious Purpose they had set forth the map false that they might deceive strangers if any gave the attempt to travel that way that they might perish by running off to the sea rather than touch with any part of the land of America."[14]

Captain George Vancouver was one of the next captains to seek the location of Drake's landing. In November 1792, Vancouver was off what is now called Drakes Bay when he noted, "According to the Spaniards, this is the bay in which Sir Francis Drake anchored; however safe he might then have found it, yet at this season of the year it promised us little shelter or security."[15]

Previously, Vancouver had been to Bodega Bay (which is another modern contender for Drake's anchorage). Vancouver anchored off a nearby point overnight, "being anxious not to have any opening on the coast unexamined."[16] Vancouver found Bodega Bay dangerous; the rocky bottom cut the cable of his anchor. Thirty-four years later, the British naval officer and geographer Captain Frederick William Beechey surveyed the coast, and dismissed the idea Drake had anchored at Drakes Bay because it was "too exposed."[17]

Californians began the search for Drake's landing site in earnest in the mid-1850s with the first federal surveys of the coastline. California was a new state, and curiosity had been raised by Vaux's 1854 publication of a collection of contemporary accounts about the voyage that included Drake and Fletcher's *The World Encompassed by Sir Francis Drake* (1628), Hakluyt's chapters (1589, 1600), and other manuscripts associated with the voyage.[18]

The question of where Drake had landed was very much a matter of debate. In 1868, F. D. B. Stillman asserted that Drake and company never would have landed on the dangerous shores of Jack's Bay (soon to be renamed Drakes Bay), but must have landed in San Francisco Bay.[19] Drake and his men had explored inland, but the account is not clear concerning how many days they explored. Many historians found it difficult to understand how they could have missed finding, or being led overland to the great San Francisco Bay.

In California, the most authoritative voice in the debate was George Davidson, a marine surveyor for the United States government. He studied the currents, winds, and approaches to various bays, and determined Jack's Bay, situated under Point Reyes, was the best bay within the latitudes given in the Hakluyt's authorized account of the voyage and renamed it Drakes Bay. In 1887 Davidson wrote the first scientific examination of the subject in which he made some broad assertions, including the notion that Drake did not go further north than 42° north.[20] British maritime historian and Drake scholar Julian Corbett disagreed with Davidson on that point, and considered it highly likely that Drake sailed as far north as 48° north latitude.[21]

Nevertheless, the California populace put a lot of stock in Davidson's opinion and the shortcomings of his arguments were overlooked. Californians had begun to identify with Drake's golden legend. Davidson popularized Drake as a pirate, and built his reputation on the Drake in California theory. Davidson painted Drake as the "Captain-general of Freebooters," and his men, made up of both gentlemen and sailors, were drawn together by what he described as a "love of adventure and plunder."[22] Davidson became a popular lecturer at civic organizations, and became the first professor of geography at the University of California, Berkeley.

In 1886, Hubert Howe Bancroft in his *History of California* reviewed the arguments in favor of several of the bay candidates, and suggested that the landing may have been at the newly named Drakes Bay, but that it could not be determined with any certainty.[23]

After he retired, Davidson revisited the issue of the landing and latitudes in a book published in 1908. The book has the assertive title, *Francis Drake on the West Coast of America in the Year 1579: The Golden Hind Did not Anchor in the Bay of San Francisco*.[24] Here he systematically proceeded to discredit the accounts that gave latitudes differing from Hakluyt's 1589 account, which he took as the basic authority for the voyage.

The tug-of-war on the points of latitude shifted to Corbett's favor when John Drake's first deposition came to light in 1911.[25] John was Francis's young cousin who served as a page on the circumnavigation and was captured by the Spanish on the follow-up voyage led by Fenton.[26] John had given two depositions to his Spanish *inquisidodres*, but when Davidson wrote his analysis he only had access to his second, taken in 1587, not the first deposition taken in 1584. In his 1587 deposition John related that they found land at 44° north, and then anchored and refitted at 48° north, where Drake named the land Nova Albion.[27] Davidson dismissed this as erroneous, calling it a transcriber error, commenting "it would seem that he gave the latitude 48° instead of 38° N."[28] Julian Corbett suggested an alternate explanation: that a transcriber error corrupted the passage and confused the first and second latitudes, meaning they went as far north as 48 degrees, and then turned south and careened the ship at 44 degrees north.[29]

Corbett's contention of the higher latitude was proved correct when John's first and longer deposition was found. This deposition was taken before the Spanish tribunal in 1584 at Santa Fe, in what is now Argentina. The transcriber did not err in the manner Davidson surmised and is consistent with the later deposition in terms of the higher latitude: "They sailed out at sea always to the north-west and north-north-west the whole of April and May until the middle of June…until they reached 48 degrees. They saw five or six islands in 46 and 48 degrees. Captain Francis gave the land that is situated in 48 degrees the name New England."[30]

These latitudes are also in accordance with another early account written by an anonymous author who was on the voyage. This manuscript is in the British Library, and is Harley Ms. 280, folios 81–90.

After Davidson dismissed John Drake's narrative, he singled out Francis Drake's compatriot and Arctic navigator John Davis, who had written that Drake "coasted all the Western shores of America until he came into the Septentrionall [northern] latitude of forty eight degrees being on the back side of Newfound land."[31] Davidson criticized Davis, "Of those who give their voice for the higher latitude are John Davis the Arctic Navigator who made three voyages to the Northeast coast of America in 1585, 1586 and 1587…We are satisfied the critic can give no weight to the latitude claimed by Davis: it would be a waste of time to show his ignorance of the subject."[32]

Davidson's disdain of Davis is unexplained. Davis was an excellent navigator, and an acquaintance of Drake. He was married to Walter Raleigh's sister and named his three sons after the navigators Drake, Raleigh, and Cavendish.

Davis and the Drake and Fletcher account from 1628 both related that Drake found the land there very high and covered in snow.[33] Davidson did not address the concordance of these narratives with the geography of the Northwest coast: specifically that the high and perpetually snow-covered Olympic Mountains in Washington State are in these latitudes. Nor did Davidson address the possibility the islands in Puget Sound (Bainbridge, Whidbey, Camano, etc.) are where John Drake and several of the contemporary maps put "five or six islands."

Davidson altogether dismissed the contention that Drake was looking for the Northwest Passage, calling it a ruse. He flatly stated: "Drake did not sail northward searching for a passage to the Atlantic."[34] Martin Frobisher placed the strait at 60° north. John Dee suggested it was between 40° and 50° north latitude. It begs the question: Would Drake only look as far as 42° north (as Davidson conjectured) for a passage Frobisher placed at 60° north and John Dee thought might be as high as 50° north? Historian Arthur Davies suggested the search for the passage may have been one of the main purposes of the voyage: "It therefore would have been sheer lunacy on the part of Drake to sail 2000 miles out into the grey empty wastes of the Pacific for 49 days, and make land only at 42° N."[35]

Davidson's beliefs about the voyage prevailed in the arena of public opinion, and he effectively popularized the idea of "Drake in California," an association that enhanced his reputation. The theory Drake landed in California coalesced around the following contentions put forward by Davidson: (1) the latitudes from Hakluyt's accounts were correct (around 38° for the actual landing, and 42° or 43° for the highest latitude reached), (2) the voyage was not state sponsored, though some of the men at court supported the venture, and (3) Drake was a pirate.[36] Davidson asserted the objectives of the voyage were for booty, trade, and exploration, not to look for places to establish a colony or to search for the Northwest Passage.

The swashbuckling story of Drake, his golden hoard, and his adventures resonated with Californians, and they embraced Drake as a native son. So much so that in 1893 the Right Reverend William Ford Nichols, Episcopal bishop of California, proposed to erect a Celtic stone cross at Drakes Bay to commemorate the first English language sermon and first use of the *Book of Common Prayer* on the soil of what is now the United States at the site where Drake and his crew were thought to have landed in 1579.[37]

The San Francisco Park Commissioners thought it would be better to erect the monument in San Francisco, and offered a site on the highest point in Golden Gate Park: a rocky knob where it would be a conspicuous landmark overlooking Stow Lake. When Drake's Prayer Book Cross was built, it was the largest cross in the world, composed of sixty-eight robust sandstone blocks: It still stands fifty-seven feet high atop a pedestal over seventeen feet square and seven feet high.

Davidson took part in the dedication of the cross in 1894. Annual celebrations at Drake's Prayer Book Cross in Golden Gate Park drew hundreds of people. Though Davidson died in 1911, the concept of Drake in California became embedded in California culture and folklore. Cultural traditions, like scientific paradigms, are difficult to shift.

Taking up the slack after Davidson's death was Reverend Nichols, who gave lectures on Drake's landing and in 1913 helped form the Sir Francis Drake Association, a group that organized annual pilgrimages to Drakes Bay to commemorate the landing and the first English language sermon on the west coast. In subsequent years the association installed a plaque and erected a cross at Drakes Bay. That same year, a purported descendant of Drake was featured on a parade float that represented the *Golden Hind* during San Francisco's Portola Festival.

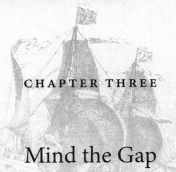

CHAPTER THREE

Mind the Gap

THE PRESENT WRITER has found that manuscript 280, folios 81–90 in the British Library's Harley collection is a handwritten draft in progress of a small portion of Richard Hakluyt's chapter "The Famous Voyage" published in *Principall Navigations* in 1589.[1] The tone and content suggest that this scribal draft was abstracted from a narrative about the voyage written by the chaplain onboard, Francis Fletcher. The only known journalists on the Pacific part of the voyage (which this manuscript covers) were Francis Drake and Chaplain Fletcher.

The manuscript is clearly a draft in progress. There are a number of interlinear additions, some passages are struck through, there are marked changes in sequence, and editorial notations and marks in the margins. Hakluyt had another manuscript or journal in hand while he was compiling the chapter as evidenced by additional passages that could only have come from Drake's account of the voyage. In short, the Harley manuscript is an abstract of Fletchers account, which when compiled with Drake's account, formed the basis for the chapter "The Famous Voyage."

The Harley manuscript is in two parts. The first part (folios 81–82) contains memoranda relating to the voyage. This will be referred to here as *Memoranda* (following Vaux).[2] The second part has no title but the first paragraph describes the contents: "A Discourse of Sir Francis Drakes iourney and exploytes after hee had past ye Straytes of Megellan into the Mare de Sur, and throughe the rest of his voyage afterward till hee arrived in England" (see Figure 3.1). This narrative, hereafter called the *Discourse*, is sometimes referred to as *The Anonymous Narrative* because it is unsigned and its original provenience is unknown.

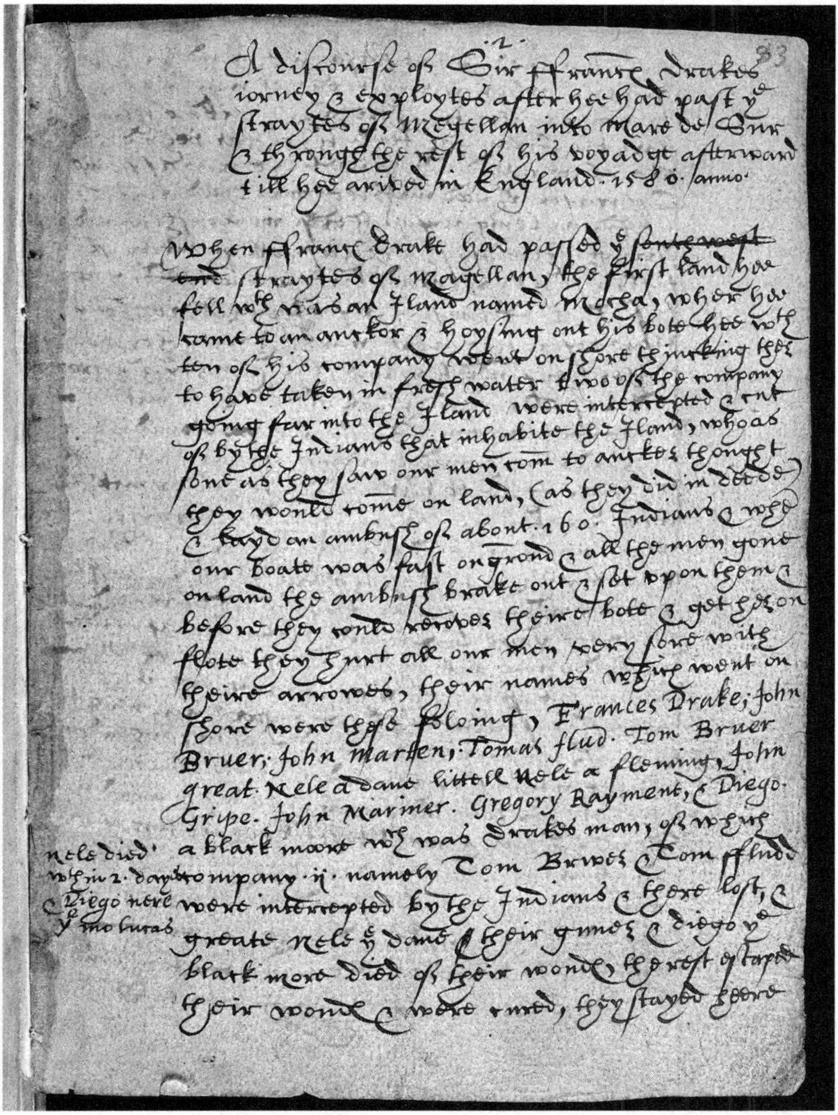

FIGURE 3.1. Harley Manuscript 280, folio 83, recto. Courtesy of the British Library (©British Library Board).

The manuscript is in the secretary hand, a type of handwriting commonly used for court documents in the later quarter of the sixteenth century. The pages were written by the same unknown scribe, on the same paper. Though most of the manuscript is in brown ink, later edits are in black ink. These include several crossed–out passages, and Greek crosses drawn in the margin to mark places in the text where the treasure taken in a particular action is inventoried and described.

One small note scratched in at the bottom of the first page of the *Memoranda* is in another hand and another ink: "Queary if this be not printed in hakluit."[3] This note may have been written by one of the seventeenth-century collectors who owned the manuscript. Where the Harley manuscript originated is unrecorded, but the provenience can be traced to Sir Simonds D'Ewes, a seventeenth-century antiquary. D'Ewes, like his father and grandfather, had studied common law at the Middle Temple, (Hakluyt's institution as well). Prior to D'Ewes, these manuscripts may have been part of the collection once owned by London merchant and antiquarian Ralph Starkey who died in 1628.[4] Starkey made transcripts of state papers, and most of his collection was from the late sixteenth century. He was an avid collector of letters, including those of Robert Dudley and Sir Francis Walsingham. D'Ewes obtained the collection when Starkey died, and claimed that besides material from Dudley and Walsingham, Starkey had forty-five packets of papers belonging to William Davison, another of Queen Elizabeth's councilors, "before the government retrieved them." These manuscripts were eventually obtained by Robert Harley (d. 1724) and Edward Harley (d. 1741), 1st and 2nd Earls of Oxford. Subsequently this collection went to the British Library. D'Ewes's biographer J. Sears McGee examined the *Discourse* and *Memoranda* and noted that most of D'Ewes's collection was from the late sixteenth century, and that "it seems very likely to me that the hand for the Drake ms. is from that period."[5]

The manuscript only details a small section of the journey, but in many places the manuscript text is word for word to the chapter, or slightly changed and made better by corrections and clarifications than an editor naturally would make. There are whole passages in the manuscript that are not in the final chapter, but these describe events that would not be necessary to include in the chapter, such as Drake's troubles with his steward, William Legge. The manuscript begins at Mocha Island off the southern coast of Chile, and continues in some detail describing events on the south and central American coast. From the Mexican coast onward the manuscript presents only a brief sketch of events.

One piece of evidence is particularly compelling and very much supports the idea that the Harley manuscript is a draft: In the margin of folio 82r of the *Memoranda* is a sketch of a pointing finger next to the following editorial notation to put some text at that location referring to the Portuguese pilot who Drake had captured in the Cape Verdes and was left in Guatulco: "The setting this ma[n] on shore should have bin recited in the latter end of the first leafe at this marck [pointing hand] the first side thereof."[6]

An examination in the *Discourse* section of the manuscript found there is only one mark of a pointing hand, and it is situated in the margin of folio 87r, just below a sentence about Tom Moone taking a gold chain from a Spanish gentlemen at Guatulco. The editor's instruction was carried out because positioned just after Moone takes the gold chain in the printed chapter, is recited the text about leaving the pilot on shore: "At this place our Generall among other Spaniards, set his Portugall Pilot, which he tooke at the Islands of Cape Verde."[7]

This correspondence could hardly be a coincidence. Further examination of the text by the present writer found that of the eleven marginal notes in the manuscript, five appear in the chapter, placed in the same position next to the same passages in the printed text as they are in the manuscript. This, also, is unlikely to be a coincidence.

Two points of importance to the question are that the author related that Drake's "fair and good bay" was at 44° north, and the text specifically mentions his search for the Northwest Passage. The latitudes reported are the same as those found in John Drake's 1584 and 1587 testimonies taken by his Spanish inquisitors while he was imprisoned.[8] The description in the manuscript of his movements in the North Pacific are as follows: "Northwards till he came to 48. Gr of the septentrionall [northern] latitude, still finding a very large sea trending toward the north, but being afraid to spend a long time in seeking for the strait, he turned back again, still keeping along the coast as near land as he might, until he came to 44 gr. And then he found a harbor for the ship, where he grounded his ship to trim her."[9]

By the time the abstract was finalized for printing the latitudes had been changed. This printed chapter (in contrast to the draft) placed the careenage at about what is now called Drakes Bay, situated just north of San Francisco and the text had been purged of disparaging comments against Drake, by then an acknowledged English hero. This alleged anchorage was in the vicinity of what was then the boundary of the northern frontier of New Spain. Drake planted his flag and claimed all the territory from this boundary north.

To date, historians have either dismissed the Harley manuscript or misunderstood its significance. Helen Wallis, the longtime map curator at the British Museum, thought it was important, even the main source that Hakluyt drew from for the second half of the voyage in the South Sea and beyond from one who was on the voyage.[10]

The new understanding presented here, that the manuscript is a draft, sheds fresh light on the unusual circumstances surrounding Hakluyt's production and insertion of "The Famous Voyage" into *Principall Navigations*. As a chapter in progress, the contents of the manuscript narrative are important when contrasted with the final published (and censored) version of the account. The differences between the draft and the published account reveal what information the Crown wanted publically known–and what they did not, i.e., content that was likely considered sensitive or subversive.

Richard Hakluyt, theologian and geographer, is best remembered as editor of *Principall Navigations*. He was a lecturer on cosmology and navigation, and had received from Queen Elizabeth a prebendary post entitling him to a portion of the income from the collegiate parish. Hakluyt's writings and analysis informed policy decisions at the Elizabethan court, and were aligned with those of his patron, Sir Francis Walsingham, Queen Elizabeth's secretary of state and chief strategist. Hakluyt and Walsingham shared the understanding that colonization would enrich the realm by creating markets for English cloth and other commodities, and by bringing in raw materials and minerals. Moreover, if England could plant her flag in the New World it would create a check

to expanding Spanish claims and effectively limit the spread of the teach-
ings of Rome in the New World.

According to Hakluyt's biographer Peter Mancall, an underlying
theme in *Principall Navigations* was that since the English Crown had
supported various early ventures in the New World (e.g., the voyages of
Sebastian Cabot), by right, England had a fair claim to the entire mainland north of Spanish Florida and south of New France.[11] This may seem
like an overreach on England's part, nevertheless, Drake's claim of Nova
Albion bolstered England's position, and their eventual claim to most of
North America was a result of these early machinations.

Proof of first discovery and possession was particularly important
during this competitive age of discovery and expansion, and one of the
accepted methods for supporting such claims was to publish accurate
maps and descriptions of the territory as supportive evidence.[12] By including a detailed description of Drake's claim, England was asserting in
Principall Navigations a coast-to-coast claim and "juste Title" to what is
now most of the continental United States.[13]

Hakluyt's treatment of Drake's circumnavigation was unusual in a
number of ways. Drake's circumnavigation should have been the center-
piece of Hakluyt's anthology because it was, after all, a crowning national achievement as Mary Fuller observed. In her article on Hakluyt's
circumnavigators she states that the "Famous Voyage" chapter presents
"an array of problems."[14] She found Hakluyt made a striking exception
to his general practice of crediting individual authors in the case of this
chapter; he attached no author's name to it in the first edition in 1589,
nor in the ca. 1598 edition. Another problem was the account is very
short—a mere twelve pages (six folio leaves), in contrast to the twenty-
five-page account of Edward Fenton's ill-fated voyage that followed it.
Fuller thought the brevity of the account was not totally explained by the
official policy of secrecy that had surrounded the voyage.[15]

In his preface to the first edition, Hakluyt commented that he had
plans to prepare an account of Drake's voyage, but he was forestalled
because a fellow writer (perhaps Drake himself) was working on a complete history to be published elsewhere, noting that he took more than
ordinary pains to include an account of "that worthie knight" into his
volume, but he yielded so that another author could publish it later.[16]

However, the author of that complete history was thwarted somehow and the promised account was not to be. If that author was Drake, he was engaged in blockades and other activities in advance of the coming Spanish Armada. Hakluyt had already written and printed the above apologetic note in the introduction, but before most of the pages had been assembled and bound into books, Hakluyt learned that, after all, the other author would not be writing an account of the voyage. Hakluyt quickly took the opportunity to compile a chapter on Drake's circum-navigation and inserted it into some or most of the still unbound copies of *Principall Navigations.* The pages of "The Famous Voyage" chapter were so hastily added, they are without pagination, and so the unnum-bered leaves appear between pages 643 and 644.

This odd insertion caught the eye of Sir Travers Twiss, a professor at the University of Oxford, who examined one of the original volumes in 1846. Twiss found the chapter was printed with the same typeface, ink, and paper as the rest of the work but the numbers printed at the bottom of the page for the printer's guidance do not correspond with the general order of the other numbers. Twiss commented, "This furnishes a strong presumption that it was printed subsequently to the rest of the work."[17]

Besides the lack of pagination, there were other problems with "The Famous Voyage" chapter that suggest a last-minute insertion. For ex-ample, the proofs were not reviewed thoroughly. Geographer and histo-rian E. G. R. Taylor noted, "The evidence for rather hasty condensation is afforded by the marginal notes, which in places do not correspond with the text, and presuppose lacunae."[18]

One of the copyeditor's errors was that a marginal note said "a pur-pose of Sir Francis to return in the North West Passage" next to text where no such purpose is described. That particular marginal statement was corrected by being omitted entirely in the second edition.

The insertion of this chapter into *Principall Navigations* meant the prohibition on discussing Drake's circumnavigation had been lifted, albeit with qualifications. An information blackout on his journal and maps was still apparently in force. Hakluyt was preparing this publica-tion in 1588, during *Annus Mirabilis*—the year of the Spanish Armada. In August of that year, England had defeated a Spanish invasion force of 130 ships carrying an army of soldiers that planned to depose Queen

Elizabeth and return England to Catholicism. General Sir Francis Drake was instrumental in England's victory over Spain. Perhaps it was felt the insertion of the chapter about Drake's circumnavigation and his depredations in New Spain could finally be acknowledged, as the inclusion of this chapter would suggest.

Fuller observed that Hakluyt walked a fine line between the competing government imperatives to report and not to report on the voyage, and commented on the result of this policy, "The narrative that eventually emerged to take a place in the collection said little about much, remaining silent about its sources and authorship while revealing a clear interest or bias in its account of events."[19]

The two Harley manuscripts are not likely in Hakluyt's handwriting, but it is possible they were written by one of his scribes. One can picture this scribe at his desk, a well-worn sea journal on one side; and his pen, ink, and paper on the other. The scribe's task was to abstract the longer journal to make the final printed version fit onto the small folio of six leaves Hakluyt was hurriedly planning to insert into the first edition of *Principall Navigations*. When the scribe finished, and the folio printed, this scribal copy and associated notes were put aside. By 1628 it was in the hands of Sir Simonds D'Ewes. Lost, however, is the original journal of the voyage that the scribe had on his desk.

This leads us to the next question: What is the evidence that Fletcher's journal was the one that the scribe was abstracting? The manuscript is written in the first person and it provides details that could only have come from someone who was on the voyage.[20] Julian Corbett commented that it gives several details not given elsewhere, but questioned its authority because the words "pirate," "thief," and "robbery" are freely used, and it contains "vulgar slanders a dissatisfied seaman would naturally invent."[21] He concluded that the person who wrote it had a grievance against Drake.

It so happened that Chaplain Francis Fletcher had a grievance against Drake. Custom dictated that a clergyman was an essential part of the crew in the Tudor Navy, as well as on Spanish ships during this era. They served as officers and their duties included keeping a daily calendar of events and a record of decisions made by the leaders of the voyage. A chaplain could gather evidence in the case of a dispute or disagreement over the best way to follow the given plan of the voyage. They also took testimony and evidence in the case of legal infractions. This power served as a deterrent to bad behavior because infractions would be punished upon their return.

The idea that the original source was Chaplain Francis Fletcher is not a new one. In 1854 Vaux posited that the document may have been testimony by Fletcher as *piéces justificatives* in a grievance against Drake regarding the Doughty mutiny.[22] The *Memoranda* in particular reflects on Drake's character and provides more detail on Fletcher's disgrace while he was shackled to the hatch.

Chaplain Fletcher's grievance against Drake came to light when the *Golden Hind* became grounded on a reef and was almost lost in what are now the waters of Indonesia. In a desperate effort to escape, Drake and the crew lightened the ship by throwing overboard several cannon, firewood, several tons of cloves and pepper, and crates of cloth. But she was still stuck fast after twenty hours. Thinking the worst was about to happen, Drake instructed Chaplain Fletcher to conduct a communion service.

Fletcher, emboldened by their dire circumstances to express his feelings about Drake, made an impassioned sermon openly declaring God was punishing them because Drake had executed Thomas Doughty for treason and mutiny.[23] He was referring to the Doughty affair, a mutinous incident that had occurred over a year before, just before they entered the Strait of Magellan. That Fletcher brought up the execution of Doughty at this time of peril demonstrates a significant rift had existed between Fletcher and Drake for most of the voyage.

A day after Chaplain Fletcher gave communion to the imperiled crew, by providence or chance, a gale blew up that pushed the *Golden Hind* off the reef and she floated, not the worse for wear. While everyone was greatly relieved, the acrimony in Fletcher's sermon had to be addressed. The company was called together and Drake had the parson shackled to a hatch while Drake sat cross-legged on a chest, held a shoe in his hand and–with pointed jocularity–excommunicated Fletcher, and denounced him to the devil and all the angels. After that, Fletcher was not allowed before the mast, "for if he did, he sware he should be hanged."[24]

While Fletcher was shackled to the hatches in the forecastle, Drake had a "posy" hung on his arm; it read "Frances Fletcher ye falsest knave that liveth." Following this sentence in the *Memoranda* is a crossed-out but readable phrase: "Save Francis Drake, quoth the writer hereof."[25] It is interesting to contemplate whether this was a direct quote written verbatim from Fletcher, or an editorial comment by an opinionated scribe. It should be noted that although Drake was at the peak of his popularity when Hakluyt was compiling *Principall Navigations*, Drake's contemporary William Monson wrote that he was despised in some quarters due to the "baseness of his birth and education, his ostentation and vainglorious boasting; his high haughty and insolent carriage."[26]

Twiss remarked that the Harley manuscript "is written in rather a sober style, and is much less diffuse than might reasonably be expected."[27] This sober style would make sense if the original journal was written by the chaplain, who was neither a friend of Drake nor a promoter of his accomplishments. Perhaps it is no coincidence that the document includes information a chaplain charged with keeping records on the voyage would have found necessary to record, such as a careful inventory and description of the silver chalice, two silver cruets, and an altar cloth Drake gave Fletcher after the crew sacked a church in a town called Saint Yago.

How much the Harley manuscript reflected the original journal, and what was filtered out by the copyist, are unknowns. Even without knowing the scribe, the manuscript may be considered a more perfect account than "The Famous Voyage" chapter in *Principall Navigations*. Taylor thought so and commented, "The unvarnished account of the Anonymous Narrative probably comes nearer to the truth [of the voyage]."[28]

Hakluyt's exception to his general practice of crediting individual authors can be explained by the animosity that existed between Drake and Fletcher. Drake had just been instrumental in defeating the Spanish Armada, and was at the peak of his public popularity when Hakluyt was compiling his anthology. Would Drake have been pleased that within the most important book on English exploration published to date, there was an account of his greatest achievement coauthored by his chaplain, a man he did not like and who may have testified against him in the Doughty inquiry?

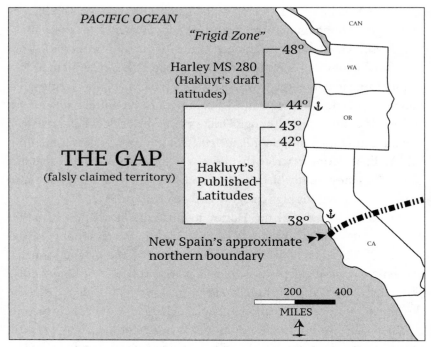

FIGURE 3.2. The Gap: The west coast showing the latitudes reported in the Harley Manuscript and the Hakluyt account, and the gap of territory that Drake could not have legitimately claimed.

The latitudes were falsified, and it begs the question: To what end? It likely was a ruse to claim more land. If Drake came in on the North Pacific gyre at 48° and only coasted a few degrees south beyond his anchorage at 44° north before he headed west back out to sea, by the conventions of the time he could not have legally claimed the wide swath of territory that he did.[29] By claiming all the territory north of the frontier boundary of New Spain (at about 38° north on the Hondius Broadside and other English maps), Drake's claim effectively checked Spain's expansion and gave England all the territory above the boundary, leaving no gap and no land unclaimed on the west coast of America (see Figure 3.2).

The contention presented here is that "The Famous Voyage" account was designed to subscribe to the tenants of an official land claim by providing proof of first discovery and possession. The account describes Drake fulfilling the four symbolic acts of sovereignty used by navigators and explorers of the colonial powers of Europe. These included (1) conducting a religious ceremony, (2) marking the territory (with a metal plate in this case), (3) conducting a symbolic ritual by which ownership or sovereignty was obtained (the crowning of Drake by the Natives), and (4) the formal attestation.[30] The Hakluyt account went to some length describing the installation on a post of an engraved metal plate that displayed "Her Majesties right and title" as well as the day and year of their arrival, with a sixpence of current English money set under the plate.

Besides the correct points of latitudes on the coast, the Harley manuscript describes events the sanctimonious Chaplain Fletcher would have found important to include. Discreetly removed from the published version is the pregnancy of the Black woman who accompanied the voyage and her abandonment on an island with no water: "The negro wench Maria, she being gotten with child in the ship, and now being very great, was left here on this Island."[31] This incident, descriptions of conflict between Drake and members of his crew, details of Doughty's misdeeds and execution, any statements considered discreditable to Drake, and other sensitive information found in the manuscript did not appear in Hakluyt's chapter.

Incidental support that the narrative was an abstract from Fletcher's journal is that we know his journal was broken into two sections after the voyage. Though there is a copy of the first half (MSS Sloane 61 at the British Library), the second half that began just after they passed through the Strait of Magellan is lost. The first sentence describes its contents as "a discourse of the journey of Francis Drake after he had passed the Straits of Magellan." Scholars have searched for the second half of Fletcher's journal. Historian Warren Hanna, for one, thought it may have been filed with the papers of Joseph Banks or Charles Darwin, and overlooked.

An explanation of its loss may be that the second part of Fletcher's journal was in the possession of Hakluyt, and was never reassembled with the earlier Atlantic part of the journal after they finished abstracting it. It seems Hakluyt collected in his valise only the section of the journal he wanted to abstract. He already had Captain Winter's journal of the Atlantic portion of the voyage, so he needed an account of the voyage from the South Sea and onwards.

In Hakluyt's second edition of *Principall Navigations*, he added another chapter (referred to here as "The Course") about the voyage that, like the "Famous Voyage" chapter, was also apparently abstracted, in part, from Fletcher's original journal because at the point on the voyage where these two accounts overlap, the manuscript and this chapter are almost word for word.[32] Again no author is attributed, and it is written in the first person. The chapter's long preface describes the official latitudes (the ruse latitudes), and how the Natives offered Drake the dominion of the country and Drake took possession on behalf of Her Majesty. Where the Harley 280 manuscript and this account differed is where Hakluyt inserted information, or misinformation, directed at the Spanish. There was a paragraph about the Frigid Zone Drake and his company found above 43° north. Though this voyage was made during the "little ice age"—a particularly cold number of years—this chapter went to some length describing the cold weather. These descriptions may have been somewhat hyperbolic with the intent to discourage the Spanish from venturing into the latitudes claimed by Drake (because the English believed the Spanish eschewed cold weather sailing). The latitudes repeated the official line, and it seems apparent that Hakluyt added this chapter to affirm England's land claim of Nova Albion, and further dissuade the Spanish from exploring north.

In 1628, Drake's nephew compiled *The World Encompassed by Francis Drake*, which included portions of Fletcher's original journal and "diverse others." It was only in 1984 that historian David Quinn observed that there were passages that could only have come from Drake himself (previous to this, many historians just referred to this publication as Fletcher's account). Quinn thought these passages were from Drake's unfinished manuscript (perhaps the very account that Hakluyt referenced in his preface to *Principall Navigations*).[33] We know Drake's manuscript existed because on New Year's Day in 1593 he sent narratives of several of his voyages to the Queen. In the letter that accompanied "the first fruits of your servant's pen" he explained that "many untruths have been published, and the certain truth concealed," so he found it necessary to correct the record.[34] From this letter we can suppose Drake's intention was to ready the book for publishing once Queen Elizabeth gave her approval. However, these were some of Drake's busiest years in service to England. The manuscript was never published, and Drake died at sea three years later.

Drake's brother Thomas inherited Buckland Abbey, along with Drake's papers. The family biographer, Lady Elliott-Drake, surmised Thomas was too tied up in lawsuits to take an interest in putting the book together.[35] Finally in 1628 Thomas's son "set forth" the work. Drake's unfinished manuscript was collated with Fletcher's larger original account, and published as *The World Encompassed by Sir Francis Drake*.

The World Encompassed is longer and contains much more detail than any of the previous accounts of the voyage. Of interest here, is that the land claim latitudes in that publication adhered to the censored conventions of the latitudes—with the important exception that nephew Drake corrected the highest latitude attained on the coast from 43° to 48° north. It is evident Drake's true northing (48°) in the Pacific was information the Drakes wanted to be known. After all, it was only the southern latitude and the boundary it created that mattered when it came to the claim.

It appears that the lower latitudes in the official accounts were a ruse to claim as much territory as possible for England, leaving no gap between the border of New Spain and England's new possession. This explains why Queen Elizabeth kept the journals and true charts made on the voyage: By doing so, Queen Elizabeth was sewing the fox's skin to the lion's.

CHAPTER FOUR

The Beginnings

Francis Drake came from humble origins. He was merely the son of a tenant farmer on Lord Bedford's estate in Crowndale, near Tavistock in Devon in the West Country of England. H. H. Drake, writing in 1883 about the family genealogy, noted the name was not associated with ancient land tenure as recorded in the Domesday Book, but he reasoned the proud symbol of the dragon found in the Drake family coat of arms suggested a family of importance because such a symbol would not have been lightly assumed by an obscure person. He did concede that in the thirteenth century around Tavistock the bearers of the Drake name "were an energetic tribe that often took the law into their own hands and broke it."[1]

The West Country was a place known for spawning England's best seafaring adventurers.[2] Drake family biographer Lady Elliott-Drake wrote Francis was born in 1542, as evidenced by a note on his portrait in the family home of Buckland Abbey.[3] Like other farmers in that era, the Drake family also was engaged in other trades. His grandfather may have been a cloth dealer, and his father, Edmund Drake, was a shearman in a wool mill, "the most skilled of all the craftsmen, who teased the nap of the cloth and then trimmed the nap with fine shears to make the surface as smooth as possible."[4]

When Francis was still quite young the family moved to a hulk in the Medway estuary near the Royal Wharf, where Drake's father Edmund had received an appointment as a naval chaplain. Hulks were old ships unfit for sea duty that often served as floating storehouses, temporary quarters for seamen, and housing for quarantine purposes.[5] Francis, the oldest of twelve brothers, grew up on these bustling docks where he and his brothers acquired a sailor's education in seamanship, and obtained a practical knowledge of marks, stars, winds, and tides while sailing small craft in the sandy shoals of the Medway.

Edmund Drake's main job was as a reader of prayers to mariners. He was a strident Puritan, as Lady Elliott-Drake noted he was a "hot gospeller" whose zeal for preaching was prompted by political as well as by religious motives. Psalms or prayers were read twice daily from the Book of Common Prayer. It is worth noting here that it was less than a generation since this book replaced the Latin liturgies of the Catholic Church, and at sea Francis himself read prayers and psalms from the prayer book to his men.

In order to provide a trade for their sons, Drake's parents sent young Francis and some of his brothers to Plymouth to apprentice with their kinsmen William Hawkins, a wealthy trader and seafarer. The Hawkins boys, William Junior and John, were a few years older than their Drake cousins: Francis, Thomas, John, and Joseph. They all went to sea and became a tight pack of seadogs on vessels belonging to the Hawkins family.

The Hawkins were merchant explorers whose exploits were being curtailed in the 1570s by a restrictive monopolistic colonial policy imposed by Spain, whereby Spain's dominions were not allowed to trade with any other country. The Spanish and Portuguese increasingly regarded the English as "Lutheran smugglers" and pirates even when their intention was to trade legitimately. Spain stepped up the confiscation of English ships and the imprisonment of ships' crews. England's mariners, the Hawkins and Drakes included, retaliated in increasingly violent exchanges that stopped just short of acts of war.

It was typical of English merchantmen during this time to carry "letters of reprisal"—permission letters that allowed a person or syndicate whose cargo was captured in peacetime to recoup losses by capturing a like amount back from any ship or merchant from the offending country.[6] War with Spain became inevitable as reprisals escalated. Queen Elizabeth deflected talk of conflict as long as she could. This was, in part, because as long as it was still peacetime, the Crown was entitled to an interest in goods taken back under letters of reprisal. The Crown's share was often up to a lucrative one-third of the cargo. As historian

Susan Ronald commented: "The holders of Letters of Reprisal or Letters of Marque made the bearer a bona fide mariner seeking reprisal…. Yet as the years rolled on, virtually anyone requesting a letter of reprisal was granted one. They [the officials who issued these letters and the Queen] became direct beneficiaries of the pirates' prosperity."[7] This device thus provided hard currency for England in this era of state formation.

Over the horizon, Spain and Portugal were building colonial empires on either side of a pole-to-pole line dictated by the Treaty of Tordesillas dating from 1494, two years after Columbus sailed. France had also made claims to parts of North America, in what is now Quebec. The Portuguese were profiting from the import of spices, cotton, and silk from India on the route around Africa, and Spain was enriching itself from the gold and silver mines in Peru and Mexico.

Among some of the Queen's advisors there was serious discussion about the possibility that an English explorer could find a navigable Northwest Passage; if it existed it would provide a direct route north of the American landmass to East Asia. A colony in North America could also be a stepping-stone to those riches. Accounts of some explorers described the unclaimed lands of America having fertile fields for planting, thick forests that could supply trees for ships' masts and planks, plants of medicinal and economic value, fur-bearing animals, and minerals in abundance. The establishment of a colony could also be a solution to the pressing problem of unemployment.

England's most important commodity at the time was broadcloth—a dense, tightly woven woolen. English wool had a fine staple, and the fibers were curly and serrated, which provided strength and a heavy dense quality.[8] By the 1560s the woolen cloth industry was in decline. Besides new sources of wealth, it was thought that establishing an English colony or colonies in the New World would expand the market for English cloth. Richard Hakluyt specifically suggested that if merchant explorers encountered people that "hath need of cloth" that it should be ascertained what commodities the savages have to trade for cloth.[9]

The whole of the Spanish Main (i.e. the Caribbean and Gulf of Mexico), and the Pacific Ocean were considered by Spain to be off limits to English and French merchants, who had to conduct a sort of trade by force. They would sail into a port with guns blazing, or at least visible, and negotiate a trade with the port administrator. Failing that, they would loot the town of particular goods and valuables, then leave their goods on the dock as an exchange before they sailed away. Kelsey called this method "request, refusal, scuffle and trade."[10] Though the Spanish officials called the English and French "pirates," they were basically traders, and frequently local merchants and port authorities were in collusion with them.

A defining moment for Francis Drake (and a pivotal episode in the cold war between Spain and England) occurred during John Hawkins's disastrous trading voyage to the Caribbean in 1567–68.[11] Hawkins had conducted two prior slaving voyages that proved so lucrative that Queen Elizabeth contributed a ship, the *Jesus of Lubeck*, as Hawkins's flagship to the fleet. These voyages were before the advent of slavery as an institution in Europe. Tudor historian Miranda Kaufmann noted, "Hawkins was the only English merchant to attempt the trade before the 1640s, and he was an interloper, selling [only] to the Spanish Caribbean."[12]

On the Guinea coast Hawkins loaded about four hundred slaves and sailed for Dominica. By the time the fleet reached the Caribbean it consisted of ten ships; six original and four captured en route. Drake, who was about twenty-two years old, was captain of the *Judith*.[13] The fleet was caught in a hurricane off the coast of Cuba, and the *Jesus* was severely damaged. They made their way to the port of Vera Cruz. The port was undefended, and they landed on the island of San Juan de Ulúa that guarded the bay. While repairs were underway, the English occupied the castle-fortress, and pulled eleven cannon out of their ships and set up a battery, pointing the cannons toward the bay as a precaution.[14]

By ill luck, the Spanish fleet arrived the next day with the new viceroy of New Spain on board. Hawkins allowed them to enter the port, but only after a truce was signed and hostages exchanged. To the dismay of the Englishmen, the Spanish viceroy did not keep his word and launched a surprise attack. The fighting was furious, and lasted several hours; over three hundred of Hawkins's men were killed including some of Drake and Hawkins's kinsmen and their closest comrades.[15]

During the mêlée a fire ship was launched towards *Jesus of Lubeck*, and as Hawkins and his men were escaping to their smaller ship the *Minion*, Hawkins signaled Drake in the *Judith* to assist. Drake either would not or could not come to Hawkins's aid, and escaped out of the harbor with much of the proceeds from the voyage, leaving his cousin with a ship so overloaded with men and undersupplied with provisions that Hawkins had to abandon over a hundred men on the Mexican coast. Some were captured and sent to the galleys or were killed, but most perished in the woods. The ones that sailed on with Hawkins scrounged for food along the Florida coast and ate every rat, cat, dog, and parrot they had on board.[16] They eventually made it back, but because there was so little food, many men died of starvation and disease along the way.[17]

Drake, believing Hawkins and his crew had been killed or captured, sailed back to England and upon his arrival told William Hawkins that his brother John was likely dead. Three days later, John and the remainder of his crew arrived, bedraggled and much reduced, in the *Minion*. John was severely critical of his cousin and wrote, "The *Judith* forsook us in our great myserie." Spanish historian Antonio de Herrera reported that Drake was imprisoned for three months on charges of desertion.[18] Drake claimed that a fire ship had blocked his path, but the accusation of desertion haunted Drake for the rest of his life and may have created a rift between him and John, though they soon worked together on other projects. The Hawkins brothers felt that the attack amounted to an act of war, and pressed the Queen to declare it. She refused, putting off the inevitable as long as she could, while her "pirates" stepped up their activities.[19]

Drake turned this disaster into a life-long vendetta against the Spanish, who had attacked under a flag of truce–an act Drake found particularly galling.[20] Patrick O'Brien suggested that Hawkins may not have blamed him as much as Drake blamed himself. Drake converted this emotion into a still more bitter hatred for the Spaniards. "Though a love for gold and a loathing for Catholics had not inconsiderable influence— he was after all brought up in a strongly Protestant atmosphere."[21]

In 1572 Drake returned to the West Indies and the Spanish Main on a privateering expedition to rob the Spanish of as much gold and silver as they could carry back to Plymouth. Historian Julian Corbett commented that they carried the most modern ammunition and artillery requisite for such a man-of-war on such an attempt, "the whole affair indeed bears very little the aspect of an irresponsible piratical adventure."[22] They reconnoitered the Panamanian section of the route where the Spanish carried gold, silver, and emeralds from Peru across the isthmus to load on ships at the Caribbean port of Nombre de Dios. Drake's company comprised a strong group of West Country seamen, including two of his brothers, and Drake's great friend and lieutenant on this enterprise, John Oxenham, who had served under Drake on other expeditions in various capacities, which included sailor, company cook, and soldier.[23]

In the Panamanian jungle, with the help of an escaped slave named Diego, Drake and Oxenham forged a strong alliance with a population of escaped African slaves and creoles known as the Cimarrons. Drake described them as: "Black people which about eighty years past fled from the Spaniards their master, by reason of their cruelty, and are since grown to a nation, under two kings of their own. The one inhabiteth to the west, the other to the east of the way from Nombre de Dios."[24]

Diego was a fugitive slave. His master was the Spanish administrator of Nombre de Dios, a small but important port on the Caribbean coast of Panama.[25] It was common knowledge that when a Black person set foot on an English vessel or on English soil, "he immediately became free, because in that Reign nobody is a slave."[26] On the occasion when Drake and his men were raiding the town on a piratical adventure, Diego ran to the shore and called out to Drake's men who were manning four pinnaces awaiting Drake's return with the silver. Diego was under fire as he approached them—three or four shots had been fired at him from the jungle—and he entreated Drake's men to let him onboard because he had an important warning for them. They fetched him aboard and Diego related the news that the Spanish had brought in 150 soldiers to guard the town. The English were grateful to Diego and found that his knowledge of the country and the people were an asset. Subsequently Diego assisted Drake in forging an alliance with the Cimarrons, which was key in the success of the venture.

One of the Cimarron kings made a particular point of bringing Drake to a high point of land where a tall tree stood. Steps cut into the tree ascended to a high bower where ten or twelve men could sit. Here, a famous scene unfolded: Drake and Oxenham climbed the tree with the Cimarron leader. From that vantage point to the east they could see the Caribbean, and to the west was the Pacific Ocean. Drake was so stirred by the scene, he swore an oath that if God gave him leave he would be the first to sail an English ship in the Pacific Ocean. Oxenham retorted with enthusiasm that he would follow him in that quest, and added words to the effect of "unless I beat you too it."[27]

They raided a town they called Venta Cruz where Drake "strictly charged the Symerons, and all his company, that they should on no account hurt any female, or unarmed man; an order which they all faithfully obeyed."[28] Historian Susan Ronald writes of this: "While there is no excuse for the terror Drake and his raiders inflicted on their victims, this level of humanity in the sixteenth century—let alone in the twentieth or twenty-first—is remarkable."[29]

The expedition captured a mule train of silver that was on its way from the west coast of Panama to the eastern port of Nombre de Dios. What Drake and Oxenham learned from this success and their reconnaissance of the isthmus was that the flota of treasure ships loaded with silver from the Peruvian mines was unprotected as it sailed up the Pacific coast from the port of Lima to Panama.

The next year (1576) John Oxenham returned with a crew of fifty men, and reuniting with the Cimarrons, the united force carried a disassembled pinnace across the isthmus. In the estuary of a river that flowed into the Pacific they reassembled the ship and sailed into the ocean. They established a base in the Pearl Islands from which they ambushed several ships on the silver route. Therefore, Oxenham did in fact beat Drake in the quest to captain the first English ship on the Pacific Ocean. Oxenham and his crew relieved two Spanish ships of treasure, but the Spanish found them out and burned their mother ships, which had been secreted in a bay on the Caribbean coast. Oxenham and his men were captured and most of the men were killed; a few became slaves on Spanish galleys. Oxenham, a cabin boy, the pilot, and the ship's master were imprisoned at Lima, and brought before the Inquisition.

Evidence in the Spanish archives suggest that England had the intention of gaining permanent control of the isthmus through the alliance that Drake and Oxenham had forged with the Cimarrons. Drake may have made a secret plan with Oxenham to join forces with him in Panama and gain control of the isthmus with the assistance of their Cimarron allies.[30] Once Drake found out that Oxenham and the others were being held in a prison in Lima, it became part of his mission to break them free.

CHAPTER FIVE

Afar the Seas Were
Blue and White

A PORTRAIT BELIEVED to be of Drake has recently been discovered in England.[1] It is the earliest known image of Drake in existence, and dates to the time just prior to his famous voyage, when he was at court promoting and planning the expedition. His stance and gaze leave no doubt that at the peak of his prowess Drake had a commanding presence.

The plan of the voyage was along the lines of the plan Richard Grenville had proposed three years before. It called for Drake's fleet to enter the Pacific through the Strait of Magellan, annoy the Spanish, plunder as much treasure as possible, and explore unknown lands for Her Majesty's realm. The Spanish did not often use the strait because they considered it too dangerous; they preferred the portage route across the Isthmus of Panama. For Drake the voyage provided an opportunity for treasure, and for revenge against depredations inflicted upon him and his family by the Spanish.

There were two camps of opinion at court about the capture of treasure from the Spanish—and piracy in general. Lord Burghley (William Cecil), who was a father figure to Queen Elizabeth and her longest serving councilor, did not want to provoke Spain to war. Burghley felt that out-and-out piracy was not a legitimate occupation of the State. Walsingham, Leicester, and Hatton, in contrast, felt England had little choice in the face of the increasing Spanish malice: England must send out her explorers to find new places to trade, reconnoiter for colonies, and harry the Spanish as they saw fit. Walsingham and Burghley agreed on the point that England needed to explore and found colonies in order to

occupy a position of importance in the world and counter the preroga-
tive the Spanish and Portuguese maintained in claiming new lands and
extending their influence and the influence of the Pope.

Queen Elizabeth profited from the plunder brought in by "her ma-
rauding brood courtiers, merchants, and close relations vying for power,
plunder, and riches."[2] The plunder provided funds that enabled her to
build up the fleet with new sleek and swift ships specifically designed
to outrun and outgun Spanish ships, and hide in inlets and shallows
where the Spanish vessels could not reach. These ships were essential for
England's budding imperialistic aspirations.[3]

With a fleet of new ships manned by merchants, young noblemen,
sailors, and adventurers, England was ready to send out expeditions to
search for better trade routes and unclaimed lands. One of the goals of
the voyage was to determine if there was a Northwest Passage that would
provide easy passage to Cathay (China) and India.[4] Evidence that Drake
was tasked to reconnoiter this passage is found in a letter John Dee wrote
while Drake was preparing for the voyage. Dee remarked that a British
subject presently intended "to accomplish that discovery which of so
many and so valiant captains by land and sea hath been so oft attempted
in vain."[5]

The plan of Drake's voyage was a closely guarded secret. The scheme
was only revealed to the crew after they had set sail. Most of the sailors
on the voyage thought they were heading to Alexandria to load a cargo
of currants. This manuscript plan with Drake's instructions only came to
light when geographer and historian E. G. R. Taylor found a burnt scrap
in a collection of manuscripts at the British Library. Taylor reported her
finding in an article titled, "The Missing Draft Project of Drake's Voyage
of 1577–80." This manuscript is Cotton MSS., Otho, E VIII. The paper
was badly mutilated by a fire. Its edges are burnt and there are missing
portions but much of the text is readable. It called for "finding unknown
shores not in the possession of any Christian Prince, and to reconnoiter for special commodities such as spice, drugs, scarlet dye, and other
commodities."[6] This founding document of the voyage listed the sponsors. Taylor noted "This authentic list of the men who set the voyage on
foot shows that it was sponsored by the Navy Board—the Lord High
Admiral, Sir William Winter, George Winter, John Hawkins—and by

the inner circle of Queen Elizabeth's advisors—Walsingham, Leicester and Hatton."[7]

The purpose of the voyage was manifold. For the sailors who had sailed with Drake before, it meant the capture of ships, "prizes," and the treasures they carried, (some of which would be shared with the sailors). In Captain John Winter's mind "they were bounde for the part of America for discovery and other causes of trade of merchandizes necessary and requisite."[8] For the gentlemen on board (often second sons of noblemen), the voyage was for various measures of fame, adventure, and profit.

Taylor, intrigued by this burnt scrap of a manuscript, surveyed several more collections for more information on Drake's circumnavigation. In the Harleian Collection at the British Library she found a manuscript titled *Navigation Manual* that was inscribed with the date 1577. This was an astonishing find, for as Taylor noted, "There was but one English seaman who needed a rutter for Magellan's Strait in 1577, and that seaman was Francis Drake."[9] Taylor had found Drake's personal *Navigation Manual*.

Looking through the pages, Taylor found a scribbled list of items to be procured in advance of a sea journey. These included a Bible, a gilt silver cup for beer, silver spoons with acorn finials, a box of balsam ointment, a gilt helmet, a case of glass bottles, a wainscot desk, a flintlock musket, a cloth gown for the sea, and a leather trunk. Taylor commented: "These are just such belongings as Drake is known to have had about him, and are too splendid for anyone less than the general of the fleet, who was served on fine china and plate. Balsam was held to be a notable heal-all for wounds and ship-board ailments, and Drake was well known for his care of the health of his men."[10]

It is not surprising that the first item on Drake's purported packing list was a Bible. Witnesses reported that Drake also brought along the Book of Common Prayer and John Foxe's *Acts and Monuments* from 1563—a history of the Protestant martyrs in the reign of Queen Mary.

Drake's fleet of five heavily armed ships sailed from Plymouth on November 15, 1577. It was a portentous day according to Gaspar de Vargas, chief magistrate of Guatulco, Mexico, because on this day, a comet appeared, which was seen in New Spain.[11] As commander of the fleet,

FIGURE 5.1. *Golden Hind at Sea*, starboard side. Drake's ship by Harold Wyllie.
© National Maritime Museum, Greenwich, London.

Drake's title was General. This fleet included his flagship the *Pelican*, about 120–150 tons (renamed *Golden Hind* on the voyage in honor of Christopher Hatton, a sponsor whose coat of arms included the female red deer or hind); the *Elizabeth*, 80 tons, owned by Queen Elizabeth and captained by John Winter; the *Marigold*, 30 tons, captained by John Thomas; the *Swan*, a flyboat of 50 tons, captained by John Chester; and the *Christopher*, pinnace of 15 tons, captained by Thomas Moon.[12]

The *Pelican* had three masts and a long slender bowsprit that carried a cross arm that supported a square spritsail. Her keel length was about sixty to seventy feet, her length at waterline seventy-five to eighty feet. She was to be small enough to approach the shore and enter small harbors, both for raiding and provisioning. Each mast carried two yardarms. The main and foremast were square rigged, and the mizzen carried a lateen rig—that is, one large triangular sail. The sails were woven from flax, and the ropes and rigging were made of hemp. The main mast was taller than the overall length of the hull. The hull was built up high astern, as was custom in those days, with a quarterdeck and short poop deck and a raised forecastle.[13]

According to one of Drake's Spanish prisoners, the *Pelican's* compliment of artillery included twelve pieces of cast iron and two of bronze, all heavy cannon.[14] Nuño da Silva (the Portuguese pilot Drake had captured off the Cape Verdes Islands and brought with him for most of the American part of the voyage), said that on one of the bronze cannons "there was a sculptured globe of the world and a North Star on it passing over." Drake had told him "these were his arms and that the Queen had given them to him, sending him to encompass the world."[15]

The placement of the North Star and the globe demonstrate that a search for the Northwest Passage was part of the plan from the beginning. (Da Silva's comment has been ignored by the California landing theorists.) When Drake returned, a south star was added to his coat-of-arms because he had sailed further south than anyone had sailed before, to an archipelago well beyond the southern tip of South America.

The men-at-arms included both gunners and archers. The arms lockers were stocked with long spears and smaller pikes. They carried powder and shot, as well as oil, pitch, sulfur, and spirits for making incendiary devices. The captain of one of the ships they captured described weaponry on the *Pelican* as follows: "Fire-bombs and darts to set fire to the sails of the enemy; chain balls for breaking top-masts and other deadly work; tackle and rigging, and many arquebuses, corselets, pocket pistols, trappings, pikes and a great quantity of many different kinds of arms."[16]

Drake's brother Thomas, and cousin William Hawkins were officers, and his cabin boy was his young cousin John Drake. Diego, the former slave from Panama, sailed as Drake's manservant and was a paid member of the crew.[17] The crew consisted of about 164 able men who served as men-at-arms or as common sailors. The ship carried a cook, a surgeon, a surgeon's boy, smiths, carpenters, and coopers (the *Pelican* carried a forge). Onboard were musicians, including a drummer, a trumpeter, and two or more violists.

Officers of the voyage included a chaplain, Francis Fletcher, and various gentlemen adventurers or noblemen who were investors in the enterprise or who were supported by their patrons at court. One of the gentlemen onboard was Lawrence Eliot, a naturalist whose drawings and botanical descriptions were published shortly after their return.[18]

During the planning and on the outset of the voyage, courtier Thomas Doughty and Captain John Winter considered themselves "equal companions and friendly gentlemen" with Drake in the enterprise, as remembered by John Cooke, an officer on the voyage.[19] On land Doughty may have regarded himself Drake's superior due to his high social standing and connections at court. By Elizabethan conventions Doughty had a major say—perhaps an equal say—in decisions and the initial direction of the undertaking, as did John Winter, who was probably a relative of the Lord High Admiral of the Tudor Navy, William Winter.

Onboard it was a microcosm of the English class system. Tudor sumptuary laws (literally a dress code for social classes) dictated the type of cloth and even the colors that social classes could wear. The officers and captains wore garments of richly embroidered silk and fine linen in scarlet, greens, and royal blues corresponding to their rank in society, and they were allowed to wear fur on their collars or fur lined cloaks. The commoners were relegated to clothes of rough wools or coarse linen dyed in shades of indigo blue, muted browns, and yellows. These base-level men quartered in the forecastle and ate simple fare. The captains and officers, in contrast, drank fine wine, ate the best food available off fine china and silver tableware; and at Drake's table they dined to the music of viols.[20]

After a false start and some damage to the fleet due to bad weather, they ventured out of Plymouth Harbor on December 13, 1577. As soon as they were out of sight of land, Drake informed the fleet that if they became separated, to rendezvous at the Island of Mogadore, in the Atlantic, just off of the coast of Morocco. This news at once informed the crew that they were not sailing for the Mediterranean. At Mogadore they gathered by Christmas Day, where they set about building a pinnace, a small ship they had brought in pieces and assembled on the island. As they continued south, they used this little ship to capture some Spanish fishing vessels and a caravel.[21]

Their first major action was in the Cape Verde Islands where they captured a Portuguese ship laden with farming tools, cloth, wine, and other goods for Brazil. Historian Oscar Spate described this event as significant in several aspects: "First, it was naked piracy: there could be no question of reprisals, the islands had been Portuguese for over a century, and it was only two years since Elizabeth had signed a treaty to stop English incursions in these parts. Second, while Drake released the rest of the company, he took good care to keep Nuño da Silva, a pilot highly experienced on the Brazilian coast."[22]

At about this time, the aristocrat Thomas Doughty began to assert himself in ways that some of Drake's men found uncomfortable. Doughty accused Drake's brother Thomas of pocketing some of the booty. Thomas made a counter charge that Doughty had inappropriately touched John Brewer, the trumpeter, on the "buttoke." As the ships made their way across the Atlantic, these troubles grew to mutinous levels in the humid doldrums: "Friction grew into disaffection: there were petty squabbles, crude horseplay, arrogant or ironic speeches, ostentatious avoidances between gentlemen and mariners, and Drake's attempts at alleviation by shifting commands were unsuccessful."[23]

Finally they arrived at their wintering place: a natural harbor occupied by the Patagonian people on the very southern Argentinean coast. Here they scuttled the Portuguese prize ship, and used her for firewood. They set up their tents, and remained for two months.

Ironically, this was the same natural harbor where Ferdinand Magellan had wintered in 1520, whilst preparing for his attempt on the strait that was to bear his name. Here on the beach Drake and his men found the ruins of the gallows Magellan used to execute members of his crew for mutiny. Doughty was accused of sedition, and in a twist of irony, he stood trial on the same beach, for not only mutiny but treason. That he was guilty there was little doubt. William Camden, a seventeenth-century historian, remarked, "the most impartiall of all the Company, did judge, that he had indeed carried himself a little sedicioulsly."[24] Doughty was found guilty, beheaded, and buried on a sandy island in the harbor.

Other authors, including Vaux and Kelsey, have discussed the story of Thomas Doughty's misdeeds and eventual execution during the voyage. Here it is sufficient to note that on the beach just after Doughty's execution Drake established himself as the undisputed leader of the expedition. John Cooke recorded the speech Drake gave where he reminded the crew that they were very far from their own country, and surrounded by enemies:

> Wherefore we must have these mutinies and discords that are grown amongst us redressed, for by the life of God it doth even take my wits from me to think on it: here is such controversy between the sailors and the gentlemen, and such stomaching between the gentlemen and sailors, that it doth even make me mad to hear it. But, my masters, I must have it left, for I must have the gentleman to haul and draw with the mariner, and the mariner with the gentlemen. What, let us show our selves all to be of a company.[25]

There was to be no more rule-by-committee. From this point on, there was a single clear chain of command on the voyage and it ended at General Drake. This command structure eventually became established in all the ships of the English Navy, a convention the Spanish did not adopt. It was never quite clear who gave the decisive orders on a Spanish ship.[26]

The slowest ships, the *Swan* and the *Christopher,* were scuttled; their fittings and iron salvaged. Three ships remained: the *Pelican*, the *Marigold* and the *Elizabeth*. On August 17, 1578, they set out, proceeding south toward Cape Virgin Maria at the entrance to the Strait of Magellan. This was their first important objective. It was here according to the Drake and Fletcher account that Drake ordered the fleet "to strike their topsails upon the bunt, as a token of his willing and glad mind, to show his dutiful obedience to her highness, whom he acknowledged to have full interest and right in that new discovery."[27] It was here that the *Pelican* may have been renamed *Golden Hind*.[28]

The reduced fleet of three ships—and at least one pinnace—entered the strait on or about August 20, 1578, and soon found that the passage had many turns and arms that led nowhere, forcing them to retreat on several occasions in an effort to find the main passage. Taken from east to west, the Strait of Magellan calls for maneuvers that are exceptionally perilous in contrary winds—and the winds are typically contrary. They had trouble keeping the fleet together, and found that sometimes one ship would pass a cape, only to have the winds change, preventing the others from joining; this would force them to anchor until the winds were favorable. The land on both sides was high and mountainous. However, there was no lack of fresh water, and finding penguins easy prey, they took in a store of three thousand of the birds that they found nesting on an island in the channel. On another island they found "scurvy grass" and other greens that were a help as Drake and Fletcher recalled "both in our diet and physick, to the great relief of the limbs of our men."[29]

At one point it was not clear whether they should take the open road on the north, or the fret southward. Drake brought the fleet to anchor under an island, and with some of his officers, rowed out to explore the way, and found the entrance to the great South Sea, i.e. the Pacific Ocean to the north. The fleet emerged from the strait on September 6, and ran northwest about seventy leagues, making for Peru.[30]

However, a relentless gale drove them two hundred leagues south of the strait. The wind was almost continuous; for much of the time the ships could not bear any sail. The crews were weakened by short rations and worn out by working in the bitter cold where monstrous waves battered them constantly for fifty-two days. This was an unaccountably long time in these conditions. Winter reported that "most of our men fell sick of the sickness Magellan speaketh of [scurvy]."[31] When the winds finally abated, and the sky cleared enough to take a navigational reading, they found they had reached 57° south (about 9° shy of what is now called the Antarctic Circle). They anchored in the lee of an island off Cape Horn. Here they found a few scattered islands, and an open expanse of sea where the Atlantic and Pacific converge. They claimed the southernmost island as an English possession and named it Elizabeth Island, after the Queen. This expanse of open sea astonished them, because until then, mapmakers believed the continent encompassed the Antarctic region, and the only path to the Pacific was through the Strait of Magellan.[32] Here is where Drake earned the southern star for his coat-of-arms. Drake is credited with the discovery of this open passage south of Cape Horn, which now bears his name: Drakes Passage.

A respite in the weather allowed them to make their way north again. Just as they were beating past the western entrance of the Strait of Magellan the weather rose up yet again. During the night watch on

September 28, they lost the little *Marigold* along with her crew of 28 men. John Brewer and John Cooke reported they heard their "fearful cryes when the hand of God came upon them."[33] On October 7 the seas had grown even more, and the *Elizabeth* and the *Golden Hind* were forced to run east to the land to find shelter. They entered a very dangerous and deep bay where the *Golden Hind* lost an anchor, forcing her back out to sea.

It was on this occasion that the flagship lost company with the *Elizabeth*. The next day Captain Winter ordered that the *Elizabeth* put into the Strait of Magellan, which was just at hand, to find better shelter. They anchored in an open bay for two days with fires lit on the shore in hopes that Drake would sight them. For three weeks they sheltered in the strait. The men at first were "very sick with long watching, wet, cold and evil diet."[34] However, this respite enabled them to recover their health on a diet of mussels and birds.

Drake, meanwhile, was looking for the *Elizabeth* along the coast. There was no sign of her, nor of the little *Marigold*, for which they still held out some hope. What Drake did not know was that Captain Winter had decided to abandon the voyage, apparently against the wishes of some of the men onboard, and turn back to England.[35] At one point, Drake sent out a pinnace with eight men "to wait upon the ship for all necessary uses," but foul weather struck and they were separated. Despite a desperate search, they lost each other, and the men in the pinnace sailed back into the strait. Peter Carder, the only survivor, reported their misadventures after he finally made it back to England in 1586.[36] There is some doubt about the veracity of his story; Sugden suggests the accounts were edited, and that the pinnace was lost off of the *Elizabeth* rather than the *Golden Hind*.[37]

The *Golden Hind* sailed north toward the appointed height of 30° south, where the fleet had orders to rendezvous in the event that they became separated.[38] On the Island of Mocha, Drake and a few officers landed to ascertain if they could water and take on fresh food. The people gave Drake two fat sheep and some hens, and thinking the work would be accomplished in peace, Drake arranged that they would return the next morning to fill their water barrels. When they landed, the Natives attacked in a bloody ambush. Drake's relative Richard Hawkins related that the Natives of Mocha betrayed Drake's trust: "They used him with so fine a treachery, that they possessed themselves of all the oars in his boat, saving two, and in striving to get them also, they slew and hurt all his men: himself, who had fewest wounds, had three, and two of them in the head."[39] The Drake and Fletcher account said 500 men attacked them; Fletcher, the likely source of the Harley manuscript, reported only 160.[40] John Drake related "they fled and attempted to embark in their boat. But the Indians shot many arrows at them, wounding all in the boat, although the arrows did not enter the flesh deeply."[41] Richard Hawkins reported that the trumpeter John Brewer was wounded by seventeen arrows, and Drake's servant Diego by "above twenty."[42]

Diego did not die right away from his wounds, and in fact lived for many more months. There has been some confusion about Diego's death because the main text reported that he died of his injuries, but a marginal note on the original document clarifies that he died near the Indonesian Moluccas Islands, which the *Golden Hind* only reached twelve months later.[43] Kaufmann conjectured he may have died as a result of one of his wounds becoming infected or turning gangrenous, or else he could have developed scurvy, which causes old wounds to reopen.[44]

While most of Drake's crew survived the attack at Mocha Island, a gunner called Great Nele, a Dane, was not so lucky, and Drake himself nearly lost his life.[45] Of the three arrows that wounded Drake, two were in his head: "The General himself was shot in the face, under his right eye, and close by his nose, the arrow piercing a marvelous way in under *basis cerebri*, which no small danger of his life; besides that he was grievously wounded in the head."[46] Their chief surgeon was dead, the other surgeon was on the *Elizabeth*—wherever she was—and the only one with medical expertise was the surgeon's assistant, a boy, "whose good will was more then any skill he had, we were little better then altogether destitute of such cunning and helps, as so grievous a state of so many wounded bodies did require."[47]

In Nuño da Silva's Inquisition testimony taken a few months later, he related that Drake could be identified by his scar: "He has the mark of an arrow-wound in his right cheek which is not apparent if one does not look with special care."[48] Drake recounted that the people of Isla Mocha mistook them for their Spanish enemies, and blamed the aggression of the islanders on the Spanish, who had driven these people from the mainland.[49]

They were more cautious as they proceeded north. They passed by Native towns on the coast, and the people came out to them in boats and traded fish for trinkets.[50] The weather improved, fresh food revived the crew, wounds healed, and news of treasure-laden ships further north boosted moral and whetted their piratical appetites.

Their raiding began in earnest at Valparaiso, where they captured a good quantity of local wine, gold, and an emerald encrusted gold cross.[51] Drake captured a pilot (one of several captured on the voyage and later released) who knew the coast. At a port called Tarapaca they landed and found a Spaniard lying asleep on the trail, next to him was a pack that contained 13 bars of silver. They unburdened him without waking him up: "We freed him of his charge, which otherwise perhaps would have kept him waking."[52]

As they met ships en route they boarded and rifled through them, taking what they wanted.[53] It might have been from the captain of one of the captured ships that Drake found out that his comrades John Oxenham, John Butler, Thomas Xerores, and an English youth named Henry Butler were imprisoned in Lima.

Drake's plan to link up with Oxenham and their Cimarron allies in Panama was foiled but a new plan took shape.[54] Drake worked out a scheme to free them from their Spanish prison. This effort was set into motion when the *Golden Hind* entered the port of Callao at Lima about ten o'clock at night on Friday, February 13. As soon as they dropped anchor they were hailed by a man aboard a Panamanian ship that had sailed into the harbor about the same time. Drake ordered one of his Spanish prisoners to call back and say that they were from Chile, so no alarm was raised.[55]

There were twelve ships at anchor in the harbor at the time. Drake's men boarded two nearby vessels, and found a chest full of silver aboard one of the ships, as well as a good stock of linen and silk. They then met with resistance; one of Drake's men was shot and killed as they began to secure the Panamanian ship. Drake, who had cannons primed, fired a cannon ball clean through her sides. No one was killed by the shot, but her crew abandoned her, and Drake's men were then able to capture the Panamanian ship.[56]

Drake's crew boarded the other ships and cut their cables and hawsers to set the ships adrift. His plan was for these ships to be carried out of the harbor by the tide and the wind, and at sea his men would then gather them and use them as ransom for Oxenham and the other Englishmen. As they were preparing to leave the harbor, however, the wind that had been blowing from the land, fell, and their sails emptied. Meanwhile, the town had been awakened by the cannon fire and burst into activity. Drake had no time to gather the drifting ships. In the end they escaped on the tide with only the Panamanian ship, which they abandoned soon after.[57] Drake's ransom plan to obtain the release of his friend and comrades had failed.

Drake's imprisoned comrades were interrogated one week after Drake's raid on Callao. It was only in 1908 in the Archivo General de Indias, in Seville, that anthropologist Zelia Nuttall found the sworn declarations taken that day of Captain John Oxenham, John Butler, and Thomas Xerores. This new light shed on the voyage included comments on Drake's means and the Crown's motives. The line of questioning by the inquisitors was about Drake, his purpose, and whether there was any state-sponsored project to arm ships and pass through the Strait of Magellan. Butler affirmed there was, and described the Grenville plan of four years prior where the Queen granted a license to found settlements in lands that were unclaimed. Butler related that Her Majesty later revoked the license, and the ships that were being fitted out for the venture were sold. When questioned about Drake's route, Butler said "it was a well known thing that, if one did not return through the Strait, one would be obliged to make the round voyage by the Portuguese Indies, the Cape of Good Hope, and the coast of Africa, and return to the Canaries."[58] When John Oxenham was interrogated he reported there was a route through "another Strait that passed into the North Sea, but nobody knows this for a certainty or has passed through it."[59]

The prisoners' testimony does not reveal their thoughts, or how much they were told about Drake's raid on Callao and his dramatic efforts to free them. Were they heartened by Drake's presence? It is a

Caca Fogo.

Caca Plata.

FIGURE 5.2. *Battle between Francis Drake's ship* Golden Hind *and the Spanish ship* Nuestra Señora de la Concepción, *nick-named the* Cacafuego. From Levinus Hulsius's *kurtze, warhafftige Relation vnnd Beschreibung der wunderbarsten vier Schiffarhten*, 1626. Used by permission, Getty Images.

pretty thought to imagine the astonishing reunion if Drake's scheme had been successful.

Drake and his crew continued north. They had information about an even greater prize: a Panama-bound treasure ship that was en route from Peru, the *Nuestra Señora de la Concepción*.[60] This ship had a nickname, *Cacafuego*, which colloquially meant "emits fire" and was the Spanish idiom for a braggart.[61] This has been translated as *Spitfire*, which has a different modern connotation. (It should be noted that this word could turn into *Shitfire* readily in either English or Spanish.) As Drake and his crew hunted the sea for the *Nuestra Señora de la Concepción*, they captured and detained several ships in an attempt to gain information on her movements and whereabouts.

On one such occasion, on the last day of February 1579, Drake captured a ship piloted by Benito Diaz Bravo, and imprisoned the crew for two days. Drake's crew had been reduced by losses to about eighty-five men. They were distributed on the *Golden Hind* and a pinnace. The *Golden Hind* was overloaded, and Drake needed another ship. He initially tried installing some of his artillery in the captured ship, and tested her sails. In the end, though, he opted to return the ship to Diaz, who thought that Drake decided not to take it because "he realized that he had too few men to distribute into two ships and the launch."[62] However, before releasing Diaz's ship, Drake's crew appropriated tackle and rigging, various cargo, and a great deal of victuals, including maize, salt pork, and hams. The food was exactly what they needed: these victuals had been destined for the provisioning of a Spanish ship for a voyage across the Pacific to the Philippines.[63]

Drake had promised that whoever first spied the treasure ship would be rewarded with a gold chain necklace. On March 1, at about three o'clock in the afternoon, young John Drake sighted her. The *Nuestra Señora de la Concepción's* captain, San Juan de Anton, related that he at first thought the *Golden Hind* was a local trader, and so changed course to intercept her. Drake had the pinnace hauled up on deck, and hung oil jars filled with water from the stern as a drag to slow his ship. This was a device to make it appear that the ship was just a slow merchant ship, even under full sail.[64] The pursuit was slow but deliberate. At about six o'clock that evening the *Golden Hind* came alongside the *Nuestra Señora de la Concepción*, guns ready, and with one shot knocked down her mizzenmast and she was captured (see Figure 5.2).[65] The Drake and Fletcher account of this action likely had more input from Drake than Fletcher, who gleefully relates what they captured:

> We found in her some fruit, conserves, sugars, meal, and other victuals, and (that which was the special cause of her heavy and slow sailing) a certain quantity of jewels and precious stones, 13 chests of royals of plate, 80 pound weight in gold, 26 tunne of uncoined silver, two very fair gilt silver drinking bowls, and the like trifles, valued in all about 36,000 pesos. We gave the master a little linen and the like for these commodities, and at the end of six days we bade farewell and parted.[66]

Hakluyt reported in *The Famous Voyage* that the treasure included jewels, precious stones, thirteen chests full of coins, forty pounds of gold, and twenty-six tons of silver. In the anonymous Harley manuscript the amount of gold was doubled and the author commented that there was "so mooch silver as did ballast the *Goulden Hinde*."[67]

As they were leaving, one young sailor yelled out that the ship's common name should be changed from *Spitfire* to *Spitsilver* (*Cacaplata*): "When the pilot departed from us, his boy said thus unto our General: Captain, our ship shall be no more the *Cacafuego*, but the *Cacaplata*, and your ship shall be called the *Cacafuego*: which pretty speech of the pilot's boy ministered matter of laughter to us, both then and long after."[68]

It was also this moment when Drake tried one more time to free John Oxenham and the others. When he set the ship free, Drake gave a message to Captain San Juan de Anton to carry to the viceroy who he knew would interview him. Drake told de Anton to tell the viceroy that he has killed enough Englishmen, and that he is not to kill the four who remain: "He charged San Juan de Anton to beg the Viceroy of Peru from him not to kill the English prisoners, and said that if they were killed, it would cost more than two thousand heads, not those of people of Spain, but of these parts adding that if he reached England alive, there would be no one there who would attempt to hinder [prosecute] him from carrying out this threat."[69]

In the version of the story told by Domingo de Lizarza, another one of Drake's prisoners, the number of men he would hang was three thousand, and the heads of the hanged would be cut off their bodies and cast into the bay at Callao de Lima.[70] De Anton mollified Drake by commenting that the Englishmen had not been killed outright, which suggested to him that they would probably be sent to Chile to serve as soldiers in a garrison to fight the Natives. "Francis rejoiced greatly on hearing this and became pacified; for he displayed much anger whenever he spoke about them."[71]

The *Nuestra Señora de la Concepción's* treasure clinched the success of their voyage and would provide a big payoff to the investors back in England. If they made a safe return to England, every man onboard would be rich—providing a Catholic sovereign had not replaced Queen Elizabeth. That was a real fear, as there had been many plots and intrigues to dethrone the queen and Drake had no guarantee that when he arrived back in England he would be well received.

On March 17, Diego de Messa was a passenger in a bark owned and commanded by Captain Rodrigo Tello. De Messa reported that off the island of Caño they saw a pinnace with about thirty men rowing fast towards them. Some of the men were archers and some carried shields, and still others had arquebuses. These were Drake's men, and when they reached the bark they ordered the crew to strike sail. Tello refused. Drake's men sounded trumpets and discharged arquebuses, wounding a man in the face and the arm. Tello surrendered, and the crew and passengers were transferred as prisoners to the *Golden Hind*, which was at anchor in a small bay on the mainland ten miles away.[72] Cornieles Lambert was a merchant on the ship, and related the following in his deposition to the Spanish officials: "The vessel was in the small bay and after the Corsair seized Rodrigo Tello's bark he began to transfer into her, for the purpose of lightening his vessel, his artillery, which he placed therein in disorder, as well as many locked chests. Then he hove down all the gold and silver that he had [onto the river bank], and repaired both sides of his vessel so far as she was out of water."[73]

Drake asked his prisoners where he could find a beach to completely careen his flagship so the whole bottom could be caulked. His prisoners did not know a suitable location. Drake, in desperation, decided to keep the little bark. Drake apologized to Tello but felt he had no choice because "he did not know in what necessity he might find himself out at sea, because his vessel was leaking, and that, even if the bark belonged to his own father, he could not desist from taking her."[74] They added oars to the bark, and strengthened the wale planks so she could carry a new main topsail. According to Lambert, who overheard Drake's plans, they hoped this would make her fit to sail all the way across the Pacific to the Moluccas.[75] Drake also took the bark's pilot as prisoner.

Just over a week later, on April 4, 1579, off the coast of Guatemala, in the early morning hours Don Francisco de Zarate saw a ship in the moonlight coming very close to his ship. Only six of his men were awake at the time. His steersman shouted to the other ship to get out of the way and not come along side, but the crew on the other ship pretended to be asleep. Suddenly, the *Golden Hind* veered across their poop deck and a voice ordered them to strike sail, as seven or eight arquebus shots flew over them.[76] Zarate and his crew were captured. Zarate wrote: "On our part there was no resistance…so they entered our ship with as little risk to themselves as though they were our friends. They did no personal harm to any one beyond seizing the swords and keys of the passengers."[77]

Zelia Nuttall discovered a note in da Silva's logbook that mentioned that Don Francisco de Zarate was a nobleman and cousin to the Duke of Medina.[78] De Zarate was on his way to Panama, and planned to subsequently sail to Manila with letters from the King of Spain to the governor of the Philippines. Onboard were luxury goods that included four crates of Chinese porcelains, bales of taffeta, linen, and silk, and chests of expensive clothing. The Harley manuscript relates the following exchange about de Zarate's cargo that illustrates this point: "The owner of this ship earnestly entreated Drake and besought him not to take away from his apparel, which he [Drake] promised not to do, and the gentleman gave him a falcon of gold with a great emerald in the breast thereof for his favorable dealing with him."[79] Drake kept de Zarate and his ship captive for three days and entertained him at his table. He thought de Zarate might be a relative of the viceroy (the man that betrayed Hawkins at San Juan de Ulúa) and asked one of the pilots he had captured if this was true, but that particular pilot did not know.[80] Drake freed that pilot, but took as a prisoner de Zarate's own pilot.

Drake also took de Zarate's slave, Maria, who was referred to by the author of the Harley manuscript (almost certainly Chaplain Fletcher) as: "A proper negro wench called Maria, which was afterward gotten with child between the captain and his men pirates, and set on a small island to take her adventure as shall be hereafter shewed."[81]

Whether, like Diego, Maria became a free person once she stepped onboard is unknown. Historian Miranda Kaufmann remarked that Drake had eschewed slavery since the events with his uncle at San Juan de Ulúa, and recounted that when Drake was offered "a woman, a Moore'" off the coast of Mauretania he refused because this was the sort of merchandise in which Drake "would not deal."[82]

Though Drake took the porcelain wares and some cloth from de Zarate's ship, his most important acquisitions were the sailing directions and charts that would lead him across the Pacific. Francisco de Zarate was freed, and as he took his leave Drake spoke to him: "His last words were to beseech me, earnestly, to tell certain Englishmen [Oxenham and the others] who were in Lima that I had met him on April 6th and that he was well."[83]

It is not known if de Zarate delivered the message to the Englishmen in Lima. Perhaps the date Drake gave de Zarate had an embedded message to the men. These men would consider the date, and it may have occurred to Oxenham, who had sailed with Drake, to refer to the psalms read on that day from the Book of Common Prayer.[84] The proper psalms to be read the sixth day of April are Psalms 30–34.[85] Psalm 30 speaks to "God lifting me out of the depths," not to have "my enemies gloat over me," and being "spared from going down into a pit," and that "weeping at night will give way to rejoicing in the morning."

Whether Drake's message of April 6 was an embedded message of hope is interesting to contemplate. If the imprisoned men were told that Drake was on the coast, and of his efforts to free them, then they must have been heartened. The Spanish interrogated Oxenham and the other English prisoners, and when Oxenham was asked about Drake and if the Queen would have sanctioned his voyage, his response as related by the interrogator is as follows: "Witness thinks that if the Queen were to give a license to Captain Francis Drake he would certainly come and pass through the Strait, because he is a very good mariner and pilot, and

there is no better one than he in England who could accomplish this."[86]
Despite Drake's threats of murder and beheaded corpses, Oxenham,
Xerores, and Butler were not released. They were hanged at Lima by
the civil authorities in November 1580, a little more than a month after
Drake returned to Plymouth Sound.[87] Writing in 1843 John Barrow considered Oxenham: "Drake had the highest opinion of him, and he was
beloved by the whole crew."[88]

Drake anchored at Guatulco on April 15, 1579. At first the towns-
people were not alarmed because they mistook the *Golden Hind* for a
Spanish ship. About twenty men came ashore in a launch, while Drake
remained on the ship. According to the anonymous account, they apparently walked up the street and into the courthouse, where a judge
was handing down a sentence to three Black men who were on trial for
conspiracy to burn the town. Drake's crew took the prisoners and the
judge to the ship where Drake induced the judge to write a letter to the
townspeople telling them to avoid Drake's men and allow them to safely
water there and take the spoils of the town.[89]

Subsequently, Drake's men proceeded to loot the town. In addition
to the seizing of goods, they broke up the stone altar in the church and
slashed the graven images therein. A red-haired, pockmarked man, who
was identified as a boatswain, took a crucifix belonging to the chief factor
of the port and struck it against a table breaking it into pieces. Seeing that
the chief factor was grieved, the boatswain said that they were not Chris-
tians but "idolaters, who adore sticks and stones."[90] Nuttall noted that
the "English writers observe absolute silence about the acts of religious
fanaticism perpetrated in the church of Guatulco."[91] Nuttall conjectured
the boatswain's motives for the vandalism might have been because
he may have been one of John Hawkins's men who suffered under the
Inquisition.

As they were embarking Guatulco, Drake invited the Black men who
had been on trial to join him. Two stayed on board, and one was freed
onshore where he disappeared into the woods.[92]

Licentiate Valverde was the local Spanish official who reported
Drake's activities to King Philip II in a letter. He related that they car-
ried off the town traders' entire supply of *huipiles*, which he described as
"Indian women's petticoats." These are the light woven dresses that are a

traditional garment of various Mayan groups. He cited this as proof that Drake planned to go north, and suggested his plan for the garments was as follows:

> [To] trade them for victuals and articles of necessity and keep them contented during the time when he would have to repair his ship and be in his winter quarters. This would necessarily have to be done with the warlike Indians who inhabit the coast beyond New Spain and New Galicia [central Mexico]. He would not otherwise have carried off the said Indian clothing; for he was not going to wear it, nor would it be of utility in England.[93]

At Guatulco Drake and his crew unmounted the ordnance and caulked the portholes in preparation for the open sea. They took in a supply of fresh water and wood. Another prisoner, Cornelius Lambert, observed that they had "much flour and meat, fish and Spanish wine, preserves and vegetables, and a quantity of biscuit."[94]

It was also at Guatulco that Drake left Nuño da Silva. This was a surprise move by Drake, and da Silva was quite distressed that Drake left him on shore "for the poor man very unwilling to have been left to ye Spaniard for a prayer."[95] Da Silva was immediately deposed before the Inquisition—racked to make him confess—and testified that Drake was bound to go explore for the Strait de los Bacallaos (the Northwest Passage). (Evidence that da Silva did not hold a grudge against Drake was a document found by Nuttall in the Archivo General de Indias, Seville, that mentioned that a few years later da Silva was living in Plymouth and serving as pilot on English ships.)[96]

Valverde believed Drake would winter on the California coast beyond New Spain and careen his leaking ship "in those small bays or deep coves that are there."[97] He noted that Drake carried all that was necessary for caulking and careening the *Golden Hind*, which was ballasted with silver, chests of gold, and reales of eight.[98]

Drake left the coast of Mexico and sailed northwest. In order to avoid the calms and current along the coast, the course Drake took is described as follows: "He saw that of necessity he must be enforced to take a Spanish course, namely, to sail somewhat northerly to get a wind. We therefore set sail, and sailed 800 leagues at the least for a good wind."[99] The

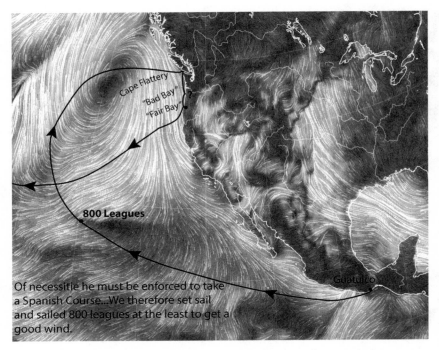

Cape Flattery

"Bad Bay"

"Fair Bay"

?

800 Leagues

Of necessitie he must be enforced to take
a Spanish Course...We therefore set sail
and sailed 800 leagues at the least to get a
good wind.

Guatulco

FIGURE 5.3. Drake's probable route to the Northwest coast from Gualtulco,
showing the prevailing surface winds on a typical day in spring and summer.

Golden Hind was best before the wind. They sailed northwest, out into
the Pacific on a bowline so as to catch the wind and current that would
swing them north then east in a clockwise spiral (see Figure 5.3). By late
May or early June, they found the coast. This was the first certain exploration of latitudes north of 43° by Europeans. They were in a position to
secure a place for "thorough careening well beyond any risk of Spanish
interference; fill in time until a less hazardous season for crossing the
ocean; and perhaps disclose a short and safe passage for home; should
there really be a Strait of Anian."[100]

The North Pacific Gyre is situated between the equator and 50° north
latitude. In June, July, and August the prevailing surface winds and currents circulate clockwise.[101] The uncensored accounts suggest that Drake
took advantage of the gyre by sailing west for many leagues, then north
on a bowline that eventually swung them east to approach the west coast
at about 48° north. This route is consistent with sailing directions for

the wind sailor in *Ocean Passages of the World* (1973) for early summer from lower California, which instruct the sailor to proceed west until the variable winds are reached, in about 130° longitude, and then make a northing to sail on this clockwise wind around and then point eastwards.[102] As planned, this course put them in a good position to search for the Strait of Anian, the entrance for the fabled Northwest Passage that purportedly connected the Pacific and Atlantic Oceans. They may have searched from early June to mid-June or later. Eventually the leak in the *Golden Hind* forced them to find a haven to repair her.[103]

Drake and company found that the west coast "did not trend so much as one point in any place towards the East, but rather running on continually North-west, as if it went directly to meet with Asia."[104] The geographical trend of the coastline was an important observation that astronomer and the Queen's personal astrologer, John Dee, in particular, had hoped to ascertain. Drake could not have described the American coast trending northwestward if he had reached latitudes short of 48° north. It is significant that after Drake's voyage Mercator maps showed the Northwest coast with surprising accuracy, and the Northwest Passage was no longer depicted as a broad open expanse of water.

Martin Frobisher thought he had found the strait's eastern entrance in 1576, the year before Drake began this voyage. Frobisher caused quite a stir with the announcement that he had found entrance to the strait at latitude 60° north, though he had actually found an inlet on the south of Baffin Island that now bears his name. Frobisher was there late in the season, and what he thought was the passage to China was blocked by ice. However, to prove his claim he brought back three people he thought were from the Orient because of their "black hair, broad faces, flat wry noses, of a swarth and tawny color."[105] Actually, they were not Asians but Inuit people, who died soon after he brought them to England.

If Drake had found a passage that summer, what a coup it would have been. He would have discovered a short route from England to the Orient that avoided Spanish colonies, and importantly for Drake, if it was as some mapmakers imagined at the time, the passage would have been a shortcut home, with prevailing winds at his back.

As it turned out there was no passage, and the window for catching the wind to cross the Pacific was closing. From the sailing directions and charts of the route across the Pacific that Drake had obtained from two captured pilots, he would have understood that the best time to begin the journey across the Pacific was in late summer. These instructions must have warned that it would be fatal to arrive in the South Pacific during the typhoon season, which typically ended in late October or early November. Calculating a crossing time of two months, they could begin the Pacific crossing at the end of August to safely avoid the typhoon season. Within this window of time, the crew explored the coast of North America for perhaps two weeks in early June before the leak forced them to seek a careenage.

The company coasted south looking for a careenage. Henry Wagner noted that the worst cargo a vessel can carry is bars of metal, as was true with the *Golden Hind*, with a full cargo being exceedingly dangerous, "as it is perfectly rigid."[106] It was vital to find a bay with the necessary conditions to careen the ship, and prepare her for the journey across the Pacific Ocean. They briefly touched in a "bad bay, the best road we could for the present meet with," but the exposed bay was dangerous and they were forced to leave in search of better mooring.[107] A protected bay and a gently sloping sandy beach—one with no large breaking waves—were the necessary requirements.

The *Golden Hind* was a remarkably small and tough ship. She was double hulled, and designed in the new sleek manner favored by the new administrators in the Tudor Navy. These were fast ships that could outmaneuver the typically larger Spanish ships, and they could shelter and refit in small bays. The *Golden Hind* was well down to her marks with the weight of the treasure, so her draft would have been perhaps thirteen to fourteen feet due to the load.[108]

Exploring the coast with the pinnace or Tello's bark for close-in reconnaissance, they found a bay that met the specific careenage requirements. There they encamped for several weeks, explored the country, and prepared the ship for the long Pacific voyage. (The crew's interactions with the Native inhabitants of the area will be described in future chapters.)

Nautical archaeologist Peter Michael Goelet commented on the requirements for a good careenage: "The preferred location for a careening was a place where the land configuration would afford some protection against the prevailing winds and provide calm water for the low-freeboard work platforms or floats hauled close along the exposed hull…the site had to be defensible, and if possible some of the ships guns would be positioned to defend entrances to the careenage."[109]

Careening, or "heaving down" as the English preferred to call it, was the act of tipping a vessel on one side to expose the other side. Besides repairing the leak, they would have cleaned off the barnacles that had built up on the hull, cleaned out the old caulking material from the seams of the planks and driven new oakum, cotton, or rope fibers into each seam.

Drake had heaved down the ship a few months previously, but the conditions were such that the ship had been only partially careened. This was sometimes called half-careening or partial heeling. This episode was described as follows by Cornieles Lambert, a Flemish merchant taken prisoner by Drake on March 20, 1579: "The vessel [*Golden Hind*] was in the small bay and after the Corsair seized Rodrigo Tello's bark he began to transfer into her, for the purpose of lightening his vessel, his artillery, which he placed therein in disorder, as well as many locked chests. Then he hove down all the gold and silver that he had, and repaired both sides of his vessel so far as she was out of the water."[110]

Tello's bark was still their consort two months later as they searched along the Northwest coast for a safe careenage. According to the Drake and Fletcher account, they anchored in their "fair and good bay" on June 17, 1579. On the third day, "our ship having received a leak at sea, was brought to anchor nearer the shore, that, her goods being landed, she might be repaired."[111] A vessel could be careened against a shore, a floating hulk, a pier or wharf projecting from the shore, or it could be hoved down against another ship. The heaving down gear consisted of tackles with blocks affixed to one or two of the *Golden Hind's* masts. The advantage of careening the ship against a floating craft, such as Tello's bark, was that the tackle falls needed less adjustment. If the ship was careened against the shore, then the lines would have been attached to heavy posts set in the ground and connected to a capstan. In this case, the tackle falls needed constant attention, for as the tide rose they needed to be slackened, and tightened as it fell.

The accounts do not describe the careening process. We know that Drake carried ship carpenters who probably supervised. Before she could be careened, the gundeck ports would have to be sealed, and her stores, armaments, toprigging, and ballast of bullion had to be landed. As later happened on Crab Island in the Moluccas, it is likely that "there was order given and followed for the burning of charcoal" and that a smith's forge was set up, both for making some "necessary shipwork," and for the repairing of some iron-hooped casks.[112]

The landing in the fair and good bay is noteworthy because the crew was composed of the first Europeans as well as the first people of African descent to set foot on the Northwest coast of America. Of the Black Moors or Cimmerons, we only know the names of two: Maria and Drake's manservant Diego. It is possible that Diego and the two other Black men on the crew organized the construction of the stronghold at the fair and good bay. It was Diego with the help of the other Cimmerons that built a fort for Drake and his men in the Panamanian jungle in 1572. Their fort was tightly built out of branches and boughs and they named it Fort Diego.[113]

With the ship successfully repaired, Drake's main problem at this point in the voyage was that there were too many men for the *Golden Hind* to carry back to England. Licentiate Valverde of Guatemala had reported Drake's actions and details of Drake's equipment in a letter to Philip II, and in the letter he expressed doubt that Drake would cross the Pacific: "He cannot convey, in one ship only, the provisions sufficient for the eighty men he carries, during such a long voyage, even if his ship were to carry no other cargo but victuals."[114]

Of the eighty men counted by Valverde, only fifty-eight or fifty-nine men made it back to Plymouth.[115] There are about twenty men unaccounted for. Samuel Bawlf conjectured that these men were assigned to Tello's bark, which he thought may have been left behind in order to continue explorations further up the Pacific in search of the Strait of Anian.[116] These men and the ship remain unaccounted for and are lost to history.

In his first deposition, John Drake related to his captors that the complement was reduced in the Moluccas: "There they took in a supply of meat and provisions and lightened their ship by reducing their company to sixty men."[117] However, there is no Spanish or Portuguese record of Englishmen being landed in the Moluccas. In his second deposition,

John Drake said that they left the smaller ship in the "Californias," which was probably the truth.[118] Nuttall noted in several instances that John misled his inquisitors in order to avoid disclosing sensitive information, and that was probably the case here: "It is noteworthy that he speaks most guardedly of California and entirely omits any allusion to the fact that Francis Drake took possession of the land and named it New Albion—an action which would scarcely meet with the approval of his Spanish examiners."[119]

It seems likely that when the *Golden Hind* embarked on the cross-Pacific leg of the journey there were about sixty-two men and one woman onboard. One day after leaving the bay, they paused at a rocky archipelago where they took in a plentiful supply of seal meat and birds, which they found "completely serve our turn for awhile."[120] There are many rocky islands along the Oregon coast where birds make their nests and seals haul out. These islands may be the ones situated off of the white cliffs of Cape Blanco.

They steered west the next day (July 25, 1579, according to the Drake and Fletcher account, though it may have been the later part of August as related by the Harley 280 manuscript); leaving the land behind them they began their journey to the Moluccas:

> And our General now considering…that the wind blowing still (as it did at first) from the Northwest, cut off all hope of finding a passage through these Northern parts, thought it necessary to lose no time; and therefore with general consent of all, bent his course directly to run with the Islands of the Moluccas. And so having nothing in our view but air and sea, without sight of any land for the space of full 68 days together, we continued our course through the main Ocean till September 30 following.[121]

For our purposes, their adventures beyond America are not material to the vexed question, and subsequent chapters detail the events that took place at the Nova Albion fair bay. Beyond America they had some dangerous close calls. To summarize, they crossed the Pacific Ocean, which was no small feat. They sailed to the Moluccas, or Spice Islands, where Drake furthered the interests of England by negotiating a trade agreement with the sultan of Ternate to establish a clove trade with England.

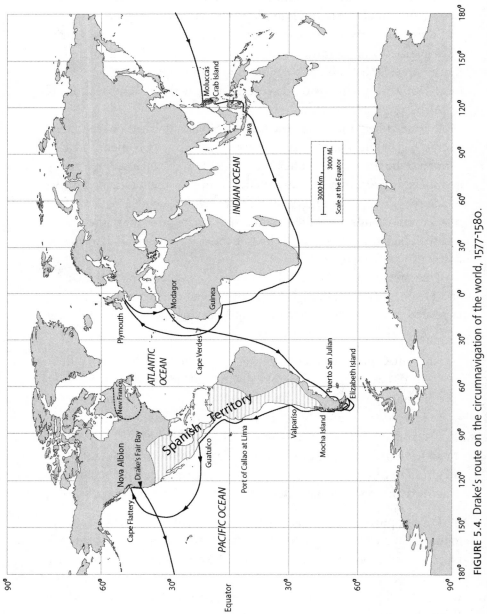

FIGURE 5.4. Drake's route on the circumnavigation of the world, 1577-1580.

There is one episode on their homeward-bound journey that seems significant to this discourse because it describes the fate of Maria and the two Africans whose names are not known to us. Diego had died at sea sometime before the crew made landfall on Crab Island. This island, situated somewhere between the Moluccas and Java, was where Maria and her two fellow Africans were left behind to make their new lives. The expedition had rested and refitted on this island over a period of several weeks, and the chroniclers noted that the island had an abundance of wood and crabs; however, the island lacked fresh water, which compelled them to make regular trips to the neighboring island to obtain water. According to John Drake, they provisioned the heavily pregnant Maria and the other Africans on the island with a supply of rice, seeds, and a means of making fire so they could found a settlement.[122] John Drake noted that people occupied the neighboring island, but they "never saw them nearby."

In her book *Black Tudors: The Untold Story*, historian Miranda Kaufmann reports that Drake's treatment of Maria and her abandonment on an island seemed so callous that "even his contemporaries remarked on his shameful conduct."[123] Kaufmann considered that Maria may have already been pregnant when she came aboard, because she was "very great" with child thirty-six weeks later when she was left on the island, and childbirth usually takes place at around forty weeks.[124] As to the reason why she was abandoned: "The cynical answer is that being heavily pregnant, she was no longer of use to a ship full of lustful sailors…A kinder interpretation would be that Maria was left on the island because Drake feared that she and her child would not survive the long journey home."[125] Kaufmann's last word on Maria was that though Drake and the crew may have considered Diego and the other Africans compatriots, and equal to some extent, "invariably the lot of women at sea was to be exploited."[126]

Though Drake was criticized about Maria's treatment and abandonment on an island with her two fellow Africans (or men of African descent), Drake and Fletcher's description of the island characterizes it as a paradise that "afforded all necessaries" of provision, which refreshed their wearied bodies so that the "sickly, weak, and decayed (as many of us seemed to be before our coming hither), we in short space grew all of us

to be strong, lusty, and healthful persons."[127] Following is a description
of the coconut palm trees and fireflies they observed there:

> The whole Island is a thorough grown wood, the trees for the
> most part are of large and high stature, very straight and clean
> without boughs, save only in the very top. The leaves whereof
> are not much unlike our brooms in England. Among these trees,
> night by night, did show themselves an infinite swarm of fierie-
> seeming-worms flying in the air, whose bodies (no bigger than an
> ordinary fly) did make a show, and give such light as if every twig
> on every tree had been a lighted candle, or as if that place had
> been the starry sphere.[128]

After bidding farewell to Maria and the Africans, the voyagers headed
towards Java. They hit a reef and almost wrecked, and encountered
storms that nearly drove them upon a lee shore. Once at Java they purchased ornate daggers, a sample of Java papyrus, and replenished their
store of rice.[129] In the Indian Ocean they almost perished for want of
water off of Mozambique, rounded the Cape of Good Hope, and saw
elephants when they landed in Guinea to buy lemons and other fruits.

On the September 26, 1580, a crisp westerly wind brought them into
their homeport of Plymouth. The Famous Voyage took two years, ten
months and a few odd days. Drake and Fletcher concluded *The World
Encompassed* with these words: "We safely with joyful minds and thank-
ful hearts to God, arrived at Plymouth, the place of our first setting
forth…in seeing the wonders of the Lord in the deep, in discovering so
many admirable things, in going through with so many strange adventures, in escaping out of so many dangers, and overcoming so many dif-
ficulties in this our encompassing this nether globe, and passing round
about the world which we have related."[130]

The legacy of the Famous Voyage on the west coast is a small foot-
note in the whole scheme of the voyage's many accomplishments. Drake's
daring peacetime raids in New Spain exposed Spain's vulnerability in
the Americas and challenged the dominance of Spain and Portugal on
the high seas. He established a colonial foothold in America, trade with
the Spice Islands, and brought back a shipload of treasure that helped to

finance England's buildup for the inevitable war with Spain that followed not long after.

Drake had ambitions to return to Nova Albion as revealed by the last document anthropologist Zelia Nuttall published in her compilation of contemporary documents from the voyage titled *New Light on Drake*. This was an application by Drake for a "project of a corporation" to return and be governor of the country:

> In consideration of the late notable discovery made by Francis Drake of such dominions as are situated beyond the said Equinoctial line yet it may please her Majesty that he may during his natural life supply the place of Governor of the said company: and in consideration of his great travail and hazard of his person in the said discovery to have during his said life a tenth part of the profits of such commodities as shall be brought into this realm from the parts above remembered. Item that there shall be reserved unto her Majesty a fifth part of the profit of such mines of gold and silver as shall be found in these countries that are hereafter to be discovered and are not lawfully possessed by any other Christian Prince.[131]

Plans called for ten ships to be prepared, but the plan had to be abandoned as Nuttall commented, "Drake's services could not be spared when political complications were increasing and a war with Spain seemed more or less imminent."[132]

CHAPTER SIX

Either Here or There

WITHIN A WEEK after he returned to Plymouth from his circumnavigation of the globe, Drake presented Queen Elizabeth with a hand-drawn,
colored and gilded map of the world. This is often referred to as the
Whitehall map, also known as the Queen's map. It was hung next to
Sebastian Cabot's map just outside the Queen's chamber at Whitehall.[1]
This map has not survived, though there are several derivatives, including those brought to light by Nuttall.[2]

Helen Wallis, the authority on the cartography of the Famous Voyage,
was map curator at the British Library in 1979 when she wrote *The Voyage of Sir Francis Drake Mapped in Silver and Gold*. She followed its publication with *The Cartography of Drake's Voyage* published in 1984.[3] In
her analysis of the surviving contemporary maps, Wallis found that one
of the most important derivatives of the Whitehall map was the Hondius
Broadside. There are only six known surviving copies of this map and
Wallis had difficulty establishing the map's place and date of issue, which
she attributed to its being unauthorized by the censors, but she determined that it was probably issued twice: first in England in 1590, and
later in the Netherlands in 1595.[4] The nineteenth-century geographer
and historian Johann George Kohl thought the original Hondius map
might date from 1589. The map showed Drake's track, and Kohl noted:
"We see on it he also added a little plan of "Drake's harbor" (near San
Francisco). Perhaps this plan of Hondius was after an original survey of
Drake himself.[5]

The Hondius plan of Drake's "fair and good bay" was likely derived from an original painting composed during the voyage. In the sixteenth century official painters would sail on maritime expeditions as artists and mapmakers whose job it was not only to make maps, but also to keep a record of profiles of the coastlines, hazards, depths of anchorages, and the character of the seafloor. These painters also painted flora and fauna, portraits of Natives, and important events on the voyage.[6] In the graphic style that was popular at the time, people were often depicted standing in the landscape, and maps were not drawn to scale but meant to represent the geography in a generalized way that was descriptive.[7]

On the Famous Voyage, Francis and John Drake were the "painters" aboard, as da Silva described, "[Drake] kept a book in which he entered his navigation, and in which he delineated birds, trees and sea-lions. He is an adept in painting and has with him a boy, a relation of his, who is a great painter."[8]

In April 1579, Don Francisco de Zarate wrote a letter to Don Martin Enriquez, the viceroy of New Spain, to give him an account of what happened when Francis Drake captured his ship and crew off of Guatemala. De Zarate related, "He also carries painters who paint for him pictures of the coast in its exact colours. This I was most grieved to see, for each thing is so naturally depicted that no one who guides himself according to these paintings can possibly go astray."[9]

The Hondius derivative of the Whitehall map illustrated the port of Java in the top right hand corner, and Drake's harbor in the upper left corner of the map. This plan of the harbor has the title "Portus Novae Albionis." No other account except the Hondius Broadside describes the sacrificial fires on the mountainside.[10] Wallis commented that the Hondius illustration of the port of Java is clearly recognizable, and thought the careful engraver Hondius "would surely have made a faithful copy of the manuscript plan."[11]

The illustration shows the *Golden Hind* as Drake and his men were preparing to leave the bay. Here the Natives are depicted burning items as sacrifices to the English on the point or peninsula, in the hills, and on the beach. The caption translated from Latin describes the scene: "By horrible lacerations of their bodies and by frequent sacrifices [by fires]

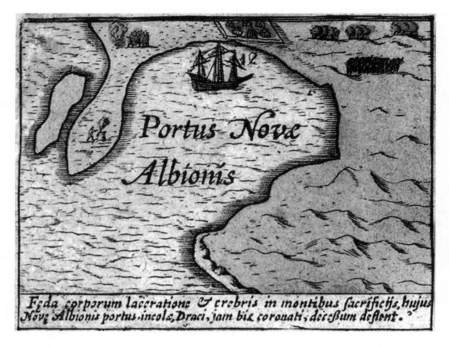

FIGURE 6.1. The Portus illustration, from the Drake Broadside map, by Jodocus Hondius, probably issued in Amsterdam, 1595.

in the mountains, the inhabitants of this port of New Albion bemoan the departure of Drake, now twice crowned."[12] Other details in the Portus illustration include a depiction of the rectangular enclosure Drake and his men had constructed for protection, and it even shows rows of tents set up inside the stronghold. The cove is pocket shaped, and the geographical features depicted include the cliffs and ridge of a headland south of the cove. The two features that may be the most diagnostic geographic details of Drake's actual fair bay are the point and an island or islet that appears to be located just offshore.

The Portus illustration has been famously compared to every bay in contention for Drake's "fair and good bay." If the fit was poor, then the advocates reasoned that the map was not faithful, or that the bay configuration had changed over the last four centuries. Wallis commented: "Whether this is a true depiction of that historic site has been endlessly debated, all the more so because there is no harbor on the California

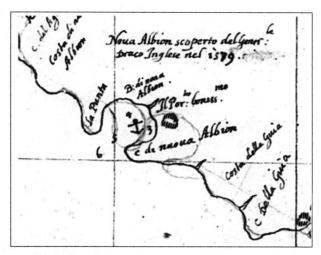

FIGURE 6.2. Detail in Italian of Robert Dudley's ca. 1636 manuscript chart of the west coast of America describing the geographical features of "Nova Albion discovered by General Drake the Englishman in 1579." From the top is the Coast of Nova Albion, the Extremely Good Port (Porto Buonissimo), the Bay of Nova Albion (including the depths of the bay in fathoms), the cape and point (punta) of the bay. Further down the coast is the Coast of the Guide, and Cape of the Guide. Not shown further south is Coast of Canoe Trees, and Desert Land.

coast which exactly fits its topography."[13] Robert Dudley labeled it "*Baia di Nova Albion*" on his chart, with the added note "porto bonissimo."[14] (see Figure 6.2) Historian Justin Winsor wrote in 1884 that Dudley's "porto bonissimo," meant "the best of harbors," which was an expression that prompted Winsor to comment that this description "certainly does not belong to Jack's Bay [Drakes Bay, California]."[15]

Given that the Harley 280 manuscript is an early and uncensored draft of Hakluyt's account, a match for the bay where they made landfall should be situated at or around 44° north latitude on the central coast of Oregon.[16] A candidate that fits this latitude was put forth in 1979 when Bob Ward, a British engineer, searched and found a geographic match with the Portus illustration. This match is Whale Cove, Oregon.[17]

During prohibition, Whale Cove was referred to as Bootlegger Bay. It was one of the few hidden bays smugglers could navigate and became famous for its association with the Canadian trade in black market

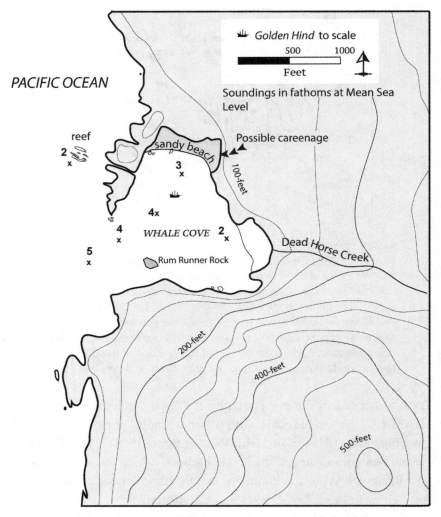

FIGURE 6.3. Topographic map of Whale Cove showing the depths of the cove in fathoms and conjectured location of the careenage.

liquor: "Vessels ran down the coast from Canadian ports with fortunes in Canadian liquor. They'd sneak into the cove, at night, anchor and transfer the hootch to the beach in skiffs for distribution throughout the country by shore gangs."[18] In February 1932, one of the bootleggers' ships, the thirty-six-foot *Sea Island* out of Victoria B.C., attempted to enter the bay during a storm at night. It crashed into the prominent rock in the cove's south entrance where it caught fire and sank.[19] The rock the ship hit is now known as Rum Runner Rock (see Figure 6.3).

Safe harbors are few on the Oregon coast, and river bars are exceedingly dangerous in bad weather. Only the mouths of small streams and a few good size rivers (including the Umpqua and Rogue) break the coastline. Multiple small rocky islands and rock islets along the coast are dangerous to navigation, but provide nesting sites for seabirds and ledges for seals to haul out. While most of the Oregon coast is mountainous, there is a narrow zone of relatively level topography at sea level, closely bounded to the landward by the densely forested Coast Range.

A navigators' landmark is the prominent and sheer white cliff of Cape Blanco, at about 43° north. This is the westernmost point of land on the Oregon coast. These white cliff walls extend several degrees along the central coast, including at Whale Cove, and may be the white cliffs that reminded Drake of England, and prompted him to name the new region Nova Albion.[20]

Besides Hondius, cartographer, navigator, and ship builder Robert Dudley made depictions of Drake's fair bay.[21] These depictions portray the shape, and geographic features of the point and the cape found in the Portus illustration. Dudley's manuscript charts are the drafts of the maps in his published atlas, *Arcano del Mare*, or *Secrets of the Sea*, his life's most important work that he began in 1630 and published in Florence in 1646–1647. Drawn prior to making the final engravings for his atlas, these manuscript charts include two pencil sketches and an inked-in sketch of the bay of Nova Albion indicated at about 38° north.[22]

Dudley wrote that he had his information from an English pilot.[23] His depiction of the fair bay includes the depths of the bay, information no other mapmaker had. The depth at the mouth of the bay was recorded at six fathoms, a point just inside at five fathoms, and two more points taken along the cove's inner shore.[24] It is compelling that these soundings match the depths at the corresponding points at Whale Cove. Dudley's chart depicts a creek entering the center edge of the cove—and it corresponds to the location of Dead Horse Creek, which falls down the cliff face as it flows into Whale Cove. There is also a Native hamlet noted on Dudley's drawing that appears to correspond to the general vicinity where a prehistoric archaeological site has been recorded.

The English pilot apparently did not provide Dudley with exact data, and Dudley noted that his calculations of the distance to the frigid area ("Costa Scoperta da l'Drago Inglese nel 1579 è freddissima") where Drake turned back were not exact: "The distance to the high cold is unknown and the error is great, but there can be no accommodation for it."[25] Dudley's manuscript notes in pencil about the distance from Acapulco to the coast of Quivera (North America) demonstrate the problem. First he wrote 1000 leagues, crossed it out and wrote 790, then crossed that out and put 720.[26]

The latitudes of the points of discovery are just as inconsistent. The northern-most point Drake reached in the Pacific Dudley indicated at 46½° north on his manuscript chart where he noted, "Port of Quivera discovered by Drake the Englishman in 1582 [*sic*]. It was so cold in the month of June there was no comfort." On the published version of this map, this note is adjacent to two bays indicated as anchorages at 44° north and just south at 43½°.[27] If we discount the apocryphal Juan de Fuca, only two other explorers had ascended to the southern coast of Oregon by 1646, when Dudley's atlas was published, but they did not sail as far north as the geography recorded on Dudley's map.[28]

Dudley was apparently trying to reconcile information from more than one source, and evidently his sources were contradictory. These two anchorages may have come from Drake's records, and may actually indicate the "bad bay" at 44° where Drake had stopped briefly while moving south in search of a careenage, and Porto Nova Albion at 43½° (the "fair and good" bay). Dudley recorded Drake's Porto Nova Albion at about 38° north. This and the text regarding the extreme cold suggest that Dudley was not aware of what the present author argues is the Queen's ruse.

Dudley noted place names both north and south of Porto Nova Albion in his manuscript chart. Some of the place names were definitely from the Spanish voyages on the California coast (for example Cape Mendocino is indicated), but perhaps several of the place names were from the English pilot, and may be place names from Drake's charts. If so, these names may be the only record of what Drake and his men saw on the coast. In general these do not describe geographical features but they are evocative, such as the River of Holy Sparrows, Cape of Sardines, and the River of Kingfishers. One reference to geography is an area named Majestic and Tempestuous Chalk Cliffs situated north of the Porto Bonissimo of Nova Albion. South of Porto Nova Albion is the Coast of the Guide, further south is the Costa Xagnia, which translates to Coast of the Canoe Trees (see Fig 6.1).[29]

Canoe making trees such as cedars (*Thuja plicata or Chamaecyparis lawsoniana*) or redwood (*Sequoia sempervirens*) are not found south of California's Drakes Bay, or even in the vicinity, which is compelling evidence that these place names are describing the Oregon coast. The place name Dudley indicated south of the Coast of Canoe Trees is Desert Land, which may correspond to the desert-like sand dune hills known as the Coos Bay dune sheet. This dune sheet extends along over eighty kilometers of continuous coastline. Commonly called the Oregon Dunes, this formation is situated about a degree south of Whale Cove. It is likely that Drake coasted south a degree or two to these latitudes where he knew he could begin his westward tack to catch the Pacific Gyre, and the winds that would take them across the ocean.

Bob Ward's Whale Cove hypothesis was largely based on the present shape, geographic features, and depths of Whale Cove. These features are a match for Drake's fair bay depicted in the Portus illustration and on Dudley's charts. The Oregon coast is dynamic, and there was some question whether the shape of Whale Cove would have substantially changed over the last four hundred years. Two geomorphic studies of the area have concluded the shape of Whale Cove has persisted because the bay is a basalt-armored pocket cove, though the size of the bay has expanded as the cliff walls eroded back.[30]

Whale Cove is navigable by a careful sailor. The mouth of the bay is five fathoms, or about thirty feet. The mean draft of the *Golden Hind* was about thirteen and a half feet, but loaded with bullion and leaking it may have been as low as fourteen feet. Sounding the depths as they made their way, the *Golden Hind* could have avoided the shallow rocky area on the southern edge of the cove and been brought to a careenage on the sandy beach that lay on the northeast margin of the cove. If Drake's landing was actually at Whale Cove, the ship would have been protected from the prevailing summer winds by the basalt arm of the peninsula that encompasses the northwest part of the bay like a jetty. Waves do not break hard on this beach, and the sandy near shore area has a gradual incline, which was a necessity required for a careenage.

There is one particular detail that supports Ward's Whale Cove landing theory: there is a rocky reef outside the cove where an island is indicated on the Portus illustration. The water is shallow over this reef, and from a vantage point on the peninsula, one can observe that the foul area breaks in moderate seas. Over the last 430 years the direct force of the prevailing ocean waves and possible subduction from the 1700 earthquake has reduced this reef, but whether it was a rocky islet just above sea level in Drake's day and drawn on the Portus illustration can only be conjectured.[31]

In support of Drake being on the Oregon coast, we have some scant physical evidence. An English silver shilling dating from circa 1560 was reportedly found on the beach at Nehalem Bay after the 1962 Columbus Day storm, though the source of this information and the coin remain elusive. Recently another coin was found near Victoria, British Columbia, by a metal detector hobbyist. This artifact is a hammered silver shilling that dates from 1551–1553. The coin was in a buried archaeological context, but the finder also found a nickel from 1891 in the same vicinity, which casts doubt on the provenience of the shilling.

There have been several archaeological projects at Whale Cove and its surrounds (including a brief survey by the present writer), but these excavations found no historical artifacts that could be attributed to a 1579 European occupation. The lack of soil buildup on the bench above the cove may be evidence of a tsunami event that washed in after the Cascadia earthquake in 1700. The lower elevations of the terrace were scoured by the waves, and any evidence of an Elizabethan presence likely would have been removed or displaced. However, archaeological investigations in a recorded archaeological site on higher ground less than an English mile away may be more productive.

CHAPTER SEVEN

The Great Discoveries

ONE FEBRUARY DAY in 1908, in the National Archives in Mexico City, anthropologist Zelia Nuttall was searching for documents relating to the trials of Natives by the Spanish Inquisition. Incidentally, she was also looking out for any Inquisition documents that might throw light on the fate of the members of the John Hawkins expedition who had been captured by the Spanish during the battle of San Juan de Ulúa—the famous battle where Drake forsook Hawkins.[1] Her interest was heightened in that topic because the Hakluyt Society had recently published the harrowing personal accounts of two of the one hundred men John Hawkins had put ashore to lighten his overloaded ship after fleeing from the Spanish after the famous battle.[2]

Nuttall was a great linguist and fluent in Early Modern Spanish. Sixteenth-century books and manuscripts had been her daily companions for over twenty-five years when on that auspicious day in 1908 she made a discovery of profound importance. She described the moment of discovery in the introduction to her book *New Light on Drake: A Collection of Documents Relating to His Voyage of Circumnavigation 1577–1580*:

> The volume which chance literally threw across my path...lay on the floor in a dark and dusty corner from which I carried it to the light. On turning its pages my attention was arrested by the superscription: *Declaration by Nuño da Silva as to how he was taken prisoner by English pirates on his way from Oporto to Brazil, May 23, 1579.* Attracted by the unexpected subject I scanned the

FIGURE 7.1. Zelia Nuttall. On the back is a note, "Zelia Nuttall taken in Lausanne, 11 Jan 1897 years Aged 40 years [*sic*]." Photograph courtesy of Ralph Falkiner-Nuttall.

document with growing curiosity. It was not, however until I read on the first line of the page, the name "Fran^{co} Drac," [Francis Drake] that my interest became thoroughly aroused.[3]

It was an Inquisition testimony, but not of Hawkins's men: it was the testimony of Nuño da Silva, the Portuguese pilot Drake had captured off the Cape Verde Islands and later released in Mexico after fifteen months aboard Drake's ship. In the testimony, da Silva related vivid details about the voyage, and a description of Drake: "This Englishman calls himself Francis Drake and is a man aged 38.... He is low in stature, thick-set and very robust. He has a fine countenance, is ruddy of complexion and has a fair beard. He has the mark of an arrow-wound in his right cheek, which is not apparent if one does not look with special care. In one leg he has the ball of an arquebuse that was shot at him in the Indies."[4] Nuttall soon found a second deposition of da Silva that gave particular personal details about Drake. For example, this account explained how Drake had received that scar in his cheek; he was struck with an arrow on Mocha Island. Though da Silva's deposition had been found and a portion published before, this account was of interest to Nuttall, a native of San Francisco. Her interest was piqued in part because, as she later wrote in the introduction to *New Light on Drake,* Drake had been her childhood hero.

Zelia Maria Magdalena Nuttall was born in San Francisco in 1857 to a family prominent in the city's social, diplomatic, and banking circles. Her Irish father was a physician who had come to California during the Gold Rush, tending to gold miners in his hospital tent. Nuttall's grand-mother, Magdalena Barrera, was a native of Mexico City. In 1864, when Zelia was seven years old, the Nuttalls left for Europe, where she at-tended schools in France and Germany, principally because her father thought his children should be fluent in those countries' languages—in addition to the Spanish and English they heard at home. In London she attended a finishing school administered by a well-known suffragette leader.[5]

At Harvard, Nuttall began work in the Peabody Museum for Ethnol-ogy and Archaeology under the tutelage of Frederic Putnam and Alice Fletcher. Anthropology was in its infancy, and Putnam was a luminary and pioneer in American archaeology and ethnology, and the long-standing director of the museum. Fletcher was an ethnologist, anthro-pologist, lecturer, prolific writer, and an important champion of the civil rights of Native Americans. Nuttall and Fletcher became life-long friends, and Fletcher later spent considerable time in Mexico with Nuttall.[6]

Nuttall became a specialist in pre-Columbian Mesoamerican cul-tures and conducted archaeological fieldwork in Mexico for the Peabody, where she was "Honorary Assistant in Mexican Archaeology," a post she

held for forty-seven years.[7] In Mexico she was also named Honorary
Professor of Archaeology at the National Museum of Anthropology.
By the 1890s Nuttall belonged to the elite cadre of the first professional
anthropologists. She lectured at major conferences and universities in
the Americas and Europe. She wrote articles for prestigious journals
and traveled throughout the world to collect archaeological and ethnological specimens for museum collections, as well as for a select group
of wealthy patrons. She was one of the first women honored by being
selected as a fellow of the American Association for the Advancement
of Science. Including *New Light on Drake*, her major contributions to
the field of anthropology are classics: *The Nuttall Codex*, *The Island
of Sacrificios*, and the *Fundamental Principles of Old and New World
Civilizations*.[8] The Nuttall Codex is recognized as one of the "greatest of
pre-Columbian finds, as one of the great works of manuscript art of all
civilizations, and as one of the most important New World documents."[9]

One of Nuttall's patrons, and a particularly good friend and one-time
neighbor, was Phoebe Apperson Hearst, who supported much of her research and many of her archaeological endeavors.[10] Under Mrs. Hearst's
sponsorship in 1896–1899, Nuttall took part in a mission organized by
the University of Pennsylvania Museum to collect ethnographic specimens in Russia. While she was in Moscow she attended the coronation
of Tsar Nicholas II; she attended all the official coronation fêtes, due in
part to her social connection to Mrs. Hearst.[11]

In 1901, Mrs. Hearst provided financial support to Nuttall and her
colleague, anthropologist Franz Boas, in order to establish the anthropology department at the University of California, Berkeley. Nuttall and
Hearst tried to convince Boas to come west and be the first professor of
anthropology at Berkeley. They settled on Alfred A. Kroeber, Boas's star
pupil who had received Columbia's first PhD in anthropology.[12]

As part of her mission to further the study of anthropology, Mrs. Hearst
established a museum at the university, which purchased artifacts and
collections provided by archaeologists, and included items from Nuttall's archaeological and ethnographic expeditions. With Hearst's support Zelia returned to her work in Mexico under the auspices of the
anthropology department.[13] Mrs. Hearst provided the funds for Nuttall to purchase a large old Spanish colonial house just north of Mexico

City—Casa Alvarado. This became Zelia's beloved home for many years, and also served as her archaeological headquarters and laboratory.

Nuttall's manuscript discoveries in the Mexican archives pertaining to Drake's voyage compelled her to do a thorough search in other archives before presenting her work. Over the next two years she tracked down leads and traveled to archives in New York, London, Paris, Spain, Italy, and the Vatican. She found documents relating to the cargo of Nuño da Silva's ship, Spanish documents relating to Nuño da Silva after his release from the Inquisition, and the first official reports concerning Drake's voyage received by King Philip II. There were legal briefs on the case and proceedings against Sir Francis Drake for his depredations in New Spain. She found official reports to the viceroy and King Philip of Spain relating to Drake's actions at Guatulco, and eight letters, including one from the mayor, describing Drake's Guatulco raid in detail.

In Seville Nuttall was astonished to find Nuño da Silva's logbook, uncataloged and found only by chance in a bundle of papers within a file of documents relating to the Strait of Magellan. The logbook was unbound and its pages were stitched together and out of order. She marveled that the exterior pages were much thumb marked.[14]

This was perhaps her most important find; this log is the *only extant log* of any part of the voyage, and one of only a handful of artifacts from the voyage. The log ran from da Silva's capture on January 19, 1578, to April 13, 1579, when Drake released him just before sailing to the Northwest coast. Nuttall was struck with the importance of this find, but she was frustrated because the logbook proved extremely difficult to translate and edit. The calligraphy and orthography of its sixteen sheets were almost undecipherable, the entries were short and obscure, and they were in Portuguese. An accomplished Portuguese paleographer helped with the translation, and at long last Nuttall was able to compare Nuño da Silva's account of the journey with the English accounts, verifying nearly every statement in the log.[15]

Nuttall's other important discoveries included the papers that the viceroy of New Spain had methodically collected. These were depositions from nearly everyone Drake encountered that described each action, what Drake's ship was like, his armaments, his crew and many details that flesh out Drake's encounters in New Spain.

The details about Drake himself found in these documents show that he spoke "a fluent and forcible foreign Spanish."[16] The viceroy had forwarded these depositions to King Philip II, and Nuttall found them in the archives of Seville. Ross Parmenter, Nuttall's biographer, wrote: "Next to the log of da Silva, the Drake adventure that thrilled Zelia most was coming upon the first batch of depositions of men, whom Drake had taken prisoner.... When she had coordinated the stories of the 20 prisoners, she found she had a complete chain of evidence, furnishing accounts by eye-witnesses of the seizure of every ship or boat taken by Drake in the South Seas."[17]

In particular, it was the record of the evidence about Drake given under oath by his imprisoned comrades, John Oxenham, John Butler, and Thomas Xerores that enthralled Nuttall. One detail she found compelling was their statements that Drake could not possibly, and would not, have set out on a voyage without the sanction and aid of Queen Elizabeth.[18] Oxenham testified under oath "Captain Francis had often spoken to witness saying that if the Queen would grant him the license, he would pass through the Strait of Magellan and found settlements over here in some good country."[19] Nuttall wrote: "The tragic circumstances under which their testimony was taken and the wonder that, after a lapse of centuries, their last utterances should have first reached me, have caused me to sometimes feel as though, in some strange way, messages from those men, long dead, had been entrusted to me for transmission to their living compatriots."[20]

In 1913 the Hakluyt Society accepted Nuttall's proposal to publish the documents. It was intended that her book would be a complement to the W. S. W. Vaux volume on Drake that the Hakluyt Society had published in 1854. The day after the announcement of the proposal, the *London Times* printed both a news article and an opinion piece about the trove of documents she had amassed. The news article included a description of the documents, including details of the first deposition by Nuño da Silva that Zelia had discovered four years previously in Mexico City.[21]

New Light on Drake was published in 1914. Nuttall had included sixty-five Spanish documents; the vast majority had not been published before. In her introduction she described the sources of the collection:

I doubt whether it would be possible to match so complete and varied a set of official documents, all relating to a single subject and written, within a few years, by men of such different degrees as the King of Spain, members of his Council, Viceroys of Mexico and Peru, military and naval commanders, governors of provinces and ecclesiastical dignitaries down to alcades, notaries and petty officials filling humble posts in Mexico and on the Pacific Coast of South and Central America.[22]

In her introduction she directed her readers to the French Drake map considered a close copy of Queen Elizabeth's Whitehall map.[23] Nuttall pointed out that the map is inscribed with the note "seen and corrected by Sir Francis Drake." Apparently, Drake had defined England's claim to most of what is now the continental United States by drawing two lines of demarcation. The land north of a line from the Gulf of California to Florida is depicted as England's territory, and includes Florida. Another line encloses "New France" the French possessions on the eastern coast of North America. The crowned arms of Queen Elizabeth are placed to indicate two new English possessions claimed by Drake; New Albion and Elizabeth Island, south of Cape Horn. Nuttall credited Drake with laying down the concept of an English possession stretching from the Atlantic to the Pacific: "He also drew lines to indicate the boundaries of New Spain & New France, & his project of a New England extending from the Pacific to the Atlantic Coast."[24]

In England her findings were hailed as a triumph. A reviewer in the *Geographical Journal* of the Royal Geographical Society noted: "The evidence of the whole series appears to Mrs. Nuttall to furnish final solutions to several of the most important disputed questions concerning Drake's voyage of circumnavigation. Not only is it seen that Drake was sent on the voyage by Queen Elizabeth herself, but that it was regarded and described as a *voyage of discovery*, of which the purpose was 'to discover good lands where settlements could be established.'"[25]

Another reviewer wrote, "Mrs. Nuttall, in her 'New Light on Drake,' has not only swept away a pile of calumny and misrepresentation: she has placed Sir Francis Drake in a much higher niche in the temple of fame than he held before."[26]

Nuttall had even more astonishing new findings to present. She wrote that this new material had "assumed proportions which will compel me to publish it later on, separately, as a monograph."[27] She noted, "Nothing short of a series of such monographs and a revised and complete version of the history of Drake's voyage around the world, will, indeed, suffice as an adequate means of distributing the fresh knowledge gained concerning it and its true purpose."[28] Since the Hakluyt Society did not publish monographs, her new project would have to be published elsewhere. Thus she began her second project on Drake and the circumnavigation.

As Nuttall gathered and analyzed maps, manuscripts, and contemporary accounts, the evidence was building that Drake and Company had not—after all—landed on the California shores. We cannot know whether that revelation came to Nuttall in a thunderclap, or in a slow realization. However, these findings posed a problem for Nuttall: to dislodge Drake from California would be a radical shift in the dominant paradigm.

Nuttall passively opened the discussion in *New Light on Drake* by introducing her theory on Drake's movements in the north Pacific by referring her readers to the latitudes depicted in the French Drake Map, which shows he ascended to 50° north or more, and made landfall at about 45° north. This map was the second illustration she included in her book—second only to Drake's portrait in the frontispiece. She also asserted three times in her introduction that Drake had "sailed along the entire Pacific Coast of America," and made the "first survey of the entire Pacific Coast," and explored "the entire Pacific Coast of America with a view of taking possession of the regions beyond the limits of Spanish occupation."[29]

Her new project also had other, cultural, implications. Her finding that Drake and Company landed further north meant that the people at the landing were from a Northwest coast culture, therefore Drake could not have met the Coast Miwok or Pomo people of California. Nuttall's project included an ethnographic investigation that took her to the Northwest coast as she pursued her inquiry into what particular Native group it might have been that greeted Drake and his company during the summer of 1579.

CHAPTER EIGHT

The California Juggernaut

ZELIA NUTTALL'S BOOK came out during the time when Drake's swashbuckling legend was being polished by the fraternal organization known as the Native Sons of the Golden West, a group that extolled California history.[1] As one author noted, this group did more than put up plaques and fly flags; in the early-twentieth-century California, the Native Sons were aggressive proponents of white supremacy.[2]

While British scholars hailed Nuttall's book, the reception of *New Light on Drake* in California was cold. Her findings on Drake on the Pacific coast were disparaged because they cast doubt on a California landing, and asserted that the voyage was a state-sponsored voyage of discovery, which meant Drake was therefore not a pirate in the strict sense of the word (at least not on that voyage anyway).

Members of the Native Sons were a who's who of California: civic leaders, judges, senators, wealthy capitalists, and history professors.[3] At that time it was a large, busy, and influential organization. In 1915 there were 146 chapters (called "parlors") throughout California, and meetings were held twice a month. Often meetings included lectures presented by one of their Grand Orators. There was a monthly magazine (*The Grizzly Bear*), and an annual Grand Parlor conference. They created grandiose titles for themselves that expressed the importance they placed in the organization and its ranks. At the 1914 Grand Parlor meeting, for example, they elected a Grand President who was visibly overcome by emotion in appreciation of that honor. They also had a Junior Past Grand President,

Grand First Vice President, Grand Second Vice President, Grand Third
Vice President, Grand Organist, and several other officers down the line,
including a Grand Historiographer.[4]

One particularly prominent member of the Native Sons was James
Rolph. San Francisco was in the midst of rebuilding in the years following the 1906 earthquake and the fires that followed. Rolph and his
fellow businessmen "longed to redesign their hometown from the ashes
of the 1906 earthquake into the capital of a new Pacific Empire."[5] San
Francisco had a bawdy reputation and had the nickname of "Sin City"
because of the abundance of saloons and brothels. Rolph controlled one
of the brothels, and it was one of the first buildings to be rebuilt after the
earthquake because half the profits went to city hall.[6]

In 1909 Rolph served as head of the San Francisco Merchants Association, and as such had a major role in planning the Portola Festival that
took place that year. The Portola Festival celebrated the discovery of San
Francisco Bay by Captain Gaspar de Portola in 1796 and was full of historical references, including a planned commemoration of Drake. The
festival was envisioned as San Francisco's version of Mardi Gras, and was
originally planned as an annual event, though it only lasted a few years.[7]

Rolph gained the mayor's chair in 1911. He served ten terms as mayor
of San Francisco, and then was elected governor of California. He became known as Sunny Jim, the self-proclaimed "mayor of all the people."
He was a master showman and politician, and continued to be a promoter of popular spectacles. The next extravaganza he promoted was a
world's fair that was designed to showcase San Francisco. It was named
the Panama-Pacific International Exposition in honor of the opening of
the Panama Canal, and it specifically celebrated San Francisco's position
as a port and great city on the Pacific.[8] The promotional literature touted
the fair as an aid to business interests and an opportunity to "upbuild"
the state, and noted that the assets would include magnificent buildings
that "will cover the remaining vacancies in the burned area, while new
car lines to reach the Park and ocean will fill the residential districts with
substantial homes."[9]

Rolph capitalized on California's assumed Drake connection. In 1913
an emissary was sent to England to promote the festival. As a result,
Rolph received a letter from Winston Churchill, who was then First Lord

of the British Admiralty. Churchill wrote: "It is especially gratifying to me, as chairman of the committee which is promoting a national memorial to Drake in this country, to find that his memory is kept alive in those regions of the new world where his exploits were performed, and I am glad that you have given me an opportunity to send you all my good wishes for the success of the celebration."[10] Churchill's words resonated, and made the organizers feel their work was important. The Portola Festival successfully demonstrated to the world that San Francisco had the ability to sponsor a major civic event, and it bolstered the city's case for hosting the Panama-Pacific International Exposition in 1915.

One of the events planned in conjunction with that yearlong exposition was the Panama-Pacific Historical Congress of the American Historical Association, a large conference of historians set for July 19–23, 1915. It was at this conference that Nuttall would present her paper titled, *The Northern Limits of Drake in the Pacific.*

One of the conference organizers was Henry Morse Stephens, a professor of history at the University of California at Berkeley, and the newly elected president of the American Historical Association. Stephens was the first person west of the Mississippi to hold that position.[11] Stephens was eager that the conference would showcase both the history program at Berkeley and the Bancroft Library, an important archive and research library.[12]

Herbert Eugene Bolton, Stephen's colleague in the department, assisted him with preparations for the Historical Congress. In 1911 Stephens had recruited Bolton from Stanford (previous to Stanford, Bolton had been a professor in Texas). Bolton was an influential historian. At Berkeley, Bolton lectured to large classes of undergraduates—frequently the class size was in the hundreds. Bolton called his graduate students his "knights of the round table." These were "his boys" who received his support often in the form of fellowships provided by the Native Sons of the Golden West.[13] He promoted his students' careers by writing countless glowing recommendations and finding them positions throughout the United States as graduate assistants, professors, archivists, and in positions on editorial boards. These were relationships of patronage and reciprocity, and Bolton used all of these connections to forward his own work.

Bolton's empire was not an idyllic Camelot. Many of his colleagues disliked him. His detractors thought of him as a huckster and "glory seeker" who courted publicity.[14] He subscribed to a newspaper service that sent items about him from papers across the country (the Bancroft Library has several folders of these clippings).[15] Bolton's biographer, Albert Hurtado, suggests Bolton's detractors were just jealous because he had great influence within the university; in the department his power was nearly absolute.[16] The animosity some of his colleagues felt against Bolton persisted to the end of his career. Hurtado wrote: "Everything about Bolton's life bespoke a man who was a great success. He had risen to the top of his field, and he possessed all of the things that symbolized his arrival: many publications, hundreds of graduate students, excellent salary, titles, authority, national and international acclaim…. If some of his colleagues were jealous, there is no need to puzzle out the reasons."[17]

There must have been more to his colleagues' distain of Bolton than jealousy. Two of his former graduate students, who later became history professors, became disillusioned with Bolton and his machinations. It got back to Bolton that these two men "hated him like a snake."[18]

This unflattering opinion about Bolton was shared by historian William Gates. Gates sent Nuttall a letter requesting that she copy parts of a book for him while she was at Berkeley during her visit ahead of the big historical conference.[19] The book could be found in the Bancroft Library collections where Bolton's presence was frequent. Apparently there was animosity between Bolton and Gates, because he cautioned Nuttall not to mention his name to Bolton.

Gates's letter contained what turned out to be prophetic words, warning her about Bolton with the comments "as suspected in our talk the other day and by Dr. Hewett it may be necessary to look out for Bolton," and "Bolton might try to obstruct her."[20]

About this time Nuttall received a letter from Bolton himself, requesting her help to secure Mexican historians to present their research at the conference, in particular in the Spanish American session.[21] This was during the early chaos of the Mexican Revolution, and Nuttall replied that Mexico was in such throes that of the two most important historians in Mexico, one was probably guarding the archives, and the other the monuments.[22] She suggested that he should get as many presenters as he could for the Spanish American session, even if they were solely American scholars. As she closed the letter, she asked if the Bancroft Library had any material relating to Sir Francis Drake. She wrote that she "shall have to consult them before finishing the lecture I am preparing."[23]

Nuttall then wrote a cheerful letter to Gates and related that she had informed Bolton that she wanted to do research at the Bancroft Library before giving her lecture on Drake.[24] She also wrote a cordial note to Benjamin Ide Wheeler, the President of the University of California, Berkeley, letting him know that she would be at the Shattuck Hotel, and that she was "looking forward with much pleasure to seeing you and Mrs. Wheeler and to working in the libraries. With kindest regards to you both."[25]

In these times white supremacists controlled many of the levers of power. President Wheeler was a proponent of eugenics and advocated sterilization of people deemed unfit to procreate. Belief in eugenics was particularly widespread in California, and these white men feared that the "pure white race" would be "polluted by intermarriage with blacks, Mexicans, Jews, Asians and Indians, who were thought to be a lesser order of humans."[26] In California, "Golden State eugenicists were especially concerned about Mexicans, who they racialized as dark-skinned, mixed-blood mongrels who should be kept south of the border."[27]

Nuttall arrived in Berkeley in early April. She expected to be invited to the graduation ceremony in May—after all, she was a founder of the Department of Anthropology. Though President Wheeler had, in fact, invited her to attend, he had sent the invitation to her Harvard address— despite knowing full well that she was staying at the Shattuck Hotel. The invitation would not arrive in time for the ceremony. Nuttall's biographer Ross Parmenter noted that Nuttall felt President Wheeler purposefully mishandled her invitation to the commencement ceremonies. This slight may have been because Wheeler backed Bolton in most of his endeavors. Parmenter thought that the coldness from Wheeler was because he had somehow found out that Nuttall concurred with her friend Gates's poor opinion of Bolton, though some of the coldness may have been because President Wheeler viewed Nuttall as a "mixed-blood mongrel."[28]

Bolton, Stephens, and Wheeler—and later Henry Wagner—were all cold to Nuttall for a myriad of reasons that no doubt also included the fact that she was a woman. An example that reflects the contemporary world view of these men can be found in the autobiography of Henry Wagner, who barely mentioned his own wife, but wrote how he was horror stricken the first time he saw a woman smoking a cigarette.[29]

Nuttall traveled in elite circles. She had met two presidents, at least one pope, and attended the coronation of Tsar Nicholas II in a silk ball gown she had bought in Paris. When she arrived at Berkeley, the *Berkeley Daily Gazette* printed the headline—"Mrs. Zelia Nuttall, world-famous archaeologist, is again at the Shattuck."[30]

Hurtado made this observation about the men in academia at that time and their attitudes: "WASP faculty and university presidents maintained their sense of ethnic, religious, and gender exclusivity wherever they could by raising barriers against Catholics, women, and Jews."[31] Being a divorcee from a Catholic background was another mark against her. (Nuttall had left her husband—French explorer and ethnographer Alphonse Pinart—two years after their daughter Nadine was born.) She may have been further marginalized because she was often in the company of other equally beautiful and accomplished women.[32]

Bolton was no equal to Nuttall as a scholar. She had been working in the Mexican archives since 1881, spoke five languages well, could translate pre-Columbian Aztec codices, and was a more proficient translator of old Spanish texts than either Bolton or Wagner.

Nuttall's research at the Bancroft for Gates was not fruitful, however. The librarian in charge could not find "No. 59178" (the book Gates needed), and there was nothing substantial in their collections on Drake.

Behind the scenes at the Bancroft Library there was a power struggle between Bolton and Frederick John Teggart, a history professor who had been custodian of the Bancroft library materials since the university purchased the library's core collection from Hubert Howe Bancroft. The great Bancroft collection was one of the reasons Bolton left Stanford for Berkeley, he called the collection "the greatest in my field," and from the time he arrived in Berkeley his sights were set on taking over the library. Bolton felt he could freely borrow from the collection. His attitude annoyed Teggart, who asserted that he had the authority to restrict Bolton's access to the library and its materials. Bolton, in turn, threatened to "knock Teggart's false teeth down his throat if he tried it."[33] In 1916

Bolton had his way, and through some subterfuge Teggart was ousted from the Bancroft and Bolton was appointed in his place. This was a circumstance Teggart resented deeply for the rest of his life.[34]

Hurtado wrote that feuding with Bolton was foolish. President Wheeler gave Bolton both leeway and support because Bolton was emerging as a public figure in the state and his academic accomplishments elevated the reputation of Berkeley among academics throughout the United States.[35] "He represented the University's history department before the regents and the state legislature. Newspapermen asked his opinions about local topics and he provided them."[36]

The faculty in the Department of Anthropology were much more receptive to Nuttall than the historians. She had been in charge of the department's Crocker-Reed archaeological investigations in Mexico during the early years of the department, so as a returning former faculty member and founder of the department she was afforded special attention. Department chair Alfred Kroeber was in Europe at the time. Acting department head Thomas Talbot Waterman invited her to lecture at the summer session, writing, "I think you would get a very interested and sympathetic audience, and that your lecture would be much appreciated."[37] Nuttall readily agreed. Waterman was especially excited to have her lecture because he was fascinated by her *Book of the Life of the Ancient Mexicans*, which the university had published in 1903.[38]

For Nuttall's entertainment Waterman made arrangements for postgraduate student Ralph Roys, an aspiring Mayan expert, to keep her company and take her "motoring" in his automobile—a novelty at that time.[39] Roys called on Nuttall at the Hotel Shattuck, and as they drove in his car they became "pretty well acquainted" as Roys later described. He recalled that she was planning a trip to Neah Bay on the Washington coast, believing that Drake and Company may have landed there: "She had gotten the idea that one place further up the coast, which the Drake material tells about, must have been at Neah Bay up near Cape Flattery."[40]

The Women's Board of the Exposition invited Nuttall to be their guest of honor for the week of April 22. As part of the celebration, she presented a lecture on Sir Francis Drake, which was a version of the lecture she was planning for the history conference.

The *San Francisco Examiner* had a one-column story announcing her appearance.[41] The newspaper article noted that in Nuttall's lecture she described the expedition as being luxuriously fitted; musicians were part of the crew, and among the items they carried were fine cloth and perfumed water. Nuttall stressed that these were not the trappings of a pirate, but of an expedition that enjoyed royal support. She concluded with the point that Drake was "not the pirate king that he is popularly supposed to be, but that his explorations and discoveries contributed much to the advancement and progress of the world."[42] The next day, the headline of the *San Francisco Chronicle* touted, "Lecturer Says Drake Not Pirate King."[43]

Parmenter believed Nuttall's findings about Francis Drake, the person, were among her most important achievements with *New Light on Drake*. As noted in an earlier chapter, the Fletcher and Drake account is likely an amalgam of Chaplain Fletcher's diary with material from Francis Drake's account, which were put together by Drake's nephew after Drake died.[44] However, there was clear animosity between Fletcher and Drake that was evident in the portions of the account attributed to Fletcher. As Parmenter wrote:

> Fletcher was Drake's chaplain on the voyage, and his many unfavorable comments on Drake were to provide a constant fillip to Zelia's subsequent researches. Again and again she was to find documents revealing that Drake was a chivalrous and cultivated gentlemen, and she was always delighted when she did...Fletcher and others, became targets as her book idea expanded to become not only an account of the circumnavigation based on new documents, but a detailed defense of Drake's character.[45]

On Monday, July 19, 1915, the Panama-Pacific Historical Congress opened. Nuttall's paper, "The Northern Limits of Drake's Voyage in the Pacific" was scheduled for the *Spanish America and the Pacific Ocean* session held in the Argentine Building on the fair grounds for Wednesday afternoon, July 21. She was scheduled for the podium just before Herbert Bolton, who was to give his paper on Father Kino. She requested a last-minute venue change to Berkeley for the Thursday morning session, *Exploration of the Northern Pacific Ocean and Settlement of California.*

She told Bolton that the logistics of transporting her slides and maps across to San Francisco were difficult, so she preferred to present the next morning at Berkeley. Parmenter conjectured that it was not just logistics that prompted her to request a venue change, but also because her paper was more pertinent to the northern Pacific exploration theme.[46] Although she had not yet explored Neah Bay and the ethnographic considerations of her theory, she felt her cartographic and manuscript evidence could stand on its own. The schedule change also meant that Bolton would not be taking the podium after her.

Her request was granted. Nuttall presented her address in the morning, and that evening Judge John F. Davis delivered the keynote address of the conference. It was titled "The History of California," and he presented it in a formal session at the Native Sons' Hall, in San Francisco. Judge Davis at the time was the Grand President of the Native Sons. This evening session was planned to honor the Native Sons in recognition of their financial contributions to the study of history.[47]

If Judge Davis's speech reflected a consensus among California historians on Francis Drake, it was that Drake was a pirate and that his anchorage was at Drakes Bay.[48] Nuttall's astonishing findings published the previous year in *New Light on Drake* were not referenced. Further, Davis assiduously ignored the new findings she had presented that morning for the academic conference audience, which was a version of the lecture she delivered to the Women's Board in April—a lecture that had been widely reported in the press.

She must have understood the game Judge Davis and his protégés were playing. To underscore her presentation and counter Davis, she installed a pictorial display of the original material she had gathered in her research on Drake in an exhibit space in the library at the University of California at Berkeley. There were twenty-four items on display with her handwritten captions describing the particular importance of each map or picture. Luckily, these caption cards survive and are preserved at the Bancroft Library. They provide an outline of the arguments she presented in her lecture.

A review of her lecture in the *American Historical Review* noted that Nuttall established careful comparisons between noteworthy maps covering Drake's Pacific voyage.[49] Her presentation included a discussion

FIGURE 8.1. Detail of North America, from the world map or French Drake map, by Nicola van Sype, ca. 1583 or later. Map is in the Public Domain.

of the six maps and one very large globe of the earth.[50] The first map in her display was Hakluyt's map from *Principall Navigations* (1589) and then both the Dutch and French versions of a map engraved by Van Sype (ca. 1586), where her exhibit captions noted that these were new to Drake scholars and "brought to light by Mrs. Z. Nuttall."[51] The globe she referred to was one of the two Molyneux Globes made for Queen Elizabeth in 1592 that was updated in 1603. This globe was displayed in the Middle Temple, which was Hakluyt's home base, and Drake's frequent lodgings. The other maps she displayed were the Silver Map of the World, the Hondius map from 1595 that shows both Cavindish and Drake's tracks, and an unnamed map from Venice that showed the last time Nova Albion was used on a contemporary map.

Nuttall's intent for the exhibit was to illustrate Drake's movements in the Pacific with the early maps produced after the voyage.[52] The map engraved by Jodocus Hondius that was printed for *Principall Navigations* shows a star where a note in Latin read that "Drake turned back because of the cold." The star is set at latitude 48° north.[53]

The Dutch version of the map engraved by Nicola Van Sype shows the track of Drake's voyage ascending to above 50° north latitude along the Northwest coast of America. Nuttall conjectured in the caption: "This map probably dates from 1586 when Drake visited Holland and may have been made by one of the Dutch mariners who had accompanied Drake on the famous voyage."[54] Nuttall's reasoning was that if a mariner on the voyage made this map, the latitudes would likely be accurate.

The later version of the Van Sype map is the French edition of the map that was "seen and corrected by Drake."[55] This map, too, was new to Drake scholars when Archer P. Huntington, president of the Hispanic Society, brought it to her attention. Her exhibit caption described Drake's corrections as follows: "He reversed the order of the numerals marking the meridians...drew the arms of England and Ireland and the crowned arms of Queen Elizabeth under Elizabeth Island and New Albion. He also drew lines to indicate the boundaries of New Spain and New France and his project of a New England extending from the Pacific to the Atlantic Coast, as it practically does at the present day."[56] The implication of Drake's placement of the crowned arms of Queen Elizabeth was that Drake wanted the map to reflect that he had claimed two strategic landfalls for the Crown: Elizabeth Island south of Cape Horn, and Nova Albion, placed clearly north of any Spanish claims.

Nuttall's exhibit at the library included a photograph of a silver medallion called the "Silver Map of the World" that was engraved ca. 1589 to commemorate Drake's voyage, perhaps even made with some of the silver he brought home. This—and the photograph of the updated Molyneux Globes—both depict the west coast of America in remarkably correct detail with indications of Drake's advance to about 48° north.

Hakluyt admired the Molyneux globe and wrote that it was "[a] very large and most exact terrestrial Globe, collected and reformed according to the newest, secretest, and latest discoveries."[57] On the globe a faint track shows Drake's path ascending to 48° north where Drake's name is indicated, and the path then descends to about 43° north where Cape Mendocino is incorrectly indicated.[58]

Nuttall must have come to the same conclusion as historian Ken MacMillan subsequently came to regarding the details in these early maps depicting Drake's famous voyage. In MacMillan's discussion of the Nicola van Sype map editions he wrote: "Like other contemporary published maps of newfound lands, neither of these maps was detailed enough to disclose secret intelligence, but each contained expressions of sovereignty that would have pleased the English crown and served as texts of possession."[59]

Other items in Nuttall's exhibit included photographs of Nuño da Silva's logbook, a chair made from the timber of the *Golden Hind*, a view of Buckland Abbey that was Drake's home near Plymouth, various portraits of Drake, and an image of a deposition signed by forty-nine members of Drake's company once they returned from the voyage around the world.

The exhibition of Drake material at the Berkeley library continued for several days after the historical congress adjourned. Nuttall presented her lecture to the anthropology summer session. Her talk was a repetition of her paper to the congress, and the student newspaper had the headline "Drake was no Buccaneer."

After her lecture the Watermans invited Nuttall to dinner where she was introduced to Ishi, who "graciously agreed to show her how he could make an arrowhead."[60] Ishi was a Yana who had escaped the genocide of his tribe by living in a remote area near Mount Lassen. He was living with the Watermans for the summer. Ishi made an arrow point out of bottle glass and presented it to Nuttall. It is a treasure her family still retains.[61]

The Bancroft Library has correspondence from Nuttall to both Bolton and Stephens during her time in Berkeley in 1915. On July 16, a few days before her presentation, she asked Stephens to dine with her to "obtain your advice" and just after the conference closed in August she cordially asked him for a meeting to discuss "certain questions, of interest to us both being historical."[62] To Bolton, Nuttall corresponded cordially, often signing off with "kind regards" or "kind remembrances" to Mrs. Bolton.[63]

Whatever the substance of her discussions with Bolton and Stephens, it was decided in late summer 1915 that her monograph, *The Northern Limits of Drake in the Pacific* was to be included in a forthcoming publication that Stephens and Bolton were editing. This publication, *The Pacific Ocean in History*, was the collection of papers and addresses presented at the Panama-Pacific Historical Congress.

In September Nuttall wrote to Bolton asking what agreement he had made with Macmillan, the publisher, regarding the reprints. She was curious about how to request additional copies beyond the number given to contributing authors, and what the cost would be.[64] She was clearly excited about the chance to publish her theories about Drake's landing.

A month later Nuttall sent Bolton a note to inform him that she had suspended work on her paper for several weeks because she had to undergo "dentist's treatment," but that she had since returned to Berkeley. She wrote, "Encouraged by your definite statement about reprints I am taking up the work again and shall finish as soon as possible."[65]

Despite their earlier assurances to Nuttall that her monograph would be included, Bolton and Stephens notified Nuttall in spring 1916 that they would not include her monograph in *The Pacific Ocean in History* after all. Nuttall's contribution was completely cut out. (When the volume came out it included the writings of Bolton's fellow faculty members and students, as well as two articles that Bolton himself authored.)[66]

Nuttall wrote back, clearly unhappy about the change of circumstance. She responded with the request that Bolton at least allow the title of her monograph—*The Northern Limits of Drake in the Pacific*—to be published in the volume, along with a preliminary statement detailing her results, with an explanation that the completed monograph would be published separately.[67]

Nuttall reminded Bolton that she had just provided the Bancroft Library with the negatives of several important documents that she had found in the Public Record Office in London. One of the documents was "a detailed list of every gold and silver bar delivered by Drake to the Queen's Commissioners—one of these Tremayne, a member of her Council, has never been published *in extenso* and may yield curious results if analytically studied by a specialist."[68] She then referred Bolton to page 408 of Corbett's book on Drake for "a very curious and interesting account."[69] Therein was a description of the amount paid to the investors of the voyage, including Sir Francis Walsingham, the Earl of Leicester, and Christopher Hatton who were members of the Privy Council.[70]

Calling Bolton's attention to these documents was Nuttall's way of underscoring that Drake's voyage was state-sponsored, and that these important findings would be in her monograph. At the time, Nuttall did not realize how little Bolton cared about the historical record (as detailed in a later chapter). As to the photographic negatives that she deposited at the library, she requested, "they not be referred to until my publication is out, in a years time—as they are not available for inspection now."[71] Here she was attempting to entice Bolton with her important findings, and to get him involved in her process.

In the same letter, Nuttall asked Bolton's advice about where she could publish.[72] If he responded to her request, there is no record of it. Bolton could have helped her: he was editor of two series of University of California publications, and coeditor of two historical magazines, and was influential on other editorial boards.[73] Bolton did not help her, or include the title or any preliminary statement of her forthcoming paper in *The Pacific Ocean in History*, which came out in 1917.

The same day she wrote Bolton, she penned a letter to Carl Ewald Grunsky, the president of the board of trustees of the California Academy of Sciences:

It having been suggested to me that the California Academy of Sciences might be willing to publish a monograph I have almost completed, I venture to address you on this subject. The manuscript deals with the question how far north Francis Drake sailed in his famous voyage and embodies a mass of fresh material. It would cover about 100 pages and include reproductions of 10 or 11 maps and charts...It is the outcome of years of research and labour.[74]

She received an encouraging answer three days later from the Academy's director, Dr. Barton W. Evermann, who wondered if the monograph would be entirely germane, but was willing to seek funds for its publication.

It seems likely that behind the scenes, an effort (perhaps led by Bolton) had been coalescing and was set to counter her promulgations of a more northerly landing by Drake by overwhelming public opinion about Drake's voyage. The California legislature was prompted to adopt a series of resolutions to establish a spectacular commemoration of Drake to take place in May 1916 in Marin County concurrently with the Marin Flower Pageant. Ostensibly, the purpose was to honor Drake, who "landed on our shores and raised the English flag at Drakes Bay."[75]

The strongest effort to influence public opinion came about when William Kent, a U.S. congressmen from Marin County, introduced a resolution in the United States House of Representatives authorizing President Woodrow Wilson to appoint a representative of the government to appear at the forthcoming Drake's landing commemoration. Woodrow Wilson signed the bill and appointed one of Mayor Rolph's friends, James H. Barry, as his representative. The resolution is as follows: "Resolved by the House of Representatives (the Senate Concurring) that the President of the United States is hereby authorized and requested to appoint a representative of this government to appear at the celebration of the landing of Sir Francis Drake on the shores of Marin County, California."[76]

These strong measures must have given Nuttall an inkling as to how determined the powers-that-be were to subvert her findings and promote their version of history. Three days after the resolution was introduced on the House floor, Nuttall wrote again to Evermann to remind him that he had promised he would let her know in a timely manner the result of his consultation regarding the publication of the Drake monograph. She needed an answer, "May I now trouble you to give me a definite answer, for I am planning to have it published elsewhere if it is not convenient for you to do so."[77] He answered Nuttall right away, letting her know that he had discussed it with President Grunsky and Mr. John W. Maillard, who were the other members of the publication committee: "We all feel that it is more than likely the funds can be raised but as a necessary preliminary step you should send on the manuscript, which would be at once referred to the Committee on publication for recommendation."[78] Evermann's comments included the remark that they were also anxious to have her lecture on Drake before the Academy at the long anticipated opening of their new museum in Golden Gate Park that was scheduled for September. Parmenter suggested that Evermann's rapid reply to Nuttall was because Nuttall's celebrity was increasing, and Evermann did not want to lose the public attraction of Nuttall's Drake lecture at the big opening. On May 7 Nuttall replied to Evermann's letter: "Now that I have your opinion that it more than likely that the Academy will be able to publish my paper I shall proceed at once to make a final revision of my MS. preparatory to submitting it to the Committee on Publication."[79] Nuttall spent several months getting her material into publishable form.

The big Drake celebration in Marin County took place over three days beginning on May 19, 1916. It was held in a natural amphitheater on the estate of Congressman Kent. Representatives of the embassies of Great Britain, Spain, and Russia took part in the celebration. On the opening day they were treated to a reception hosted by Governor Hiram Johnson. The whole Drake fête included choral concerts, balls, historical pageants, and a parade in Drake's honor.[80] The Sausalito newspaper reported that thousands of people attended the celebration where "Drake's praises were voiced in song and story and commemorated in colorful pageantry of parade and tableau."[81]

The celebration was not without controversy. After Governor Johnson's remarks, Reverend G. M. Cutting of the Episcopal Church gave the principal speech of the day, wherein he objected several times to the speech Johnson had given that had lauded Drake as a pirate. Apparently Nuttall was not present, but Johnson's comments about Drake not being a pirate echoed Nuttall's. The fête was not a financial success. After all the receipts had been added up, it was found that expenses exceeded receipts by about $200.[82]

How she felt about the resolution authorizing President Woodrow Wilson to send a representative of the government to appear at Drake's landing fête is unrecorded. That circumstance, the Drake fête itself, and the rejection of her monograph by Bolton, all must have daunted Zelia. Parameter suggested that her grandmother Abby Parrott, or perhaps Phoebe Hearst, thought she needed a "long, life-restoring trip" and so one of them provided the funds to make the journey.[83] She left California in the later part of May for points north. This may have been her way (or her benefactor's way) of making sure she was out of town during the Drake fête. The *Oakland Tribune* reported that her trip included "a most inspiring trip to Alaska, in the region of British Columbia, where the Spanish explorers had one time been, going along the inside passage."[84] Nuttall traveled with a friend, and their itinerary included going above the Arctic Circle where they would witness the solstice and photograph the midnight sun at Fort Yukon.

As part of Nuttall's final research for her monograph on the northern limits of Drake's voyage, she visited the Makah Tribe, at Neah Bay, Washington, on the Olympic Peninsula at the tip of Cape Flattery at 48° north, in waters where she suspected Drake had sailed. Nuttall reached Neah Bay via a cannery boat out of Port Angeles—the only conveyance that regularly made that remote port of call—which was met in the bay by Makah fishermen paddling splendid cedar canoes.[85] Nuttall was the guest of a missionary woman, who also kept a little museum that displayed crafts and artifacts made by the Makah.[86] Parmenter wrote:

> What excited Zelia most about this visit was not having been where Drake gave up his quest for the Northwest Passage, but what she wrote her brother George. "She felt sure," he summarized, "she had identified Drake's 'Bay of New Albion.'" So she had the material she wanted to add to her Drake monograph for the

Academy. The topography of Neah Bay and its Indians, it seems, convinced her that the young John Drake had not been wrong in saying where Drake had caulked the *Golden Hind*.[87]

Nuttall's final stop before returning to San Francisco was a visit with Phoebe Hearst, who was residing for the summer at Wyntoon, Hearst's country mansion on the McCloud River in Northern California. Parmenter speculated that Nuttall discussed her findings with Mrs. Hearst and expounded on her theory that Neah Bay was a more likely candidate for the honor of being Nova Albion than the popular California candidates: Bodega Bay, Drakes Bay, or San Francisco Bay. Nuttall's cultural and ethnographic observations at Neah Bay have not survived, though Parmenter speculated that her observations with Mrs. Hearst included "the way the Makahs lived in houses of cedar boards proved the presence of plentiful wood from which Drake could have built his huts."[88]

Nuttall's ethnographic observations of the Makah people were incorporated into her monograph, which was ready a few months after she returned to San Francisco. On January 13, 1917, she submitted the manuscript to the California Academy of Sciences. Her typing and photographic expenses came to a total amount of $250 for its preparation. This was a large sum at the time, and she included a request for reimbursement for her expenses.

She must have had confidence her book would be published by the Academy, because eleven days later she gave an interview to a newspaper reporter who wrote the following: "Miss Nuttall has finished a book dealing [with] the voyage of Sir Francis Drake along the Pacific coast of America which is now in the hands of her publisher in San Francisco. In this book she brings to light many facts concerning this courageous explorer obtained from archives in Mexico and Spain."[89]

The Academy publications board read and reviewed her monograph, which by then exceeded one hundred pages and included eleven maps. Three months after it was submitted, on March 17, 1917, they rendered the following decision: "The committee on Publication submitted a report on the paper offered for publication by Mrs. Zelia Nuttall to the effect that it appeared inadvisable to publish the same, since historical papers, in the judgment of the Committee, are not within the province of the Academy."[90] This was a heavy disappointment for Nuttall, but she was not yet defeated. Her monograph was primed and ready to be published somewhere. At the same time, the people who wanted to protect the "Drake in California" paradigm knew what evidence her monograph contained. With the threat of her finished monograph at hand, one of them initiated a potent subterfuge: a hoax designed to eclipse her findings.

Nuttall left Berkeley in May for her home and work in Mexico. In a last attempt to get it published, on July 26, Nuttall wrote to Bolton:

> I was disappointed just before leaving California in the Spring to receive word from the Secretary of the Academy of Sciences that after all they thought it best that my monograph on "the earliest authentic records of Drake's Landing of the North Pacific Coast" should be published by some historical society, as the Academy can't hardly depart from its specialty on works on Natural Sciences. I have taken no steps about publishing it since having been travelling and too unsettled to think about the matter. If only your department would undertake to bring it out in quarto size and promptly I would be glad to send it to you...Perhaps you can suggest some way to publish the monograph which embodies much entirely new material and has given me a great deal of work.[91]

She also requested a refund of the expenses she incurred for photographs and copyists. The Academy had not reimbursed her, and after all, she had incurred these expenses while she had the understanding that Bolton and Stephens would be including her paper in their compendium. She noted that she was in strained circumstances owing to altered conditions and the diminished value of her property.[92] There is no record that Bolton made any effort to have her compensated.

Nuttall's monograph on the northern limits of Drake's voyage is as lost as Drake's journal of the circumnavigation. Nuttall died in 1933, and many of her papers were burned shortly after. Some were collected by her grandson and taken to London, but lost during World War II when a German bomb destroyed the building where her papers were held.[93] We are deprived of Nuttall's full and reasoned analysis of the question.

Parmenter wrote: "So Zelia's contribution to what has continued to be one of the great debates of California historians, archaeologists and ethnologists—which bay was Nova Albion—has been lost."[94]

The juggernaut the Californians put up was too much. Her work could have created a sea change that swept away the "Drake in California" model, or at least spurred more scholarship and discussion. She trespassed on the high ground of a California myth and found that to take Drake out of California was akin to pulling up the redwoods.

CHAPTER NINE

Henry Wagner Huffs and Puffs
and the British Blow Him Down

IN 1918 HENRY WAGNER retired from his job as an executive in the mining and smelting business and moved to San Francisco.[1] He was an avid book collector and aspired to be a historian. In his memoirs Wagner recalled going to a meeting of the Sir Francis Drake Association in a garden in Marin County where the founder, Bishop Nichols, gave an address to the members. Wagner related that the bishop presented "the most extraordinary ideas that I had ever heard as historical facts. I gathered that he had been reading Mrs. Zelia Nuttall's book, *New Light on Drake.*"[2]

Wagner related that the large number of English people in the audience "swallowed it [Nuttall's theories] without difficulty."[3] At the garden meeting, he thought the bishop was promulgating English propaganda by his remarks that Drake was on a mission for the Queen and reconnoitering for a colony: "This was English propaganda, and I am still of that opinion. Mrs. Nuttall's book appeared in 1914, published in London by the Hakluyt Society. The "New Light" consisted of one document, a diary or log of Drake's Portuguese pilot, Nuño da Silva."[4]

There was more than one new document that Nuttall brought to light, so this was a patently false statement. It reveals that Wagner, even sixteen years after his first efforts at writing history, was cavalier about the tenets that bind trained historians regarding the historical record.

After the meeting in the garden, Wagner said he immediately went home and reread Nuttall's book, which he found "to be a tissue of misrepresentations, mistranslations and misconceptions, so I sat down to write an article for some magazine, showing it up."[5] Thus began Wagner's mission "to show up" Nuttall. Wagner traveled to Europe in 1919 to do research on an article he planned about the purpose of Drake's voyage: "Further study of the subject had convinced me that I had obtained the clue to the object of his voyage. To proceed therefore with simply a destructive criticism of Mrs. Nuttall's *New Light on Drake* hardly seemed worthwhile. It would be better to prepare a constructive book on the voyage, its aims and achievements."[6]

One of Wagner's main objections concerned Nuttall's interpretation of the French Drake Map that was "seen and corrected by Drake" and that Nuttall affirmed dated to the sixteenth century.[7] Wagner had found the same map in a seventeenth-century book on Drake, and became convinced the map was not as old and important as Nuttall asserted it to be. This map is now believed to be the second closest surviving copy of the map Drake gave Queen Elizabeth, and it has even more historical significance than Nuttall realized.[8] Further, Wagner blamed the Hakluyt Society for "having been taken in by Mrs. Nuttall in publishing a map, which she had found in a French book printed in 1641, as a sixteenth-century production."[9]

Wagner had built up a head of steam about the subject, and was scheduled to address the California Historical Society and present his arguments on the purpose of Drake's voyage at their meeting on April 22, 1923.[10]

A few days before Wagner's presentation, Nuttall and prominent labor lawyer M. F. Michael made some sort of protest at a meeting of the board of directors. The nature of their protest is unknown, but it can be conjectured that it was about Wagner's declared crusade against Nuttall.[11] The minutes of the meeting are just a sketch, but what is known is that Nuttall and Michael were unsatisfied with the outcome, submitted their resignations from the Society—which were accepted by the board—and they walked out.

If Nuttall had any hope that the *Quarterly* would publish her work on Drake or allow her to address Wagner's criticisms, it ended with her walking out of the meeting. Nine months later, the *Quarterly* did publish an article she had written about two important Native American baskets (the article had been written the year before).[12] According to Parmenter,

Wagner had even arranged its publication.[13] Women, it seems, were allowed to write about baskets but not about explorers.

In Wagner's address to the Society he brought up the French Drake Map. He noted that map experts in England consider it a "seventeenth century map beyond question."[14] Parmenter wrote that Wagner "was then too cocksure in denouncing Zelia's map on the basis of inadequate evidence, but in his talk his criticism of Zelia was mild compared to what he was to publish later."[15]

His criticism of Nuttall was walloping. Wagner's book, *Sir Francis Drake's Voyage around the World: Its Aims and Achievements* was published in 1926. Within its pages Wagner's misrepresentations and labored refutations of Nuttall's conclusions devolved into personal attacks on Nuttall. In one particularly sarcastic passage Wagner mocked Nuttall's theory that the Nova Albion landing was on the Northwest coast: "Not content with the discovery of her 'Drake's Dream,' Mrs. Nuttall attempted to prove that when he sailed from England in 1577 his greater object was to found an agricultural colony on the Northwest Coast of America."[16]

Nuttall fired back in a five-page rebuttal that was published in the *Hispanic American Historical Review*. She particularly disputed Wagner's chief conclusion, that Drake's expedition was an inglorious one undertaken "entirely for trading purposes." In response to Wagner's particular statement about her theory of Drake on the Northwest coast, we have her only published comment on the subject: "Attention is drawn here to the extraordinary fact that whereas in his sentence already quoted, Mr. Wagner charges me with attempting to prove that Drake's objective was to found an agricultural colony 'on the Northwest Coast,' he here attributes to me another 'theory' that can only be qualified as absurd and ridiculous. I therefore must challenge him to point out a single statement made by me to the effect that the objective of Drake was *California*."[17]

It seems Nuttall enjoyed toying with Wagner on the point of Drake on the Northwest coast. Parmenter noted that "scholars are notably unfriendly to interlopers from the outside, and Wagner, after all, was a mining engineer."[18] A few months later, Nuttall was invited to review Wagner's book for the *American Historical Review*. Her criticism here, too, was pointed: "Limitations of space prevent the reviewer from pointing out certain misstatements, misreadings of Spanish words, mistranslations, and omissions, which render it advisable for the student to read Mr. Wagner's text and theories with caution. Notwithstanding its defects, however, because of the valuable collection of material it contains, not only relating to Drake's Voyage, but also the Fenton expedition, Mr. Wagner's publication and its many bibliographical notes will prove to be a useful and convenient *book of reference*."[19]

Parmenter noted that Nuttall's summary of Wagner's book was cogent and level, and the points she made were worth making, "But the blood Zelia had drawn with the rapier of wit must have rankled."[20]

Parmenter pointed out that many historians were positively on Nuttall's side. The assistant keeper of the map room at the British Museum was cartographer and historian Frederick P. Sprent, who dismissed Wagner's conclusion about the French Van Sype map. Sprent's book described two contemporary maps of Drake's voyage around the world, including the French map that Nuttall had brought to light and that Wagner supposed to be unimportant.[21] Sprent demonstrated that the French map was probably made in Antwerp—out of reach of the Crown's censor—and that the paper, the lack of folding, the general style and content of the map, were "points in favor of an early date."[22] Historians now consider this map to be one of the earliest we have of the voyage, and it is thought to date from ca. 1583 or shortly thereafter.[23]

In 1927 John Wooster Robertson argued that Drake may have run as high as 48° or 49° north latitude, or even the current border of Alaska. He reflected that "many of our local historians" had attempted to locate Drake's fair bay, but the problem is that the descriptions in the narratives are scanty and there are no specific topographical details. "The various harbors named have been proved to be the result of personal preference rather than a selection based on authentic data."[24] His book, titled *Francis Drake and Other Early Explorers along the Pacific Coast*, was chosen as one of the best fifty books of 1927. His dismantling of George Davidson's analysis prompted one California reviewer to call him a "destructive critic."[25]

British historian E. F. Benson had relied heavily on *New Light on Drake*, for his book *Sir Francis Drake* published in Harper's Golden Hind series of books in 1927, just after Wagner's tome came out. The Golden Hind series included biographies by well-regarded authors.

Nuttall's book contained what Benson described as "a quantity of most important new material (depositions, etc.) concerning the Voyage of Circumnavigation."[26]

Benson was, like Sprent, critical of Wagner's analysis and misunderstanding of the record, and openly attacked him in several passages. He supported Nuttall's finding that the voyage had a greater purpose than trade. Drake's objective, as Benson characterized it, was to "sail through the Strait of Magellan, furrow the waters of the Pacific with an English keel. And play havoc with the Spanish treasure ships, which, built at Panama, brought to the Isthmus the golden harvests of Peru."[27]

Benson's most pointed criticism was in a note in response to Wagner's theory that the expedition was bound for the Moluccas and perhaps China. Benson wrote: "Among the many fatal objections to this view are, (i) there would have been no reason for concealing it from Burghley [the dove on the Privy Council and a father figure to Elizabeth], if this was the case; and (ii) the expedition, instead of taking the fabulously difficult route which included the passage of Magellan Strait, would have sailed eastwards."[28]

A new edition of Benson's book came out in 1932 published by The Bodley Head Books—a precursor to Penguin Books—and was widely distributed in the U.K. and in America. The publisher found that large audiences existed for history books, including a book about Francis Drake. The popularity of this book and the assertion that Drake ascended to 48° north must not have sat well with the powers-that-be in California.

Nuttall died a year later, at her beloved Casa Alvarado, eight miles south of Mexico City. Philip Ainsworth Means wrote an appreciation of her for the *Hispanic American Historical Review*. He called her a *savante* and reflected on her battles: "Mrs. Nuttall could, and did, hit—hard and well. Many a cocksure person who differed with her on scientific questions received a sound drubbing for his pains, her weapons being the bludgeon of authentic fact and the rapier of valid argument."[29]

E. F. Benson was not the only British historian who found the Americans' understanding of the social and political context of Elizabethan England lacking. Shortly after Benson published his Drake biography, E. G. R. Taylor discovered two documents that validated his and Nuttall's conclusions, and exposed Wagner's bias.

E. G. R. Taylor was a distinguished professor of geography and a
Tudor expert at Birkbeck College, London. Taylor challenged the "Drake
in California" theory in a series of articles and in two books published
between 1929 and 1934. In 1929 when her first article appeared, she reported on the evidence she found that Drake was seeking the Straits
of Anian. In 1930 she published portions of a document that "must be
reckoned of first class importance" concerning Drake's famous voyage—
the draft plan of the voyage.[30] It consists only of two pages, and they
are badly burned. The surviving portions contain enough information
about the expedition's purpose to call it a voyage of exploration, with the
additional purpose of reconnaissance for trade. With this find, Taylor
effectively put to rest the contention that Queen Elizabeth was only passively involved in the venture. The plan's directive, as best can be made
out, is as follows:

> The pole…the South Sea then…far to the northwards as…along
> the said coast…as of the other to find out…to have traffic for
> the vent…of Her Majesty's realms…they are not under the obe-
> dience of princes, so is there great hope of…spices, drugs, co-
> chineal and…special commodities such as may…Her Highness's
> dominions, and also…shipping a-work greatly and…gotten up
> as aforesaid into 30 de[grees]…to the South Sea (if it shall be
> thought…by the forenamed Francis Drake…to…far) then he is
> to return the same way…homewards, as he went out which voy-
> age by God's favor is to be performed in 12 months. Although he
> should spend 5 months in tarrying upon the coast to get knowl-
> edge of the princes and countries there.[31]

Taylor noted that the plan of Drake's voyage was modeled after a plan
proposed by Sir Richard Grenville in 1574 that was found in the State
Papers, and was in the handwriting of Queen Elizabeth's chief advisor,
Lord Burghley.[32] Queen Elizabeth revoked Grenville's license almost
immediately. She had come to the conclusion that the voyage would be
seen as too provocative during a time when relations with Spain were
improving.[33]

In 1576 the voyage was given to Drake, and the scheme was expanded
to include exploration of the western entrance of the "northern strait"

i.e., the Strait of Anian. Taylor explained that the reason for attempting the fabled strait from the west came from Sebastian Cabot's experience. The eastern entrance from the Atlantic was considered a difficult approach due to prevailing winds. Exploring from the further or Pacific end would be easier to navigate because of the prevailing westerlies.[34] It was reasonable to infer that the best way of exploring the strait was from the west, with a small agile ship that could navigate narrow passages and ice floes. It was thought it might be possible to do it in late summer when the ice conditions would be most favorable.[35]

The manuscript plan for Drake's voyage also listed the sponsors, which brought Taylor to the conclusion: "This authentic list of the men who set the voyage on foot shows that it was sponsored by the Navy Board—the Lord High Admiral, Sir William Winter, George Winter, John Hawkins—and by the inner circle of Queen Elizabeth's advisors—Walsingham, Leicester and Hatton."[36]

Taylor's discovery put the important point of whether Drake was on a mission in the interests of the Queen and England beyond dispute. By one account, the origin of the scheme came from Walsingham, who summoned Drake and asked him where he thought the Spanish could be most annoyed. Drake and Walsingham then "roughed out a plan for harassing the Pacific coast settlements and seeking a north-west passage by which to return."[37]

In searching for more manuscripts on Drake's activities in the Pacific, Taylor discovered an important passage from the private diary of Richard Madox. Madox served as chaplain and recorder on the Fenton voyage, which was intended as the follow-up voyage to Drake's circumnavigation. The passage indicated that Drake found land on the "backside of Labrador"—i.e., North America. Taylor wrote: "The document then contains the categorical statement that Drake graved and trimmed his ship in 48° N., which agrees with a later account by John Drake. Now there can have been no possible reason for any falsification of the facts in a shipboard discussion, or in a diary jotting meant for the writer's eye alone."[38]

Taylor concluded that Drake's anchorage must be sought on the Northwest coast, rather than in California. She suggested the anchorage may have been at Gray's Harbor, or the mouth of Raft River in the state of Washington. Taylor commented that Drake could not have described the North American coast trending northwestward if he had reached latitudes short of 48° north, and pointed out that after Drake's voyage Mercator maps showed the Northwest coast with surprising accuracy, with the Northwest Passage no longer depicted as a broad open expanse of water. To assume that Drake was not the source of this information "is to fail to understand the intellectual outlook and mental equipment of the men of the expansionist period,"[39] Taylor wrote. After Taylor's publications, it became increasingly difficult to argue that Drake did not go farther than 42° north.[40]

The "Drake in California" theory was losing ground. Benson's popular history on Drake and the articles from other British historians were undermining the entire Drake in California paradigm. The British had searched their archives for documents relating to the voyage, and found them. Since the British historians had access to records, and better insight into the political and social context of the Elizabethans than the California historians did, their findings were authoritative. The result was a shift in thinking about the circumnavigation and its goals—including the northern limits of the voyage and the location of the landing. It seems likely that the cumulative evidence presented in these books and articles was what prompted the hoax that followed.

Just as the evidence for a more northern landing was building to a crescendo, the tune abruptly changed as if the arm of a record player was grabbed and the needle scratched across the record to a whole new tune.

CHAPTER TEN

The Historian on the Hill

ON A DRIVE in Marin County, California, a tire on Beryle Shinn's car went flat, and he pulled over to the side of the road to fix it. It was a summer day in 1936, and he and his unnamed passenger—a young woman—decided to go for a hike. They climbed through a hole in a barbed wire fence and walked up the adjacent hill.[1] On a small terrace he found a small cairn of rocks stacked on one side of an outcrop.[2] As the story goes, he began to playfully throw rocks from the stack down the hillside, and in so doing he discovered a corner of metal sticking out of the base of the cairn. He pulled the metal out. Beryle Shinn did not know it at the time, but he had found what would later be celebrated as "Drake's Plate of Brass." He tossed the plate in his car, thinking he could use the metal later to repair his car frame, and then forgot about it for a few months.

Subsequently, one of Shinn's friends—a student at Berkeley examined the plate. The friend recognized the word "Drake" on the plate, and advised Shinn to show it to the famous Berkeley history professor and director of the Bancroft Library, Herbert Bolton. Shinn called Bolton, and met with him in his office the very next day to show him the plate. Bolton wrote of these events: "I surmised its identity even before seeing it, from a very general description, which he gave me over the phone. My mind leaped to the conjecture at once, because for years I have been telling my students to keep an eye out for Drake's plate and the silver sixpence bearing the image of Queen Elizabeth."[3]

The day after he met Shinn, Bolton announced the great find to the students in his large History 8-B class in the Wheeler Auditorium. He

FIGURE 10.1. Beryle Shinn and Herbert E. Bolton with the Plate of Brass. Portrait file of The Bancroft Library, Bolton, Herbert-POR 53. Courtesy of The Bancroft Library, University of California, Berkeley.

heralded the plate with great enthusiasm in his lecture that day, and roused his class into action, saying they should all go over to the ocean immediately and look for more artifacts from Drake. Triumphantly, he led them out the doors of the lecture hall like he was leading seventy-six trombones in a big parade, though it soon dawned on the class that they were not actually going out to the shore, and so they disassembled.[4]

It is almost certain that Bolton himself initiated the Plate of Brass hoax, and this enthusiastic show for his students was part of the ruse. Bolton was implicated in the scheme in 1977 by the testimony of the daughter of one of Bolton's accomplices. Her name was Dolores Barron Scoble, and her father had been the curator at Park Memorial Museum in Golden Gate Park. In her 1977 statement, she recounted the day her father went to a meeting with several men at the home of a historian who lived in Berkeley. Barron had brought along his wife and Dolores, who was twelve years old at the time. At some point Dolores left the company of her mother and the others who were visiting in the house, and went out to see what the men were doing in the garage. Dolores watched them, and heard them laughing and discussing a metal plate. When Dolores recounted these events many years later, she provided the only firsthand eyewitness account of the plate and its perpetrators to James Hart, the investigator of the plate hoax. As detailed in a subsequent chapter, among the revelations in her testimony was that the Plate of Brass was made in ca. 1917 and that the plate hoax was initiated by the Berkeley historian who lived in the hills above the University of California, Berkeley.[5] The events in the garage took place twenty years prior to the eventual launch of the hoax, but was at the critical moment when Zelia Nuttall's theory of Drake's landing was gaining traction.

As it happened, the hoaxer and his accomplices did not launch the plate hoax that year. Perhaps because Bolton was worried Nuttall would see that it was not an authentic artifact from Drake. Perhaps there was no imperative to launch the hoax: Nuttall's efforts had been foiled, she had not found a publisher for her monograph, and never did.

The plate was kept in hiding for several years, until another opportunity presented itself. In the 1930s the "Drake in California" theory was again in jeopardy. It was then that the plate hoax was launched using a different set of accomplices—the Clampers, as is related in a subsequent chapter. The plate was found by Shinn in 1936, and was brought to the public's attention in 1937.

A thief does not begin his career with a bank heist, and if Bolton was the perpetrator as argued here, the plate was not Bolton's first attempt at pulling the wool over the eyes of the public. The following accounts of Bolton's other schemes show a similar *modus operandi* to what was found in the plate ruse, and demonstrate a pattern of deceit that a historian would normally eschew.

Spanish treasure was a theme in no less than three of Bolton's schemes, and pirate treasure was in two. The first episode occurred early in his history career while he was teaching in Texas, where he had learned the utilitarian value of wealthy friends and old documents. Rumors of a rich Spanish silver mine prompted a group of Texans to organize and seek the legendary long-lost San Saba silver mine.[6] Bolton had copies of old Spanish maps and records of the mine sent to him from a Mexican archive, and in exchange for these documents and his expertise, he was paid for his services and became a partner in an investment group that planned to find and exploit the mine. The group found the mine exactly where the Spanish map indicated—or at least *a* mine. The mine was unproductive, and may have been little more than an exploration or assay site that the Spanish abandoned after not finding productive ore. Nevertheless, this episode taught Bolton the value of his expertise, a map, a good story, and wealthy acquaintances.[7]

Bolton's second "Spanish treasure" episode began in 1920, when a prospector named John Mayeroff found an old document wrapped in a tattered cowhide tucked under an unusual and precariously balanced rock in Imperial County, California. In 1921 the prospector brought it to Bolton, who confirmed the document was authentic (it was not), and that it was written by Francisco Leyva de Bonilla and Antonio Gutierrez de Humaña. These men were leaders of an ill-fated Spanish exploration party that set out in 1593 to explore what is now New Mexico (though the newspaper said the date of their exploration was 1572). The members of the expedition never returned and it was supposed that Natives killed them. The spurious document pointed the way to the location of a rich gold and silver mine where the expedition had obtained a great amount of bullion that they loaded on twenty-nine horses and twenty-nine mules. The party was besieged and forced to bury the gold and silver in three different places, which were noted on a sketch map in the document. De Bonilla and de Humaña were writing this note, the document said, at the *very moment* when four thousand Natives surrounded the party.[8] The explorers related that they felt they might not survive and wanted their children to inherit the mine and buried treasure they had stowed, so they made a record and put it under a rock. There is no doubt that the document and the whole scenario are absurd, and a historian of Bolton's expertise would have figured that out immediately.

The *Oakland Tribune* printed a picture of the supposed manuscript and the man who found it.[9] The *Los Angeles Times* added a drawing of the discovery, and an artist's illustration depicting a battle between the explorers and the Natives.[10] Bolton was quoted as saying that there was no doubt as to the authenticity of the document because the pages were "sixteenth-century paper and bear every proof of genuineness."[11] This gave Bolton a convenient out if it was found to be a fraud. This statement in itself is suspicious—as a historian, he would know that forgers were known to use blank sheets cut from the back pages of old books or manuscripts to create frauds.

The manuscript's text is fantastical, and says in part: "In an encounter with the savages our forces were reduced so that we…have been obliged to bury our fabulous riches as we do not have hope of living…We have deposited these records of the nobles and the civilized peoples in the belief that our children may some day find them in the name of the Saint and the Holy Mother."[12]

An expedition to find the treasure was announced in the newspaper, though the expedition never actually happened. In Bolton's files is a contract between former U.S. congressman and *Oakland Tribune* publisher Joseph R. Knowland (the capitalist funder), Bolton, and Mayeroff. Knowland was an important and influential man: he had served in the U.S. House of Representatives from 1905 to 1915, and was past president of the Oakland chapter of the Native Sons of the Golden West.

According to the contract, Bolton was to finish the translation of the document, assist in the search in the desert for the treasure, and that all three partners "shall own" the document.[13] The contract stipulated that Mayeroff was to be advanced $1000 for his expenses. If any gold was found, Bolton would receive 30 percent of its value, and Knowland the remainder. In addition, the contract called for the original and a photographic copy to become the property of the Bancroft Library to use for historical purposes.[14]

Bolton's files include subsequent letters from Mayeroff in which he asked when Bolton was going to meet to translate the rest of the document, requested the money, and flattered Bolton by writing "you are the most superior educator in America." In his last letters, Mayeroff expressed disappointment that Bolton had not answered any of his letters.[15]

It is not clear if Knowland paid Bolton to translate the document. Knowland backed out on financing the expedition, as evidenced by one of Mayeroff's letters to Bolton in which he expressed his frustration: "Now you just go to that newspaper man and tell him to put up some cash."[16]

There is absolutely no record in the Bancroft Library of this purported old Spanish treasure document, ostensibly written by the long-lost explorers Francisco Leyva de Bonilla and Antonio Gutierrez de Humaña, and found under a precariously balanced rock. There is no mention of this document or of the alleged treasure by any author in any subsequent history of the de Bonilla and de Humaña expedition.

Bolton's former student and history professor George P. Hammond later coauthored a book about these early explorers, wherein he did not mention this important manuscript that solved the mystery of their disappearance—a document that his mentor allegedly translated and copied for the Bancroft Library.[17] One may reasonably suppose that this was a fraud—and that Bolton's colleagues and students saw it as such, and it raises the question of who planted the document. Did Bolton write a spurious account on old paper and plant it in the desert? Was he paid to translate a forgery he had made himself?

An even more fantastic—and perhaps related, but completely different—report of a Spanish treasure appeared in July 1921, only three months after the first. A reporter at Knowland's *Oakland Tribune* reported that Bolton had showed him a newspaper clipping from the *New York Times* reporting that an unnamed man had found 8,646 gold bars and 4,560 silver bars on Saddle Mountain near the city of Monterrey, Mexico. This is an implausibly large amount of bullion.

Bolton told the *Oakland Tribune* that he had translated an old document for the man, and it pointed the way to the treasure. In exchange the man had offered Bolton a half interest in the venture, which Bolton, quite nobly, had refused. The *Oakland Tribune* printed the headline "18 Millions Spurned by U.C. Teacher."[18] That same day, an article in the *Berkeley Daily Gazette* announced "Bolton Loses Share in Buried Treasure." The thrust of the articles was that Bolton had turned down the chance at millions because he was purely interested in the history, not the money—the same theme that had been stressed in the other treasure episode that year. The *Berkeley Gazette* article reported the following:

> Dr. Herbert Bolton, head of the history department at the university, may lose $36,500,000 because he was unable to take part in a buried treasure hunt in Mexico. Some time ago, Adam

Fisher of Monterrey, Mexico, came to the university with an old document which was said to have something to do with a buried treasure. The manuscript was translated by Dr. Bolton and was found to contain directions for a buried treasure hunt. Fisher asked Dr. Bolton to take part in the expedition but because of the pressure of academic duties, the latter was forced to give up the trip. Recently Dr. Bolton had a dispatch from Monterrey, Mexico stating that Fisher had applied for permission to export over 50 tons of gold bullion and Spanish gold.[19]

There was in fact an article about the treasure printed in the *New York Times* on June 4, 1921, but no other report of the fantastic find has been found in any history of Monterrey, Mexico, nor is there a dispatch from a man named Adam Fisher in Bolton's extensive correspondence files.[20] The facts cannot be substantiated. It appears that the *New York Times* report was false. Was this story planted to show Knowland that seeking old Spanish treasure was not so absurd?

A historian of merit would have corrected the record if his initial pronouncement about an important document was incorrect. Bolton made no such correction with regards to the de Bonilla and de Humaña document. Perhaps he was embarrassed and did not want to look foolish. However, it seems probable that Bolton knew the document was a forgery from the start. Eight years later the school newspaper of the University of Michigan published a story about Bolton that demonstrates he did not mind that the public believed these stories, and underscores the pattern Bolton demonstrated of narcissistic deceit. The headline read, "Professor in University of California Gains Fortune from Supposedly Abandoned Mines."[21] The text relates both stories of lost treasure but notes that Bolton actually found the exact location of the rich silver vein of the long-lost San Saba silver mine, and received a large royalty. This, as demonstrated, was not true. The article continued by relating the equally false story about the de Bonilla and de Humaña silver mine.

In another dubious story that was evidently intended to polish his image, an article in 1922 reported that Bolton had found thousands of documents on his three-week tour of the "regions inhabited by the Cliff Dwellers" that may reveal "hitherto unknown facts about Aztecs." He valued the documents at $2 million and asserted that they would be added to the collections at the Bancroft Library.[22] The entire premise of the story is absurd, not only because of the improbable valuation of the documents, but because the Aztec Empire was in Mesoamerica— thousands of miles from the regions where the Cliff Dwellers lived. The article included embellishments such as the "shadow of romance clings about the form of Professor Bolton," and that he had trekked through the Mojave Desert on horseback and that he was "often obliged to swing himself by ropes to the former habitations of the Cliff Dwellers."[23]

In both 1923 and 1926 Bolton put out the false story that the pirate Captain Kidd had allegedly buried a chest containing old Spanish gold coins and a quantity of jewelry in a cave in Maine. The story was that the chest was found by an employee of fur-trade tycoon John Jacob Astor. The first time this story surfaced was in May 1923, when Bolton gave an address before the San Jose Chamber of Commerce. Bolton asserted that the treasure brought Astor $1.4 million after he sold the treasure secretly in London.[24] Bolton's address was reported by the *Dubuque Telegraph-Herald*. The headline read: "Kidd Loot Basis of Astor Wealth? Californian Says Evidence Points to Discovery of Buried Treasure." Bolton gave himself an out by his qualification that he had not personally seen or verified the records and documents, but that persons who had access to them described them to him in detail. This story was actually a running Olmstead family joke that had been written down by a family friend and published as a spoof a few years earlier.[25] Bolton evidently had read a copy of the account and chose to embellish it further.

Three years later, a reporter from the *Dearborn Independent* (Henry Ford's paper famous for its anti-Semitic sentiments) interviewed Bolton for an article about the Captain Kidd treasure. In the interview Bolton repeated the story that a fur trapper had discovered Captain Kidd's treasure chest in a cave in Maine, and that he sold it to Astor. Bolton alleged that "Astor's fortune came out of an iron-bound oaken chest filled with doubloons, pieces of eight, sets of plate and other valuable things all looted by Captain Kidd from Dutch, Spanish, French and English merchantmen whose high prows he crossed with most influential solid shot."[26]

There is no truth to the story. Nevertheless, authorities in Maine read the account and asserted that the state has a legal claim to the treasure and "a court fight may develop in an endeavor to recover the money."[27] Why Bolton would repeat at a public meeting and two years later in an interview what he knew was a spoof and represent it as an actual historical account—with the addition of such specific details—and let the spoof go on, is an interesting question.

Four months after the 1926 article was published, Bolton received a letter from J. Neilson Barry, the director of a group of history buffs called the "Trail Seekers." Their letterhead described the organization as one dedicated to encouraging "young people to seek the footsteps of the past by searching for historic relics, historic incidents, and historic localities."[28] Barry pressed Bolton about the truth of the article, and Bolton sent his letter back with a note scribbled on the bottom that admitted indirectly that the story was a fabrication: "I told this as a good 'story' and the gulls grabbed it."[29]

This was Bolton's method: create a good story for the gullible public, and if it was exposed, call it a joke.

The present writer has found evidence that Bolton may have had some agency in another famous hoax: the Dare Stone. On November 8, 1937, a few months after the Drake Plate was brought to Bolton, a curiously engraved stone was brought to Haywood Jefferson Pearce Jr., professor of American history at Emory University in Atlanta. The man who brought the stone said his name was L. E. Hammond. The inscription was allegedly a message written in stone by Eleanor Dare, one of the colonists of the English colony of Roanoke established by Sir Walter Raleigh in 1585. Eleanor had arrived in Virginia the summer of 1587 with a group of colonists that included her husband, Ananais, and her father, John White, who Raleigh had appointed as governor of the colony. A few months later White sailed back to England to obtain help for the struggling colony. Over one hundred colonists remained, including Eleanor and her new baby, Virginia, who is celebrated as the first English child born in what is now the United States. War with Spain and other troubles prevented White's return for three years. In the summer of 1590 he was finally able to return and found that the settlement was deserted—and colonists of Roanoke have not been heard from since.

The message from Eleanor on the Dare Stone, as it was soon called, was to her father and related the fate of the colony, including the deaths of her daughter and husband. Half the colony had died of sickness or had been murdered by "Ye Savages," and asked that if any Englishman found the stone they should show it to her father, John White, the governor of Virginia.[30]

By 1937 the disappearance of Sir Walter Raleigh's Lost Colony had become an American legend. Playwright Paul Green, fascinated with the mystery, wrote *The Lost Colony*, first produced in summer 1937, which is now one of America's longest running plays.[31] It can be seen all summer at Fort Raleigh, North Carolina.

The stone brought to Pearce was hailed as the discovery of the century. It was thought that finally after 350 years the first tangible evidence of the fate of the people had been found.

Seven months after the stone was brought to Pearce he published an article in the *Journal of Southern History* titled, "New Light on the Roanoke Colony." He described the stone as a possible "rare piece of Americana." He even brought up Bolton and the Plate of Brass: "With the putative Drake plate of brass, recently reported in California, the Dare stone, if genuine, is one of the earliest historical records made by English hands on the soil of North America."[32]

Pearce looked for more stones, and offered rewards to any finders. Soon enough, a Georgia carpenter brought two more to Pearce, and subsequently the carpenter found even more inscribed stones. Then an Atlanta handyman found some, and subsequently two others brought even more carved stones. In all forty-six more stones allegedly inscribed by Dare or another member of the colony were found, and the finders were paid rewards for the stones.

In September 1939, Pearce invited a select group of historians, archeologists, and geologists to examine the stones. Bolton was one of the invitees, and Pearce noted on Bolton's invitation that he should "bring with him any other member of your faculty who might be able to add anything of value to the discussion."[33] The assembly was to hear a "recital of all the circumstances, not yet made public surrounding the discovery and history of the stones."[34] Bolton did not attend, and a year later Pearce invited Bolton to another meeting to see even more stones, and visit a cave where he said, "Eleanor Dare appears to have lived for six years."[35] Bolton did not attend that meeting either.

Pearce enjoyed the spotlight for almost four years when the stones were considered authentic. That changed in 1941 when Boyden Sparkes, an investigative reporter from the *Saturday Evening Post*, was sent to investigate the Dare Stones. Sparkes became suspicious of their authenticity after his first interview with Pearce, who he found very defensive.[36] Soon enough Sparkes's investigation revealed that all of the stones were forgeries—with the possible exception of the first stone that the mysterious L. E. Hammond had brought to Pearce. Historian David La Vere suggested Pearce had lost his professional objectivity because, "He just wanted to believe too much."[37] La Vere noted that Sparkes was not sure Pearce was the hoaxer: "That sort of lie would have been the absolute worst crime an academic could be accused of. But Sparkes did think Pearce was guilty of the second worst: playing up speculative evidence while suppressing that which countered his argument, and, further, failing to pursue the necessary research to uncover the truth."[38]

Pearce's behavior, however, seems to be a page out of Bolton's playbook. Sparkes noted that Pearce had lied to him on several points, including when Sparkes found out that Pearce had pitched a movie idea about the Lost Colony to filmmaker Cecil B. de Mille, though Pearce had asserted to Sparkes that someone else had contacted de Mille.

Pearce was implicated in the hoax and disgraced, though he said he was actually a victim of the hoax. He joined the U. S. Army in 1942, and after the war accepted a teaching position at Eastern Michigan University. He rarely published after his disgrace, though in 1947 he wrote an article about the Catholic Friars of Georgia, and in the second paragraph singled out Bolton and his students' work on the Spanish borderlands of Georgia.[39]

There is still a persistent question about the authenticity of the first Dare Stone brought by Mr. Hammond to Pearce and his colleagues at Emory. La Vere concluded that there is only circumstantial evidence that the first Dare Stone is a forgery, and that it may, in fact, be authentic. L. E. Hammond's story to Pearce was that he and his wife were on vacation and that he was a retired produce dealer from California. He alleged that he had found the stone while looking for hickory nuts on the bank of the Chowan River near Edenton, North Carolina. It was arranged that Mr. Hammond would receive a reward for finding the stone, and so

Pearce paid Hammond either $1000 or $500 for the stone (the accounts vary).[40] The money was sent to a general delivery post office box in Oakland, California.[41]

Emory officials soon became suspicious, and hired the Pinkerton National Detective Agency to investigate L. E. Hammond. Though it had been less than a month since Hammond left Georgia, the Pinkerton agency could not find L. E. Hammond or his wife, and it became evident Hammond was not who he appeared to be. Who was he, and is the first Dare Stone authentic?

In 2018 Andrew Lawler writing for *National Geographic* called for archaeologists and specialists to take another look at the stone.[42] The present author read Lawler's article in *National Geographic* about the Dare Stone and was struck with parallels between the circumstances surrounding the first Dare Stone and the Plate of Brass hoax. The behaviors of both Bolton and Pearce when they first examined the artifacts, how an aura was created around the artifacts, how the public's fascination was exploited, and even the money that was offered as a reward seemed too similar to be a coincidence.

In addition, the superficial resemblance of the alleged old English text on both the stone and the plate suggested they were somehow related. They were both brought to light in 1937, and touted to be either a "clever fraud" or a genuine artifact from the Elizabethan age of exploration.

The Dare Stone's finder, L. E. Hammond, said he lived in the Oakland-Alameda area, and that is where the money was sent—a location virtually next door to Berkeley. One of Bolton's students frequently mentioned by Bolton's biographers was named George P. Hammond. George was one of Bolton's "boys" who metaphorically was a knight at Bolton's round table. Bolton and George Hammond were close colleagues and friends. When Hammond was a student he had worked for Bolton at the Bancroft Library, and was one of the recipients of the fellowships awarded by the Native Sons of the Golden West. After graduation George taught history at a number of universities, including the University of Southern California. Hammond and Bolton traveled together on exploring expeditions. They retraced the trails of both the Domínguez–Escalante and the Coronado expeditions. Retracing the Domínguez–Escalante trail was especially arduous; Bolton and Hammond and their group had to travel twelve hundred miles through southwestern deserts, sometimes on horseback.[43]

In 1937 when the first Dare Stone was brought to Emory, George Hammond was at the University of New Mexico where he was not only a history professor, but head of the history department, dean of the graduate school, and president of the national honor society for students and professors of history. The deanship relieved him of half of the usual teaching load of a history professor, but his duties included frequent travel for his research, and for meetings and conferences, so it was not uncommon for him to be away from the university for several days or more.[44]

No photographs of L. E. Hammond were taken and the only physical evidence was his signature on each of four notarized contract documents at Emory University. The present writer compared the four notarized signatures of L. E. Hammond to twenty documents with the known signatures and handwriting of George P. Hammond.[45] There were significant morphological resemblances. Copies and photographs of these materials were sent to four handwriting and document examiners to determine if the known genuine handwriting shows substantial agreement in handwriting characteristics to the signatures of L. E. Hammond. Three of the examiners came to the conclusion that it was probable that the L. E. Hammond and George Hammond signatures were written by the same hand.[46] Brenda Petty found that "the similarity is quite extraordinary." With regards to the final letter "d" she noted, "In researching the cursive scripts used in the 1910s to the 1930s, not one of the scripts taught the letter 'd' with the formation used in the signatures. That makes it unique in formation."[47] (See Figure 10.2.)

Marcel Matley concluded, "I have arrived at the opinion that the available, relevant and reliable evidence shows that it is probable, more likely than not, the one person wrote both the LE Signatures and the George Signatures."[48] One final examiner, Jacqueline Joseph, was sent the materials for a preliminary verbal analysis. After reviewing the examples she was sent Matley's finding. Without writing a formal report, Joseph concurred with his results. She wrote, "Marcel took the entire body of handwriting evidence and went beyond the basic preliminaries to apply logic and to consider the rarely encountered situation that we

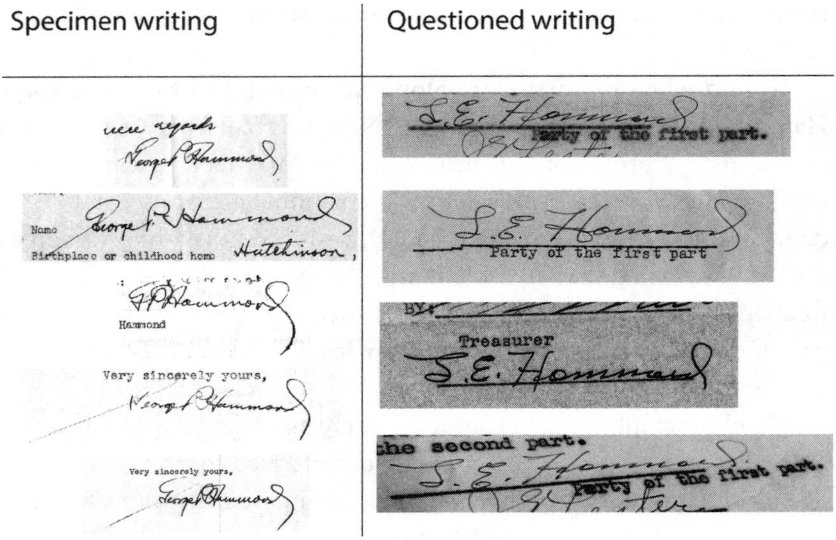

Specimen writing	Questioned writing

FIGURE 10.2. L. E. and George Hammond handwriting comparisons. The questioned writing is from the Dare Stones Collection, 1937-1987. Volume/Box: 1 TN: 59254. Stuart A. Rose Manuscript Archives, and Rare Book Library, Emory University. The specimen writing is from George Hammond Faculty File, 1935–1940, Center for Southwest Research, University Libraries, University of New Mexico.

have in the Hammond case."[49] However, the fourth examiner cast strong doubt on the idea that George signed the documents at Emory, but noted that "the evidence is not quite up to the virtually certain range."[50]

Therefore, it is probable, and more likely than not, that George Hammond posed as a retired produce dealer and was an important agent in the Dare Stone hoax. The plan for the hoax seems to have included having the contract documents notarized to add an element of importance or underline the significance of the find. Notaries are required to witness or attest the signatures on the documents, so it was imperative that Hammond present a piece of legal identification so that the notary could compare the signature on the document to the signature on his identification card. He may have altered the first name or initial on an old drivers license from the time when he lived in Los Angeles.[51] This may explain why the Pinkerton agency began their search for L. E. Hammond in Los Angeles.

Haywood Pearce must have been complicit in the scheme because George Hammond would not have risked being recognized by Pearce at a future meeting of the American Historical Association. They were both members and if Pearce did not know George's identity, George would not have risked "blowing his cover" by being recognized later.

This trail of circumstantial breadcrumbs leads to Bolton. It seems likely that he was involved somehow with the Dare Stone hoax. This can only be inferred by the resemblance of this scheme with his other schemes, his closeness with George Hammond, and that the money was sent to Oakland. It was well known that loyalty had its rewards in Bolton's Camelot, and it may or may not be significant that in 1946 Bolton arranged for George Hammond to be appointed director of the Bancroft Library, a position Hammond held until 1965.

If George Hammond was involved in the Dare Stone hoax, it follows that he was aware of some of Bolton's other fraudulent activities. When the alleged letter and treasure map from the de Bonilla and de Humaña expedition was brought in for Bolton to translate in 1921, Hammond was working for him at the Bancroft Library.

Only the broad strokes of the Dare Stone hoax are presented here. Whether anyone else at Emory was complicit in the scheme is unknown. Further research may answer the remaining questions, including whether the first Dare Stone was a quartzite rock from California rather than North Carolina. There was an opportunity for a stone delivery. One of Bolton's students came to visit George Hammond in Albuquerque three weeks before the Dare Stone was presented at Emory. The student had arrived from Berkeley and was traveling to Texas. Was he delivering a heavy package from Bolton containing a quartzite stone, we will never know, but George commented in a letter to Bolton after the visit, "It is always a pleasure to meet someone who has come from 'headquarters' recently, and to hear something about you and 'your boys.'"[52]

Both the Dare Stone and the Plate of Brass hoaxes required considerable planning, coordination, and execution. The hoaxers' motives were probably about dazzling the public with historical artifacts, polishing reputations, and gaining fame, students, and funding support for their universities and particular projects.

However, these hoaxes were concocted by important historians who risked their reputations if their machinations were uncovered. Written history is a powerful tool in a historian's hand because it influences the public's perception of historical events. The darker undertone of these hoaxes is that they may have been designed partly in the interest of promoting the English-speaking heroes of early American history in order to underscore and exaggerate America's white national identity.

The writings of both Pearce and Bolton demonstrate a strong racially biased ethos that may help explain their motivations. Bolton's doctoral dissertation was titled "Free Negro in the South," and contained comments such as: "Their general standing was no doubt largely determined by their origin, they were the descendants of heathens"; "The free [N]egro was idle"; "In his ignorance and poverty he was a public burden"; "They are people of such base and corrupt natures that the credit of their testimony [in court] cannot be certainly depended upon."[53] Haywood Pearce Jr.'s dissertation was on U.S. Representative Benjamin Harvey Hill of Georgia, who argued that the South could not accept racial equality even though it accepted military defeat. In a subsequent publication meant as a high school text book for students in the south, Pearce and his coauthors wrote a defense of the Ku Klux Klan, arguing that they helped rid the south of carpetbaggers and kept social order, though the authors did not mention lynching.[54] They romanticized the Klan noting: "Long white robes were chosen as a society regalia, with the old Scotch 'Fiery Cross' as its emblem. It was decided for fun to ride together at night upon white-sheeted and muffled hoofed horses" terrorizing those "whose consciences were not clear; especially Negroes."[55]

Raleigh's Roanoke, Eleanor and Virginia Dare, and Francis Drake became potent symbols of white manifest destiny. Virginia Dare, in particular, had been venerated among white supremacists since the 1860s. Though the message on the Dare Stone related that Virginia had died shortly after her birth, this information did not dash the idealistic vision white supremacists held of a romantic blond, blue-eyed white girl of the lost colony who lived among the adoring Algonquin and wore a white doeskin robe off one shoulder.[56] The Dare Stones had the effect of bringing the Lost Colony of Roanoke into popular consciousness.

How much a racially biased ethos was a motive in these hoaxes is debatable, but it is indisputable that these prominent and respected men provided much of the fabled narrative that vaunted and furthered the goals of their white supremacist/separatist supporters.

George Hammond retired as director of the Bancroft Library in 1965. He continued to maintain an office as Director Emeritus in the library until the late 1980s. He even served as chairman of a session in the conference on Sir Francis Drake in 1979.[57] During this time James Hart was director of the Bancroft Library and the chief investigator of the Plate of Brass hoax. When Hart was puzzling over who concocted the hoax, or at least why it was made, Hammond's office was just down the hall.

CHAPTER ELEVEN

Behind the Scenes

HERBERT BOLTON's storied exploits with Spanish treasure were one thing, but the Drake Plate of Brass raised up an Anglo hero who was a potent symbol in California. The plate enabled Bolton to turn his sights to the largely white and Protestant California elites, who embraced Drake: "For them, the plate was not just a metal document or a valuable antique. It was the holy grail—a venerable Anglo-American, Protestant, religious relic…As such, the Drake plate figured in a struggle for California's cultural high ground, and afforded Bolton a unique opportunity to ingratiate himself with a California elite who identified with the state's non-Hispanic pioneers."[1]

Hurtado claimed that Bolton derived power and fame from associating himself with the heroic exploits of historical figures. Bolton crafted his image to reflect not merely a historian who haunted dusty archives but "a striving young professional historian [transformed] into a romantic adventurer, at least in his own mind."[2]

The plate brought Bolton not only local attention, but international fame as the historian associated with the find. He probably did not expect all of the attention the plate attracted, but he certainly rode the wave it created and exploited the public's fascination with it. He understood, above all things, that publicity (and paying money for artifacts) lends enchantment.

The timing of the find suggests that Bolton's objective was to counter the cumulative evidence Eva Taylor and others had found that struck at the core of the "Drake in California" theory. He had foiled Zelia Nuttall's efforts, but the Drake in the Northwest theory had reared up again. Taylor and others had been writing books and articles over the previous years that were changing the paradigm and put forth the conjecture that Francis Drake–by then the golden hero of California—had landed elsewhere.

Bolton needed accomplices, and the fun-loving fraternal organization known as the Clampers fit the bill. The revived order of the Clampers was established in 1930 or 1931 by three lawyers who were history enthusiasts: Leon Whitsell, George Ezra Dane, and Carl Wheat.[3] The first chapter was the Yerba Buena chapter, and Bolton was a member. The Clampers were another advocacy organization that—like the Native Sons of the Golden West—extolled pioneers and put up interpretive plaques.

The Clampers were, and still are, a history satire organization, and a counterpoint to the Native Sons, though at the time many were members of both groups. Their antics during these early years were fraternal and comedic—they sought to emulate the hard-drinking miners and pioneers whose history they were dedicated to preserving. They told tall tales and went on camping trips to historic sites, and their ribald humor included a note in their charter that they "were dedicated to protecting lonely widows and orphans, but especially the widows." The official Clampers motto is *Credo Quia Absurdum*: "I believe because it is absurd."[4]

One Clamper related that the plate was placed in an area where there were several popular hiking trails so that they could stage a "surprise" find by Bolton. One of the Clampers recalled "the whole discovery was mixed up because it was picked up by somebody and thrown in a car."[5] It seems that while most of the members of the Yerba Buena chapter of the Clampers may have thought it was just a joke on Bolton, there was an inner circle working with him and knew that Bolton was orchestrating the hoax.

Curiously, the date when Beryle Shinn made Bolton aware of the plate is not recorded in Bolton's files, nor was the date he brought the plate to Bolton. This gap is unusual given the meticulous records Bolton kept about the plate that are still in his files in the Bancroft archives.

Bolton's problem was that if he declared the plate to be an authentic relic from Drake, and it was later found to be a fraud, he needed a cover story to deflect the blame in order to protect his reputation. The plan in this contingency seems to have been that if the plate were proven fraudulent, Bolton would have claimed that he was just overeager, and that his Clamper brothers perpetrated the joke as a fraternal prank.

In 1978 Hart interviewed Shinn about his first meeting with Bolton. Shinn related that the first thing Bolton wanted to know was how much money he wanted for the plate. Shinn was surprised by this first line of questioning, and had no idea of the Plate's possible worth, so Bolton suggested $1,000.[6] Many years later Shinn recalled that he "did not take the plate to Dr. Bolton to sell. After I learned that there was a Drake plate and that this might be it, I thought it should belong to some institution like the Historical Society or the University."[7]

In order to obtain the "artifact" from Shinn, Bolton enlisted the help of Allen Chickering. Chickering said he was suspicious that the plate might be a forgery, and so tested Shinn to see if he could take them to the location where he had found the plate: "Naturally, when the Plate was brought to my attention, I was suspicious that it might be a 'plant.' Dr. Bolton had passed [on] this and relied on Shinn, but I insisted on testing him out for my own satisfaction. This was easily arranged on the pretext that Dr. Bolton and I wanted to see where he had found it."[8]

On Sunday, February 28, 1937, a few days after Shinn brought the plate to Bolton, Chickering, Bolton, and Shinn drove out to the place that Shinn said was where he had found the artifact a few months prior. He showed them the barbed wire fence he and his female companion had crawled through, and the rocks where he had found the plate six or eight months before he brought it to their attention. During the hike, Bolton and Chickering convinced Shinn that the relic needed to be in a museum, and offered more money this time: $2,500 as a reward for finding the relic.

Chickering contacted several members of the Historical Society and University of California alumni and made a collection to pay Shinn a reward for the artifact. Chickering was a believer in the importance and authenticity of the plate, and was tasked with raising money to obtain it. Bolton spoke with great gravity about the Drake plate to possible benefactors; enabling Chickering to raise money from donors who were dazzled by this find that Bolton spoke about in such reverential tones.

One day later, Shinn balked. His uncle had warned him that if the plate were found to be fake, he could have legal complications, so Shinn informed Bolton that he was going to ship it out of state. Bolton quickly offered to assume any risk regarding the authenticity of the plate, including any legal complications that might arise if it were found to be a fraud. The two men also made an agreement that Bolton would have the opportunity to meet any price offered to Shinn from a third party, and if Shinn sold the plate to a third party, Bolton would get 10 percent of Shinn's proceeds from the transaction.[9] This agreement was recorded on a handwritten note found in Bolton's file, and is reminiscent of the treasure hunter agreement Bolton had signed with Mayeroff for his professional services in authenticating that particular forged document and assisting with the treasure hunt.

Shinn promised to bring the plate to Bolton the next morning, but did not show up. On Friday he brought Bolton the plate, and the reward offered was higher: $3,500. This would have been a huge sum for Shinn, who earned $800 a year at his job at a department store. He accepted, and the money enabled him to buy a house.

The spurious plate is inscribed as follows:

BEE IT KNOWNE VNTO ALL MEN BY THESE PRESENTS
IVNE 17 1579
BY THE GRACE OF GOD AND IN THE NAME OF HERR
MAIESTY QVEEN OF ENGLAND AND HERR
SUCCESSORS FOREVER I TAKE POSSESSION OF THIS
KINGDOME WHOSE KING AND PEOPLE FREELY RESIGNE
THEIR RIGHT AND TITLE IN THE WHOLE LAND VNTO HERR
MAIESTIES KEEPEING NOW NAMED BY ME AN TO BEE
KNOWNE VNTO ALL MEN AS NOVA ALBION
CG FRANCIS DRAKE

Word of the find had spread even before Bolton made the official announcement. A chauffeur named Caldera told Chickering that he had actually found the plate at Drakes Bay in 1933 while his boss hunted birds and he waited around the car. He had put the plate in the side pocket of his car door, and forgot about it, and later threw it out of his car in the general vicinity of where Shinn had found it. This story has a false ring that is entirely absent from Shinn's account. It appears to have been a deliberate deceit from another quarter designed to support the idea that Drake was at Drakes Bay rather than one of the other bays in contention. Shinn reported, "After he [Caldera] said that he had found the same plate I had found neither Dr. Bolton nor Mr. Chickering ever again called me or came to see me."[10] Chickering did, however, help Shinn get a job at Pacific Gas and Electric two years later.[11]

Bolton used his personal charisma and his authority and standing to convince people that the plate was undoubtedly from Drake. In 1936— when Shinn found the plate—Bolton was sixty-six, and was by then one of the most honored American history professors of the century. He had several honorary degrees and in 1925 the King of Spain had decorated him Comendador de la Real Orden de Isabel La Catolicà.[12] He had held important positions in the history establishment, was an endowed professor, had overseen hundreds of students, and was a favorite of the Native Sons of the Golden West. Who would not believe the word of this man?

Bolton wanted to "make a bang" with the news of the find.[13] On April 6, 1937, Bolton officially announced the plate's discovery at a meeting of the California Historical Society, which fittingly took place at the Sir Francis Drake Hotel in San Francisco. Zelia Nuttall had died in 1933, but had she still been alive she surely would have bristled at the title Bolton chose for his talk: *Newer Light on Drake and the Location of His Anchorage in California.* His speech was reproduced in the *California Historical Quarterly*, where Bolton described the find as: "One of the world's long-lost historical treasures apparently has been found!.... I surmised its identity even before seeing it, from a very general description which he gave me over the telephone."[14]

The following portion of Bolton's speech has language that not only demonstrates his ego and swagger, but was intended to firm up the theory that the Drake and Fletcher account was the most authoritative with regards to the plate: "Either the plate is a clever fraud, perpetrated by someone who carefully studied Fletcher's words; or, if it is genuine, as I fully believe, Fletcher made a remarkably accurate record of what it was like and what the inscription said. Between the relic and the eyewitness record there is a spectacular and convincing harmony which no fraud would be likely to attain."[15]

With the aid of this fantastic artifact and some tortured logic, Bolton argued that the Plate of Brass made *The World Encompassed* account the authority and last word. This declaration settled several questions, including the California latitude of the landing. *The World Encompassed* did not mention Drake's exploration for the Northwest Passage, nor any reconnaissance for a colony. In short, the Plate of Brass supported the paradigm that Drake landed in a bay in California and was not searching for the Northwest Passage.

In his speech, Bolton referred to W. J. Harte's recently published article, which he noted had "new information" and expressed "recent changes of opinion regarding the voyage." Harte's article was a brief note titled, "Some Recent Views on Drake's Voyage round the World," which had appeared in the journal *History*.[16]

The new information Bolton was referring to was a statement Harte had made about E. G. R. Taylor's discovery of the passage about Drake's landing in Richard Madox's diary from the Fenton voyage. In that passage Madox noted that Drake had graved and trimmed his ship at 48° north; this, as Taylor observed, agreed with a later account by John Drake. Taylor presented the case that maps after Drake's return showed that the American coast trended northwestward and that "he could not have come to the decision he did, namely that the American coast trended northwestward, if he had reached a latitude much short of 48°."[17]

Taylor's most sensitive finding drawn from the diary was as follows: "Thus it would appear that Drake's anchorage must be sought in Oregon [or around 48° north] rather than in California."[18]

Taylor concluded, "In view of the detailed work done by Mr. Wagner and Professor Davidson and the present writer's lack of local knowledge, it seems best merely to submit the new evidence and leave the question open."[19] Harte, however, mischaracterized that sentence with the misleading comment "[Taylor] does not feel the evidence strong enough in face of what Professor Davidson and Mr. Wagner have written."[20] Harte's mischaracterization of this sentence is clearly disingenuous.

With his remark about new information Bolton deftly deflected discussion of a more northerly anchorage. A difference of professional opinion can be understood, but Bolton deliberately spun these distortions and omissions in order to mislead his audience.

In his speech Bolton reasoned that if the plate was a hoax, the hoaxers would have known about the landing controversy and planted it at the more believable Drakes Bay rather than close to San Francisco Bay— ergo, it was not a hoax. The motive for a hoax would only be for financial gain, Bolton reasoned, so the absence of a profit motive spoke to its genuineness.

Money was a likely motive, as was a particular kind of fame that Bolton reveled in. Bolton wrote to one correspondent about the plate on April 25, 1937: "You would be surprised if I were to tell you how much time I have had to spend over the little piece of brass which Drake nailed to a 'firme poste' and after three hundred and fifty years chanced to come my way. It is not highly important, but has been intensely interesting to the general public, and I have had to play my part, hoping that the incident may be worth one or more millions to the university."[21]

The address to the California Historical Society was a huge success for Bolton. His correspondence files are full of congratulatory notes about his "masterful address," and the "sensational discovery." *Time Magazine* wrote an article about the plate.[22] Bolton was interviewed on a nationwide radio broadcast in a program titled *A Pirate Leaves His Calling Card.*[23]

Before the Plate of Brass was found, student enrollment at Berkeley had dropped off, and the Great Depression had slowed the flow of funds from benefactors for the purchase of manuscripts and materials for the Bancroft Library. The Native Sons of the Golden West had cut back their funding for student fellowships from $3000 to $1000 per year.[24] The plate did not just put Bolton in the limelight—which he craved—it also attracted new students, and bolstered private support for Bolton's programs. In 1940–1941 he was paid to travel to Ohio, Pennsylvania, and Colorado for speaking engagements at six colleges.[25] The years following the plate's discovery were successful fundraising years, which enabled the Bancroft Library to purchase important acquisitions.[26]

Though many were convinced of the authenticity of the plate, according to one student on the Berkeley campus it was a widely held secret among the undergraduate students in history that the newly begotten plate was phony.[27] Herb Caen, a columnist for the *San Francisco Chronicle*, had doubts about the plate and wrote the following in his column on July 9, 1938: "Around University of California, they're willing to bet 5 to 1 now that the 'brasse plate' of Sir Francis Drake is a phony—Professor Herbert Bolton is still testing the metal for signs of authenticity. And the California Historical Society (which paid $3500 for it) is holding its collective breath."[28] Just over a week later in a subsequent column Caen raised the question of the plate's authenticity again:

> You might be mildly interested to know that the case of the "brasse plate" of Sir Francis Drake isn't dead yet. A year ago you'll remember a battered copper plaque, supposedly the original one left behind by Sir Francis to prove England's claim to the new land, was found near San Quentin point by a youth who turned it over to the California Historical Society for some $3500. Since then its authenticity has been alternately confirmed and denied. Nobody seems to know whether the society got a bargain or a hunk of copper (all right a bad penny, then). So right now Professor Herbert Bolton of California is putting the metal through new, rigid tests. Within a month he'll have an announcement ready.[29]

Bolton was uneasy with the questions about the plate's authenticity. He had to do some damage control with Chickering, on whose loyalty he depended. Chickering was Bolton's lieutenant in the matter of the plate; he handled the fund raising, most of the correspondence, and defended the plate against attacks. On the day Caen's second column was published Bolton wrote a letter to Chickering that began with "My Dear Mr. Chickering": "Apparently the San Francisco chronicle is trying to get a rise out of somebody about the Drake Plate. I have noticed two or three articles in which they pretended to have heard something which I have said about it, but they are entirely untrue. I am writing this note so that you may not obtain a wrong impression regarding the matter."[30]

CHAPTER TWELVE

The Authentication of
the Plate of Brass

CHALLENGES TO THE authenticity of the Plate of Brass were numerous and authoritative, as were demands for analysis of the relic. Journalists at home and abroad, as well as historians and archaeologists, sent requests for at least a good photograph of the plate. Herbert Bolton demurred, put off analysis, and did not follow up with experts on specific questions they had about the plate that could help determine its authenticity. A good photograph was not available even by August 1937 when the editor of *Antiquity* wrote to Bolton "surely in the case of an object which, if genuine, is of the highest historical importance, at least one really adequate photograph should be made available!"[1]

What would an authentic Elizabethan plate such as the one left by Drake look like? There is an interesting example of a plate from Edward Fenton's last voyage that may be a good corollary to the one that Drake purportedly left on the west coast. The Fenton plate was recorded by his chaplain, Richard Madox, who noted it was a square plate of copper that they fixed to a rock at their watering place in Sierra Leone. The inscription was in Latin, and said "Edward Fenton is the bearer of Queen Elizabeth of England's fleet destined for the regions of China and Cathay." It was dated August 26, 1582. Chaplain Madox sketched the plate for his journal record of the voyage. The shape and design on the copper plate is reminiscent of the royal arms of England; it is an escutcheon divided into four sections by a cross, with a *fleur-de-lis* in each field.[2]

The Drake Plate of Brass is crude compared to the above example, and the experts were pretty well unanimous that the plate was not right. Captain R. B. Haselden, the curator of manuscripts at the Henry R. Huntington Library in Pasadena, was astonished by how quickly Bolton authenticated the plate, and was one of the most vocal critics. He warned that "fraudulent metal tablets of this sort are by no means uncommon,"[3] and that the University of California should take more caution before pronouncing the brass plate genuine. In response to Bolton's reasoning about financial gain, Haselden countered: "It is quite possible that a hoax was perpetuated without any thought of monetary gain whatsoever. The fact that the plate tallies in a most astonishing way with Fletcher's account does not at all preclude fraud, but is, in itself, enough to give rise to suspicion."[4]

The British Museum offered to conduct the investigation on the plate, as did the British National Maritime Museum, which offered the services of their metallurgical laboratory. Bolton did not take them up on their offers, and delayed analysis for as long as he could. Vincent T. Harlow, keeper of Rhodes House Library at Oxford, observed that the phraseology of the text and the format of the plate violated Elizabethan conventions. "It is inconceivable that Drake could not have produced a more imposing piece of brass…that he could not find among his ship's company someone capable of producing a better effort than this illiterate botch."[5]

Dr. Thomas Rickard of the British Columbia Historical Association wrote to Bolton with concerns about the plate. He noted that "in 1579 the English word for 'brass' (the alloy of copper and zinc) was 'laton' and that brass or 'brasse' was the word for copper. The composition of the plate should be ascertained."[6] If Rickard was right, then Drake's original plate would have been made of copper and not of the alloy that we now call brass.

Allen Chickering sent some sort of a facsimile of the plate to Dr. Robin Flower of the manuscripts department at the British Museum. Flower responded: "The crude forms of the letters, particularly those of BPRMN, which you indicate, are at once apparent and I cannot parallel them from any Elizabethan writing, inscription or printing known to me…On the other hand it might be argued that such devices might be adopted by anyone anxious to give a quaint and old fashioned appearance to a fabricated inscription."[7] Flower's colleagues in the Department of British and Medieval Antiquities authorized him to add that "the lettering on the plate does not recall any inscriptions on metal of the period known to them, and that the plate is not authentic."[8] Flower copied this letter to Haselden, and added the note, "I cannot myself believe that such forms as these were possible in 1579 in any circumstances. In any case the onus of proof seems to me to be on those who maintain the genuineness of the tablet."[9]

Haselden's correspondence files reveal that he gathered experts' opinions so that he could present sound and reasoned evidence about the plate—and explain the basis of his conclusion of why it was not authentic—in an article planned for the *California Historical Society Quarterly*. Harlow told Haselden that he had "been of the opinion for some time that the alleged plate of Sir Francis Drake, discovered at San Francisco, was probably forgery."[10] Harlow pointed out that the lettering is sharp while the plate itself looks weathered. He also thought that the format of the inscription was odd, and noted that the name of the Queen was not in a prominent position.[11]

In May 1937, Robert Sproul, the president of the University of California, Berkley, wrote Bolton, pressing him to at least have a chemical analysis done on the plate. Sproul also informed Bolton of a forthcoming article where there was going to be a "blistering" attack on the genuineness of the Drake plate.[12]

A critical essay appeared in the *American Historical Review* in July, and was written by Haselden. He pointed out that the plate had not been subject to any analysis, other than the opinion of an unnamed sea captain "who expressed the opinion that it might have been cut out of a brass track of a gun carriage."[13] He listed several problems with the plate, and suggested that the investigation had to include an analysis of the writing, the position on the plate of the date, the orthography, and the extent of erosion in the crevices and on the plate as a whole. He concluded his comments as follows: "The importance of this discovery makes it essential that the utmost care be taken to establish the genuineness or expose the spuriousness of this plate. It is hoped that due consideration of the above questions will not be obscured by uncritical enthusiasm."[14]

In September, the *California Historical Society Quarterly* published a second article by Haselden that had even more pointed criticism of the plate.[15] In the same issue, Chickering rebutted Haselden's criticism of the plate in his own article.[16] After the articles came out, Chickering wrote a note to Bolton disparaging Haselden. This note exhibited Chickering's naïveté about frauds and how they are investigated: "I have read Captain Haselden's article with some care. It seems to me, although it bristles with prejudice, it is quite weak. Further it seems to me Capt. Haselden assumes an entirely undue and uncalled for interest in this matter."[17]

For the next year, Bolton refused to enter into any public debate about the plate, but in his private correspondence he continued to tout the plate as authentic until proved otherwise, and said that he would leave the "task of disproof to others."[18] He referred questions to Chickering, who was not a historian and had no expertise in the matter, but served to insulate Bolton from direct questions. Bolton downplayed any evidence that called the plate's authenticity into question, and fended off criticism as personal opinion, and not evidence. He postponed analysis with statements such as, "We feel reluctant to mutilate the metal of the unusual relic in any way until we are confident that this procedure will be justified."[19]

Bolton did not weigh in on the bay location debate. For example, in a letter from April 1937 he wrote, "You probably noticed that I avoided all question of controversy as to the place where Drake landed, and devoted myself solely to the drama enacted on the California Coast."[20]

Chickering defended Bolton's cautious stance publicly, but after almost a year, in two letters to Bolton he pressed him on the point that it was time to get the plate analyzed.[21] Hurtado later opined that Bolton delayed analysis because he knew the plate was a hoax even before it was analyzed: "Now it was obvious that Bolton did not intend to cooperate in exposing a hoax that made him look foolish."[22] Hurtado explained Bolton's reaction by saying that his promotion of Drake as a California hero clouded his critical judgment, but it enabled him to "strike a blow for his people, his hero, and his religious roots. At last Bolton could extol English heroes whose blood and beliefs he shared and whose exploits he saw reflected in the golden sheen of the plate of brass."[23]

On January 31, 1938, the plate was finally sent out for analysis, just short of one year from the day it was first brought to Bolton by Beryle Shinn. It was sent to Colin Fink, head of the Division of Electrochemistry at Columbia University.

Three months later, Chickering wrote to Bolton and expressed some frustration with Professor Fink, who he thought was treating the plate like a holy relic, and to date had not sampled it to determine the character of the plate:

> Mr. Phelps informs me that Prof. Fink is so impressed with the sanctity of the plate that he did not show it to Mr. Christie, the metallurgist of the Bridgeport Brass Company. Personally after having heard almost hundreds of people talk about how easy it would be to determine the character of the plate by making a small drilling on one side, which would not interfere with its appearance, it is a marvel to me why Prof. Fink had not done something of the character since it got there. He has had it for over six weeks now and, as far as I know, has done nothing whatever.[24]

Professor Fink approached the test with the assumption that he was defending its genuineness rather than determining its authenticity. From the beginning this was not a rigorous scientific examination. He and E. P. Polushkin, who assisted him, found organic and mineral matter in crevices, confirming in their minds that it had been buried "for a long time." Near the grooves made by the letters, they saw parallel lines that were similar to marks made by a pneumatic tool rather than a hand chisel. These marks seemed unusual, but an expert in armor at the Metropolitan Museum of Art told them that these marks sometimes were found on armor.[25]

In due course, Fink and Polushkin concluded that the impurities in the alloy, chemical inhomogeneity, and varied grain sizes indicated that the plate was of old origin. Consequently, one whole special issue of the *California Historical Society Quarterly* was devoted to the report, published September 16, 1938.[26] Bolton was delighted and wrote, "the results of Dr. Fink's investigation speak for themselves."[27] In a letter to Fink, Bolton wrote: "Everybody here to whom we have divulged the nature of your report is very enthusiastic over what you have accomplished...We are trying to keep the news under cover until we can bring it out with a bang, as was done with the announcement of the discovery of the Drake Plate."[28]

It was not the scope of Fink's investigation to address the orthography or language on the plate, but Bolton stressed that if the metal was old, then so was the text.

James Hart wrote about the views of the time decades later after conducting his own investigations on the plate: "A sizable number of skeptics had their say on questionable particulars in opposition to the more general feeling of acceptance expressed by some scholars at the University of California and local historians of the region, fascinated by the subject of the first English visit to California."[29]

One of the skeptics was Earle R. Caley of Princeton's chemical laboratory, who wrote to President Sproul. Caley called much of the evidence worthless. In a detailed three-page report he outlined numerous problems with Fink's analysis and commented: "I do not agree with the authors' broad conclusions given at the end of their report nor do I agree with Professor Hildebrand's comment that the 'evidence has been presented completely and conclusively.' The thing I like least about the report is the ignoring of alternative explanations and contrary evidence... that the plate is of rather old metal I have no doubt, but I do not see that this proves that the plate is not a forgery."[30]

About this time, yet another spurious treasure story arose. In March 1939, Allen Chickering wrote to Bolton to inform him that a man had delivered a document to his office that was purported to be a copy of a letter written by Francis Drake himself in 1579. Drake's purported letter described a treasure of silver he left behind at his landing in Nova Albion. A note with the letter said it was a duplicate and that the original letter was in the archives of one Lord Heathfield, but this was supposed to be a faithful copy of the original, which was on parchment paper and signed "Captain Francis Drake, of the Privateer *Golden Hinde*."[31] It was dated June 25, 1579, and the first paragraph is as follows: "To lighten the burden of my ship I have removed from my own cabin a quantity of silver bars most of which came from the ship 'Grand Captain of the South.' The gold and jewels and the rest I will take with me for her majesty's keeping."[32]

Chickering told Bolton that he thought the letter was entirely a fake and that the man who delivered it seemed at first to want money for it, but then had just given it to him because it might have some historical value. This letter was, of course, a hoax. However, it gained some traction with a group of treasure hunters and became the catalyst for the formation of the Drake Navigators Guild according to one newspaper report.[33] The members believed the letter written by Drake was authentic. According to the newspaper account, they crisscrossed west Marin County in a member's vehicle looking for Drake's long lost silver bars.[34]

Soon after the Plate of Brass was declared authentic, the Episcopal bishop of San Francisco wrote to Bolton requesting a replica of the Plate of Brass. The bishop led annual celebrations for his congregation at the Drake Prayer Book Cross in Golden Gate Park, and felt that it was important for the congregation to have a replica of the plate. Bolton wrote back to the bishop noting that a committee had been appointed to consider the preparation of replicas of the plate but it had not met yet. He added "your request will be one of those most welcome to the committee when it assembles."[35] Bolton defended the Fink report in a later passage in his letter as follows:

> As to Haselden's comment on Fink's report on the authenticity of the Drake Plate, I have only to tell you that he has never taken the trouble to come to see the relic but has merely said to everything, "I don't believe it."...I regard Haselden's statement in the American Historical Review as of no consequence whatsoever, a feeling which I think is shared by nearly everyone who has read Fink's report. The article was just a last squeak.[36]

Bolton continued to deflect arguments, and minimize any criticism of the plate. In 1941 Dr. Joseph Ellison of Oregon State University sent a letter to one of Bolton's colleagues inquiring about the plate for an article he was planning, and asking for information on "the present status of the plate controversy."[37] Bolton was forwarded the letter, and replied as follows:

> To what extent is there a controversy? I have been so busy at other things and away from Berkeley so much that I have paid little attention to discussions which may have appeared in print...The question of the authenticity of so spectacular a relic as Drake's "Plate of Brasse" is bound to be discussed on many intellectual

levels. Most of the prattle...will have no more value than cracker-box politics or campus gossip...Miscellaneous debates by the butcher, the baker, and the candlestick-maker do not justify saying that "authorities differ."[38]

Despite Bolton's dismissive note about the "candlestick-maker," Professor Ellison's piece was published two years later in the *Saturday Evening Post* in an article titled "True or False," which was highly critical of the plate.

Investigative reporter Charles Dunning asked Henry Wagner to lend him money to conduct an investigation into the plate for the article he was proposing.[39] It was well known that Wagner did not believe that the plate was genuine on the grounds that the spelling is not Elizabethan and that the brass is not the kind that was being made in Sir Francis Drake's time.[40] Dunning thought that he could persuade Wagner to follow up on some of the objections scholars had raised—specifically, about the wording on the plate and the metal content of the brass.

Dunning also wanted to do a related story, this one about his search for the hoaxers. Dunning did not suspect Bolton, but noted that Dr. Bolton frustrated him with his biases about the plate: "Dr. Bolton is, regrettably, the one primarily at fault, I believe. Apparently through the years he built up in his own mind, and in the minds of a great many others, the belief that the plate was undoubtedly in existence and that it would be found. A will-to-believe as intensive as that can, and does, produce ghosts, floating tambourines, and apports."[41]

Wagner refused to fund Dunning's investigation and responded that he would lose friendships over it: "The fact is that the people who have sponsored the Drake plaque are all intimate friends of mine and if the plaque was found to be a hoax they would almost lose their faith in God Almighty."[42]

CHAPTER THIRTEEN

Investigations and Resolutions

THE VEXED QUESTION remained unanswered: At which bay on the west coast of America did Francis Drake and his crew land and refit the *Golden Hind*? In the 1970s the tenor of the debate changed. The discussions between the various bay proponents devolved into a competition for public support. The proponents of this or that particular bay put up plaques, nominated—or tried to nominate—their preferred landing site to historic registries, courted the press, and got politicians and historians to sanction their preferred bay.

In an effort to resolve this issue of the landing, the *California Historical Quarterly* invited the three leading bay proponents at that time to present their arguments for their preferred bay (Bolinas Bay, San Francisco Bay, or Drakes Bay).[1] The proponents presented their cases, but in the end there was no resolution of the matter. University of California archaeologist Robert F. Heizer commented that the "quality of the arguments [of where Drake landed] displayed by the several partisans (Aker, Neasham and Power) in the recent *California Historical Quarterly* makes this whole matter one that can only be called ludicrous."[2]

Heizer was, at first, one of the believers in the authenticity of the Plate of Brass, as he commented decades later:

> In 1935 or 1936 I had a course from Dr. Herbert Bolton at Berkeley during which he talked about Drake, pointed out that nobody knew where he had landed, and told us to keep our eyes open for the brass plate which he said he left. Thinking that some Indian

might have picked up this brass plate at Drakes Bay, where most people at the time seemed to think Drake landed, I suggested to Bolton that perhaps I might do some digging in the shellmounds in search for the plate. He was encouraging, and so we did carry out a good deal of digging.[3]

Bolton arranged for Allen Chickering of the California Historical Society to raise funds to support Heizer's archaeological excavations at Drakes Bay in the summers of 1940 and 1941.[4] Heizer and others conducted over thirty excavations between 1937 and 1974 in and around Drakes Bay, San Francisco Bay, Bolinas Bay, the rock outcrop where the plate was found, and other locations, but as he noted, "found nothing that could be associated with Drake the Englishman."[5] By 1974 Heizer had formed serious doubts about the brass plate, and in a letter to James Hart he suggested that the plate be reanalyzed: "Perhaps in order to inject a little objectivity into that part of the problem which involves the brass plate itself, as an object, a new and careful study of the plate by real scholars might turn the question into new avenues—at least this might give us some relief from the stupidities of the Drake Navigators Guild, the Vacaville restaurateur, and the champion of the Bolinas Bay duck pond."[6]

Later in the letter Heizer warned Hart of the many "self-styled experts" on Drake who may want to borrow the plate to conduct their own studies, and advised him to form a committee to determine the best course of action in the event of this type of request.[7]

Heizer was unfriendly to the bay booster groups, particularly the Drake Navigators Guild. When it was announced that Heizer would be included in the International Conference on Drake, Guild member Raymond Aker complained to Norman Thrower, President of the Sir Francis Drake Commission:

> Dr. Heizer has long been a vitriolic critic of the Drake Navigators Guild and its identification of the Drakes Estero site. His attitude is unreasonable and petty, and I suspect that it is merely due to jealousy. Because Dr. Heizer had been involved in the question of the Drake landing place and had favored Drakes Bay as the

location before the Guild had entered the picture, he was one of the first to be notified of the guild's discovery of the site in 1952... the news of the Guild's discovery was met with indifference by Dr. Heizer.[8]

In 1973 California historians and politicians began to plan the celebration of the 400th anniversary of Drake's west coast visit. Drake's famous voyage was being commemorated in England in concert with the California commemoration, which meant that international attention would be focused on the proceedings in California. It was therefore important for the California historians to put on a good show, and that meant that they had to try to clear up the debate on the vexed question: Where was Drake's fair bay?

The debates rose to a fever pitch, and the Plate of Brass figured in the discussion. James Hart was tasked with conducting a new investigation of the plate. Hart's archive about the plate at the Bancroft Library is extensive. Much of the discussion below is based on material contained in Hart's thick file in the Bancroft Library marked "CONFIDENTIAL," that provided a paper trail of his ten-year investigation into the plate hoax.

Hart authorized a new analysis of the plate, and not surprisingly, the result was that the plate was not a piece of sixteenth-century brass, and could not have been fashioned by any member of Sir Francis Drake's expedition. In 1977 the Bancroft Library issued Hart's report titled *The Plate of Brass Reexamined*.[9]

Although the Plate of Brass would continue to have some defenders after the 1977 report, for scholars, it settled the suspicions they held about the plate's authenticity. To finally settle the question for some of the more ardent plate believers, two years later Hart authorized new analyses that were conducted by staff at the Lawrence Berkeley Laboratory. Their scientific investigations included X-ray diffraction and X-ray analysis, and their results left no doubt about it: the Plate of Brass was not associated with Drake.[10]

"Who did it?" and "Why?" were the questions, and everyone wanted to know the answers, though in his report, Hart would not speculate on the identity or motives of the perpetrator except to suggest it was a prank. In an interview Hart posed the question, "If the plate is indeed a modern creation, numerous questions about it remain unanswered, including who created it and why it should be left in an isolated spot where it might never be found."[11] Hart did not have the answer, and continued to add to the confidential file even after his reports were published.

It is evident from the information amassed in Hart's file that his intention all along was to find out who made the plate, and why it was made.

One of the most important pieces of evidence Hart investigated was a letter written in May 1954 by Herbert Hamlin, a Clamper and editor of *The Pony Express Courier*, a Placerville paper that was associated with the Clampers and printed articles on local and California history. The letter was from Hamlin to Henry Wagner and contained a formal statement from another Clamper, art dealer Lorenz Noll, regarding who made the Plate of Brass.[12] Hamlin requested that the information be kept confidential "until such time as we decide to release same."[13] Noll related that in a conversation with sculptor George Clark, Clark admitted he crafted the plate from a piece of old brass provided by George Barron, and that it was a joke on Bolton.[14] For the text and lettering, they had some sort of drawing or a model of what the forger had specified. According to Noll, the plate was taken to a chandler who had tools for punching brass, and after it was done they dipped the plate in acid several times to make it look old.[15]

Noll stated that he admired George Clark and enjoyed the stories he told about the bohemian colony of artists, poets, writers, and sculptors in Oakland who included Joaquin Miller, William Keith, Gertrude Boyle and her husband Takeshi Kanno. Noll related the following: "As they were all artists, painters, and sculptors and had much in common, they fraternized, and gathered at Clark's home for drinks, after an afternoon at Gertrude's studio. George Barron knew most all of them, and being curator of de Young Museum he was well accepted among the superb gathering of Bohemians."[16] The Noll deposition demonstrated that the time frame the plate was created was when Barron, Clark, and the various artists George Clark mentioned to Noll were active in Oakland, which was generally between 1900 and 1922, though Joaquin Miller died in 1913.[17]

Hart received another large part of the puzzle from George Barron's daughter. The newspaper stories about the Plate of Brass hoax prompted Dolores Barron Scoble to telephone Hart with information about the

hoax. Hart immediately arranged to interview Scoble at the Bancroft
Library. In their first interview, Scoble said that the man who was in
charge of the hoax was a historian, and that there was another man at the
meeting who she remembered was a newspaper reporter. She also had a
strong memory of when the plate was made.[18] Hart interviewed Dolores
twice that August. The first interview occurred on August 10, 1977. Here
is a portion of Hart's memorandum from his "CONFIDENTIAL" file:

> Mrs. Barron-Scoble recalls walking in on a conversation her father
> was having with one of his acquaintances who she had seen sev-
> eral times before but whom she does not characterize as a friend
> of Mr. Barron. She is certain that the date was 1919 or 1920 since
> she also insists, despite my repeated questioning, that this conver-
> sation occurred when she and her family were living in the Fruit-
> vale area of Oakland [the records show they lived in Fruitvale in
> 1917–1918]. She insisted that it occurred about a decade before
> she was married (1930). The conversation that she overheard
> concerned the making of a plate of brass to claim the landing of
> Francis Drake in California. She does not believe the plate was
> there and she has the impression that the man was telling her
> father this as a great joke but that her father was not involved. She
> also has the impression that there were other men involved. She
> describes it as a prank. She does not recall how old the man was
> but she says he was younger than her father who was about 45 at
> the time. She says that she believes that he was a teacher in the
> East Bay but not at the university. She does not know why her fa-
> ther was told. She believes that he may have been told because he
> had an interest in California history and his acquaintance wanted
> somebody to know about the hoax that he and his friends were
> perpetrating…She said her father laughed about the joke at the
> time that the plate was found 16 or 17 years later but that he never
> to her knowledge spoke of the person responsible for it.[19]

In Hart's file is a second account of Scoble's recollections of that visit
to the historian's house, with more details on the people who were involved:

On August 24, 1977 I talked with Mrs. Harry Scoble [contact information for Mrs. Scoble redacted] about her recollections of the time when she accompanied her father, Mr. George de Haviland Barron, later the Director of the De Young Museum, to a visit that turned out to involve discussion of a fraudulent Plate of Brass. She was positive that it could have occurred only during the year that her family lived in the Fruitvale section of Oakland, that is in 1918. She thinks that the visit occurred in the summer of that year. She was then 13 years old. She accompanied her mother and her father to a house in Berkeley that she believes may have been in the hills but not necessarily close to the University campus. It was the home of a man, aged perhaps 30, who taught history, but not at U.C. There this gentleman, whose name she cannot recall, took her father and another man, a newspaper reporter, Mrs. Scoble recalls, to have some conversation in a workshop or garage area. As a child Mrs. Scoble was left to entertain herself with the two young children, aged three or four, of the gentleman whose house she was visiting. Naturally she did not find this very appealing so she wandered away from the youngsters and joined her father and the two other men, who perhaps did not even know that she was present. The three men were laughing over a joke which she discovered pertained to a plate, presumably of brass, that the other two men had concocted and that dealt with the landing of Drake in California and his taking of that land for the Queen. She recalls her father reading a text and laughing about it a good deal. She cannot remember whether he was reading from a plate of brass or from a piece of paper. She thinks she may have seen a plate of brass but her recollection of it is that it was smaller than the Plate of Brass in The Bancroft Library and she does not remember the hole for the sixpence. She had occasion later in the day to tell her mother of this. While her father thought this presumable hoax was a great joke, her mother thought that what was being done was wrong or improper. However, she did remember hearing her father say in the company of the two men; This [plate] would never convince anybody and that people would detect that this was not an honest effort. He said something like, "This is ridiculous."

[Hart's note:] As I know from other sources, Mr. Barron had occasion to laugh about the Plate at later dates and to say that he knew it to be a fake. Mrs. Scoble, however, never had occasion to talk to her mother or father about it again and when it was discovered in 1936 she was married and living elsewhere and did not bring up the subject with her father.[20]

In a letter to Dolores a few days later, Hart included a typed copy of the text she dictated. He commented that "As I continue to piece together information about the fabrication of the Plate of Brass, I hope you will give even further thought to this matter and that the present memorandum may jog your recollection sufficiently to allow you to recall the name of the man whose house you visited or that of the newspaper reporter."[21] Hart was very interested in whether she could remember the name of the historian whose house they visited, but his files show he did not search into directories or other records to find this historian's identity (which suggests he knew who it was).

Hart received a call from another key witness. After hearing about Hart's investigation, Mrs. Gordon White decided to come forward with what she knew. Hart recorded the details in the following memorandum to his file: "I received a telephone call from Mrs. Gordon White...occasioned by her reading of newspaper stories on the recent reexamination of the Plate of Brass. Her two uncles Ray Taylor and Will knew who made it...Will Taylor was a neighbor of Clark."[22]

White's information inadvertently provided Hart with the identity of the newspaper reporter who was in the garage that day with Scoble's father; it was White's uncle Ray Taylor. White related to Hart information from conversations she had with her Uncles Ray and Will Taylor who said that their friend and neighbor, sculptor George Clark, crafted the plate.[23] One of her uncles told White that Clark's wife was unhappy with her husband for creating the plate, and Clark responded that it was just a practical joke.[24] White's information confirmed Noll's testimony—though there were inconsistencies between the narratives told by White and Noll—the general facts matched, and the stated motive was as a joke on Herbert Bolton.

Taylor was a reporter for various newspapers in Oakland and San Francisco beginning in 1897.[25] He reported on political news, and reported on the planning and execution of the Panama-Pacific Exposition in 1914–1915. He was no longer a reporter when the plate was found. Taylor's willing involvement in the fraud is unexplained, though he was a close associate of Mayor Rolph who had championed the Panama-Pacific Exposition. Taylor was a friend of Clark and knew Barron. In an article he was described as "the most widely known newspaperman of San Francisco [who] has a wide acquaintance among civic organizations and holds a high position in their councils."[26] Taylor's part in the hoax scheme may have been to control the information received by the public.

Later, Mrs. White added another detail to Hart's investigation: she said that Clark had stamped his intertwined initials "GC" in the plate to the left of "Francis Drake."[27] When the plate was found these initials were interpreted to be an abbreviation of Drake's title "Captain General." Hart looked at the plate and found the initials exactly where White described, which confirmed that Beryle Shinn's find on display at the Bancroft Library was, in fact, the plate made by Clark. There had been several reports of so-called Drake plates over the years (and Heizer looked into most of them), but the initials confirmed for Hart that this was the same plate associated with the historian who lived in the hills above Berkeley.

Hart's intention was to find out who was involved in the plate, and why it was made but he was frustrated because he was unable to reconcile the date the plate was found with the troublesome early dates (ca. 1917–1918) implied by Noll's testimony and Scoble's depositions.

Though Hart did an extensive investigation into the three men known to be associated with the hoax (Clark, Barron, and Taylor), there is no evidence that he ever tried to find the identity of the historian described by Scoble who lived in a house above Berkeley. Hart's silence on the matter and the absence of any investigation into the identity of that historian is telling. In Hart's thick file labeled CONFIDENTIAL, among the many pages of memorandums, newspaper clippings, and notes from city directories, there are over thirty notes or clippings about Barron, half that many for Taylor and Clark, but no compilation of information, lists, or notes on historians who lived in the Berkeley hills and who had young children at home in about 1917. This would have surely made for a short list of suspects.

This omission suggests that Hart may have known or suspected it was Bolton. Hart did write a memo to a staff member with a request, "Do our very old files contain any correspondence from George Haviland Barron? None in Bolton's papers under his name."[28] If Hart suspected or knew the historian was Bolton, and had chosen to publically discuss Bolton as the hoaxer, it would have been sensational. This was the kind of information that would have embarrassed the University of California, the Bancroft Library, and California in front of a worldwide audience.

One note in the file infers that Hart did, in fact, suspect Bolton. In a memo dated February 2, 1980, he related a conversation he had with Leon D. Adams, a feature writer who had written a series of interviews with prominent professors over the years for the *San Francisco News*. Bolton, who died in 1953, had been one of Adams's interview subjects. Aware of Hart's investigations into the brass plate, Adams remembered something odd about Bolton and felt it was important enough to contact Hart with his suspicions. He related a conversation he had with Professor Bolton, "who wanted to take the reporter on a hiking expedition in Marin County, and that it was somehow associated with Drake."[29] This event occurred in the 1920s, and Hart evidently thought it was suspicious enough to make a note of it in a dryly worded memo in his CONFIDENTIAL file. Hart may have suspected that Bolton perhaps intended for the plate to be accidentally found during their hike. It also speaks to Bolton's calls to his students to look for Drake's plate while hiking in Marin County. Evidently Bolton had set up a treasure hunt with hints and encouragements that spanned almost two decades.

Herbert Bolton fits the general profile of the historian described by Scoble, though her memory that he did not teach at U.C. is one of several points of inconsistency. Scoble said that this historian lived in a house that "may have been in the hills but not necessarily close to the University campus."[30] From the nearest trolley stop it would have been an uphill walk into the hills above Berkeley to Bolton's house on Scenic Avenue, north of the campus. Scoble said that there were two young children in the house; Bolton's youngest children were three and seven years old in 1917 (the year the Barron family lived in Fruitvale).[31] Scoble described the man as younger than her father, who was in his early forties. In fact, Bolton was about the same age—an understandable mistake for a young girl to make when her father drank excessively, was overweight, and whose hair had turned completely white.

It seems likely that Bolton's part in the cover-up was to be enthusiastic about the discovery, and quickly authenticate the plate, and if it was immediately debunked and found to be a joke he could be forgiven for losing his professional objectivity and being so enthusiastic—recall the parade of students he led out of his classroom the day after the find was brought to him.

Hart's investigation revealed that Dolores' father, George Barron, had a colorful and tarnished reputation. The newspaper clippings and notes in Hart's file shed light on Barron's character and career. In the 1890s Barron became involved with a married woman who left her husband for him, but later accused him of embezzlement, resulting in his arrest. In a newspaper article she called him a "base deceiver."[32]

In 1910 Barron was appointed curator at the Park Memorial Museum in Golden Gate Park (the museum was later renamed the M. H. de Young Memorial Museum). By that time he was married, and had three children. He was part of the historical establishment and worked as a professor, a writer, and an expert on Spanish Missions in California. He had been appointed the second "Grand historiographer" of the Native Sons of the Golden West and was one of their great orators.

However, there were irregularities with the collections at the museum. Barron was accused of inattention to duties and suspended on April 12, 1917, during a special meeting of the San Francisco Board of Park Commissioners, which oversaw the museum.[33] The minutes of the board meeting on May 3, 1917, indicate that the contents of a large safe were inventoried after he was fired.[34] Barron returned some items to the museum, and a receipt was recorded for "a number of articles, property of the Memorial Museum."[35]

Barron, his wife, and three children—including Dolores—had been living in a cottage on the museum grounds, rent-free.[36] When Barron was sacked, they were forced to move away from their home in Golden

Gate Park to the Fruitvale section of Oakland across the Bay. This was quite a step down from their former abode. The 1918 City Directory for Oakland shows that the Barron family lived in Fruitvale at the time.[37] A newspaper article on November 20, 1920, had the headline "Former Curator Sued for Divorce." In the complaint, his wife said that Barron was blatant about his womanizing and even called women for dates on their phone in front of their three children.[38] By 1921 the directory lists Barron as living in San Francisco.[39]

In her two depositions, Scoble asserted that a historian who lived in the hills near the Berkeley campus was the perpetrator of the plate, and that the plate was made during the year they lived in Fruitvale, which could only have been between 1917 and 1918.[40] Hart referred to the dates stubbornly asserted by Scoble as "troublesome" because the plate was not found for many years after it was made.[41] He interviewed her twice to clarify this point.

A twelve-year-old girl would have remembered details about when and why her father was fired from his job. The firing would have created an indelible memory because it resulted in a forced move from a cottage in Golden Gate Park to a lesser abode in Fruitvale. Though her perception was imperfect, she would have remembered the event in the garage, especially since she had discussed the matter with her mother who had voiced strong disapproval of the scheme. Hart noted that Dolores knew that the plate was to be a hoax, and that her mother had explained to her the substance of the plate hoax. Dolores Scoble would have certainly remembered whether the event in the garage happened before or after her father left her mother, which was in 1920. Scoble's own daughter, Vicky, also reiterated to Hart that her mother had always maintained that the plate was made during the year they lived in Fruitvale.[42]

Among the people Hart interviewed about Barron was Thomas Howe, an acquaintance of Barron's. When asked if he thought Barron himself might have been involved in such an affair as the plate, Howe said that he thought it was extremely unlikely because, as Hart summarized: "[Barron] wasn't inventive enough. He didn't create things. He called him a jolly old fraud, very affable who drank a great deal."[43]

Hart also interviewed a woman who worked with Barron at the museum. She said that at one time she mentioned that the museum had been approached to display the plate but that Barron "very definitely rejected it."[44]

In fact, Barron's participation appears to have been to act as a straw man to cover for the real perpetrator. If the plate was exposed as a fraud they had a ready motive and believable fall guy, whose explanation was that it was a "joke that got out of hand." People would believe Barron capable of such a thing because of his character and past foibles. It is possible that George Barron's involvement was in exchange for getting his curatorial job back—which he did in 1922.

Hart found that the records in the city directories and newspaper accounts of George Barron's behavior substantiated Scoble's testimony regarding the troublesome dates, but he had difficulty understanding the motive for the hoax. If Barron had created the hoax to make a fool out of Bolton, it would be illogical to wait almost twenty years between the creation of the plate and the launch of the hoax. Once Hart began to suspect Bolton, he must have wondered what Bolton's motive had been, and it may have been difficult to ascertain without an understanding of Zelia Nuttall's unpublished theory.

In 1979 Hart hoped that a private investigator would be able to finally solve the riddle. With the financial assistance of Warren Hanna, a historian and authority on Drake and the circumnavigation, he hired a private investigator. Hart made a note about this in his file: "Warren Hanna introduced me to Mr. Schneider to whom (in the company of Peter Hanff) I told the whole story about Clarke, Barron, the Taylors, etc. and all information concerning possible forgery of the Plate of Brass. Thanks to the aid of Warren Hanna, Mr. Schneider will undertake a confidential investigation for Bancroft: Chalmers & Schneider Inc."[45]

If Mr. Schneider ever submitted a report about his own investigation, it is not in the open files or in Hanna's papers at the Bancroft Library. It is unlikely that Hart understood the possible Nuttall connection to the plate hoax, so it also seems unlikely that Schneider's investigation ever revealed the motive behind it.

Nuttall's findings jeopardized the gilded legend of "Drake the freebooter and Captain general of pirates" that California historians and leaders had crafted. If Nuttall had been able to publish her monograph in 1917–1920, the hoax may have been triggered at that time. The plate either would have had the effect of eclipsing any further discussion of a Northwest coast landing (as it effectively did in 1937), or at least it would have confused the issue. If the plate was found to be a hoax, then the "just a joke that got out of hand" cover story could then be implemented— Barron would confess, and Bolton would be in the clear and everyone would have a laugh.

If the plate was made in the spring of 1917—just after Barron lost his job—there was almost a nineteen-year gap between when the plate was made and when it was found. In spring 1932, a streetcar struck Barron and he suffered a broken pelvis and fractured ribs; he retired the next June. Bolton's problem was that by then, no one would believe that Barron would pull a prank such as this. When the plate was found, Barron, Clark, and Taylor were still living in the Bay area, but they were not part of the final implementation of the hoax; though Dolores Barron Scoble said that her father laughed about it when the plate was found.[46]

With Barron out of the picture, Bolton needed a new straw man to take the blame if the plate were revealed to be a hoax, and thus shield him with the "joke that got out of hand" smokescreen. The solution was the Clampers. Bolton was the Grand Historian of the Clampers, and letting his fraternal brothers cover for him may have suited the situation. Shinn's discovery in 1936 was probably accidental, and it may have disrupted the planned schedule for the launch of the hoax.

Seven weeks after Bolton made the formal announcement of the find, the Yerba Buena Clampers chapter nailed a look-alike plate (called the Tuolumne Plate) to a post at a Clampers gathering and dinner. The summer before they had published a booklet *Ye Preposterous Booke of Brasse*. The booklet and the look-alike plate may have been intended as evidence of a practical joke that the Clampers could point to if the analysis of the plate showed it to be a fraud.[47]

In 2002, an article written by several history enthusiasts was published by the journal *California History*.[48] The authors asserted that *Ye Preposterous Booke of Brasse* was written as a warning with hints to Bolton that the plate was not authentic because—as the argument goes— the Clampers were too embarrassed to tell him that it was just a joke. They further speculated that the Clampers thought that the *Preposterous* booklet was packed with more than enough clues to lead the scientific team to conclude the plate was a hoax. Bolton would have to admit that his identification had been wrong, but no individual hoaxers would have to be identified.[49] A recent book titled *An E Clampus Vitus Hoax Goes Awry: Sir Francis Drake's 1579 Plate of Brasse* revisited the hoax, and made some of the same assertions except that the authors speculated that Barron and Clark made the plate at the behest of a mystery man who gave them instructions through an intermediary.[50] The mystery man these authors identified as the man behind the hoax was a George Ezra Dane.

This speculation seems contrived. This was a lot of plotting for just a joke. Bolton was the Grand Royal Historian of the Clampers, he had a phone, and one of his fellow Clampers could have just called and told him that the plate was a joke before Bolton made the big announcement in front of the California Historical Society at the Sir Francis Drake Hotel. In fact, just before the *Preposterous* booklet was printed, fellow Clamper (and the person accused of the hoax) George Ezra Dane, sent Bolton a promotional flyer soliciting preorders. Printed in the flyer was an interesting comment that may have alluded to the truth of the scheme: "As history thunders down the corridors of time, the name of E Clampus Vitus and the Francis Drake Plate will be forever joined."[51]

Another piece of evidence that the plate was intended as a hoax and that Bolton was behind it, is found in a letter written by Clamper brother Eric Falconer in 1949—over a decade after the brass plate was found. In Falconer's letter addressed to "Dear Brother Bolton," he related how he and "a certain Banker, Paper Merchant, Historian and Ex-Regent"[52] had recently reminisced about how Bolton "dearly loves a joke."[53] In the letter this statement is immediately followed by the Latin abbreviation "Verb. Sap,"[54] for *verbum sapienti sat est* for "a word is enough to the wise"—this was, in effect, a wink between conspirators, including the paper merchant, banker, and ex-regent.

In 1939 the plate went on display before an international crowd of several million people at that year's Golden Gate International Exposition in San Francisco.[55] Bolton gave a presentation at the Exposition that was ironically titled "The Stuff History is Made Of."[56]

George Ezra Dane knew the Plate of Brass was a hoax, and as president of the Yerba Buena Clampers chapter he may have been the one assigned to step forward and announce it as a Clampers joke. What he did not know is that he may have been set up by his fellow Clampers. There would be no big reveal unless the plate was analyzed and found to be a fraud.

Dane was a young admiralty lawyer at an important law firm in San Francisco. He was from a prominent Pasadena family, and according to his family he had a brilliant intellect. He had graduated from high school at the age of fifteen, studied law in The Hague in the Netherlands, and then attended Harvard Law School where he served as associate editor of the *Harvard Law Review*, a high honor.[57]

However, Dane's true calling was as a writer and editor of folk tales and tall tales of the frontier and mining camps. In partnership with his mother, who was also a writer of merit, he wrote stories and edited story collections, including a compendium of tall tales written for the Clampers in 1935 called *The Curious Book of Clampus*. Bolton contributed a particular bawdy article to that edition.[58]

Above all else, Dane was an expert on Mark Twain. His stories were often told in the spirit of Twain, and he coedited a book about Twain's letters titled *Mark Twain's Travels with Mr. Brown*, published in 1940.[59] Dane was steeped in Twain's writings, and there is no doubt that he was aware of a particular satirical hoax that Twain played on the public.[60] Twain was amused by a flurry of hoaxes regarding petrified mummies and bemused by the public's mania for such stories, and surprised at how easily they were taken in. While he was working for a newspaper in Nevada in 1862, he made up a story about a petrified stone mummy found in the mountains. He described the mummy as "perfectly preserved," and caught in the position of his thumb to his nose. Despite the absurdity of a mummy thumbing its nose, the public thought it was a real story, and newspapers reprinted it all over the United States. Twain was dismayed that his story was believed and had spread so far. After several months he revealed that he created the hoax. Twain later wrote, "I chose to kill the petrifaction mania with a delicate, a very delicate satire. But maybe it was altogether too delicate, for nobody ever perceived the satire part of it at all."[61]

James Hart investigated Dane and his possible nexus with the plate hoax but later discounted the idea that Dane was responsible. In a confidential memo Hart described conversations he had with Berkeley

English professor and author George Stewart. His reasoning is that Dane had a great interest in the plate and was amused by the claim for its authenticity.[62] Stewart knew about the Clampers' part in the hoax: in an interview conducted many years later with Charles Camp in 1972, Stewart said "let's come clean," and prodded Camp to talk about the plate hoax. At first Camp was reluctant to talk about it:

> **Camp:** It seems to me as though it was settled—
> **Stewart:** Well, let's come clean here, now. We've got a real opportunity here to say your say about the Drake plate.
> **Camp:** [laughter] Yes. Well, of course, there are so many things about the Drake plaque that are peculiar. The whole discovery was mixed up because it was picked up by somebody and thrown in a car, and was all covered with grease when I first saw it. It looked as though it had been hammered by somebody recently. Maybe not recently but anyway it looked as though it had been. Oh, it was the most peculiar situation.
>   And then the story came out that it was picked up over here on San Quentin—near San Quentin Point instead of over at Drakes Bay. Oh, I don't know, I suppose we have to say that it was genuine. That's what we have to say now. It's like a sort of a canon [law]. It's like some—
> **Stewart:** We don't <u>have</u> to say that here. She [fellow interviewer Reiss] won't tell what we say about it.
> **Camp:** Like the Ten Commandments or something, that [it] was dug up, that its got to be genuine?[63]

Camp revealed that they were sworn to secrecy about the plate. One or two of the Clampers may have understood the real objective, but the rest evidently thought it was done as a joke on Bolton. Later in the interview Stewart and Camp commented on Bolton and the authenticity of the plate:

> **Stewart:** Bolton said it was [genuine] and he really put it across.
> **Camp:** Well, Bolton danced around and didn't make any real scientific investigation of it. Then Wagner got busy and advised him to get it analyzed or something…[64]

Stewart asked Camp about Dane in the last passage of the interview. Camp said he knew Dane very well, but he didn't think George had anything to do with "this plaque business."[65]

Much of the blame for the Plate of Brass hoax has been placed on Dane's shoulders.[66] If Dane did not mind having his name associated with it, was he to be the main fall guy or main jokester amongst the Clampers? Did Dane expect the plate to be revealed as a satirical joke in the same manner that Mark Twain had revealed his hoax?

In April 1937 George Dane inadvertently revealed in a quickly scribbled note that another Clamper, Harry Peterson, had a hand in the Plate of Brass hoax, and this note provides the proof that Dane did not initiate the hoax or even was the chief Clamper coconspirator. Dane's note to Peterson had the following congratulatory comment: "We thought you had reached the climax of your career of humbuggery with the Bear Flag, but this Drake Plate hoax of yours tops all. Congratulations!"[67]

Dane wrote the note to Peterson on April 11, just three months after the plate was brought to Bolton. This was early in the hoax timeline, and Dane may have expected that it would be revealed as a spoof and everyone would have a laugh. What Peterson did to contribute to the hoax and prompt Dane's congratulations is not clear. At this point in time there was a lighthearted fraternal camaraderie about the plate expressed by Dane. Did the rank and file believe that it was just a folly—nothing too serious—as opposed to the forgery that it actually was?

Dane was an artist, writer, and a lighthearted spirit like Twain. Taking part in a forgery may not have squared with his conscience. Once Dane began to realize that there was to be no big reveal of the plate's true nature in contrast to the reveal of the Bear Flag, or the climax of silliness that gave away Twain's petrified mummy, he may have come to the understanding that the plate was designed to fool the public and distract scholars from an important historical question. It does not fit Dane's profile to be part of a hoax—a fun joke, yes, but not a hoax that grew into a fraud of the magnitude that the plate did.

As a lawyer, Dane may have observed that this so-called joke had crossed the line into fraud, perhaps even a crime—an actionable tort of deceit that exposed Bolton to legal prosecution and put Dane himself in jeopardy as an accessory. Bolton and Chickering had collected $3,500 from wealthy donors in order to obtain the plate from Shinn. Dane's choices at that juncture would have been to expose Bolton, or not. It would have reflected badly on Dane himself if he blew the whistle: he would be seen as a coconspirator who ratted out his fraternity brother— the most famous historian in California. Betrayal of a brother meant social ostracization from the San Francisco society that Dane and his wife engaged in.

In fall 1941, Dane was clinically depressed and sought help for his condition from his physician.[68] Dane was thirty-seven years old, and had a wife whom by all accounts he loved very much along with two young daughters, ages four and six. Dane's book on Twain's letters had been published the year before, and he had just finished collaborating with his mother—author Beatrice J. Dane—on a collection of short stories set in Gold Rush days and told in the vernacular of Mark Twain, titled *Ghost Town*.[69]

The story Dane wrote in Chapter 17 of *Ghost Town* was about the theory and practice of practical joking and how a rogue chapter of the Clampers "took charge of the Community's Morals and what it did to a Sucker."[70] The story opens with a gravestone inscription: "When I am dead and in my grave, No more whisky will I crave." The story is about a group of Clampers in a hard drinking town who thought that their local chapter had gotten on the wrong track and forgotten the true principles of Clamperdom. They seceded and formed their own renegade chapter. The "morals committee" of this chapter was led by a man named Doc, and they proceeded to pull a hoax on the "too moral for comfort towns-people" to make them look foolish. They turned their sights on a guileless man, and made a "sucker" out of him. This story could have been Dane's way of criticizing his fraternal brothers. Could this story have been meant as a veiled indictment of the men involved in the plate scheme, including a man called Doc? Was Dane himself the poor "sucker"?

On October 19, 1941, a newspaper article announced the formation of the California Folklore Society, and Dane was to be one of the organization's vice presidents. This was a plum position for Dane—the type of position he must have considered the pinnacle of his folklore-writing career (and the type of reward Bolton may have proffered for Dane's co-operation in the scheme). The officers of the new organization included several Clampers.[71] The society's quarterly journal was to be published by the University of California Press where Bolton had editorial authority. The first issue was due to be released in December.

On Sunday, October 26, Dane, his wife, and their little girls returned to San Francisco after having spent three weeks at their vacation cottage at Pedro Point, on a cliff overlooking the Pacific Ocean. Dane's book *Ghost Town* was to come out the day after they returned to their little Victorian house on Union Street, five blocks from the Presidio. Dane's wife said later that her husband had shown signs of a breakdown, and on that day, Dane dropped from sight.[72]

The next night was mild, partly cloudy, with a waxing moon that must have reflected on the still waters of Stow Lake in Golden Gate Park where Dane planned his last act. In the moonlight stood the fifty-seven-foot tall stone cross—Drake's Prayer Book Cross—perched on a rocky outcrop overlooking the lake where he sat. Sometime that night, in the shadow of the Drake's cross, a gunshot blast shattered the peace as Dane ended his life.

In his pockets were sealed letters to his mother, his boss at the law firm, and his wife Yvonne. A note on his body said that this was "from my own hand," and gave instructions on how to contact his wife. The note to his boss asked him to help his wife and girls.

To his mother, he wrote "to go on would be much worse for all concerned."[73] The note to Yvonne addressed her as "Sweetheart" and asked for forgiveness, expressed his deep and abiding love for her and their daughters, and advised her to be careful and "don't get involved in anything that you can't see the end of."[74]

Questions still remain about Dane's suicide, and nothing further can be safely inferred from the existing evidence. Did Bolton and his brethren betray him? Was the *Folklore* position a *quid pro quo* for his involvement in the Clamper scheme? Why did Dane choose to end his life on the very day that his book came out? Was his story in *Ghost Town* a parable and an indictment of Doctor Bolton and his Clamper associates? Why did he choose that particular location—by Drake's Prayer Book Cross? In his note to his wife he warned her not to "get involved in anything that you can't see the end of." Was this an allusion to a scheme of which he himself could not see the end?

DRAKE'S PRAYER BOOK CROSS AND FALLS, GOLDEN GATE PARK, SAN FRANCISCO, CALIF.   58

CALIFORNIANS, INC. PHOTO   4A-H846

FIGURE 13.1. Postcard from ca. 1930 showing Drake's Prayer Book Cross, in Golden Gate Park, San Francisco.

In 1949, when Bolton was seventy-nine years old, Pope Pius XII knighted him with the Equestrian Order of Saint Sylvester. The Franciscan brothers invited him to Washington, D.C., to address the Academy of American Franciscan History. Many in the audience that day were priests. Bolton's presentation was titled *Confessions of a Wayward Professor*.[75] In his address he noted that the confessional occupies a prominent place in Catholic practice, and it seemed to him to offer a fitting approach for his remarks. Despite the title of his talk, there was no confession, and he expressed no regrets or remorse for anything he had done in his life. In one part of his speech, he described his family's genealogy that he said had recently been published in Boston. He then made a flippant joke that his colleagues found humor in the fact that he was a blood relation to Black Bart, the most notorious highwayman of the Gold Rush days in California.

This was another untruth. Though it is true that one of Black Bart's aliases was Charles Bolton, it was just an alias: Black Bart was no relation to Bolton and there was no Boston genealogy published about Bolton's family.[76] Lying about facts to embroider his reputation, and being self-deprecating at the same time was typical of Bolton's style. If he had been called out on the lie, he probably would have said it was "just a joke."

History, of course, will now be the judge of whether Bolton was worthy of his accolades, medals, titles, honorary degrees, and knighthood. His legacy endures because he was an influential presence in the profession of history. Hurtado notes that Bolton's students taught in twenty-three states, and "During the course of his career Bolton's students held at least ninety-eight jobs in sixty-five colleges and universities."[77]

However, the record now shows that Bolton had a pattern of perpetrating historic deceits and hoaxes, and further, that he disguised his behavior with false statements. In hindsight it seems likely that an academic would not have put off analysis of the Plate of Brass with such weak excuses, or fail to provide a good photograph of the artifact so that archaeologists could study it. He was unprofessional in the way he played the plate up in an over-enthusiastic way, and was, at the same time, dismissive and belittling of the experts who questioned its authenticity.

It seems likely that James Hart also suspected the perpetrator of the hoax was Bolton, but chose not to reveal it because it would have embarrassed California at an especially sensitive time: just before the impending 400th anniversary of Drake's landing. As Hart may have realized, Bolton was most likely the mystery historian who lived in the hills above Berkeley as Dolores Scoble recalled. The details she remembered about the man and his family closely match the details of Bolton and his family, which seems too remarkable to be just a coincidence.

CHAPTER FOURTEEN

The Commission and
the Commemoration of Drake's Voyage

IN 1973, the California legislature established the Sir Francis Drake Commission and charged it with planning the celebrations to commemorate the 400th anniversary of Drake's landing. Events planned for the commemoration included student essay contests, visits to elementary schools by a living history group in Elizabethan costumes, and the creation of a postage stamp. The year 1979 was declared "Drake year" in California. Commemorations that year included speeches at the Berkeley campus by the British Ambassador to the United States and the American Ambassador to the United Kingdom. At UCLA there were seminars and a six-week program in which six postdoctoral fellows studied the influence of Drake's circumnavigation. An international history conference on Drake took place over seven days in June that ended with a Drake Landing Day parade and a sermon at Grace Cathedral by the Lord Bishop of London.[1]

One of the most spectacular events of the commemoration was the dramatic arrival of the *Golden Hinde II* into San Francisco Bay in 1975. Two American businessmen commissioned the full-size replica of Drake's ship that was built in Devon, England, by shipwrights using traditional methods. The ship left the West Coast and continued on its own journey around the world, traveling to Japan, Hong Kong, Singapore, across the Indian Ocean, through the Suez Canal and the Mediterranean, then back to England in time to commemorate the 400th anniversary of Drake's return from the Famous Voyage.

The problem of the vexed question needed to be addressed before the main events of the commemoration. During the run-up to the

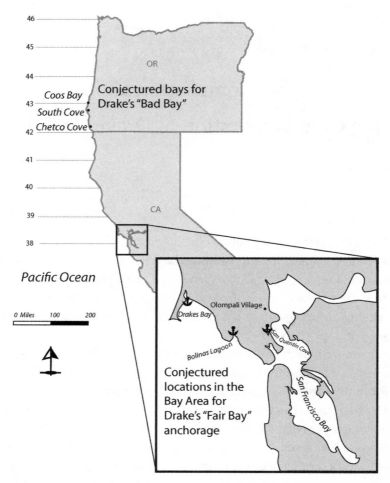

FIGURE 14.1. Map showing the contenders in the 1970s for Drake's "Bad Bay" on the Oregon coast, and the "Fair Bay" contenders in the San Francisco Bay area.

commemoration there was an effort to solve the riddle. In fall 1974, a group of more than 150 people boarded buses and set out on a tour of the main bays in contention for Drake's famous landing. These included Bolinas Lagoon off of Bolinas Bay, Drake's Estero that drains into Drakes Bay, and San Quentin Cove within San Francisco Bay. The group included interested historians and various advocates of one bay or another and their supporters. The *Los Angeles Times* reported that "the group endured heavy thundershowers and hours of bus riding over the hills of

Marin County, listening to the presentations and arguments of assorted advocates. A participant reported 'raised voices' but no fisticuffs."[2]

For a while, San Francisco Bay seemed to be the answer to the vexed question. The bay proponents supporting the idea that Drake landed in San Francisco Bay were elated by one particular discovery that occurred in 1974. Archaeologists from Dominican College in San Rafael found an English sixpence coin during excavations at a Miwok village site known as Olompali, located north of San Quentin Cove in Marin County.[3] Native American house pits and other features were uncovered and over fifty thousand artifacts recovered. The coin, two glass trade beads, and several fragments of Chinese ceramics were thought to be artifacts from Drake's visit.

Charles Slaymaker was the archaeologist in charge of the excavations. He had been living at the site during the excavations. The owner of the property was planning to build a twelve-hundred-unit mobile home and condominium development. Just as the construction was to begin, Slaymaker found the coin and the beads. The timing of the find seemed suspicious, but soon the coin was hailed as evidence of Drake's visit.[4]

When he found the coin, Slaymaker said that he undertook an investigation to make sure it had not been fraudulently planted. As he told *The Los Angeles Times*, "I had to check out my people [student volunteers who assisted him at the site] and try to make sure no Drake person had salted it."[5] Slaymaker's anthropology department supervisor, Mike Moratto, wrote that he had reason to suspect that the coin was not found *in situ*.[6] Historian Warren Hanna discredited the coin with a terse statement that the coin could not be archaeologically authenticated.[7] Nevertheless, these finds effectively stopped the planned development and eventually the California State Parks obtained the property. In an interpretive video, Park Ranger Fred Lew admitted that the provenience of the English sixpence was suspect; he was convinced that the archaeologists planted it to stop the condominium project.[8]

The vexed question eventually spilled over into Oregon in a series of unfortunate events. It began in 1975 when a member of the Drake Navigators Guild met with Thomas Vaughan, who was executive director of the Oregon Historical Society. Vaughan was given the impression that there was some evidence that Drake anchored the *Golden Hind* in

South Cove under Cape Arago to take shelter from a storm.[9] This was conjectured by the Guild to be Drake's "bad bay."

With the assistance of members of the Drake Navigators Guild, Vaughan began to plan an Oregon event to commemorate Drake's arrival in the "bad bay." The major event would have been the placement of a plaque at South Cove. Accordingly, Vaughan invited the Sir Francis Drake Commission to send a representative to the Oregon commemoration.

Vaughan received a terse reply to this invitation from Norman Thrower, the president of the commission, who informed Vaughan that the Sir Francis Drake Commission was not empowered to designate a possible Drake landing site; not Cape Arago nor any potential landing site.[10] Thrower did not want Vaughan to get the impression that the presence of a member of the Sir Francis Drake Commission meant that the commission was sanctioning an anchorage promoted by the Drake Navigators Guild.

Thrower considered the members of the Guild to be rogue when it came to discussions of possible landing sites of Drake: "Whenever these rogue members tried to talk about a Drake site in California, Alfred Newman, lawyer and SFD [Sir Francis Drake Commission] secretary would strike it from the record. They were not to discuss or determine Drake landing sites."[11]

Vaughan at the time did not understand that Thrower considered the Guild's research to be unreliable, so Vaughan continued with his plans for the plaque at Cape Arago. He wanted the unveiling of the plaque to take place at the same moment that Queen Elizabeth II unveiled a plaque in Plymouth during her official visit to commemorate Drake's Famous Voyage. Scheduled for August 5, 1977, this was one of the events in recognition of her Jubilee year.[12] Vaughan tried to get radio and television coverage through the BBC for the event: "We would be especially pleased if some reference might be made to our Pacific Ocean event by the commentator in Plymouth or by some distinguished personage in the Royal party, and that some exchange of messages might be arranged with our rock promontory."[13]

A few weeks before the dedication, a reporter for the *Oregonian* newspaper interviewed Vaughan for a story. Vaughan is quoted as follows: "The society has records that prove beyond a doubt that the South

Cove of Cape Arago is the anchorage Drake used between June 5, and June 10, 1579. We know that he did not sail north of this site and that harsh weather caused him to move south toward his eventual careening camp on the California coast (Nova Albion). California historians agree."[14]

Vaughan was referencing the Guild's *Report of Findings Relating to Identification of Sir Francis Drake's Encampment at Point Reyes National Sea Shore.*[15] Vaughan's confident assertions of Drake's movements in the Pacific came as a surprise to Kenneth Holmes, chair of the history department at Western Oregon University. He responded in a letter to the editor:

> I am surprised that Oregonians of some prestige are falling for the California Drake Navigators Guild claim that Francis Drake sailed into Coos Bay [*sic*] in June of 1579. In studying Drake's voyage here and in London over some 17 years, I have looked at all the known documentation from the period and find that all but one of them tell of the *Golden Hind* reaching 48 degrees of north latitude. The one authority who has Drake sailing up to our Pacific coast at any other latitude was Richard Hakluyt who on one occasion in a work called the *Famous Voyage* gave the latitude as 42 degrees and in a later edition changed it to 43 degrees.[16]

The die was cast, both literally and figuratively. The commission appointed historian Aubrey Neasham to be their representative at the Cape Arago plaque unveiling. Neasham was a good choice to bring some common sense to the proceedings and to keep the Guild in check. He was a professor and the regional historian for the National Park Service. Neasham and Vaughn were acquainted, and soon enough, Vaughan learned that Neasham, like Holmes and Thrower, was also skeptical about the Guild's bay assertions. In fact, in 1974 Neasham had coauthored with archaeologist William E. Pritchard an article titled *Drake's Landing in California: The Evidence for Bolinas Lagoon.*[17]

The official program announced that it was "a concurrent program with Plymouth, England and the Royal visit to Drake's departure site."[18] In the end there was no concurrent program or BBC coverage with Plymouth as Vaughan had hoped. The Queen and Prince Philip visited Buckland Abbey, Drake's home outside Plymouth, where they met with the visiting commissioners of the California Sir Francis Drake Commission. Instead of a concurrent unveiling, the people gathered at Cape Arago were read a telegram from the Queen's private secretary, conveying Her Majesty's warm wishes to those attending the commemoration. The Queen quite properly stopped short of naming the location of Drake's "bad bay" with the remark that the commemoration honors "the first landfall of the North Pacific coast by the *Golden Hinde* and her gallant crew."[19]

When the bronze plaque was unveiled, it was immediately obvious there were several errors in the text. Among them the date Drake embarked from Plymouth was wrong by several months. Mistakenly it was dated August 5, 1577, which was the date of the commemoration, minus four hundred years. The most unfortunate error was that it stated Drake went home around Cape Horn—he actually shaped his course west around Africa's Cape of Good Hope and circumnavigated the globe. The next day the *Oregon Journal* reported the reaction when the bronze marker was unveiled: "But no sooner was it put on view than the horrified eyes of Thomas Vaughan, the society's executive director, noticed that it credited Drake with sailing the wrong way home to England."[20]

That night at the banquet in Coos Bay, Vaughan assured the audience that the plaque would be corrected as soon as time and metalworking permitted. Vaughan took responsibility for the mistakes, though it is unclear who wrote the text.

Neasham gave the keynote address at the banquet, and took the opportunity to set the record straight about the bay debates. He opened his remarks by saying he was not speaking for the Sir Francis Drake Commission, and though he believed Drake may or may not have been near Coos Bay, it was also possible he landed in Chetco Cove or as far north on the coast as 48° north, near Cape Flattery. He made it clear that the various anchorages of Drake on the west coast were unknown, and that there was no consensus among historians. He also suggested that wherever the "bad bay" was, it was likely a landing party came ashore to reconnoiter for water and wood (something the Guild disagreed with as they believed that Drake only anchored and did not go ashore). Neasham suggested that Oregon form a state commission to research the question, and possibly even a national Drake commission of some sort should be created.

These comments rankled the members of the Guild who were in attendance at the dinner. On October 12, Guild president Raymond Aker sent a stern letter to Vaughan criticizing him for not allowing equal time for Guild members to rebut Dr. Neasham's remarks pertaining to Drake's landing sites, for not answering his previous letters, and for his "devil-may-care" attitude in replacing the incorrect plaque.[21]

Ever eloquent, Vaughan's measured response to Aker was searing:

I have read your letter over several times. At first I thought of telephoning you, but perhaps it is best to send you a letter. Several misunderstandings seem to have developed. I think principally this is from lack of better communication, or any other kind, which then gave rise to suppositions which have ended finally in your letter, the tone of which I much regret, by the way. Let me say at the outset that I travel a great deal in the Society's behalf, and it is possible your letters may have not been answered as rapidly as you wish. Please accept my apologies.

With reference to Francis Drake, whom all of us here much admire, I should tell you that the formal recognition of his voyages is one of many, many projects in which the Society is involved. I am sorry not to seem to give it the top and immediate priority that your Guild gives the event, but we cannot operate in this single-purpose way....

I am sorry to appear so dense but it simply wasn't in our thinking that rival representatives would appear.... Now of course we are in a quandary because of the serious criticisms you level against our society. Because of the nature of your disagreements in California, we are withdrawing from the discussions and plans for future programming.... We are taking no position presently concerning Drake's activities after he left Cape Arago. We have no other choice in the matter at the present time, and it seems here most improper for me to offer any comment on what is obviously a thorny problem which I am certain you must all find vexatious in the extreme.[22]

Neasham, the historian, was right to comment. The Plate of Brass had only just been declared a forgery. The Guild had argued for many years that the Plate of Brass supported their theory that Drake landed in Drakes Bay because the plate was made of brass as described in *The World Encompassed* rather than "a plate of lead" as described in the Harley 280 manuscript.[23] The loss of the plate as evidence meant *The World Encompassed* was no longer considered the authority or the last word on the subject of the latitudes. The other contemporary accounts became, once again, just as important. Neasham knew these accounts had details that conflicted with *The World Encompassed*, including the latitudes Drake attained in the Pacific, and where the "bad bay" stood.

After he received Aker's letter, Vaughan wrote to a maritime historian who had been at the Coos Bay event expressing his dismay about the bay controversies, "I had no idea that there are not only two very oppositely inclined groups but several. We have far too much to do to allow ourselves to be diverted by such unproductive arguments."[24]

The Guild members could not let the matter drop. They sent another stern letter, this time to Norman Thrower complaining about commissioner Neasham's comments to the gathering in Coos Bay. The author of the letter was Robert W. Parkinson, secretary of the Guild. He related that Dr. Neasham spoke about how "he was not convinced that the Cape Arago site was the proper one," which they objected to: "The California Drake Navigators Guild strongly objects to the conduct of Dr. Neasham as the representative of the Sir Francis Drake Commission to this Oregon function...[He] attempted to undermine and confuse the positive and officially accepted research by the State of Oregon, the Oregon Historical Society, and the Drake Navigators Guild—the very research Dr. Neasham was sent to Oregon to honor at the unveiling."[25]

Parkinson and Aker were not trained historians, and they did not understand the concept that there was no "officially accepted" research to be "honored."

Aker wrote another letter to Thrower a few months later. He was still angry about Neasham's comments to the assembled group at the banquet, and wrote, "Tom Vaughan claimed to be a friend of Aubrey's, and I do not doubt that he has been for some time back. Perhaps it is no coincidence then that Tom now takes a cavalier attitude about replacing the plaque with a properly worded one."[26]

The ongoing bay controversy is largely unknown outside of California, and unique in that it is a tussle among mostly nonprofessional boosters like the Guild. That Vaughan got caught up in these machinations is understandable—who would suspect anyone of this type of behavior? In subsequent years the advocates of the various bays continued to compete with each other. It became a contest to see how many historians they listed that supported their favored bay, or how many plaques they placed here and there on the California shoreline.

In October 1978, the California State Historical Resources Commission called a meeting to hear testimony regarding a National Register Nomination to give Drakes Bay National Landmark status. Members of the Drake Navigators Guild were the proponents, and the nomination was to recognize the significant association with Francis Drake and the voyage of circumnavigation. The agenda included presentations by members of the Guild as well as Robert Power, who advocated for a San Quentin Cove landing. In addition, the commission listened to testimony from several historians, including Aubrey Neasham, who advocated for a Bolinas Bay landing but excused himself from a formal presentation by saying his work was ongoing. He requested that the commission wait for more definitive facts before they decided the matter.

In the end, the commission was not persuaded by the advocates, and concluded there was not enough evidence to register Drakes Bay or any other California bay as a historic landmark. Though the commission did not endorse any particular bay, they issued commemorative medallions and placed two bronze plaques in Marin County, including at Drakes Bay. Despite not receiving an endorsement for Drakes Bay, the Guild inexplicitly declared the contrary in their promotional literature: "The scholarly consensus for Drakes Bay was achieved. Drake's California haven is found!"[27]

Vaughan decided not to attend the Sir Francis Drake Commission's international conference on Drake. Alex Cumming, director of the Museum at Buckland Abbey also declined. He withdrew for the reasons he noted in a letter to Art Blume of the Sir Francis Drake Commission:

"I am sending my paper to Norman Thrower at the end of the month together with a few slides. Somebody is going to read it. In the circumstances it is the best I can do. I gather that the battle between the DNG [Drake Navigators Guild] and Bob Power still rages and seems to be having a destructive effect on the Drake 400, which is another sadness."[28]

The vexed question was a settled matter as far as the Drake Navigators Guild was concerned. In 2010 the Guild tried once again to nominate Drakes Bay to National Landmark status. In their draft nomination they cited the Chinese porcelain sherds as evidence of Drake's cargo. The original title on the nomination was "The Port of Nova Albion Hisotric [*sic*] and Archeological District," which was nixed by the peer reviewers not because the title had a spelling error, but because the reviewers refused to support the Guild's assertion that the geographic bay named Drakes Bay was the Port of Nova Albion.

Four peer reviewers were given this first draft of the nomination. Though their names were redacted, at least two of the reviewers were archaeologists. The Guild based their claim that Drake landed at Drakes Bay on the Wanli period (1573–1619) Chinese porcelain sherds that had been found by archaeologist Robert Heizer and others in archaeological sites in the Drakes Bay region. This is despite Heizer's opinion that the sherds had not come from Drake's cargo. In 1941 Heizer had sent a collection of the porcelain sherds for analysis to Theodore V. Hobby of the department of Far Eastern Art at the Metropolitan Museum of Art in New York. Hobby's report was that there were two types of porcelains in the collection: those that were from the late Ming period (1550–1644) and some that could be identified within the subperiod called the Wanli (1573–1619).[29] Heizer, who had excavated in the area for over forty years, had concluded that all of the sherds were from the wreck of the *San Agustín*, which occurred just sixteen years after Drake was on the coast.

The Guild felt Heizer was wrong, and that they could differentiate subsets within the collection (based on decorative attributes and vessel style) indicating that some of the porcelains could only have come from Drake's cargo. The Guild built their argument on the assumption that porcelain items in a single cargo were manufactured shortly before they were shipped so there would be some homogeneity of design and manufacturing technique. A further assumption they held was that sherds originating from the *San Agustín* would be clearly sand and water worn because they had eroded out of the shipwreck, whereas the sherds from Drake's cargo would not be water worn because these were from whole vessels given to the Native people. Within that subset, the Guild club members asserted that they could identify motifs and vessel shapes from sherds that were from Drake's cargo. The technical aspects of the methodology are not explained so the analysis cannot be replicated.

The archaeologists doing the peer review for the Drakes Bay Landmark nomination scrutinized the Guild's analysis of the Chinese porcelain sherds at Drakes Bay. They also reviewed Matthew Russell's research for his dissertation on the reuse of ceramics and other historical material in the Point Reyes area by the Native population. In his dissertation Russell removed from consideration the findings of the porcelain analysis done thirty years prior by Shangraw and Von der Porten of the Guild. He found that the porcelains were not from Drake's cargo: "My findings, based on a detailed examination and analysis of all porcelain fragments recovered from Point Reyes Peninsula in both the PAHMA and PRNSM collections, suggest that the entire collection of sixteenth-century Chinese porcelain can be attributed to a single source. For the purposes of the present study, therefore, I assume that all sixteenth-century introduced objects found at *tamál-húye* [Drakes Bay area] are from the 1595 *San Agustín* shipwreck."[30]

The peer reviewers agreed with Russell's protocol, and insisted on the removal of the Chinese porcelains as evidence of Drake. It was not only the National Park Service archaeologists who found the Guild's conclusions unsupportable. Two experts in Chinese porcelain motifs and manufacture techniques, archaeologists Harvey Steele and Jessica Lally, both dismissed the theory that any of the porcelains at Drakes Bay were from Drake's cargo.[31]

Understandably, Guild members were not pleased with the removal of the porcelains as evidence to support the National Landmark Nomination because these artifacts were absolutely crucial to their case. This is one thing they were right about: with the loss of the Chinese porcelain artifacts as supporting evidence, the vexed question becomes untethered to geographical Drakes Bay.

One of the peer reviewers of the Landmark application was a historian who was familiar with the general California Drake narrative supplied by the Guild, but was unfamiliar with Zelia Nuttall's Northwest coast landing theory or the major works on the topic by English historians. The Guild has an orthodox view of the historians who addressed the issue of the landing, preferring Wagner and Davidson—historians who wrote before 1927—to later historians such as Taylor who challenged the earlier historians' findings with fresh data found in contemporary sources.[32]

The National Park Service would have better served the public if it had enlisted the help of a historian who was instructed to conduct an in-depth critical analysis that included a discussion of the findings and theories of Nuttall, Taylor, Kelsey, and the other historians who have conducted original research and have discussed and discredited many of Wagner's findings, and most of Davidson's.

The National Park Service—after many redactions, edits, changes, and back-and-forth discussions—agreed to an awkwardly qualified statement about the landing. Interior Secretary Ken Salazar approved the nomination in 2012, officially making Drakes Bay a national historic landmark. The National Park Service staff had worded the important and key "statement of significance" to reflect the doubts brought up by the archaeologists:

> The Drakes Bay Historic and Archeological District is a nationally significant sixteenth-century landscape that includes 15 California Indian sites that provide material evidence of one of the earliest instances of European contact and interaction with native peoples on the West Coast of the United States; the most likely site of Francis Drake's 1579 California landing, the first English encampment on land that is now part of the United States; and the site of a sixteenth-century Spanish shipwreck, the Manila galleon *San Agustín*, which wrecked in Drakes Bay in 1595.[33]

The NPS allowed the words "most likely site of Francis Drake's 1579 California landing" to be put into the nomination. Those qualifying words disappointed the Guild as well, and they not only chose to ignore them, they asserted to the news media that the Chinese porcelain sherds from archaeological sites at Drakes Bay did, in fact, provide definitive evidence of Drake's presence. Immediately after the announcement of the Landmark status, the Guild put out a press release stating that the designation of Drakes Bay National Historic Landmark gave "formal recognition to Francis Drake's landing site at Drake's Cove in 1579."[34]

The National Park Service did not correct this misinformation, nor did it comment on the misleading statements that Guild members made to the print media and on national television. Erika Seibert, the archaeologist in charge of the National Register of Historic Places and National Historic Landmarks Program, fielded objections to the nomination in the following communication:

> As you may know, the nomination for this property has been closely reviewed by the National Park Service for decades. Most recently, our peer reviewers have included scholars both inside and outside the National Park Service. Based on these reviews and considerable archeological and historical scholarship during the last decade, the nature of the argument for the national significance of the Drakes Bay Historic and Archeological District has changed and expanded considerably. We would like to emphasize to you that the current documentation awaiting signature by the Secretary is not definitive with regard to the Drake landing site. This is clearly stated in the nomination and we believe that the nomination will encourage future research here and elsewhere... Furthermore, and more importantly, the national significance of this property as articulated in the documentation does not rest on Sir Francis Drake.[35]

The public was thus given the impression that the landmark designation was some type of "stamp of approval" granted by the federal government, confirming that Drake had landed at Drakes Bay. The National Park Service did, however, invite further study on the subject, and it should be noted that nominations can be amended as new information comes forth.[36]

CHAPTER FIFTEEN

The People at the Landing

DRAKE "THE DRAGON" made it a point to show a warlike readiness whenever he met Natives, as he did in the Moluccas when he greeted the people with peals of English ordnance, "rolling like thunder, valiantly and liberally discharged" upon his arrival there.[1]

The Native people at the fair and good bay were clearly astonished at the specter in their bay. We do not have the Native's perspective of the events that unfolded at the landing and it should be stressed that Drake and Fletcher's observations of the Natives were from the imperfect perspective of Elizabethans. The language barrier was difficult, and the difference in cultures was a wide gulf to bridge.

The first action by the Natives of the country was to send a gift to Drake.[2] A headman paddled out to the *Golden Hind* three times in succession, orating each time as he came. On the third approach he brought a feathered headdress and a bag of what was probably tobacco to Drake, as recounted in *The World Encompassed by Sir Francis Drake*:

> The next day, after our coming to anchor in the aforesaid harbor, the people of the country showed themselves, sending off a man with great expedition to us in a canoe. Who being yet but a little from the shore, and a great way from our ship, spake to us continually as he came rowing on. And at last at a reasonable distance staying himself, he began more solemnly a long and tedious oration, after his manner: using in the delivery thereof many gestures and signs, moving his hands, turning his head and body many

182

ways; and after his oration ended, with a great show of reverence and submission returned back to shore again. He shortly came again the second time in like manner, and so the third time, when he brought with him (as a present from the rest) a bunch of feathers, much like the feathers of a black crow, very neatly and artificially gathered upon a string, and drawn together into a round bundle; being very clean and finely cut, and bearing in length an equal proportion one with another; a special cognizance (as we afterwards observed) which they that guard their kings person wear on their heads.[3]

From his canoe, the man tossed a rod tied with the feather bundle and a basket of herbs or tobacco into a launch that was tied alongside the *Golden Hind*. Drake dropped into the boat, and offered the man gifts—even putting them on a plank that he pushed off to the man—but the man "could not be drawn to receive them by any means, save one hat, which being cast into the water out of the ship, he took up (refusing utterly to meddle with any other thing, though it were upon a board put off unto him) and so presently made his return."[4]

Drake did not trust the Natives. He had a fresh scar on his cheek from an arrow shot by one of the Natives of Isla Mocha—off modern day Chile—seven months earlier where one of his men died of arrow wounds.[5] After that melee, Drake did not blame the Natives of Mocha, but blamed the Spanish for the violence because the Natives had mistaken them for their Spanish enemies, who had previously used bloody methods to subdue them. Drake, critical of Spanish cruelty, prided himself in his humane treatment not only of Natives, but also of the Cimarrons—whom he partnered with in Panama—as well as the Spanish and Portuguese prisoners that he captured during his raids on ships and towns.

Drake envisioned the English as conquerors who would do credit to England by bringing to the Native people England's particular type of Protestant Christianity, which he thought was more progressive and humane than Catholicism.[6] In this fair bay on the Northwest coast of America, where the Natives had never met the Spanish, Drake ordered that there be no breach of the peace and that they would meet the people with gifts "bestowing upon each of them liberally good and necessary things."[7] If there was a breach of the peace, it was not recorded even by the sanctimonious Fletcher who took pains to record events that showed Drake in a bad light.

It took three days to position the ship to an anchorage close to shore so that she could be lighted and careened along with Tello's bark. The *World Encompassed by Sir Francis Drake* takes the narrative up from there:

Our ship having received a leak at sea, was brought to anchor nearer the shore, that, her goods being landed, she might be repaired; but for that we were to prevent any danger that might chance against our safety, our General [Drake] first of all landed his men, with the necessary provision, to build tents and make a fort for the defense of ourselves and goods: and that we might under the shelter of it with more safety (what ever should befall) end our business; which when the people of the country perceived us doing, as men set on fire to war in defense of their country, in great haste and companies, with such weapons as they had, they came down unto us, and yet with no hostile meaning or intent to hurt us: standing, when they drew near, as men ravished in their minds, with the sight of such things as they never had seen or heard of before that time: their errand being rather with submission and fear to worship us as Gods, than to have any war with us as with mortal men. Which thing, as it did partly show itself at that instant, so did it more and more manifest itself afterwards, during the whole time of our abode amongst them. At this time, being willed by signs to lay from them their bows and arrows, they did as they were directed, and so did all the rest, as they came more and more by companies unto them, growing in a little while to a great number, both of men and women.

To the intent, therefore, that this peace which they themselves so willingly sought might, without any cause of the breach thereof on our part given, be continued, and that we might with more safety and expedition end our businesses in quiet, our General, with all his company, used all means possible gently to entreat them, bestowing upon each of them liberally good and necessary things to cover their nakedness; withal signifying unto them we were no Gods, but men, and had need of such things to cover our own shame; teaching them to use them to the same ends, for which cause we did eat and drink in their presence, giving them to understand that without that we could not live, and therefore were but men as well as they.

Notwithstanding nothing could persuade them, nor remove that opinion which they had conceived of us, that we should be Gods.

In recompense of those things which they had received of us, as shirts, linen cloth, etc., they bestowed upon our General, and diverse of our company, diverse things, as feathers, cauls of net-work, the quivers of their arrows, made of fawn skins, and the very skins of beasts that their women wore upon their bodies. Having thus had their fill of this times visiting and beholding of us, they departed with joy to their houses....

As soon as they were returned to their houses, they began amongst themselves a kind of most lamentable weeping and crying out; which they continued also a great while together, in such sort that in the place where they left us (being near about 3 quarters of an English mile distant from them) we very plainly, with wonder and admiration, did hear the same, the women especially extending their voices in a most miserable and doleful manner of shrieking.[8]

On the second day after anchoring, the Natives gathered in a great assembly of men, women, and children at the top of the hill, and prepared to make a formal visit to Drake's encampment:

Against the end of two days (during which time they had not again been with us), there was gathered together a great assembly of men, women, and children (initiated by the report of them which first saw us, who, as it seems, had in that time of purpose dispersed themselves into the country, to make known the news), who came now the second time unto us, bringing with them, as before had been done, feathers and bags of *Tobah* [tobacco] for presents, or rather indeed for sacrifices upon this persuasion that we were gods.

When they came to the top of the hill, at the bottom whereof we had built our fort, they made a stand; where one (appointed as their chief speaker) wearied both us his hearers, and himself too, with a long and tedious oration; delivered with strange and violent gestures, his voice being extended to the uttermost strength of nature, and his words falling so thick one in the neck of another, that he could hardly fetch his breath again: as soon as he had concluded, all the rest, with a reverend bowing of their bodies (in a dreaming manner, and long producing of the same) cried *Oh*: thereby giving their consents that all was very true which he had spoken, and that they had uttered their mind by his mouth unto us; which done, the men laying down their bows upon the hill, and leaving their women and children behind them, came down with their presents; in such sort as if they had appeared before a God indeed, thinking themselves happy that they might have access unto our General, but much more happy when they saw that he would receive at their hands those things which they so willingly had presented: and no doubt they thought themselves nearest unto God when they sat or stood next to him.[9]

Though previously Drake and his men had heard some of the Native women's plaintive cries from the village in the distance, they had not witnessed their behavior of bloody self-mutilation. As the women approached Drake and his men, their frenzy and anguish became amplified. The women began again their doleful moans and gouged their own cheeks with their fingernails, causing the blood to flow down onto their breasts:

This bloody sacrifice (against our wills) being thus performed, our General, with his company, in the presence of those strangers, fell to prayers; and by signs in lifting up our eyes and hands to heaven, signified unto them that God who we did serve, and whom they ought to worship, was above....

Our General having now bestowed upon them diverse things, at their departure they restored them all again, none carrying with him anything of whatsoever he had received, thinking themselves sufficiently enriched and happy that they had found so free access to see us.[10]

Three days later there was an even larger contingent of people gathered to meet Drake and his men, as Drake and Fletcher related:

Against the end of three days more (the news having the while spread itself farther, and as it seemed a great way up into the country), were assembled the greatest number of people which we could reasonably imagine to dwell within any convenient distance round about. Amongst the rest the king himself, a man of a goodly stature and comely personage, attended with his guard of about 100 tall and warlike men, this day, viz., June 26, came down to see us.

Before his coming, were sent two ambassadors or messengers to our General, to signify that their *Hióh*, that is, their king, was coming and at hand. They in the delivery of their message, the one spake with a soft and low voice, prompting his fellow; the other pronounced the same, word by word, after him with a voice more audible, continuing their proclamation (for such it was) about half an hour.[11]

The two ambassadors' behavior included a complicated oration accompanied by body movements as described:

Which being ended, they by signs made request to our General, to send something by their hands to their *Hióh* or king, as a token that his coming might be in peace. Our General willingly satisfied their desire; and they, glad men, made speedy return to their *Hióh*.

In their coming forwards they cried continually after a singing manner, with a lusty courage. And as they drew nearer and nearer towards us so did they more and more strive to behave themselves with a certain comeliness and gravity in all their actions.

In the forefront came a man of a large body and goodly aspect, bearing the Scepter or royal mace, made of a certain kind of black wood, (and in length about a yard and a half) before the king. Whereupon hanged two crowns, a bigger and a less, with three chains [of shell beads] of a marvelous length and often doubled, besides a bag of the herb *Tabáh*.[12]

The headdresses were made of "knitwork wrought upon most curiously with feathers of diverse colors, very artificially placed and of a formal fashion."[13] Next to the scepter bearer was the king himself with his guards.

Drake and his men were assembled, "prepared to stand on sure ground"[14] to defend themselves if necessary. When the Natives got closer, they called out a salutation and then quieted for a moment, perhaps awaiting a response from the Englishmen. The Natives then continued towards the enclosure the English had built. The Native men began singing and dancing. Drake perceived that they were not going to attack, and gave the order to his men to allow the people to enter, so they entered the bulwark singing and dancing. Drake and his men were aghast at the appearance of the women, many of whom had bruised and cut bodies, and cuts on their faces that still bled in streams onto their breasts.[15]

By signs the leader asked Drake and his officers to sit down. After further orations, he presented Drake with a feathered headdress, the large black wood scepter, and strings of shell beads. Drake thought that the gift of the crown and scepter was the act of making him their king and transferring to him the "riches and treasures" of the country.[16] This concept of giving Drake the country, as Heizer noted, is "hardly ascribable to the Indians."[17]

These things being so freely offered, our General thought not to reject or refuse the same, both for that he would not give them any cause of mistrust or disliking of him (that [bay] being the only place, wherein at this present, we were of necessity enforced to seek relief of many things), and chiefly for that he knew not to

what good end God had brought this to pass, or what honor and
profit it might bring to our country in time to come.

Wherefore, in the name and to the use of her most excellent
majesty, he took the scepter, crown, and dignity of the said country into his hand; wishing nothing more than that it had lay so
fitly for her majesty to enjoy, as it was now her proper own, and
that the riches and treasures thereof (wherewith in the upland
countries it abounds) might with as great convenience be transported, to the enriching of her kingdom here at home, as it is in
plenty to be attained there; and especially that so tractable and
loving a people as they showed themselves to be.[18]

After the dancing and the ceremony, Drake and his officers sat together with the Native leader and his guard. Then the "common sort" of
people "dispersed themselves among our people, taking a diligent view
or survey of every man."[19] Each Native person selected an Englishman
to present him or herself to—the youngest Englishmen were preferred—
and they then began again to cut themselves and bleed, offering their
blood as a sacrifice to that chosen man.[20]

Drake's men gripped the Natives' arms to stop them from cutting
themselves, but as soon as they let go, the people would be as violent as
before. Drake's men tried to stop the hysteria and to get away from it.
Some of the men escaped the bloody clutches of the people by diving
into their tents, but the tents offered little protection, and these men the
people with "fury and outrage" sought to grasp again.[21]

Drake and Fletcher recounted that they "groaned in spirit" to see the
power of Satan prevail in seducing "these so harmless souls."[22] Drake
with his company fell to prayers, and by signs lifted up their eyes and
hands to heaven, trying to communicate to the people that it was God
above that they should worship. They sang Psalms, followed by reading
certain chapters in the Bible. At the end of every pause in the reading, the
Natives signified their assertion of the reading by saying "*oh*."[23]

Drake and his companions demonstrated to the Natives their great
dislike for the sacrificial behavior, and the people became "a little qualified in their madness," settled down and then began to show the English
their wounds and other diseases. The chronicle summarized their ail-

ments as: "Some having old aches, some shrunk sinews, some old sores and cankered ulcers, some wounds more lately received."[24] The English brought out lotions, plasters, and unguents to tend to the people's wounds.

The Natives were with the English almost every day, even surrounding their rowboat in canoes—the people "wondering at us as at gods, they would follow the same with admiration."[25] But, on every third day, the Natives arrived to perform their ceremonial bloody sacrifices. Finally, after some days or weeks, their zeal abated when the English strongly forbid these behaviors by making it very clear that they were displeased with these sacrifices.

Once the repairs were underway, Drake made a journey inland, accompanied by his officers and much of the crew:

> After that our necessary businesses were well dispatched, our General, with his gentlemen and many of his company, made a journey up into the land, to see the manner of their dwelling, and to be the better acquainted with the nature and commodities of the country. Their houses were all such as we have formerly described, and being many of them in one place made several villages here and there. The inland we found to be far different from the shore, a goodly country, and fruitful soil, stored with many blessings fit the use of man: infinite was the company of very large and fat deer which there we saw by thousands, as we supposed, in a herd.[26]

The number of days they trekked is not recorded. The Willamette Valley would have only been fifty or sixty miles inland on one of several trails that crossed the coast range, so it is not out of the question that Drake and his men explored that area. The valley was once a mosaic of broad grassy plains, oak savannahs, and lush wetlands, and it is likely that the landscape and even the stars in the night sky would have reminded Drake of England. Large herds of elk—which resemble England's red deer—still abound in the Willamette Valley.

The chroniclers did not record such details as how they repaired their ship, nor did they mention any further events or excursions that may have taken place while they were encamped at Nova Albion. Before their anchorage at the fair and good bay, the expedition had been searching for the Northwest Passage. If they did in fact reach Cape Flattery, sail through the Strait of Juan de Fuca, and see what John Drake described as six islands there (perhaps the San Juan Islands), then they must have encountered Natives of that region as well, but they left no record of it. The loss of Drake's records and material collections is especially profound when one considers that Drake's diary was filled with maps, sketches, and drawings of the country, flora, fauna, and (not least) the people they encountered. Among the collections Drake brought back would have been the gifts he received: shell and feather decorated baskets, two feathered crowns, a carved and burnished staff, and various assorted shell necklaces.

CHAPTER SIXTEEN

An Ethnographic Assessment
for an Oregon Landing

THIS ETHNOGRAPHIC assessment of the Oregon hypothesis is an applied anthropological analysis that uses specific historical analogies where the ethnohistorical source analog is compared to the ethnographic record in order to determine how closely the two are related. This method follows a similar process that archaeologists have used to determine ethnicity in specific cases mandated by the Native American Graves Protection and Repatriation Act—i.e., comparing the archaeological record against the ethnographic record.[1] Here, however, the chroniclers' ethnohistorical descriptions of the Native people and their culture are compared with ethnographic records to determine the closeness of fit with regards to material culture, food ways, and cosmology analogs.

The primary data used in this analysis comes from unpublished field notes made by the ethnographers who worked with Native speakers on the Oregon coast intermittently from the 1880s to the 1940s.[2] Note that any discussion about the geographic distribution and persistence of cultural norms and language from a time that was 300 to 340 years before the ethnographers were working must be considered speculative. The cultural cataclysm that came with the arrival of Euro-Americans was profound, and it created conditions where traditions were difficult to maintain. The amount of knowledge that was lost as a result is incalculable. No matter how insightful the anthropologist or archaeologist, forgotten traditions are specters that are usually out of our reach.

Following the conventions in the Northwest Coast volume of the *Handbook of North American Indians*, the Native people on the Oregon

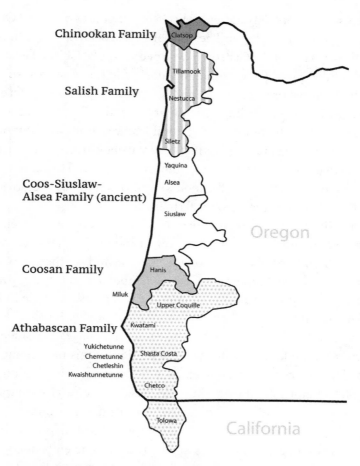

FIGURE 16.1. Cultural area map on the Oregon coast, after Homer Barnett, *Culture Element Distributions, Oregon Coast*, 1937.

coast and very northern California coast are described as southern groups within the Northwest coast cultural complex. The people in this region made elegant dugout canoes and lived in plankhouses typically made from the wood of the western red cedar (*Thuja plicata*), though in the southwestern most part of Oregon it has been reported that Native houses were more often made with planks from Port Orford cedar (*Chamaecyparis lawsoniana*), redwood (*Sequoia sempervirens*), or sugar pine (*Pinus lambertiana*). The basic social division was between free and slave, and rank was determined by wealth and inherited status.[3]

There were marked differences between the groups of coastal Oregon, both linguistic and cultural. The northern coast of Oregon was the traditional homeland of the Clatsop. These people spoke Chinookan proper. South of these groups were the Tillamook and the Nestucca, southern Salish groups whose traditional lands extended south to the Siletz River drainage. Despite their linguistic differences, the Chinookans and the Tillamook shared a number of cultural features. Both the Chinookans and the Tillamook practiced artificial cranial deformation (i.e., head flattening) that was achieved by strapping an infant's head to a cradleboard. The Chinookans and the Tillamook were also more sharply conscious of wealth and prestige than groups farther south.

The Siletz River drainage formed a cultural divide between these more complex groups of northern Oregon and the peoples of the central and southern Oregon coast. Along the central and southern coast were the related Alsean, Siuslawan or Lower Umpqua, and Coosan peoples; the latter were divided into the Hanis or Coos proper and the Miluk or Lower Coquille.

Farther south were people who spoke languages classified with the Athabascan family. Language distribution in this mountainous region along the coast was complex, and the historical distribution is not completely understood by anthropologists. The cultural similarities of Oregon's central and southern coastal groups mask a complex mix of languages unknown elsewhere. The ethnographical map of the region reveals a complicated mosaic of small groups, some embedded within larger groups in discontinuous islands.[4] The languages or dialects spoken here included the Upper Coquille, Shasta Costa, Chetco, Tututni, and the Tolowa.

Unlike those to the north, the people from central and southern Oregon coastal areas did not practice artificial cranial deformation and also had markedly different basketry traditions than the Salish people.

In addition, they were known for their frequent dancing.[5] Anthropologist Melville Jacobs's informants related that each individual had a dream song that was recited during certain celebrations and occasions. Dream songs represented that person's power. If a person obtained a new power song, they would sing it for several minutes standing in the center of the ceremonial space.[6] When the people sang their songs they also danced a specific choreography—their dream dance that went with their song—and sang their song three times. During one ceremony Jacobs's informant noted, "Everybody who wants his song sung has a chance, until by midnight they may have run through them all."[7]

Another difference was that men slept together in communal sweat-houses rather than with the women in the main house. In these more southern areas, women slept in the main house where everyone ate. Additionally, unlike their neighbors to the north, the southern groups slept on floors rather than on bed platforms.[8]

It may be said that these southern groups were relatively more peaceful than the northern groups. They had fewer slaves, smaller houses, and a less stratified society. Women often occupied positions of leadership, and among the Coos, women were frequently the recordkeepers who memorized their traditional stories and civic legal matters.[9] Anthropologist Mark Tveskov remarked: "If one measures cultural complexity by the degree of coercive authority in economic or political decisions wielded by an individual or household, the Coos-Coquille may indeed be less complex than their neighbors on the Columbia River and further north."[10]

Ethnographer Homer Barnett compiled a "Culture Element Distributions" list, wherein he compared various cultural elements and their distribution among groups who traditionally resided on the Oregon coast.[11] In the following comments he characterizes the people of the south coastal regions (and a very northern California area) within the broader Northwestern coastal cultures, and concludes the influence from the south (the Yurok and their immediate congeners) was "a striking secondary elaboration." He explained: "That is to say, for all their distinctive characteristics, the cultural flow as far as these less colorful people are concerned has been not from the far north, but from the California hearth in an ever-fading overlay. This backwash extends as far as the Coos, there to blend with the more precise manifestation of North Pacific Coast features."[12]

The people were cosmopolitan. Despite linguistic and cultural differences, there was a measure of cultural continuity among the northern, central, and southern groups of the Oregon coast, and with groups further afield. Dentalium shells were traded south from what is now the Canadian coast. Headbands made with the whole scalps of pileated woodpeckers were reported from the mouth of the Columbia River south all along the Oregon coast and into central California. Flicker quill headbands were worn by medicine men in southwest Oregon, but were more common among the traditional people of central California, including the Pomo and Miwok people.[13] A few basket designs were copied throughout the region. The relative ubiquity of particular designs may, in some cases, suggest greater antiquity. The "quail tip" design on baskets, for example, is considered to be of some antiquity, since it is found on baskets ranging from British Columbia to southern California.[14]

Writing about the prehistory of the Oregon coast, archaeologist Richard Ross noted that the southern Oregon coast shows interesting connections to the northern California coast and some of the interior valleys. In contrast, he found that the central section of the coast has a somewhat different archaeological background, less like the California cultures, which he attributed to distance and possibly more influence from the interior (Kalapuya) valley and the Columbia River region.[15]

Some theorize demographic shifts on the coast may have been brought about by the impacts of tsunamis on coastal populations and habitat.[16] In archaeologist John Draper's model for the development of southern Oregon coastal cultures he argued that epidemic diseases introduced ca. 1790 reduced indigenous populations by more than 60 percent, which meant that the models of settlement based on ethnographic data are not an accurate reflection of the situation prior to 1790.[17]

Melville Jacobs found that the Oregon-Washington beachline had fairly fixed coastal language enclaves. Using grammatical comparisons Jacobs postulated that an ancient language "which may be named Coos-Siuslaw-Alsea resided along the Oregon coast in about the same area where its modern descendant dialects are found."[18] He noted that the Siletz-Nehalem-Tillamook had less variation than the Coos-Siuslaw-Alsea dialects, suggesting relatively recent Salish entry in northwestern Oregon, extensive oceangoing journeying, or a combination of factors.[19]

Jacobs was one of a new generation of anthropologists that ventured to the Northwest between 1926 and 1934 under the direction of Franz Boas at Columbia University. Elizabeth Jacobs wrote that they recorded the peoples' stories and narratives in a nondirective, respectful Native-led approach.[20] Melville Jacobs felt this method was "less violent to the Native attitude."[21]

The anthropologists made observations and recorded cultural details. In the early to mid-twentieth-century anthropology, the preferred units of analysis were "cultural traits," or "elements" as Alfred Kroeber and Homer Barnett called them. Anthropologists brought printed word lists into the field for collecting Native vocabularies, and schedules with itemized lists of cultural traits that were to be filled out during interviews with their Native American informants. These lists and schedules elucidated everything from vocabulary and grammar to kinship terms, raiments, regalia, basketry, and so on.[22]

Jacobs also brought to the field a device that enabled him to record the voices of Native speakers. This streamlined translating and transcribing tasks, and he developed a method of ethnographic recording that focused on the structure and integration of traditional stories. In the 1930s with funding from the Council of Learned Societies' Committee on Research in American Indian Languages, Jacobs conducted ethnographic fieldwork throughout Washington and Oregon, and helped direct and coordinate the work of other students and researchers. Jacobs was a disciplined anthropologist, as Lawrence C. Thompson wrote, "He conscientiously sought out the last surviving speakers of language after language and recorded extensive materials in them, at the same time covering to the extent possible their cultural background."[23]

In 1925 Alfred Kroeber was one of the first anthropologists to address the question of Drake's landing with ethnographic data. Zelia Nuttall must have discussed her new opinion on the northern limits of Drake in the Pacific with Kroeber, who was chairman of the anthropology department at the University of California, Berkeley (a department that Nuttall had helped found). Kroeber, however, did not agree with Nuttall's findings: "Documentary evidence has recently led to the theory that Drake's landing occurred some 10 degrees of latitude farther north than has generally been believed. The question thus raised is for historians and geographers to solve. Should their views be favorable to the new opinion, it would follow that an attempt would have to be made to fit Drake's Indian descriptions to the customs prevalent farther north. Whether this could be accomplished with equal success seems very doubtful."[24]

Nevertheless, Kroeber was particularly troubled that Fletcher and Drake described the watercraft used by the people at the landing as "canoes," which he felt presented a discrepancy with the tule rafts of the Miwok and Pomo. He wrote that there was "no record of true canoes on the whole coast from near Cape Mendocino to the vicinity of San Luis Obispo," but he did not address the northern theory any further.[25]

The Drake chronicles do not describe the canoes in any detail. Dudley's manuscript map named the land south of the fair bay as "Coast of the Canoe Trees,"[26] which does not fit the landscape south of Drakes Bay, California. We can conjecture that if the canoes Drake and his men saw were unusual they would have commented on them, as they did for the "reed straw" canoes they saw in Valparaiso's harbor, the bark canoes they saw in the Strait of Magellan, and the large double-prowed, burnished-wood canoes they described in the Moluccas. It seems that if the English saw men paddling tule balsa rafts, they would have noted it in the chronicle.

On the southern Oregon coast canoes were not as elaborate as the double-pointed canoes that had attachable prow ornaments found farther north among the Chinookans.[27] Oscar Brown, who was from the Sixes River area, related to Homer Barnett that double-pointed canoes were made in the north by the "flat head" people (Salish and Chinookan speakers).[28] Brown remembered canoes with a sharp prow and blunt stern.

Sebastian Cermeño had described Miwok watercraft as "small boats of grass, which look like the bulrushes of the lake of Mexico."[29] Kroeber reasoned: "Either custom changed after Drake's day, or his [Fletcher's] canoe is a loose term for the tule balsa which was often boat-shaped, with raised sides, especially when intended for navigation."[30]

Robert Heizer was Kroeber's student, and besides looking for archaeological evidence of Drake, he also conducted research into the Native languages of the people who lived along the central California coast. He conjectured that if it could be shown that the Native language and culture described in the accounts of Drake's voyage were clearly those of one or another of the coastal tribes, then there would then be "definite and unequivocal reasons for believing that Drake landed on that part of the coast inhabited by that group."[31] To Heizer, the question was whether

Drake met the Yurok people of Trinidad Bay, the Pomo of north Marin County, the Costanoan people or the Coast Miwok people who lived along Bodega Bay, parts of San Francisco Bay, and Drakes Bay. Left out of the discussion were the people of the Northwest coast. This was due, in part to the Plate of Brass, which for many years Heizer considered an authentic artifact from Drake.

Heizer remarked: "Historians and geographers have long since stated their reasons and qualifications for presenting certain conclusions about the location of Drake's anchorage, but anthropologists have never insisted vigorously enough that their contribution might be the most decisive of all in solving the problem."[32]

Heizer revisited the ethnographic comparanda several times. Of all the ethnographic comparators, perhaps the most puzzling to Heizer was the discord between the ethnographic record and the English chroniclers' descriptions of the warm houses that reminded the English of the scuttle of a ship. In his 1947 treatment of the architecture of the people Drake contacted, Heizer reasoned that the informants did not remember plankhouses because these dwellings had not been used during the historical period. Heizer's explanation was that they changed to less permanent mat or grass-covered houses because they were inexpensive and more convenient to erect, and by 1790 the Spanish had destroyed their settlements.

Ethnographer and linguist Isobel Kelly had conducted interviews with several of the last speakers of the Coast Miwok dialect in 1931. She described the Coast Miwok houses as conical and grass covered, built on a willow frame. The door was a tule mat, and people slept on mats with their feet towards the central hearth. When it rained, the structure was covered in sealskins. Kelly, too, could not reconcile the ethnographic record with the Drake chronicle. Her best informants asserted the houses were not semi-subterranean.[33] Kelly did note that in large Coast Miwok villages a sizeable sweathouse was dug four or five feet into the ground.[34]

Miwok dwellings are depicted by at least one early explorer. Russian artist Mikhail Tikhonovich Tikhanov drew two drawings that were drawn in the interior of houses. The depictions are consistent with ethnographic informant Tom Smith's description, and show houses framed with multiple small poles to which a thatch covering is attached.[35]

Though Henry Wagner wrote about Drake's landing before Kelly and Heizer's research on the subject, it was clear to him that grass-covered huts like those in the paintings were not the plank-roofed houses that Fletcher and Drake had described. Wagner noted that Cermeño's report described the Native's dwellings as "pits made in the sand and covered with grass, in the manner of the Chichimecos Indians."[36] Another Spanish explorer described the houses in nearby Bodega Bay as "poor little houses of brush very scattered and in small numbers."[37] Based on Fletcher and Drake's descriptions, Wagner opined that Drake made landfall among the Yurok people because they were the only people on the California coast who had plank houses.[38]

A more logical explanation is that the houses Fletcher and Drake described were the vernacular plankhouses particular to the southern portion of the Northwest coast. In this region men slept in semi-subterranean sweathouse lodges that were sometimes built into embankments or the sides of hills. The roof peak was above the grade and the rafters touched the ground.[39] Coquille Thomson said the roof was two and one-half feet above the ground, and he further described the house as follows: "The house was round and a rafter went from the pole to each corner. There was a dirt wall, boards were placed over the top and dirt thrown on. The fire was in the middle of the back wall, two feet deep."[40]

Sweathouse lodges had a trench draft for the hearth dug through one wall adjacent to the hearth to facilitate the heating of the sweathouse. The hearth was typically in a corner. Peterson noted that among the Coos the roofs of sweathouses were topped with dirt and people slept on boughs and mats on the floor and the floors were clean sand or packed clay.[41]

The following is Drake and Fletcher's description of the houses they observed, which offers a good analog for Coquille Thompson's and Annie Miner Peterson's descriptions of the men's sweathouse found in traditional times on the central and southern Oregon coast. Note that the houses were sometimes built into the slopes of hills, standing slope wise as Drake and Fletcher noted, and they were "digged round" as Coquille Thompson noted, with dirt walls:

> [H]ouses are digged round within the earth, and have from the
> uppermost brims of the circle clefts of wood set up, and joined

FIGURE 16.2. Native Tolowa men's house, southern Oregon or northern California. Courtesy of the Del Norte County Historical Society.

close together at the top, like our spires on the steeple of a church; which being covered with earth, suffer no water to enter, and are very warm; the door in the most part of them performs the office also of a chimney to let out the smoke: its made in bigness and fashion like to an ordinary scuttle in a ship, and standing slopewise: their beds are the hard ground, only with rushes strewn upon it, and lying round about the house, have their fire in the middest, which by reason that the house is but low vaulted, round, and close, giveth a marvelous reflection to their bodies to heat the same.[42]

The next cultural analog considered here is the basketry. One of the earliest ethnographers to address the landing question with ethnographic data was Samuel Barrett. In 1908 Barrett argued that since Fletcher described baskets "wrought upon with the matted down of red feathers, distinguished into diverse works and forms" and ornamented with shell beads, it was his conjecture that Drake and his crew encountered the Pomo people.[43]

The aboriginal women of the Pomo—and later the Miwok—wove special baskets that display unique specializations with regards to feather decoration. The most visible aspect of the special baskets with feathers (which were typically gift baskets) was that they had raised tufts of feathers projecting from the body of the basket. Typically these baskets were decorated with shell disc beads that in prehistoric and early historical times were used as currency. These baskets were often made with the crests from the topknot feathers of quail. The Pomo were also the only people to completely ornament baskets with a layer of feathers woven into the coiled basket wall. These baskets had a raised knap on the exterior, giving the basket a furry appearance. If Fletcher and Drake saw baskets with feathers and shells, Barrett reasoned, it meant that Drake and company were on the California coast.

The idea that Drake saw "fully feathered baskets" may have come from the Drake Navigators Guild's self-published booklets, wherein these avocational historians made several unqualified statements that Drake saw "fully feathered" baskets made by the people at the landing.[44] The Drake and Fletcher account does not describe the baskets as "fully feathered" though this statement has unfortunately been repeated so often in professional meetings that this idea has become embedded in the minds of the public and professionals alike.

An objective reading of the English account reveals that Fletcher and Drake were not describing fully feathered baskets, nor were they describing baskets with designs made with raised or tufted feathers. There is not enough detail to determine if the baskets were coiled or twined. Drake and Fletcher's account also conflates two basket types (water baskets and trinket baskets) into one description, showing some lack of clarity on the part of the chronicler. Here is the Drake and Fletcher passage in question:

> Their baskets were made in fashion like a deep bowl, and though the matter were rushes, or such other kind of stuff, yet it was so cunningly handled, that the most part of them would hold water: about the brims they were hanged with pieces of the shells of pearls, and in some places with two or three links at a place, of the chains forenamed, there by signifying that they were vessels

FIGURE 16.3. Coos Basket with lid. Courtesy of Coos History Museum, Coos Bay, Oregon. Magee Collection, Coos History Museum, CHM 958.797. This is one of several local baskets in the collection that are decorated with beads and shells.

wholly dedicated to the only use of the gods they worshiped; and besides this, they were wrought upon with the matted down of red feathers, distinguished into diverse works and forms.[45]

While it is clear that this depiction would fit the description of feather overlay and disc shell beads found on Pomo gift baskets, an Oregon landing cannot be ruled out on the basis of this basketry description. In southwest Oregon the red feathers from redheaded woodpeckers were used to make a striking red thread employed as decoration on baskets, basket hats, and regalia. Beads and shells also decorated baskets, and examples of these are found in the Sarah McGee basket collection at the Coos History Museum. Sarah was an early resident of Coos County, Oregon, who came to the town of Empire about 1873 with her husband.

The continuity of Native basketry styles and designs through time and in specific cultural areas has been demonstrated to be remarkably persistent over hundreds, even thousands, of years (for example in the Great Basin). Several examples of baskets with red thread and dangling shell bead decorations—a unique basket type to the south coast of Oregon—can be found in the collection at the Coos County Historical Society, including the basket illustrated in Figure 16.3. These baskets are reminiscent of the baskets Drake and Fletcher described.[46]

Red thread was made from red feathers plucked from the heads of woodpeckers. The feathers were matted and twisted onto sinew to make a striking red thread that was used to decorate baskets, basket hats, and regalia. Some of the oldest baskets had red feather decoration, as described by basketry expert Leone Kasner: "The color came from woodpecker feathers or the bright stains of barks [alder] or berry juices used to dye grasses and roots. Red was the hue of courage and pride. Yellow denoted success, fidelity and joy; white represented riches and generosity; and black was the color-symbol of beauty and was associated with quail tail patterns."[47]

Kasner lamented, "The absence of red in later weaving, and the presence of European designs, are the two most regrettable phenomena found in 20th century Indian basketry."[48] Red woodpecker feather thread was also used to wrap the ends of dentalium shells used for currency, embroidered onto dance regalia and quivers, and applied to special containers (including money boxes). Billy Metcalf, a Chetco man, told the ethnographer Homer Barnett that this thread was used to apply designs onto men's armbands and headbands for dances. Red feathers and woodpecker scalps also functioned as wealth displays in traditional times.[49]

In traditional times, women on the Oregon coast wore basket hats that were bowl shaped and the finer ones were decorated with eagle down and feathers, as well as dentalium and abalone shell.[50] Annie Miner Peterson related that the "prettiest baskets" were decorated with star and lightning motifs.[51] The symbols fulfilled two purposes according to Kasner: "The weaver used them for decorative color and the formation of the design itself constituted an act of protection [possibly from thunder] or blessing."[52]

Men's headwear provides another cultural analog that was considered by Heizer. The English chronicle describes two types of men's headwear: "knitwork" headbands with feathers set in the band; and cauls or hats of "net worke." The first comparator considered here is the net caul, which, as Heizer speculated, may have described a kind of hairnet common to both southwest Oregon and central California groups. Heizer thought this description referred to the "well-known net caps of central California, a type so widespread that exact localization or provenience is impossible."[53] Museum examples of these nets are made from two-ply native hemp closely woven in a fishnet weave. Men wore them to keep the hair out of their eyes during certain tasks and in ceremonies. Women wore them less frequently.[54] In Oregon, Frank Drew related that the Coos decorated these hairnets with amulets or flowers.[55] The hairnets were ephemeral and went out of use in early historical times in both Oregon and California.

The chronicle shows the English were particularly curious about the down-like seed fluff or cotton laid down on the cauls:

> Some [of the people] having cauls likewise stuck with feathers, or covered over with a certain down, which groweth up in the country upon an herb much like our lettuce, which exceeds any other down in the world for fineness, and being laid upon their cauls, by not winds can be removed. Of such estimation is this herb amongst them, that the down there of is not lawful to be worn, but of such persons as are about the king.[56]

Baskets of this plant fluff were presented to Drake as a gift during the processional, and Drake observed that the people burned this fluff to sacrifice to their gods.[57]

Warren Hanna conjectured that Drake and Fletcher's plant fluff descriptions were nothing more than evidence of a fertile imagination.[58] Counter to that argument, it is likely that Drake, who was originally a merchant trader, would have naturally understood the qualities of fiber, and taken an interest in such a plant fiber for its economic potential. One of the ways Drake's father earned a living was in a wool mill where his job was to tease up and trim the nap on broadcloth with fine shears to make the surface as smooth as possible. Moreover, Drake's instructions included an order to find commodities that might be beneficial, and these descriptions of this seed fluff, which resembled cotton, suggest that Drake might have seen this as a potentially exploitable fiber.

The ethnographic record of the Miwok and neighboring groups is silent on any specific use of plant fluff. Heizer postulated that Drake might have been describing milkweed fluff (*Asclepias*), which was readily available in the environment around Drakes Bay and Bolinas Bay, though Heizer had no ethnographic reports indicating that it was ever used in the area.[59]

On the Northwest coast there is a clear record for the use of seed fluff from milkweed and cattail (*Typha* spp.) for various purposes, though the most important of all the plant fluff material was the white fluff of fireweed (*Charmerion angustifolium*), which has a long staple. Among some groups in the Northwest there is evidence that land was burned to enhance fireweed's growth, and that it was pruned and selectively harvested.[60]

Drake and Fletcher's botanical description of the plant was brief: "[This plant] groweth up in the country upon an herb much like our lettuce."[61] Like lettuce, fireweed grows on a single stem and has glabrous leaves. Fireweed is often found "up in the country" growing on old burns or clear cuts. It blooms and goes to seed in July to September in the Northwest, and the seeds floating on their fluff are spread in the wind.[62] The timing of seed formation concurs with the date of Drake's departure as related in the Harley manuscript, which noted they set sail at the end of August.

The second comparator for men's headwear is the "knit work" headbands set with feathers. These were the feather crowns presented to Drake and his men: "The crowns were made of knitwork, wrought upon most curiously with feathers of diverse colors, very artificially placed, and of a formal fashion."[63]

Heizer could not find a specific analog for the gifting of feathered headdresses among the Coast Miwok,[64] whereas Tveskov described that the most enduring traditional activities that continue or have been revived on the southern Northwest coast are seasonal gatherings where elaborate ceremonies include ritualized dancing and the display and exchange of obsidian wealth blades, feather headdresses, basketry, and other exotic regalia.[65]

The English were well acquainted with knitting, and their words "knit work" used in describing the headdresses can be taken to mean that they were given headdresses with yarn that was worked into a band or a cap. While yarn is not known ethnographically among the California groups, the use of mountain goat (*Oreamnos americanus*) wool yarn was well attested among the Native people of the Northwest coast.[66] It may have been fireweed fluff spun with other fibers into yarn, which was then crafted into the knit work headbands or caps that were the base of the feathered headdresses Drake and Fletcher described.

The archaeological evidence of textile manufacture on the Oregon coast is unequivocal. Most notably, a spindle whorl made of whalebone, and fragments of a wooden loom were recovered at the Par Tee archaeological site, located near the town of Seaside on the northern Oregon coast.[67] In early historical times textile weaving was more commonly found north of the Columbia River where mountain goats were more common, but it should be noted that also in early historical times mountain goats ranged as far south as the Cascade Mountains of central Oregon, and in prehistoric times there is evidence of their presence in northern California.[68]

There is only one mention of Native use of mountain goat wool recorded by an ethnographer working in southwest Oregon, but it is an early one. In 1882 anthropologist Willis Everette interviewed Baldwin Fairchild, a Chetco informant, who related that his people used the twisted hair from mountain goats in tunics.[69] In historical photographs there are various depictions of women wearing what appears to be mantle shawls made of white yarn.[70]

Historical portraits of the people (both men and women) from the central and southern Oregon coast frequently show elaborately embroidered clothing, caps, and regalia. The richness and complexity of design, motifs, and artistic composition is ornate and unique. The compositions distinguish these people from their neighbors. See, for example, the elaborate embroidery on Depoe Charlie's clothing and regalia in Figures 16.4 and 16.5. There is a remote but nevertheless real possibility that the elaborate embroidery—and even the cut of Depoe Charlie's pants and jacket—could, in fact, be cultural memes of Elizabethan visitors who wore embroidered doublets, jerkins, and breeches—elements that could have potentially been passed down for generations.

In Figure 16.4 there are fleur-de-lis style designs embroidered on Depoe Charlie's pants. Could these be mnemonic devices recalling the repeated fleurs-de-lis on the Queen's standard, the flag Drake carried with him on the voyage?[71] Are the lacey collar necklaces made of

FIGURE 16.4. Depoe Charlie wearing traditional regalia. Photo provided by the Lincoln County Historical Society, Lincoln City, Oregon. Catalog Number 790.

Depo Charley, Newport, Ore.

FIGURE 16.5. Depoe Charlie posing with his regalia. Note the container with what appears to be a long fringe of yarn attached to the rim. Photo postcard provided by the Lincoln County Historical Society, Lincoln City, Oregon. Catalog Number 1316.

dentalium (and sometimes yarn) found only in this region reminiscent of the ruffs worn by Drake and his officers? An illustration of this type of collar necklace is seen in Figure 16.6, on Kate, who was a Coos woman born circa 1839. Though this theory is highly speculative, there are precedents for mnemonic devices found in the art work of Native societies that support unrecorded episodes of European contact in their past.[72]

FIGURE 16.6. Photograph of Old Blind Kate. Photo courtesy of the Douglas County Museum, Catalog number 048/N12126.

Some of the early debates on the whereabouts of Drake's landing re-volved around the fauna his officers encountered on their march inland, where they found "herds of deer by a thousand in a company, being most large and fat of body."[73] The interior valleys of both Oregon and Califor-nia are habitat for elk and so the large fat deer Drake and his men saw were probably elk, an animal that is similar in size and body to England's red deer (*Cervus elaphus*).

The chroniclers described "multitudes" of an animal they called a strange kind of "conie." In early modern English, the word "conie" usually referred to rabbits or hares, but not always.[74] Drake and Fletcher de-scribed this animal as resembling the "Barbary conie" (*Procavia capensis*, or commonly called the cape hyrax); a fur-bearing mammal they were familiar with from the North African coast. Drake and his men described this Nova Albion conie as a burrowing animal that had a long hairless tail like a rat, and paws like a mole, and carried its food in its cheeks. They noted that the Native people used this animal for meat, and that the robes of their leaders were made of its skins.[75] This is their description of this animal:

> [T]heir heads and bodies, in which they resemble other Conies, are but small; his tail, like the tail of a rat, exceedingly long; and his feet like the paws of a Want or mole; under his chin, on either side, he hath a bag, into which he gathereth his meate, when he hath filled his belly abroad, that he may with it, either feed his young, or feed himself when he lists not to travel from his borough; the people eat their bodies, and make great account of their skins, for their kings holidays coat was made of them.[76]

In 1877 historian J. D. B. Stillman devoted three pages to the identification of this animal in his book *Seeking the Golden Fleece*. He asserted that Drake and Fletcher were describing the ground squirrel (*Citellus beecheyi beecheyi*). He concluded that since these squirrels do not live near the coast, or in Marin County, Drake must have been in San Francisco Bay, which he reasoned was closer to ground squirrel habitat (which is in the forested region to the east of the bay).[77]

Against the ground squirrel conjecture, other theorists pointed out that if Drake and company had seen a squirrel they would have called it a squirrel—a common animal in England. Wagner suggested that the passage may have conflated two different animals, but he supported the notion that Drake's conie was a ground squirrel.[78]

Stillman commented that the only other small mammal that is numerous at Drakes Bay is the pocket gopher, which the proponents of Drakes Bay have since concluded was the mystery animal. Stillman, and later Neasham, discounted this assertion because pocket gophers are solitary, are almost never seen above ground, have a short and obscure tail, and are so small that it would take many pelts to make a coat.[79]

After reviewing the ethnographic record Heizer wrote that he was "unable to find any ethnographic data on a special skin coat for chiefs or ceremonial leaders."[80] He tentatively suggested that the king's coat might have been a rabbit skin blanket, common to both Pomo and Coast Miwok.[81]

Drake's interest in this animal was probably not just curiosity. It seems likely that Drake's interest was more about the economic potential of the pelts of this conie than curiosity about a furry animal. Drake's mission was to reconnoiter for commodities and raw materials in any new-claimed land. He hoped that Nova Albion would be a stepping-stone for trade between England and the Far East. England's great promoter of exploration, Richard Hakluyt, noted in *Diverse Voyages* that there was also a market for fur in China.[82] There was at this time a developing European market for furs from the New World. French and Basque fishermen had begun collecting furs from the Amerindians as early as the 1540s from the coastal region of Acadia and the St. Lawrence estuary, in New France (modern-day Quebec). These included beaver, otter, and sable pelts, as well as deer and sea lion skins.[83]

Drake's conie was likely a muskrat (*Ondatra zibethicus*). While rare in California, and not present around Drakes Bay, these animals are common in wetlands in the Pacific Northwest, and in particular these animals abounded in the wetlands of the Willamette Valley.

In support of this contention, there are numerous ethnohistorical and ethnographic accounts that include descriptions of the Native American use of muskrat skin robes in western Oregon. In 1849, artist Paul Kane observed that the clothing of the Chinook men consisted of "a musk-rat skin robe, the size of our ordinary blanket, thrown over the shoulder, without any breech-cloth, moccasins, or leggings."[84] Women, he noted, wore the blanket in very severe weather. Kane painted a woman wearing a muskrat robe in one of his most famous paintings.[85] In 1805, William Clark mentioned that people at the mouth of the Columbia River "procure a robe from the natives above [Wapato Valley] which is made from a small animal the size of a cat, which is light and durable and highly prized by those people."[86] One of Clark's sergeants on the expedition, Patrick Gass, observed that these robes were made of "muskrat skins sewed together."[87] While his ship was anchored in the Columbia in 1835, the naturalist John Kirk Townsend described in his journal that the women of the region wear little clothing, but added "some, however cover their shoulders with a blanket, or robe made of muskrat or hare skins sewed together."[88]

The fit between the Northwest coast ethnohistorical accounts and the descriptions of conies and their uses in the English chronicle is a compelling match on every particular: muskrats have long bald tails, they have paws like moles, their heads are the same size as rabbits, and they store food in their cheeks. In the summer they live in warrens in the ground where they give birth to their young. Archaeological evidence suggests that muskrat meat was an important winter food source for the Native people who lived on the extensive wetlands of the Willamette and Columbia Rivers.[89]

The people that Drake and Fletcher observed wore conie skin robes. If the muskrat was in fact Drake's conie, then the cultural analog between coastal groups in Oregon with the English chronicle is strong. The advantages of muskrat skin robes were that they were lightweight, warm, and the pelt is also waterproof, which would have been an important attribute for a robe or mantle worn by the people of the maritime environment of the Northwest coast.

The above comparanda between the ethnographic record and the historical accounts of the people Drake and his men encountered are as good as, or better than, the comparisons Heizer, Barrett, Kroeber and others have made for the Coast Miwok and/or Pomo people. The architectural comparanda seems particularly striking, and the theory that Drake's conie was the muskrat would appear to solve a long pondered mystery.

CHAPTER SEVENTEEN

Linguistic Analysis

IN 1598 HAKLUYT published the first account of Francis Drake's voyage and included a single Native vocabulary word from the people of Nova Albion, and its English translation. This word was *Hioh*, thought to mean "king" because it was the word uttered as a Native herald was announcing the arrival of the leader, or *Hioh*.

In the Drake and Fletcher account published in 1628 three more words were added to the word list. These were *petáh* (a root); *tabáh*, spelled four different ways (an herb); and *gnaáh* (entreat to sing).[1] In that account the word for king was spelled in two different forms, *Hioh* and *Hyoh*, with emphasis on the second syllable (see table 17.1). The Hakluyt account from 1598 stated that the herb they were given was tobacco, but the later Drake and Fletcher account did not equate *tabáh* with tobacco, and simply called it an herb. The Native word for bread (*cheepe*) and two phrases—*huchee kecharo* (sit down) and *nocharo mu* (touch me not) were added when E. G. R. Taylor found Richard Madox's diary in 1931, as well as a Native song: *Hodeli oh heigh ho heigh ho hodali oh.*[2]

In 1908 Samuel Barrett was the first ethnographer to consider the English chronicles as a record of the people of the region.[3] Barrett found the accounts too vague to determine in which bay Drake landed, but he addressed the language of the people Drake contacted with the following speculation: "From the few Indian words given...no conclusion as to the language of the people with whom Drake came in contact can be drawn. It may be noted however that among Moquelumnan [Coast Miwok] peoples the word signifying captain is ho'ipu, which may be the same as the "Hioh" given as the name of the king in this account."[4]

TABLE 17.1. Word Lists and Translations as Interpreted in the Three Primary Sources

Drake & Fletcher	Hakluyt	Madox	English Translation as Interpreted in source
1 *Hióh, Hyóh*	*Hioh*	*Hioghe*	king
2 *Tobáh, Tobâh, Tabáh, Tobàh*	*Tabacco*		herb or tobacco
3 *Gnaáh*			entreat to sing
4 *Petáh*			root
5		*Cheepe*	root meal or bread
6		*Huchee kecharo*	sit down
7		*Nocharo mu*	touch me not

In 1925 Alfred Kroeber compared the original four words (*Hioh, tobah, gnaáh,* and *petáh*) to several Native vocabularies. He called the language comparison "the final test" to determine what language group Drake encountered, but noted that the evidence "is too scant to be conclusive, but is at least favorable to the interpretation of Drake's friends having been Coast Miwok."[5] Kroeber based his conclusion on only one of the four words, which was *Hióh.* Kroeber followed Barrett's conjecture that *Hióh* had a fair parallel to the Coast Miwok word *hoipa,* or "chief," and a closer match to the Sierra Miwok word for chief, *haiapo.* He interpreted *gnaáh* (the word given for sing!) as a meaningless interjection. Kroeber suggested that the words *tobáh* and *petáh* were borrowings from the English words for tobacco and potato because, as he noted, the narrative does not specify if it was the "English or the natives who called these plants thus."[6] Against Kroeber's conjecture about potatoes being *petáh,* Drake purchased potatoes—and referred to them as "potatoes"—from the Natives of Mocha Island, Chile, where potato was a staple foodstuff.[7]

The jotted vocabulary list in the diary of Richard Madox was compiled by the chaplain on the follow-up voyage who had taken notes from men who had previously sailed with Drake. Madox's list gave an alternate spelling (and perhaps a better indication of the pronunciation) for *Hióh,* as *Hioghe.* This word list also had a new word, *cheepe* for root bread, and two new phrases that translated as "touch me not" and "sit down."[8]

Taylor sent a facsimile of the manuscript to Alfred Kroeber at Berkeley to determine if any of the words were a match for a language group on the Northwest coast. Writing from London on February 11, 1932, Taylor asked him if he could "throw light on a little 16th century fragment of evidence about a visit to the coast of California, which I transcribe in the enclosed sheet."[9] Taylor wanted to know if the Native words could be identified to a particular group in or around the latitude of 48° north, where the manuscript said Drake had graved and breamed his ship. Taylor noted that this fragment was from 1582, and "forms a link, (possibly a frail one) in a chain of argument I am developing."[10] She noted that she had found this fragment of evidence on a page in Richard Madox's diary describing Nova Albion and the people that Drake met there. Madox was relating the details as told to him by one Mr. Haul who was on the circumnavigation. Taylor transcribed this as follows: "The latitude mentioned is MS 48 N. The people are for nature, color, apparel, diet, and hollow speech like to those of Labrador and as is thought kingless [for they crowned Sir Frances Drake]."[11]

Kroeber asked his colleague in the department, Ronald Leroy Olson, to respond to Taylor's request. This was a reasonable request, as Olson's area of expertise was the cultures of the Northwest coast. Taylor was concurrently posing the same question to anthropologist and linguist Edward Sapir. Sapir was head of the anthropology department at Yale, and had extensive experience with speakers of indigenous languages in the Northwest, as well as in California. Taylor's quest to narrow down Drake's place of landfall by identifying the language spoken there was only partly fruitful, as she noted in the article that presented her findings: "It had been hoped by the present writer that the few Indian words transcribed by Madox might form a decisive clue to Drake's landing place, but Professor Sapir, who kindly examined them, could come to no definite conclusion and Professor Olson could say no more than that a Chinook tribe of the Columbia River area might be in question."[12]

This finding, however, may have been enough to shiver the timbers of the "Drake in California" protectors. Shortly after this finding was published, it is likely Bolton initiated the Plate of Brass hoax, which, as related above, had the effect of ending any further speculation of Drake landing on the Northwest coast.

The Plate of Brass, however, did spur more investigations into the landing and more curiosity about the people Drake and his men met. In 1941 Heizer initiated a second attempt to apply the new word list to a

Native language, though he limited his search region to the California shoreline because the Plate of Brass was then thought to be authentic. At the time, Heizer was a young graduate student at Berkeley, and Kroeber was his advisor. During the winter break of 1941, Heizer, William Elmendorf, and Ronald Olson worked on the word list to see if they could determine what particular California language the people at the landing were speaking.

While Heizer was under the assumption that the plate was authentic, it must be noted that Olson was a member of the Clampers; in fact, he was a member of the particular chapter that had conspired with Bolton to cover up the Plate of Brass hoax if it became necessary. Whether Olson knew about the scheme is unknown, but his initial idea that the word list may have been Chinookan was understandably discarded after the plate was found.[13]

In a letter to Kroeber, Heizer wrote that most of the linguistic work was done by Olson, and that they had "roughed it out during one evening of Christmas vacation," and that he wanted Kroeber to "look it over" and let him know if he missed something important.[14] He also requested that Kroeber show the draft to Professor Kline in the English Department, who could offer judgment on Elizabethan English.[15]

The article came out in the summer of 1942, with Heizer and Elmendorf the authors. Olson's contribution was not acknowledged.[16] On the basis of the linguistic and ethnographic evidence they concluded that Drake landed in territory inhabited by a Coast Miwok-speaking group. This would have included Bolinas, Drakes, Tomales, and Bodega Bays but eliminated Trinidad Bay as a contender. They conceded that there were problems with the word list. For example, they thought that *cheepe* was a close match for *tci'pa* (the Coast Miwok word for bread), but they could find no Coast Miwok cognate of *tobáh*, *gnaáh*, or *petáh*, and the Coast Miwok word for king or chief, *hoipa*, is not very close to *Hióh*. The two phrases from Madox were *huchee kecharoh* (sit down) and *nocharo mu* (touch me not), and both phrases were problematic for the authors because they contained the [r] sound, which is not found in the Coast Miwok language.[17]

Heizer revisited his linguistic analysis in 1974. He also revised his hypothesis on the location of the landing: "I now believe that it is most probable that Drake did, on June 17, 1579, enter San Francisco Bay and after going through the Golden Gate turned north, and anchored."[18]

Heizer's frustration over the vexed question is evident in the following sardonic comments:

> As of 1974 it appears that we may never know for certain the exact place where Drake stayed in 1579. It would be nice to be able to have it proved beyond doubt that Drake entered a particular bay, because local politicians and history buffs could cooperate and raise there an impressive and expensive monument commemorating this unimportant event. Further, if it could be absolutely proved where Drake landed, a lot of scholars who puzzle over the question would be freed to go on to puzzle over other questions.[19]

Linguist John Lyon reviewed the previous linguistic studies during the course of his own survey to determine if the words recorded by the English were from an Oregon or Washington group, particularly one of Salishan, Coosan, Chinookan, Penutian, or an Athabaskan-speaking stock. The Drake Anchorage Research Collaboration (DARC) supported this study. DARC was a short-term, nonprofit brain trust organization that the present author founded to bring together historians and anthropologists to address the vexed question. Lyon's paper was published in 2016 and titled, "Francis Drake's 1579 Voyage: Assessing Linguistic Evidence for an Oregon Landing."[20]

Lyon surveyed and charted the phonological inventory (i.e., the sounds) of each indigenous language on the Oregon and Washington coasts to determine if particular sounds were present or absent. He then combed the existing language texts, vocabulary lists, and grammars for matches on the word list. Lyon's criteria for determining if matches were meaningful were twofold: first, the words on the word list and in the Native languages had to sound the same; second, the words had to mean what was inferred on the word list, or be meaningful within the context in which the word was uttered.[21]

Lyon included broader comparisons that consisted of sequences or phrases that are phonologically or phonetically similar to those given in Fletcher's and Madox's word lists:

This second, broader approach is necessary because of a wide margin for error stemming from the following factors. First, the orthographical conventions of Elizabethan England may not accurately represent the sounds that were actually spoken by members of the contact group, and the members of the Drake expedition might not have heard those sounds very accurately in the first place, especially given the great phonetic differences between English and many languages of northwestern North America. Second, the recorded meanings of the documented words and phrases may be "incorrect inductions of meaning" (Heizer and Elmendorf 1942, 216) on the part of the ship's crew members. Third, sound change can and does affect language, especially over the course of three or four hundred years.[22]

Lyon discussed three Chinook Jargon (also called Chinuk Wawa) words that had fair or good correspondences with the word list. These are *Hióh*, *petáh*, and *cheepe*, which may correspond to the name for a "social gathering" (i.e., a party or feast), the wapato root, and "bread cake" respectively.[23] Despite these linguistic correspondences with Chinook Jargon, and some very tentative Coosan matches, Lyon ultimately concluded, "none of the languages surveyed here present more than one or two plausible matches for the items in those word lists."[24]

Lyon qualified his conclusion with the comment that if the group Drake contacted was speaking a form of trade jargon that predated Chinook Jargon then "a reasonably full composite list of possible matches may be assembled."[25] With the significant removal of possible Chinook Jargon matches on the word list, Lyon concluded that Coast Miwok was the best match for the language Drake encountered.

There are two theories about the origin of Chinook Jargon, and Lyon takes the more conservative stance. The more conservative theory is that the jargon was born with the fur trade in the late eighteenth century as a way for the Chinookans to communicate with their English and French-speaking trade partners. The most influential voice against the existence of a proto-jargon was F. W. Howay, who, writing in the 1940s, attributed the establishment of jargon to dealings between European and American fur traders and Natives beginning in circa 1785. Over time more French, English, and Nuu-chah-nulth (indigenous peoples of the Canadian Pacific coast) words were added, so that Chinook Jargon came into full fruition during the 1840s. It was spoken from northern California to the Aleutian Islands, and from the Pacific Ocean to the Rocky Mountains.[26] Howay thought it unlikely that a system of intertribal trade and travel existed among the Native people of the Northwest coast in prehistoric times, and if it did, it must have been rare, so he theorized that there would have been no need for a trade pidgin or jargon.[27] The underpinnings of Howay's theory about Native travel are now considered incorrect, but his theory that Chinook Jargon was a relatively recent invention persists.

The alternate theory is that there was extensive intertribal trade and travel in prehistoric times that necessitated a prehistoric intertribal pidgin. Archaeological evidence and ethnographic accounts have demonstrated that shells, obsidian, fish oil, and other materials and commodities were traded in prehistoric times. It is worth noting that mollusk shells were the currency of the region and the most important shell was the tusk-like dentalium (*Dentalium* spp.), which was traded great distances from its place of origin in the waters off Vancouver Island.[28] Dentalium shells served as a demonstration of wealth and were important markers of status in the hierarchical societies of the Northwest coast and beyond. Therefore, it is not surprising that Chinook Jargon has vocabulary derived from the languages spoken by Natives who lived on and around Vancouver Island, as well as vocabulary derived from their Chinookan trading partners on the Columbia River.

Oscar Brown, one of Leo Frachtenberg's Coos informants, related an interesting anecdote that reveals a particular protocol by Coos in their use of Chinook Jargon that has been overlooked by theorists who have addressed the antiquity of Chinook Jargon, and this protocol supports the theory of a precontact jargon. Brown related that Chinook Jargon was not only used as a trade language with neighboring groups, but also to speak to fish. The protocol was that while fishing on the ocean, you and your fishing companions only spoke jargon to each other—and to the fish. Brown related that to lure the fish, they pretended they were playing a ball game called shinny with the fish, calling out game directions to the fish in jargon to bring them to their bait. But, once the fish was on the hook, it was time to be silent, and they said nothing until the fish was brought aboard.[29]

The fact that this practice (of speaking jargon to fish and to your companions while fishing) was quite widespread among coastal groups suggests that there was some antiquity to the practice. These groups included most of the Oregon coastal groups as recorded by Homer Barnett in his culture elements distribution list.[30] Brown's comments also suggest that jargon was used to communicate with other groups/teams on the shinny course during real shinny matches. He described other protocols that were followed while fishing; for example, making jokes was prohibited, as was speaking about women or land animals. The Tillamook informant Louis Fuller also related that jargon was spoken among his people at sea, and said that besides not talking about women or making jokes, talking about sea serpents was also prohibited.[31]

The prominent linguist Dell Hymes considered that it was likely that Chinook Jargon developed from a proto-jargon, which he characterized as a "stable pidgin."[32] The linguist Sarah Grey Thomason found particular phonological and syntactic features of Chinook Jargon that led her to conclude, "The most reasonable historical conclusion is that Chinook Jargon was already in existence as a fully crystallized pidgin—used by the Lower Chinook and their neighbors, by their slaves, and perhaps also by their more distant trading partners—before Europeans arrived in numbers in the Northwest."[33]

The words *petáh* and *cheepe* on the word list respectively refer to a particular root and to the cake that the Natives made from this root. As Drake and Fletcher described, "they make a kind of meal, and either bake it into bread, or eat it raw."[34] The word *petáh* corresponds well in a sound and meaning match to the Chinook Jargon word *wapato* (in particular the variant *pota*). Wapato is a carbohydrate-rich staple, and like the *petáh* of Drake, *wapato* can be eaten raw, or made into a meal or dough and shaped into bread cakes. As with many jargon words there are several variants in pronunciation. Sacagawea called *wapato* 'pota'—which is a close sound match—but wapato's variants in Chinook Jargon are many, and include *papato*, *wappahtoo*, *wapetu*, and *wapatoe*.[35]

The word Madox recorded for bread, *cheepe*, corresponds well to the Chinook Jargon word *chaplil* (bread cake) made from this root (and other roots). *Chaplil* also is used to mean wheat or flour. It has several spelling and pronunciation variants, including *sahpolel, sapelil, saplel, chaplil,* and *chap-all-ell.*[36]

Wapato is a better botanical match with *petáh* than the wild onion (called *putcu* in Coast Miwok), which was suggested by Kroeber.[37] The characteristics of wapato are also a better fit than some of the other contenders that Heizer mentioned, which included soaproot (*Chlorogalum,* called *haka* in Coast Miwok) and acorn (called *umba* in Coast Miwok). Heizer considered acorn an improbable match, but noted, "Even this remote possibility must be entertained."[38]

Wapato roots were a staple for the people who lived in western Oregon and were gathered in both the fall, when the tubers form, and in the spring before they sprout.[39] The roots can be stored fresh or dried and in taste and texture it resembles a potato.[40] Most of the ethnohistorical accounts relate that it was typically baked whole in the ashes of a hearth, but it also was made into *Chaplil* cakes, as described by ethnobotanist Martin Gorman: "When it was desired to put up the plant for future use, pit cooking was the method adopted, and the tubers after removal from the pit and husking the outer coat, were reduced to a sort of dough or paste and made into small roundish cakes about 3 inches in diameter and 1 to 2 inches thick, and were then fire dried and put away for winter use."[41]

It is striking that when George Lang addressed the antiquity of Chinook Jargon in his book *Making Wawa, The Genesis of Chinook Jargon* (2009), he singled out exactly two words to discuss the case for the existence of a proto-jargon: *wapato* and *chaplil.* Lang pondered the possibility of the antiquity of these words as follows: "Some have imagined traces of this putative precontact pidgin Chinook in Lewis and Clark's *cha-pel-el* [sahpolel] 'bread–cakes' and *wa-pa-to,* a comestible root… both entered Wawa (as *saplil* and *wapetu*), or perhaps were already part of the trade jargon before Wawa proper was born."[42]

The Lewis and Clark party recorded the word *wapato* and various versions of this word (*papato, whpto, wappato*) over forty times.[43] They purchased *wapato* from the Natives over twenty times and it became an important food for the Corps of Discovery during the winter that they spent on the lower Columbia. They noted that there was a brisk trade of this commodity that was transported in large cargo canoes from the region that Lewis named "Wapato Valley" (the greater Portland Basin) downriver to the people on the coast.[44]

Lyon was not aware of Lang's conjecture about the possible proto-jargon origins of *wapato* and *chap-all-ell*. However, Lyon noted that the ethnohistorical description of wapato "precisely matches that recorded by Fletcher for *petáh*...It is possible that *petáh* could have been the raw stuff out of which *cheepe* was made."[45] An even earlier account of *wapato* as Chinook Jargon occurs in the log kept by Captain Charles Bishop of the *Ruby* in 1795, which is further support that jargon was in existence prior to the land-based fur trade.[46]

Johnson and Zenk discussed the origins of Chinook Jargon in a co-authored chapter published in 2013.[47] Johnson found the arguments supporting a proto-jargon convincing, while Zenk took the conservative stance. Zenk considered, but did not assert, that because Chinookan proper was so difficult for non-Chinookans to speak or understand, a "foreigner Chinookan" may have been spoken that was simplified by stripping it of verb prefixes and other inflections.[48]

Whether we call it "foreigner Chinookan," "stable pidgin," or "proto-jargon," there is an increasing consensus among modern linguists that, prior to the fur trade, people in the region spoke words to each other during trade and social activities that were unique and understood by people who lived beyond the Chinookan heartland. One such word was probably *wapato*. Based on the close similarity of their names and descriptions, it seems likely that *wapato* and *petáh* are one and the same root, which would support Nuttall's theory of a Northwest coast landing.

The next word on the word list that may be a Chinook Jargon word is *Hióh*, a word interpreted by Drake and his crew to mean king. In his discussion of *Hióh*, Kroeber posited that this word corresponded to the Coast Miwok word for chief, which was *hoipa* or *hoi'pu*.[49] However, Heizer and Elmendorf were troubled by the new transcription of Hioh (*Hioghe*) found in Madox's diary because it was no longer a convincing sound match for the word chief in Coast Miwok. They suggested "very tentatively" that the Coast Miwok word for chief, *hoi'pu*, had changed phonetically since 1579.[50] When he revisited the question in 1947, Heizer revoked his earlier conjecture about the *-ghe* in *hioghe*, noting that, "It could hardly be even a sixteenth-century attempt to render the syllable

-pu."[51] Lyon also questioned the match between *Hióh* and the Miwok word *hoi'pu* on the grounds that it seems unlikely, as Heizer contended, that the English chroniclers would fail to transcribe a [p] in a source word.[52]

It is likely that the English were mistaken in their conjecture that the word *Hióh* meant king. Context is important when considering this word. On the Northwest coast when a formal social gathering was imminent, protocol called for an emissary to ask for permission to enter the village, and await a reply.[53] Just before their first formal meeting with the king, an emissary spoke the word *Hioh*. Drake and Fletcher noted, "When they were come somewhat near unto us, trooping together they gave us a common or general salutation, observing in the mean time a general silence."[54] Since *hy-yú* was the jargon word for a social gathering, it may be that the emissary was uttering this word to Drake and his crew to inform them that a formal social reception was imminent. Frachtenberg recorded that in Coos the prefix *hî-* means "to be here, to meet," and that *hîitcuu* meant to "be together, to be assembled."[55] Drake saw the leader and his entourage assembled, and he likely misinterpreted their word for assembly to mean king. Drake and his men gave no reply to the salutation, but assembled together and moved into their fenced encampment in a show of force, "forcasting the danger and worst that might fall out."[56]

The Natives approached Drake and his men with some ceremony, as was—and is—typical of Native people on the Northwest coast when greeting visitors. The Natives sent two men as emissaries to Drake while the others in the group remained at the top of the hill. One of the Native emissaries began an oration in a low voice, while the other spoke the same words in a voice that was more audible.[57] They continued their proclamation for about a half hour, alternating between them, one in a soft voice and the other in a more audible voice. When their oration ended, the emissaries approached Drake. This face-to-face meeting may have been when Drake first heard the word *Hioh*: "They by signs made request to our General, to send something by their hands to their *Hióh* or king."[58] Perhaps they were holding out their hands and saying "let's assemble."

In Chinook Jargon *hiyu* also means "much" or "plenty" and it has several variations including *hay-yu*, *hà-yu*, *hy-iu*, *hy-yu*, and *hay-yù*, among others.[59] Earl Coe and Walter Shelley Phillips included it in their lists of common Chinook Jargon words.[60] Phillips described the pronunciation as [hi] as in "high," followed by [u] as in "union," with a slight breath sound of [h] at the end: *hi-i-you-h*.[61] This pronunciation is a match for Drake and Fletcher's *Hióh*, and a perfect match for the Madox version of the word, *Hioghe*. Heizer and Elmendorf suggested that *-ghe* in Madox's transcription of *Hioghe* is silent. Lyon agreed this conclusion was likely, but he also found it conceivable the final [h] might have represented fricatives made further up in the vocal tract, a common element in Northwest coast languages.[62] With the addition of a fricative, the pronunciation of *Hioghe* is strikingly consistent with Phillips's rendering of the pronunciation of the jargon word *hiyu* as "High-you-h."

Hiyu survives today in a number of iterations, including as the name of a retired Washington State Ferry, a beer brewed in West Seattle, and the name of a Seattle service club established to produce a summer festival (i.e., a social gathering), appropriately called *hy-yú*.[63]

The word list word that probably refers to tobacco is variously spelled in the chronicles as *tobáh*, *tobâh*, *tobàh*, and *tabáh*. Perhaps the strongest correspondence Lyon found was *ta'ha*, the Hanis Coos word for tobacco. Tobacco was used by Native peoples throughout the Northwest, and according to Barnett the Native people of the Oregon coast would traditionally burn tobacco while praying.[64]

The Hanis Coos and Miluk Coos languages are closely related, as Lyon noted; their sound systems are the same, and they share a great deal of vocabulary in identical or closely similar form. Lyon noted the following about the Hanis Coos word *ta'ha*: "The Hanis word for 'tobacco' [ta'ha], seems to be a close phonological, as well as semantic, match with Fletchers [tobah], with the obvious exception of the missing [b] in the Coos form."[65]

The Hanis Coos and Miluk Coos did not have the [b] sound in their language, though they did have a labial [p] that was both aspirated and ejective.[66] Is it possible that the Hanis Coos word *ta'ha* is a derivation of the English word "tobacco," reduced to *tobah*, which came into Hanis

Coos as *ta'ha* because they could not pronounce the [b]? It should be stressed that the idea that a remnant word might have been left with the people Drake contacted—and ultimately replaced their Native word for tobacco—must be considered very speculative.

However, along these same lines, Kroeber conjectured that the Natives were trying to pronounce the English word "tobacco" during their communications, but could only pronounce it as *tobah*, which was recorded by the diarists as a Native word because the Englishmen did not understand that the Natives were trying to say an English word back to them.[67] Heizer and Elmendorf concurred and wrote, "There can be little doubt that Fletcher's tabáh and tobáh are traceable to English."[68]

The next entry on the word list to consider is *huchee kecharoh*, a phrase that Richard Madox recorded in his diary as meaning "sit down." Drake and his men might have first heard this phrase spoken just after the king and his processional came into Drake's bulwark, dancing as they came: "As they danced they still came on: and our General perceiving their plain and simple meaning, gave order that they might freely enter without interruption within our bulwark...After that they had satisfied, or rather tired themselves in this manner, they made signs to our General to have him sit down."[69]

In his analysis of this phrase, John Lyon found that *huchee kecharoh* partially corresponds with the Hanis Coos phrase *hats yî´qa tcī Lōwa ´kats*.[70] This phrase is written here in anthropologist Leo J. Frachtenberg's orthography, and can be phonetically rendered in the Americanist orthography as something like *hats ye' qa tsi tloo wa'kats*. Frachtenberg translated this as "just continually there (he) sat"; the pronoun "he" is implied and not grammatically indicated. The word in the phrase denoting "continually" is *yî´qa*, which Frachtenberg noted can also be translated as "still, anyway, at any rate, nevertheless," and it can infer something ongoing.[71] The phrase that Lyon singled out as a close match can thus be rendered "just anyway there (he) sat" or "just at any rate there (he) sat," as well as Lyon's preference, "just continually there (he) sat."

This phrase is complex. However, in Hanis Coos, *hats* serves to introduce a new idea, and was conventionally translated as "just," though it has a stronger emphasis than that, and is often used at the beginning of a sentence.[72] If *huch-* of *huchee* is the Hanis Coos word *hats*, the second syllable -*chee* could be *tcī*, which means "there."[73] Regarding *tcī*, Lyon thought that this high-frequency particle "could plausibly have been present in a phrase meaning 'sit down,' i.e., 'sit down over there.'"[74] Literally, *huchee* (*hats tcī*) alone could convey "just so," "just there," or something of the sort. There appears to be a clear sound and meaning correspondence for the first part of the phrase, *huchee*, and this phrase would make sense within the context of the king inviting Drake and his men to sit down, especially with the use of hand signs as Drake and Fletcher indicated.

Lyon considered "the match for the final syllable -*roh* is the first syllable of the verb *Lō wa ʾkats*," which is the word for "sit" or "sitting." Here the [L] symbol in the original Frachtenberg text is equivalent to the Americanist phonetic notation [ƛ] symbol, and sounds like the "tl" sound as in bottle.[75] This is not phonetically close with *huchee kecharoh*, unless the last portion was dropped, as Lyon postulated, "so assuming that this form is the source of Madox's requires that we also assume that Madox's informants forgot the last few syllables of the utterance."[76]

The Coosans did not have an [r] sound in their lexicon so it casts doubt on the idea that *huchee kecharoh* was a rendering of a Coos word except in the case of a gloss of the allophone. Lyon considered this a possibility: "An [r] sound is not particularly close to [ƛ] phonetically speaking, although one could imagine that a soft articulation of [ƛ] might be misperceived as a different consonant with a similar place of articulation, such as [l] or [r]."[77]

The next phrase Lyon considered was *nocharu mu*, which was translated as "touch me not." This also contains a soft [r] sound that could have been misconstrued from a [ƛ] allophone, and in this case it may have been either glottalized or plain. *Nocharu mu* was evidently phonetically rendered by the English source (probably in a Devonshire regional pronunciation of an Elizabethan English accent). Lyon found this word to be a close phonetic match with the Siuslaw-Lower Umpqua word *nīctcatlaᵋ mū*, "battlefield."[78] He considered this match almost as good a match as Heizer and Elmendorf's Coast Miwok form *noʾtca*, meaning "farther" or "yonder." Though Lyon found the Siuslaw-Lower Umpqua phonetic match "battlefield" interesting, the semantic match was problematic for him. This led him to conclude that, "with the absence of any close semantic and phonetic matches, Siuslaw-Lower Umpqua speakers were not likely the contacted group."[79]

Could it be that *nocharo mu* is an attempted rendering in English of the phrase "no touch me" rather than a phrase from the Native language meaning "touch me not"? This possible correspondence will be further described in the next chapter within a cosmological context that may explain what the Natives were tying to convey, which the present writer suggests was a voiced imperative uttered by the Natives not to touch or strike them.

The word recorded by Drake and Fletcher that they translated as "entreat to sing" was *gnaáh*. A possible match for "entreat to sing" is that—like Kroeber and Heizer's conjecture about *tobah* being an English word, and as the conjecture here that *nocharu mu* may be a rendering of the English phrase "no touch"—it is possible that gnaáh was also an English phrase (Go North!) said back to the English and misunderstood by Drake and his men to mean "sing." This tentative conjecture is also explored in the cosmological chapter below.

People who live in literate societies often underestimate the linguistic skills possessed by those in nonliterate societies. Native Americans in the Northwest were proficient linguists, households were often bilingual, and many people could speak three languages. It would be logical for the Natives Drake encountered to try to learn some English words and phrases in order to communicate. Early explorers noted that the people of the region had a surprising linguistic proficiency. Horatio Hale noted that "the Indians...were quick in learning languages and some of them could speak five or six native idioms."[80] In 1843 Captain Edward Belcher of the British Navy noted that one of the most prominent qualities of the people he met was their ease in picking up language, words, and even short sentences, and repeating the whole tolerably correctly.[81]

Based on this linguistic analysis, a reasonably full composite list of possible word matches can now be assembled. The close contextual, semantic, and phonetic matches between three of the words on the list and Chinook Jargon words—specifically, *hioghe* (cf. *hiyu*, a reception and social gathering), *petáh* (cf. wapato root), and *cheepe* (cf. *chaplil*, bread cake) suggest that Hymes, Johnson, Thomason, and Lang are all correct about the existence of a proto-jargon.

The hypothesis proposed here is (1) that the group Drake contacted spoke to him in a proto-Chinook Jargon or pidgin, and (2) more tentatively, that the indigenous language spoken by the contact group was from the Coosan family of languages.

There is a realistic possibility that the vexed question of "which bay" will always remain unanswered. The possible Coosan association contradicts the theory of Whale Cove as the site of Drake's summer sojourn because it is situated about one hundred miles north of the Coosan heartland, and it is geographically within the traditional territory of the Alsea people.[82] The Alsea language is related to the Coos language, according to Jacobs, who used grammatical comparisons and suggested there was an ancient language "which may be named Coos-Siuslaw-Alsea [and] resided along the Oregon coast in about the same area where its modern descendant dialects are found."[83] However, these languages diverged much longer ago than 1579, so this cannot explain the vocabulary correspondences with the word list.

It is also possible that the current models of settlement (based on ethnographic and historical data recorded in the nineteenth century) may not be an accurate reflection of the demographic situation prior to the epidemic diseases introduced ca. 1790, which reduced indigenous populations by more than 60 percent.[84] A massive earthquake and resultant tsunami in 1700 likely reduced human populations on the coastline, and the resultant demographic redistributions could have been significant.[85]

CHAPTER EIGHTEEN

Thunder and Lightning

Cosmological Correspondences

THE ARRIVAL OF DRAKE and his crew in the *Golden Hind* would have most likely been announced by cannon fire that echoed off the mountainsides. Never having encountered Europeans, this spectacle would have astonished the Native people. Whether the people believed Drake was a god or man, or something in between, it is apparent that the Natives believed that he possessed some type of power, especially if his arrival had been accompanied by what they perceived as thunderclaps.

Following Patricia O'Brien's model for tracing the cosmology of a descendant community into prehistoric times, ethnographic notes and texts were examined for correspondences that could help explain the reactions and behavior of the people Drake encountered within the context of the Native's worldview.[1] Some strong correspondences were found between the cosmology and associated ritual behaviors of the people of the southern Oregon coast and the ethnohistorical descriptions of behaviors that appear in the various chronicles of Drake's visit at Nova Albion.

Anthropologists have long pondered the extraordinary behaviors Drake and his crew witnessed. Kroeber wrote about these demonstrations: "There is no doubt that, like Cabrillo among the Chumash, Drake was received with marked kindliness. Only the extreme veneration accorded him is difficult to understand. The simplest explanation is that the Indians regarded the whites as the returned dead. Such a belief would account for their repeated wailing and self-laceration, as well as the burned 'sacrifice' of feathers."[2]

Against Kroeber's conjecture about the returned dead, it is possible some of the Natives may have mistaken Drake for either the supernatural being Thunder himself, or saw him as a man who possessed some sort of Thunder power. Thunder was an important personage in the pantheon of supernatural beings who were revered by most of the groups on the coast of southwestern Oregon.[3] The actions and self-violent demonstrations of some of the people at the landing can be explained in the context of how the Native peoples of the region envisioned Thunder, and what it would have meant to humans if he had arrived amongst them. Their behaviors seem very much like acts of homage, and perhaps the blood-letting in particular was a penitential rite performed by individuals as a way to atone for their self-perceived misdeeds that might have offended Thunder. Some of these behaviors noted by Drake were the prescribed behavior noted in ethnographic texts if one offended Thunder on the southern Oregon coast. Though archaeologists have described blood-letting as a penitential rite for other cultures, it has not been described specifically on the Oregon coast.[4]

The first meeting between the English and the Natives occurred when a man paddled his canoe out to the *Golden Hind* and sang his song. At the second meeting the following scene played out, just after an emissary who was on the hill ended his long oration, and as the Native men approached Drake's camp. They put down their bows and with the women and children behind them they came down the hill with their presents.

> In the mean time the women, as if they had been desperate, used unnatural violence against themselves, crying and shrieking piteously, tearing their flesh with their nails from their cheeks in a monstrous manner, the blood streaming down along their breasts, besides despoiling upper parts of their bodies of those single coverings they formerly had, and holding their hands above their head that they might not rescue their breasts from harm, they would with fury cast themselves upon the ground, never respecting whether it were clean or soft, but dashed themselves in this manner on hard stones, knobby hillocks, stocks of wood, and

pricking bushes or whatever else lay in their way, iterating the same course again and again.[5]

After this encounter, the people returned to their houses and some began "a most lamentable weeping" that Drake and his men could hear from their camp situated "about 3 quarters of an English mile distant."[6] After three days, at their first formal meeting (just after the presentation of a feathered crown to Drake), the following episode took place when the common people, both men and women, dispersed themselves among Drake's people. The Hakluyt account recounts the events that followed: "The common sort of people leaving the King and his guard with our General scattered themselves together with their sacrifices among our people, taking a diligent view of every person and such as pleased their fancy, (which were the youngest) they enclosing them about offered their sacrifices unto them with lamentable weeping, scratching and tearing their flesh from their faces with their nails, whereof issued abundance of blood."[7] Drake and Fletcher's account describes the hysteria of the bloodletting: "But so mad were they upon their Idolatry, that forcible withholding them would not prevail, (for as soon as they could get liberty to their hands again, they would be as violent as they were before) till such time, as they whom they worshipped were conveyed from them into the tents, whom yet as men besides themselves, they would with fury and outrage seek to have again."[8] Over the weeks that Drake and his men were encamped at the bay, it was recorded that every third day the Natives would come to make sacrifices, though Drake and his men tried to dissuade the people from this behavior: "They certainly understood our meaning, that we took no pleasure, but were displeased with them; whereupon their zeal abated, and their sacrificing, for a season, to our good liking ceased."[9]

Here it should be noted that the number three appears to have been a cosmologically significant number to the people Drake met. It will be remembered that the man who paddled his canoe out to the *Golden Hind* approached the ship three times, each time singing and making dance movements (as well as he could in the canoe). It is likely this headman was singing his power dream song, and dancing his power dream dance. The fact that the people came to Drake's camp every third day to perform their sacrifices is also significant. Ritualistic repetition based on the number three is something that several groups in southwestern Oregon and northwestern California shared.[10]

After some weeks the Natives perceived that Drake and his men were in final preparations for their departure. Drake and Fletcher related that the people demonstrated "excessive sorrow for our departing," and through signs expressed their desire that they not leave and their wish to see them again.[11] These Natives "by stealth" (i.e., against the will of Drake and his men, who repeatedly tried to dissuade them from these sacrifices), brought a sacrifice of feathers and necklaces and set them on fire: "We labored by all means possible to withhold or withdraw them, but could not prevail, till at last we fell to prayers and singing of Psalms, whereby they were allured immediately to forget their folly, and leave their sacrifice unconsumed, suffering the fire to go out; and imitating us in all our actions, they fell a lifting of their eyes and hands to heaven, as they saw us do."[12]

Drake set up a firm post, to which he nailed a plate to serve as proof of their land claim for England in the name of Queen Elizabeth. As the *Golden Hind* left the fair and good bay, the people bade their final farewells to Drake and his crew: "[They] presently ran to the top of the hills to keep us in their sight as long as they could, making fires before and behind, and on each side of them burning there in (as is to be supposed) sacrifices at our departure."[13]

The following ethnographic accounts describe Thunder and how the people of the southwestern Oregon coast perceived and acted towards this supernatural being. The ethnographic notes below detail Native perceptions of Thunder (the God of fishes), behaviors prescribed when gifting items for Thunder (sacrifice by burning), and sayings to be repeated in Thunder's presence (Go North! Don't strike me!). These ethnographic details have a remarkable symmetry with the behaviors described by Drake and Fletcher's accounts, not the least of which were the fires that the Natives kept building to burn wealth items (tobacco, shell necklaces, feathers), in spite of the English efforts to dissuade them from these sacrifices.

The following accounts come from ethnographers' unpublished notes, collected ethnographic data, and texts collected from Native

informants from the central and southern Oregon coast. These accounts
describe Thunder as a supernatural being that needed placating. Sometimes when it thundered, the Native people believed that Thunder was
chastising humans for wrongdoing.[14]

The Coos people considered Thunder to be the father of all fishes.
Jacobs noted that if people mistreated or disrespected a fish it would put
them in peril because Thunder would roar and destroy things. A storm
might come up, for example, if leftover fish was burned or thrown into
the fire, and it was important that fish entrails were carefully discarded
into the river.[15] And, as will be related, Thunder liked to sup on human
blood.

Interactions with Thunder had protocols. In the file he labeled "the
supernatural," Jacobs recorded one account as follows:

> When there are electric storms children are warned not to make
> noise or say anything that does not sound sensible. If the thunder
> becomes severe they take a piece of fish netting made of twisted
> deer sinew, throw it into the fire, and burn it, because it belongs
> to the fish kingdom above, which is making the thunder. Or they
> may throw tobacco into the fire, claiming that this quiets the
> thunder. Instead of saying something not sensible, the old people
> talk to the thunder during the storm. That is why they do not
> throw salmon into a fire and why such care is taken when fish-
> ing for salmon.... They speak to the thunder as follows: "Do not
> make it too severe for us in this country!"[16]

In Melville Jacobs's interview with Coos elder Annie Miner Peterson
he took the following notes on a page titled "Thunder—The Fishes Father," wherein Mrs. Peterson related the following about Thunder:

> Thunder was father of the fish. When Thunder comes–when it
> thunders—they believe and say he likes to smoke, so they burn
> old fishing gear, easily replaceable materials for him, whatever
> they have that was used for fishing purposes; such as a piece of old
> fish net or a stick from a fish dam. They call to the Thunder and
> say, "Go on! Do not harm us here! Go north where they burn and
> cut off the heads of your children [cut the heads off fish], where
> they make fun of your children. But do not harm us here!"[17]

Jacobs noted at the bottom of the page that Mrs. Peterson did not know why they always told Thunder to betake himself north; yet that is "what they do."[18]

He did eventually find an answer to why the people tell Thunder to go north. In Jacobs's *Coos Narrative and Ethnologic Texts* he recorded that when Thunder spoke, the people knew Thunder was angry at them for humiliating his children (the fishes). They would say "Go on north! They are insulting your children there yonder."[19] Then they would find their tobacco and throw it in the fire along with miscellaneous things such as paint or things to do with fishing, such as a paddle or a little part of a fishing net. Then the people would shout, "We are compensating you. Go away! Go on North!"[20] Jacobs's informant explained that Thunder would go away roaring: "That was the reason why if a person saw him as if he were a person ([or] had him for power), this is the way thunder would speak to him: 'When I became angry, you are to give that tobacco to me, and also paint. Those are the things I value big (highly).'"[21]

It is apparent that the Natives considered that the items they burned in the fire were transmogrified into smoke that rose up and became gifts for Thunder. The Modoc of Tule Lake, as well as the Shasta of the Klamath and Rogue River drainages, also had the custom of praying to Thunder and telling him to "depart."[22]

The following discussion appears in Jacobs's notes taken during an interview with the Coos informant Alice Malony, which further demonstrates protocols that were to be taken whenever it thundered:

> When thundering, they throw into the fire things or pieces of things they use in fishing, and also paint and tobacco. Thunder, being the salmon's and fishes father, and he wants these things for pay when his children are destroyed carelessly—heads, guts, etc. If everything were dried and later it would be all right, but when parts of fish were discarded carelessly then thunder would be angry, so they pay him by throwing things into the fire for him.[23]

Anthropologist Leo Frachtenberg's informant William Smith recalled that when the thunder was at its peak, the Alsea people would pour water out of all their buckets and upturn them to ward off lightning. When the thunder began to roar loudly, the people would shout "Take good care of yourselves, Dodge thyself my friend."[24] At the height of the storm, informant Smith related that the people would leave their houses and dance together outside in a body, "Then the storm would gradually calm down. Those people (would be still) dancing. They looked in all directions. Whenever the elements acted thus, it would sometimes thunder very (hard); people were always afraid very (much) whenever it began to thunder."[25]

The passages cited above help to contextualize Thunder—and people who possessed Thunder power—within the worldview and cosmology of the Native peoples of Southwestern Oregon. With that in mind, the following accounts provide a possible explanation for why some of the people cut themselves and presented their bloody bodies to Drake's crew: these people may have believed they were paying penance for perceived offences to Thunder, such as mishandling fish. Such bloodletting and offering of blood to Thunder—or someone representing Thunder— may have been intended as a penitential rite to appease Thunder, who likes blood. This concept is reflected in a text recorded by Jacobs (informant unnamed):

> After a mosquito alights and sucks a person's blood it takes the blood away either to a world above—not the land of the dead above but another world above, of which I have no further detail. Where it tells the people there that it was obtained the blood in the forests [sic] down below (It does not say it attained it from persons) or it flies away to the highest mountains where the forest is thick, it lets out the blood and places it on the mountain trees there, then there are electric storms, because the lightning believes that that is where blood is obtainable, the lightning does not know that persons likewise have blood. And so not understanding the desire of lightning for human blood, persons are safe because the lightning gets the blood placed by the mosquitoes all over the mountain forests. That is why there are so many mountain storms: mosquito has never revealed where he got the human blood. Nevertheless, the Coos play it safe when bitten by mosquitoes, and kill them if they can strike them fast enough. Mosquitoes do not bite and suck blood merely because they are hungry; they want to take the blood either to a land above, or to

the trees up in the mountains where the lightning can find the blood. If the thunder and lightning really did know where the mosquitoes obtained their blood supply, it would be dangerous for the people. In former times electric storms were more severe than they are nowadays.[26]

A Shasta informant related to ethnographer and photographer Edward Curtis a traditional story about Thunder asking Horsefly where blood came from, to which Horsefly responded, "Oh, I suck it out of trees and out of the ground." Thunder then struck several trees, but found no blood. He said to Horsefly, "I do not believe you get blood from trees and the ground." But Horsefly only repeated that it was so, for he feared to tell that he sucked blood from people, lest Thunder, in trying to get blood, strike them dead.[27]

The Natives' admonishment to the Englishmen not to touch them (*nocharu mu*) has not been satisfactorily explained by Heizer, Kroeber, or the other anthropologists who have addressed the question of Drake's landing. The Natives' request not to be touched seems inconsistent with their other behaviors, unless they were addressing (or thought they were addressing) Thunder. As the above ethnographic accounts describe, "do not strike us" or "do not hit us" are what one told Thunder during a storm. The Natives told Drake not to hit them, which now makes sense if the people Drake met held the belief that Drake was Thunder or had Thunder power. The Natives may have been attempting to say the English phrase "no touch me" when they uttered *nocharo mu*, which was understood—but misconstrued by the English as a Native phrase.

The troublesome word *gnaáh* was recorded as meaning "entreat to sing" in Drake and Fletcher's account, and it was described as a word uttered by the Natives to prompt the Englishmen to sing Psalms. As in the case of *nocharo mu*, it is possible that the people were speaking some English words to Thunder (a.k.a., Drake). Recalling Annie Miner Peterson's words: "They call to the Thunder and say, 'Go on! Do not harm us here! Go north where they burn and cut off the heads of your children.... But do not harm us here!'"[28] If the people were trying to tell Thunder to "go north" in English (Thunder/Drake's native language), it could have sounded like *gnaáh* to the English. This is because neither the /th/ as in "north" sound [θ] a plain alveolar /r/ sound are found in the languages on the central and southern Oregon coast.

The Psalms that Drake and his men sang when prompted by the utterance *gnaáh* may have been understood by the Natives to be Thunder's dream-power song. Dream-power songs are important in these groups, and it was typical that each person had his or her dream-power song, obtained in puberty, that was sung three times for the assembly during seasonal celebrations and important occasions. It is likely that the people would have considered that singing a dream power song was a natural response from Thunder when he was told to "go north!"

Epilogue

ONE OF THE MAIN objectives of this study is to correct the historical record and bring to light a fuller, more nuanced picture of an important segment of Sir Francis Drake's circumnavigation. Drake and his crew were likely the first European explorers to ascend as far north as Cape Flattery during their audacious search for the entrance of the Northwest Passage—a possible shortcut home with the prevailing wind at their back. It was in these latitudes they reported seeing snow-capped peaks and five or six islands. They failed to find the shortcut they were seeking, and subsequently they anchored and careened the *Golden Hind* in a bay somewhere on the Oregon coast.

To doubt that Drake could have ascended to these latitudes and sought the Northwest Passage as a way home "is to fail to understand the intellectual outlook and mental equipment of the men of the expansionist period" (to borrow a phrase from Taylor).[1] Upon their return, Queen Elizabeth confiscated the records of the voyage, and the crew was made to swear an oath not to reveal where they had traveled on pain of death. This secrecy was because Drake's land claim included a vast amount of territory he did not see, and therefore could not have legitimately claimed. Drake's claim of Nova Albion bolstered England's position, and their eventual claim to most of North America, though these machinations created profound confusion in modern California. The notion that the extended land claim was a conspiracy by Queen Elizabeth, Walsingham, Hakluyt, and Drake to foil the Spanish—and that it is only now that this has been revealed—is icing on the Elizabethan cake.

Drake and Fletcher's ethnohistorical accounts give a presence to the people of the fair and good bay, albeit through the archaic and smoky lens of an Elizabethan. This idea that Drake and his men met ancestors of the descendant societies living in Oregon today may present a problem for tribal members. After all, Drake was a would-be colonizer, and a precursor of a cataclysm that would sweep their culture. Ironically, however, the vivid descriptions and wealth of information present in the Englishmen's detailed cultural observations, though naive, could in fact have an important decolonizing role to play. These accounts have the potential to further enrich the lively cultural revivals taking place among the Native peoples of the Oregon coast.

Finally, Zelia Nuttall's original theory that Drake was on the Northwest coast is sustained. The barriers that Herbert Bolton and the other Californians threw up against her defeated Nuttall at the time, but she was never diminished by their actions, and in this new light it is clear that they are the ones diminished.

The various commemorative plaques (there are five or six) that have been erected to honor Drake's landfall in California are now depreciated. These plaques could be melted down and recast into a statue of Zelia Nuttall. Ideally, it should be erected at the University of California, on the Berkeley campus near the Department of Anthropology she helped found. Perhaps even the Plate of Brass—an artifact designed to defeat her—should be thrown into the crucible and transmogrified in her honor.

Notes

Chapter 1: The Problem

1. W. S. W. Vaux, ed., *The World Encompassed by Francis Drake, Being his next Voyage to that to Nombre de Dios* (London: 1854; repr., New York: Burt Franklin, 1963), 221.

2. Ibid.

3. Robert Dudley, "Arcano del Mare," Manuscript Charts, ca. 1621, vol. 2 (Africa and America), Chart 85, images 237–38, http://daten.digitale -sammlungen.de/~db/0008/bsb00084103/images/index.html?seite =238&fip=193.174.98.30

4. Harry Kelsey discusses the various inventories and descriptions of the treasure in *Sir Francis Drake: The Queen's Pirate* (New Haven: Yale University Press, 1998), 215–16.

5. Zelia Nuttall, as quoted in the *Oakland Tribune*, May 1, 1915.

6. The Hakluyt account and the Drake and Fletcher account note that they anchored in the fair bay on June 17, but only the Drake and Fletcher account recorded their date of departure, noted as July 23. The British Library's MSS Harleian Manuscript 280, folio 83–88 account gives no date of arrival but reported that they departed in the later part of August. There are seven early chronicles that cover the Pacific Ocean portion of the voyage and beyond. The first of the official accounts approved by the Crown is "The Famous Voyage of Sir Francis Drake into the South Sea," in Richard Hakluyt's collection *The Principall Navigations, Voiages, and Discoveries of the English Nation* [...] (London: George Bishop and Ralph Newberie, 1589). About ten years later another edition of this publication came out and some of the details in this version of "The Famous Voyage" chapter varied from the first edition. The reported latitudes were changed to 43° north instead of 42° north for the highest latitude, and the leagues sailed and some of the dates of events were also changed. In this version of *Principall Navigations*, "The Famous Voyage" chapter is properly paginated on pages 730–42, vol. 3. Hakluyt changed the title of the compilation slightly as well (see bibliography for 1598 version). Digital copies of these original books can be viewed online from the Hans and Hannie Kraus Collection of Sir Francis Drake, Library of Congress, Washington,

D.C.: https://memory.loc.gov/cgi-bin/query/r?intldl/rbdkbib:@field
(NUMBER+@od1(rbdk+d0302)).

The later edition of *Principall Voyages* has another account of the
events at the landing, with no title and no author (though it has been attributed to Francis Petty, one of Drake's men-at-arms); it is often referred
to as "The Course" from the first two words of the text (3:440–42). In
1628 Drake's nephew compiled *The World Encompassed by Sir Francis
Drake* [...], ed., Nicholas Bourne (London: n.p., 1628). According to
historian David Quinn it was likely a compilation of Drake's unfinished
manuscript from the library of Buckland Abbey, collated with Fletcher's
account. See David B. Quinn, "Early Accounts of the Famous Voyage,"
in *Sir Francis Drake and the Famous Voyage, 1577–1580*, ed. Norman J. W.
Thrower, (Berkley: University of California Press, 1984), 33–48. Perhaps
the earliest narrative of the west coast portion of the voyage can be found
in MSS Harleian Manuscript 280, folio 83–88, in the British Library. This
is referred to here as the Harley manuscript, and it is also known as the
Anonymous Narrative. This author has studied the original versions of the
above texts in the British Library. Unless otherwise noted, all of the above
sources are cited from the fine transcriptions made by W. S. W. Vaux in
his 1854 compilation of contemporary documents relating to the voyage
titled *The World Encompassed by Francis Drake* (New York: Burt Franklin
edition, 1963). Finally, there are two depositions chronicling the voyage
given by John Drake, which were taken when he was a prisoner of the
Spanish colonial administration. These are transcribed by Zelia Nuttall in
*New Light on Drake: A Collection of Documents Relating to His Voyage of
Circumnavigation, 1577–1580* (London: Hakluyt Society, 1914).

7. Manuel P. Servín, "Symbolic Acts of Sovereignty in Spanish California,"
   Southern California Quarterly 45, no. 2 (June 1963): 109–21. Edward
   Wright's *Certain Errors* (London: Joseph Moxon, 1657), calls for chart-
   ing land claims to no more than a day's sail from your sightings. See also
   Henry R. Wagner, "Creation of Rights of Sovereignty through Symbolic
   Acts," *Pacific Historical Review* 7, no. 4 (1938): 297–326.

8. "Second Narrative of the Voyage of Circumnavigation Given by John
   Drake, the Voyage of Captain Francis," in Nuttall, *New Light on Drake*, 55.
   This was a ploy.

9. "Second Narrative of John Drake," in Nuttall, *New Light on Drake*, 56.

10. Patrick O'Brien, *The Drake Manuscript in the Pierpont Morgan Library*,
    Histoire Naturelle des Indes (London: Andre Deutsch Limited, 1996), xiii.

11. "Second Narrative of John Drake," in Nuttall, *New Light on Drake*, 55.

12. See Nuño da Silva's description of Drake's journal in "Deposition by
    Nuño da Silva as to How He Was Made Prisoner by English Pirates on

His Voyage from Oporto to Brazil," in Nuttall, *New Light on Drake*, 303. The earliest account of the voyage was published by Charles de l'Écluse (pen name Carolus Clusius): *Aliqvot Notae in Garciae Aromatum Historiam* [...] (Antwerp: Christopher Plantin, 1582). Drake, Captain Winter, and Eliot met with de l'Écluse shortly after the return, and gave him specimens of the plants and seeds collected on the voyage. These included Winter's bark from Tierra Del Fuego, coconuts from the South Sea, Mexican jasmine, cocoa, and a root from Peru that de l'Écluse named in honor of Drake—the Peruvian Dragon Root, *Drakena Radix*.

13. Bruce Wathen, *Sir Francis Drake: The Construction of a Hero* (Cambridge, UK, and Rochester, NY: D.S. Brewer, 2009), 12.

14. Lancelot Voisin de la Popelinière, *Les trios mondes* (Paris: 1582), translated by Mary Fuller in "Writing the Long-Distance Voyage: Hakluyt's Circumnavigators," *Huntington Library Quarterly* 70, no. 1 (March 2007): 40.

15. Gerard Mercator to Abraham Ortelius, December 12, 1580, from Latin. Digital copy in the Kraus Collection, Library of Congress.

16. Cyndia Susan Clegg, ed., *The Peaceable and Prosperous Regiment of Blessed Queene Elisabeth: A Facsimile from Holinshed's Chronicles (1587)* (San Marino, CA: Huntington Library, 2005), 5. Large sections of the book about Scotland and the Low Countries were also cancelled or revised.

17. Ibid., 370.

18. See Matthew A. Russell, "Encounters at *Tamál-Húye*: An Archaeology of Intercultural Engagement in Sixteenth-Century Northern California" (PhD diss., University of California, Berkeley, 2011), 265. Inexplicably these sherds are still touted by Drakes Bay enthusiasts as authentic artifacts from porcelain wares that were in Drake's cargo.

19. At the time Drake sailed it was thought that a narrow passage existed, and that the west coast of North America was close sailing distance to Asia. See David Beers Quinn, *The Voyages and Colonizing Enterprises of Sir Humphrey Gilbert*, vol. 1 (London: Hakluyt Society, 1940).

20. In 1929, E. G. R. Taylor found the plan of the voyage revealing that it was backed by most of the members of the Privy Council and the director of the navy. This is the Cotton MSS., Otho, E VIII, published by Taylor in "The Missing Draft Project of Drake's Voyage of 1577–80," *The Geographical Journal* 75, no. 1 (1930): 46–47.

21. Ibid.

22. Servín, "Symbolic Acts of Sovereignty in Spanish California," 114.

23. Warren L. Hanna, *Lost Harbor: The Controversy over Drake's California Anchorage* (Berkeley: University of California Press, 1979), 4.

24. Oscar Spate, *The Spanish Lake* (Canberra: Australian National University E Press 2004), 256.

25. Paul Dean, "A Writer Rocks the Historical Boat, Sir Francis Drake Controversy Divides State Historians," *Los Angeles Times*, August 24, 1983.
26. Adam Max Cohen, "Englishing the Globe: Molyneux's Globes and Shakespeare's Theatrical Career," *Sixteenth Century Journal* 37, no. 4 (Winter 2006): 963–64.
27. Wathen, *Sir Francis Drake*, 29.

Chapter 2: The Historiography of the Vexed Question

1. Hakluyt, "The Famous Voyage," in *Principall Navigations*.
2. Kelsey, *Sir Francis Drake*, 183–84. Some of the late Ming period Chinese porcelain wares found in archaeological contexts at Drakes Bay have been conjectured to be artifacts from the porcelain vessels in the cargo of a merchant ship Drake and his men had captured off the coast of Guatemala. The theory is that Drake gave these porcelain vessels to the Natives and when the vessels broke the pieces were discarded in midden sites at Drakes Bay. Edward Von der Porten, "The Drake Puzzle Solved," *Pacific Discovery* 37, no. 3 (July–Sept. 1984). See also Clarence F. Shangraw and Edward P. Von der Porten, "The Drake and Cermeño Expeditions' Chinese Porcelains at Drakes Bay, California, 1579 and 1595" (unpublished manuscript, Santa Rosa Junior College and Drake Navigators Guild, 1981).
3. Ten years after Kelsey's book came out, archaeologists working for the National Park Service also determined these sherds are not from Drake's cargo. There were only sixteen years between voyages. In 1981 the proponents of Drakes Bay or Drakes Cove within Drakes Estero wrote a report that contended it was possible to distinguish the porcelains in Drake's cargo from the porcelains in Cermeño's shipwrecked cargo based on stylistic differences between waterworn and non-waterworn specimens. In October 2010, Chinese porcelain experts Harvey Steele and Jessica Lally also dismissed that whole premise as false during the Oregon Coast Ceramics Roundtable, in Manzanita, Oregon. See the edited and final version of the Drakes Bay National Landmark Nomination where all the references to the porcelains as evidence of Drake's sojourn were redacted. *Drakes Bay Historic and Archeological District Landmark Nomination, 2010.* See also Suzanne Stewart and Adrian Praetzellis, *Archaeological Research Issues for the Point Reyes National Seashore—Golden Gate National Recreations Area* (San Francisco: National Park Service, Golden Gate National Recreation Area, 2010).
4. Henry R. Wagner, "The Voyage to California of Sebastian Rodriguez Cermeño in 1595," *California Historical Society Quarterly* 3, no. 1, (1924).
5. Ibid., 11.
6. Ibid., 11.

7. Richard Hakluyt, "Extracts from Hakluyt's Voyages: The Course," in Vaux, *The World Encompassed*, Appendix V, 221.

8. Wagner, "The Voyage to California," 11.

9. Ibid., 12n9.

10. Ibid., 14.

11. Ibid., 13.

12. Ibid.

13. Ibid., 6.

14. Vaux, *The World Encompassed*, 79.

15. George Vancouver, *A Voyage of Discovery to the North Pacific Ocean, and Round the World*, 3 vols. (London: G. G. and J. Robinson, 1798), 430.

16. Ibid., 429.

17. J. D. B. Stillman, "Did Drake Discover San Francisco Bay?," *Out West Magazine* 1, no. 4 (1868): 333.

18. Vaux, *The World Encompassed*.

19. Stillman, "Did Drake Discover San Francisco Bay," 332–37.

20. George Davidson, *Voyages of Discovery and Exploration on the Northwest Coast of America from 1539 to 1603* (Washington D.C.: U.S. Coast and Geodetic Survey, 1887). See also George Davidson, *Identification of Francis Drake's Anchorage on the Coast of California in the Year 1579*, California Historical Society Papers, vol. 1, pt. 3 (San Francisco: Bacon, 1890).

21. Julian Stafford Corbett, *Drake and the Tudor Navy: With a History of the Rise of England as a Maritime Power*, 2 vols. (1899; repr., London: Longmans, Green, 1912), 1:289. Corbett wrote:

> He [Davidson] ground his opinion, as he kindly informs me, on the fact that Drake on June 3 reached 42°, and that 'when he struck the cold nor'wester he could not have beaten up against it to 48° in two days from June 3 to 5.' But here there seems a misapprehension. The cold did not come on till the 'night following' their reaching 42°, and was not unendurable till they had sailed two degrees higher (Authorized Narrative). Drake after this encouraged them to proceed and it was not till the 5th that the wind came N.W. and they gave it up. As they had sailed on an average thirty leagues a day since leaving Guatulco (i.e. 1,400 leagues from April 16 to June 3), there is no reason why they should not sail with a fair wind six degrees, i.e. 120 leagues, from June 3 to 5 inclusive.

22. Davidson, *Identification of Francis Drake's Anchorage*, 8.

23. Herbert Howe Bancroft, *History of California* 7 vols. (San Francisco: A. L. Bancroft & Company, 1884), 1:92.

24. George Davidson, "Francis Drake on the Northwest Coast of America in the Year 1579: The Golden Hind Did Not Anchor in the Bay of San Francisco," *Geographical Society of the Pacific Transactions and Proceedings* 5, no. 2 (1908): 2.

25. Lady Elliott-Drake, *The Family and Heirs of Sir Francis Drake*, 2 vols. (London: Smith, Elder, 1911).

26. The follow-up voyage began in 1582. The initial plan called for Francis Drake to lead the expedition, but the Queen decided Drake needed to be in England, and navigator Edward Fenton was appointed. The fleet was composed of four ships; John Drake captained the smallest ship *Francis*, forty tons. The fleet only got as far as Brazil, when Fenton changed the plan and compromised the venture. Disgusted with Fenton, young Drake sailed on, but wrecked in the estuary of the River Plate. He escaped capture for a while, but eventually was taken into custody by Spanish authorities and interviewed twice and perhaps three times under oath. A secretary of the Inquisition recorded two of his narratives. His accounts of the voyage with his cousin Francis are detailed and when checked with other sources appear to be generally accurate, though evasive on some points to do with his cousin. Zelia Nuttall included his narratives in her book *New Light on Drake*. In it, his first narrative takes up eleven pages, and his second takes up twenty-one. Both depositions describe details of the landing and describe the height of their latitude as 48 degrees.

27. John Drake, "Second Declaration of John Drake," transcribed in Nuttall, *New Light on Drake*, 50. This was recorded in 1587 at Lima.

28. Davidson, "Francis Drake on the Northwest Coast," 18.

29. Corbett, *Drake and the Tudor Navy*, 1:288n2.

30. John Drake, "First Declaration of John Drake," transcribed in Nuttall, *New Light on Drake*, 31. Samuel Bawlf suggests these were Vancouver Island and the San Juan Islands as he related in *Sir Francis Drake's Secret Voyage to the Northwest Coast of America, AD 1579* (British Columbia: Sir Francis Drake Publications, 2001), 46–47.

31. John Davis, *The Worldes Hydrographical Discription* (London: Thomas Dawson, 1595), 59. At the time Davis wrote, the distance between Newfoundland and the west coast of America was believed to be shorter than it actually is. On John Farrera's "Map of Virginia," published in 1651, Drake's landing was depicted at ten days' march to the west, and is illustrated in "The Cartography of Drake's Voyage," in Thrower, *Sir Francis Drake and the Famous Voyage*, 158. The width of North America was unknown, so the "back side of New foundland" was an apt description.

32. Davidson, "Francis Drake on the Northwest Coast," 17.

33. Ibid.; Vaux, *The World Encompassed*, 117.

34. Davidson, *Identification of Francis Drake's Anchorage*, 9. Davidson conceded that Drake had proposed it, but said he believed "the declaration to make such a wild attempt to seek for a northwest passage was as misleading as his shipping the men of this expedition for service at Alexandria." When the fleet left Plymouth in 1577, most of the crew thought they were heading to Alexandria, which was a subterfuge to confuse the Spaniards.
35. Arthur Davies, "The Golden Hind and the Tello on the Coasts of California," *The Geographical Journal* 148, no. 2 (1982): 220.
36. Davidson, *Identification of Francis Drake's Anchorage*, 8.
37. "All in a Hurry, Getting Things in Shape for Monday: Great Cross Dedication," *San Francisco Call*, December 29, 1893.

Chapter 3: Mind the Gap

1. Hakluyt, "The Famous Voyage," in *The Principall Navigations*.
2. BL Harley MS 280, folios 81–90. W. S. W. Vaux divided the manuscript into two sections and transcribed them in appendices for his important collection of contemporary accounts of the circumnavigation published by the Hakluyt Society in 1854. See Vaux, *The World Encompassed*.
3. A copy of the manuscript was reviewed by Heather Wolfe of the Folger Shakespeare Library. She found this small note and transcribed it for the present author.
4. Cyril Ernest Wright, *Fontes Harleiani: A Study of the Sources of the Harleian Collections of Manuscripts Preserved in the Department of Manuscripts in the British Museum* (London: The Trustees of the British Museum, 1972). Perhaps it was Starkey's handwriting at the bottom of the first page of the *Memoranda* querying if this manuscript was from Hakluyt.
5. J. Sears McGee, email message to author, March 7, 2017.
6. *Memoranda*, BL Harley 280, folio 82r.
7. Hakluyt, *Principall Navigations*, 1st ed. (it is the seventh unnumbered page of "The Famous Voyage" chapter).
8. These are, "First Account of the Voyage of Circumnavigation Given by John Drake," and "Second Narrative of the Voyage of Circumnavigation Given by John Drake." John's account of the voyage given in 1587 says that they sailed up to 44-degrees, anchored and refitted in 48-degrees," transcribed in Nuttall, *New Light on Drake*.
9. "Short Abstract of the Present Voyage" transcribed in Vaux, *The World Encompassed*, 178.
10. Helen Wallis, "The Cartography of Drake's Voyage," in Thrower, *Sir Francis Drake and the Famous Voyage*, 141.
11. Peter C. Mancall, *Hakluyt's Promise: An Elizabethan's Obsession for an English America* (New Haven: Yale University Press, 2007), 98.

12. E. G. R. Taylor, *Late Tudor and Early Stuart Geography 1583–1650* (London: Methuen, 1934), 14. See also Mancall, *Hakluyt's Promise*, 187–92.

13. Mancall, *Hakluyt's Promise*, 94–98.

14. Mary C. Fuller, "Writing the Long-Distance Voyage: Hakluyt's Circumnavigators," *Huntington Library Quarterly* 70, no. 1 (March 2007): 38.

15. Ibid., 39.

16. Hakluyt, *Principall Navigations*, epistle, 2.

17. Travers Twiss, *The Oregon Question Examined* (London: Longman, Brown, Green, 1846), 27. Twiss was tasked to weigh in on the Oregon territory boundary question and England's historical claim.

18. Taylor, *Late Tudor and Early Stuart Geography*, 19. Marginal notes are exactly that, small clarifications or summary notes in the margin of the page, a common medieval practice.

19. Fuller, "Writing the Long-Distance Voyage," 59.

20. David B. Quinn, ed., *The Hakluyt Handbook*, 2 vols. (London: Hakluyt Society, 1974), 227.

21. Corbett, *Drake and the Tudor Navy*, 1:407.

22. Vaux, *The World Encompassed*, xiv.

23. BL Harley MS 280, folio 82r, in "Memoranda, Apparently Relating to this Voyage," in Vaux, *The World Encompassed*, 176.

24. Ibid.

25. BL Harley MS 280, folio 82r.

26. M. Oppenheim, ed., *The Naval Tracts of Sir William Monson*, (London: Navy Records Society, 1913), 271.

27. Twiss, *The Oregon Question Examined*, 41.

28. E. G. R. Taylor, "Francis Drake and the Pacific: Two Fragments," *Pacific Historical Review*, 1, no. 3 (1932): 363.

29. Kenneth L. Holmes, "Francis Drake's Course in the North Pacific, 1579," *The Geographical Bulletin*, 17 (1979): 14. This article summarizes the authorities on navigation in the north Pacific.

30. Manuel P. Servín, "Symbolic Acts of Sovereignty in Spanish California," *Southern California Quarterly* 45, no.2 (June 1963): 109.

31. Harley 280, folio 87v. See "The Short Abstract of the Present Voyage," in Vaux, *The World Encompassed*, 184.

32. Hakluyt, "The Course," in Vaux, Appendix V, "Extracts from Hakluyt's Voyages," 219–26. The original Hakluyt publication of this account can be found in vol. 3, 440–42, in the second edition of *Principall Navigations*. Like "The Famous Voyage" chapter, the name of the author of "The Course" is omitted, and the account is written in the first person. This account has been attributed to Francis Pretty, one of Drake's officers, but this seems unlikely.

33. Quinn, "Early Accounts of the Famous Voyage," in Thrower, *Sir Francis Drake and the Famous Voyage*, 33–48.

34. Francis Drake to Queen Elizabeth, January 1, 1593, quoted in David B. Quinn, *Explorers and Colonies: America, 1500–1625* (London: Hambledon Press, 1990), 184.

35. Eliott-Drake, *The Family and Heirs of Sir Francis Drake*, 1:226.

Chapter 4: The Beginnings

1. H. H. Drake, "Drake—the Arms of His Surname and Family," in *Report and Transactions of the Devonshire Association for the Advancement of Science, Literature, and Art* 15 (Plymouth: W. Brendon & Sons, 1883): 487–89.

2. Wathen, *Sir Francis Drake*, 115.

3. Eliott-Drake, *The Family and Heirs*, 22.

4. Kelsey, *Sir Francis Drake: The Queen's Pirate*, 6.

5. Michael Peter Goelet, "The Careening and Bottom Maintenance of Wooden Sailing Vessels," (master's thesis, Texas A&M University, 1986).

6. For a general discussion of this policy see Susan Ronald, *The Pirate Queen: Queen Elizabeth I, Her Pirate Adventurers, and the Dawn of Empire* (New York: HarperCollins 2007).

7. Ronald, *The Pirate Queen*, 388n9.

8. Roze Hentschell, *The Culture of Cloth in Early Modern England: Textual Constructions of a National Identity*, (London: Routledge, 2016), 1–8.

9. Richard Hakluyt, "Notes in Writing Besides More Privie by Mouth that were given by a Gentleman, Anno 1580…, in *Diverse Voyages Touching the Discovery of America and the Islands Adjacent*, ed. John Winter Jones (1582; repr., London: Hakluyt Society, 1850), 119.

10. Kelsey, *Sir Francis Drake*, 36.

11. Ibid., 37–39.

12. Miranda Kaufmann, *Black Tudors: The Untold Story*, (London: Oneworld, 2017), 58. These Africans were transported from West Africa to the Spanish colonies, and not to England. In England at the time, slavery did not exist as an institution, and the Black men and women who lived there were considered freemen with the rights of anyone else.

13. Corbett, *Drake and the Tudor Navy*, 1:101–19. Corbett devotes a chapter to this action.

14. Ibid., 114–15.

15. Kelsey, *Sir Francis Drake*, 37–39.

16. John Fiske, "The Elizabethan Sea Kings," *The Atlantic Monthly* 76 (1895): 98–99.

17. Ibid., 99.

18. Kelsey, *Sir Francis Drake*, 42–43.

19. Ibid., 37–39.

20. San Juan de Ulúa was a fort in the seaport of Vera Cruz, Mexico. For description of the incident, see Kelsey, *Sir Francis Drake*, 36–39.

21. O'Brien, *The Drake Manuscript in the Pierpont Morgan Library*, xi.

22. Corbett, *Drake and the Tudor Navy*, 1:157.

23. William Camden, *Annales Or, The History of the Most Renowned and Victorious Princesse Elizabeth, Late Queen of England* [...], 4 vols. (London: Benjamin Fisher, 1635), 2:419–20.

24. Philip Nichols, *Sir Francis Drake Revived* (London: Nicholas Bourne, 1626), 7.

25. For a full discussion of Diego see Kaufmann, *Black Tudors*, 56–89.

26. Ibid., 60. Diego sailed back to England with Drake, a free man because "England has too pure an Air for Slaves to breath in" (15–16). Blacks had lived in England since Roman times.

27. Corbett, *Drake and the Tudor Navy*, 1:178–79.

28. John Barrow, *The Life, Voyages, and Exploits of Admiral Sir Francis Drake* (London: Jon Murray, 1843), 65. Citations are from the Forgotten Books edition.

29. Ronald, *The Pirate Queen*, 175.

30. Ann Hoffmann, *Lives of the Tudor Age, 1485–1603* (New York: Harper & Row, 1977), 348.

Chapter 5: Afar the Seas Were Blue and White

1. Angus Haldane, "A Portrait of Drake? A Belief in the Possible," *The British Art Journal* 14 no. 3 (2013/2014): 42. In 2014 a painting of an unknown gentleman caught the attention of Angus Haldane, an art historian who found several clues that suggest that this painting was a portrait of Drake painted just before his circumnavigation in 1576–1577, making it one of the earliest images in his iconography. The portrait resembles later portraits of Drake, showing his light-brown curled hair and trimmed beard, light colored eyes, high eyebrows, and a mole or wart on his nose that is depicted in other portraits. The image is striking, and the iconography demonstrates that the figure was a man of some standing, but with no coat of arms.

2. Ronald, *The Pirate Queen*, 23.

3. Ibid., 24.

4. E. G. R. Taylor, "Master John Dee, Drake and the Straits of Anian," *Mariner's Mirror* 15, no. 2 (1929): 125–30.

5. Quoted in Ibid., 129.

6. Taylor, "The Missing Draft Project," 46–47. There are plates showing two pages of the plan in facsimile. The exact origin of the scrap is unknown, but it was in the manuscript collection of Richard Cotton (1571–1631). His collection included manuscripts written by John Dee and Lord Burghley, among others at court.

7. E. G. R. Taylor, "More Light on Drake," *Mariner's Mirror* 16, no. 2 (1930): 134.

8. John Winter, "A declaration made by Captain John Winter," transcribed in Nuttall, *New Light on Drake*, 386. The original document is a manuscript in the Public Record Office, London, SP Dom. 12/139, 24.

9. Taylor, "Francis Drake and the Pacific," 361.

10. Ibid., 361.

11. "Report from Gaspar de Vargas, Chief Alcalde of Guatulco, to the Vicery Martin Eriquez," transcribed in Nuttall, *New Light on Drake*, 238.

12. Hoffmann, *Lives of the Tudor Age*, 223. The *Pelican* belonged to Sir Christopher Hatton, Vice Chamberlin to the Queen, who often acted as the Queen's spokesperson in the House of Commons. Hatton was one of the investors in the venture, and though there is a dispute about when the ship was renamed, the *Pelican* was renamed *Golden Hind* to commemorate his family crest, which bore the image of a hind (a female red deer).

13. Bray Dickenson, "Drake's Landing Place in California," *Daily Independent Journal* (San Rafael, California), October 2, 1954.

14. "Deposition of Giusepe de Parraces, Passenger, Taken Prisoner by Drake on March 20th 1579," transcribed in Nuttall, *New Light on Drake*, 186.

15. "Deposition of Nuño da Silva," transcribed in Nuttall, *New Light on Drake*, 318.

16. "Judicial Inquiry Made at Panama. Deposition of San Juan de Anton," transcribed in Nuttall, *New Light on Drake*, 173.

17. Kaufmann, *Black Tudors*, 56–90.

18. Clusius, *Aliqvot Notae in Garciae Aromatum Historiam*. This is the earliest published account that mentions the voyage.

19. John Cooke, "For Francis Drake," in Vaux, *The World Encompassed*, Appendix IV, 187.

20. "Letter from Don Francisco de Zarate to Don Martin Enriquez," transcribed in Nuttall, *New Light on Drake*, 207.

21. Drake and Fletcher, "The Voyage about the World," transcribed in Vaux, *The World Encompassed*, 13.

22. Spate, *The Spanish Lake*, 242.

23. Ibid.

24. Camden, *Annales*, 2:420.

25. Drake, quoted by John Cooke in BL Harleian MS 540, folio 93–110, transcribed by Vaux, *The World Encompassed*, 213.

26. John Mackenzie, editor Britishbattles.com 2002–2015. *The Spanish Armada*. http://www.britishbattles.com/the-spanish-war/the-spanish-armada.

27. Drake and Fletcher, "The Voyage about the World," transcribed in Vaux, *The World Encompassed*, 71.

28. Kelsey, *Sir Francis Drake*, 113–16. Kelsey points out that the renaming of the ship is not clearly supported by contemporary evidence, and it may have been an insertion by the editor.

29. Ibid., 71–78.

30. Ibid., 78–82.

31. Quoted in Taylor, "More Light on Drake," 135.

32. Drake and Fletcher, "The Voyage about the World," transcribed in Vaux, *The World Encompassed*, 86–87.

33. Francis Fletcher (attributed), from the Sloan MS, no. 61, British Library, transcribed in Vaux, *The World Encompassed*, 79.

34. "The Voyage of M. John Winter into the South sea by the Streight of Magellan," transcribed by Vaux, *The World Encompassed*, 281.

35. Ibid.

36. H. G. Rawlinson, *Narratives from Purchas His Pilgrimes* (Cambridge, University Press: 1931), 76–86.

37. John Sugden, *Sir Francis Drake* (London: Barrie & Jenkins: 1990), 117n2.

38. Drake and Fletcher, "The Voyage about the World," transcribed in Vaux, *The World Encompassed*, 92.

39. Richard Hawkins, *The Observations of Sir Richard Hawkins, Knight in His voyage into the South Sea in the Year 1593*, ed. C. R. Drinkwater Bethune (London: Hakluyt Society, 1847), 144.

40. Ibid., 98; and BL Harley MS 280, folio 83R, British Library.

41. John Drake, "Second Declaration of John Drake," translated in Nuttall, *New Light on Drake*, 44.

42. Hawkins, *The Observations of Sir Richard Hawkins*, 144.

43. Kaufmann, *Black Tudors*, 77. This marginal note is found in BL Harley MS 280, folio 83.

44. Kaufmann, *Black Tudors*, 78.

45. BL Harley 280, 83r.

46. Drake and Fletcher, "The Voyage about the World," transcribed in Vaux, *The World Encompassed*, 98.

47. Ibid. 98–99.

48. "Documents Pertaining to the Trial for Heresy of Nuno da Silva Portugese Pilot," transcribed in Nuttall, *New Light on Drake*, 301.

49. Drake and Fletcher, "The Voyage about the World," transcribed in Vaux, *The World Encompassed*, 96.

50. Ibid., 100–101.

51. Ibid., 102.

52. Ibid., 105.

53. Ibid., 110.

54. Hoffmann, *Lives of the Tudor Age*, 348.

55. "Relation of the Voyage of the English Corsair Given by the Pilot Nuno da Silva," transcribed in Nuttall, *New Light on Drake*, 265 (hereafter "Nuño da Silva's Second Relation").

56. Ibid., 264–66 (see also Kelsey, *Sir Francis Drake*, 151–52).

57. "Nuño da Silva's Second Relation," 265.

58. "The Declarations That Were Made By Captain John Oxenham and Other Englishmen," transcribed in Nuttall, *New Light on Drake*, 7–8.

59. Ibid., 10.

60. There are various theories on the nickname of the ship in question. See Nuttall, *New light on Drake*, 165; and Kelsey, *Sir Francis Drake: The Queens Pirate*, 158.

61. Elyse Bruce, "Spitfire," *Historically Speaking* (blog), https://idiomation .wordpress.com/tag/caca-plata/.

62. "Deposition of the Pilot Benito Diaz Bravo," transcribed in Nuttall, *New Light on Drake*, 146.

63. Ibid.

64. Corbett, *Drake and the Tudor Navy*, 1:274.

65. "Deposition of San Juan de Anton," transcribed in Nuttall, *New Light on Drake*, 165.

66. Drake and Fletcher, "The Voyage about the World," transcribed in Vaux, *The World Encompassed*, 111.

67. BL Harley MS 280, folio 83.

68. Hakluyt, *The Famous Voyage of Sir Francis Drake*, transcribed in Vaux, Appendix II, 242.

69. Ibid., 161.

70. "Deposition of Domingo de Lizarza," transcribed in Nuttall, *New Light on Drake*, 179.

71. "Testimony of San Juan de Anton," transcribed in Nuttall, *New Light on Drake*, 162.

72. "Deposition of Diego de Messa," transcribed in Nuttall, *New Light on Drake*, 190–91.

73. "Deposition of Cornieles Lambert," transcribed in Nuttall, *New Light on Drake*, 182.

74. Ibid., 182–83.

75. Ibid., 184.
76. "Testimony of Francisco de Zarate," transcribed in Nuttall, *New Light on Drake*, 202.
77. Ibid.
78. Nuttall, *New Light on Drake*, 199.
79. BL Harley 280, 86r–86v.
80. Nuttall, *New Light on Drake*, 197. If de Zarate had been a relative of the viceroy, then Drake might have considered using him in a prisoner swap for the Englishmen.
81. BL Harley 280, 86v.
82. Kaufmann, *Black Tudors*, 83.
83. "Testimony of Francisco de Zarate," transcribed in Nuttall, *New Light on Drake*, 206.
84. "Testimony of Juan Pascual," transcribed in Nuttall, *New Light on Drake*, 325: "Everyday before sitting down to eat at midday and before they supped, the said Francis Drake had a table brought out, without a cloth or table cover. He took out a very large book and knelt down, bareheaded, and read from the said book in his English language. All the other Englishmen who he brought with him were also seated without their hats, and made responses."
85. Book of Common Prayer, Edward VI, 1552 edition. "The Table and Calendar Expressing the Order of the Psalms and Lessons to Bee Said at the Morning and Evening Prayer." See April 6.
86. "Declaration of John Oxenham," transcribed in Nuttall, *New Light on Drake*, 10.
87. Nuttall, *New Light on Drake*, 3. See Hoffman, *Lives of the Tudor Age*, 348.
88. Barrow, *The Life, Voyages and Exploits of Admiral Sir Francis Drake*, 84.
89. "Short Abstract of the Present Voyage," transcribed in Vaux, *The World Encompassed*, 183.
90. "Deposition of the Francisco Gomez Rengifo, Factor at Guatulco," transcribed in Nuttall, *New Light on Drake*, 353.
91. Nuttall, *New Light on Drake*, 330.
92. "Short Abstract of the Present Voyage," transcribed in Vaux, *The World Encompassed*, 183.
93. "Letter from Licentiate Valverde to King Philip II," transcribed in Nuttall, *New Light on Drake*, 105.
94. "Deposition of Cornieles Lambert," transcribed in Nuttall, *New Light on Drake*, 182.
95. "Memoranda, Apparently Relating to this Voyage," in Vaux, *The World Encompassed*, 175–76.

96. Nuttall, *New Light on Drake*, 396.

97. "Letter from Licentiate Valverde to King Philip II," transcribed in Nuttall, *New Light on Drake*, 104.

98. Ibid., 105.

99. Hakluyt, "Extracts from Hakluyt's Voyages: The Course," transcribed in Vaux, *The World Encompassed*, Appendix V, 221.

100. Spate, *The Spanish Lake*, 254.

101. Holmes, "Francis Drake's Course," 14. This article summarizes the authorities on navigation in the north Pacific.

102. Commander H. L. Jenkins of the British Royal Navy, quoted in Ibid., 19.

103. Hakluyt, "Extracts from Hakluyt's Voyages: The Course," transcribed by Vaux, *The World Encompassed*, Appendix V, 219–26.

104. Drake and Fletcher, "The Voyage bout the World," transcribed in Vaux, *The World Encompassed*, 118.

105. Camden, *Annales*, 2:365.

106. Henry Wagner, *Sir Francis Drake's Voyage around the World: Its Aims and Achievements* (San Francisco: John Howell, 1926), 488n59.

107. Drake and Fletcher, "The Voyage about the World," transcribed in Vaux, *The World Encompassed*, 115.

108. The Golden Hind Limited, *The Golden Hind* (San Francisco: The Golden Hind Limited Publication 1, 1986). These estimates of the *Golden Hind* may be the most accurate based on research conducted by Loring Christian Norgaard, naval architect for the *Golden Hind II*, a replica that repeated the circumnavigation in 1980. The sources regarding the tonnage of the *Golden Hind* vary. See Kelsey's discussion of the ship in *Sir Francis Drake: The Queen's Pirate*, 84.

109. Goelet, "The Careening and Bottom Maintenance of Wooden Sailing Vessels," 23.

110. "Deposition of Cornieles Lambert," transcribed in Nuttall, *New Light on Drake*, 182.

111. Drake and Fletcher, "The Voyage about the World," transcribed in Vaux, *The World Encompassed*, 120.

112. Ibid., 149.

113. Kaufmann, *Black Tudors*, 63.

114. "Letter from the Licentiate Valverde to King Philip II," transcribed in Nuttall, *New Light on Drake*, 101.

115. "First Declaration of John Drake," transcribed in Nuttall, *New Light on Drake*, 33; see also Drake and Fletcher, "The Voyage about the World," transcribed in Vaux, *The World Encompassed*, 154.

116. Bawlf, *Sir Francis Drake's Secret Voyage*, 123–24.

117. "First Declaration of John Drake," transcribed in Nuttall, *New Light on Drake*, 32.
118. "Second Declaration of John Drake," transcribed in Nuttall, *New Light on Drake*, 51.
119. Ibid., 51n1.
120. Drake and Fletcher, "The Voyage bout the World," transcribed in Vaux, *The World Encompassed*, 134.
121. Ibid.
122. "Second Declaration of John Drake," transcribed in Nuttall, *New Light on Drake*, 53.
123. Kaufmann, *Black Tudors*, 82.
124. Ibid., 86.
125. Ibid., 87.
126. Ibid., 89.
127. Drake and Fletcher, "The Voyage about the World," transcribed in Vaux, *The World Encompassed*, 149.
128. Ibid.
129. Ibid.; and W. H. K. Wright, *The Western Antiquary*, vol. 4 (Plymouth: W. H. Luke, 1885), 135.
130. Drake and Fletcher, "The Voyage about the World," transcribed in Vaux, *The World Encompassed*, 162.
131. "State papers, Domestic, Elizabeth," transcribed in Nuttall, *New Light on Drake*, 430.
132. Nuttall, *New Light on Drake*, xxxviii.

Chapter 6: Either Here or There

1. Helen Wallis, "The Cartography of Drake's Voyage" in Thrower, *Sir Francis Drake and the Famous Voyage*, 156.
2. Perhaps the closest copy of the Whitehall map is the Drake Mellon Map.
3. Helen Wallis, *The Voyage of Sir Francis Drake Mapped in Silver and Gold* (Berkeley: Friends of the Bancroft Library, University of California, 1979). See also Wallis, "The Cartography of Drake's Voyage," 121–63.
4. Wallis, "The *Cartography* Drake's Voyage," 145.
5. J. G. Kohl, *A Descriptive Catalogue of Those Maps, Charts and Surveys Relating to America, Which Are Mentioned in Vol. III of Hakluyt's Great Work* (Washington: Henry Polkinhorn, 1857), 84.
6. For example, see *The Drake Manuscript in the Pierpont Morgan Library, Histoire Naturelle des Indes* (London: Andre Deutsch Limited, 1996), xi.
7. Baptista Boazion, *Map and Views Illustrating Sir Francis Drake's West*

Indian Voyage 1585–6 (London: 1589), Jay I. Kislak Collection, Library of Congress Map collections.

8. "Sworn Deposition III of the Portuguese Pilot Nuño Da Silva," translated in Nuttall, *New Light on Drake*, 303.

9. "Testimony of Francisco de Zarate," translated in Nuttall, *New Light on Drake*, 207–8.

10. All the painted insets may be from Drake's records of the voyage. The picture in the lower left corner of the broadside shows the *Golden Hind* being towed by four canopied boats belonging to the King of the Moluccas. Five small islands, and a large landmass are shown in the background. These islands are drawn well enough for mariners to recognize Ternate, Tidore, Mare, Moti, and Makian. In the lower right corner is a drawing of the *Golden Hind* in peril when she grounded on a reef in the Celebes. The drawing shows they were trying to kedge off with two anchors, and that they had thrown out some barrels to lighten the ship. The picture in the upper right has less detail, and may be the *Golden Hind* leaving the port of Java.

11. Wallis, "The Cartography of Drake's Voyage," 146.

12. Davidson, *Identification of Sir Francis Drake's Anchorage*, 39.

13. Wallis, "The Cartography of Drake's Voyage," 146.

14. Robert Dudley Jr., manuscript charts of *Arcano del mare*, ca. 1636, vol. 2 (Africa and America) BSB MSS 139, image 238, Bavarian State Library, Munich. The charts are online from the Bavarian State Library: http://daten.digitale-sammlungen.de/~db/0008/bsb00084103/images/index.html?seite=238&fip=193.174.98.30.

15. Justin Winsor, *Narrative and Critical History of America* (Boston: Houghton Mifflin, 1884), 77.

16. Nuttall postulated Drake careened his ship at Neah Bay, Washington, just inside Cape Flattery. Against that conjecture, Neah Bay was too rocky and not suitable for a careenage.

17. Bob Ward, *Lost Harbour Found! Where Sir Francis Drake Really Landed on the West Coast of America, and How He Also Discovered Canada* (unpublished manuscript, July 1981). See also Bob Ward, "A Degree or Six of Latitude in Drake's True Movements" (paper presented at the Northwest Archaeology Conference, Newport, Oregon, April 2009). Ward sounded Whale Cove and provided the depths on an aerial photograph of the cove, though he did not note if the soundings were from high or low tide. Sam Bawlf, a former provincial minister in British Columbia, supported the Whale Cove landing theory. Bawlf wrote *The Secret Voyage of Francis Drake*, wherein he agreed with, and expounded upon Ward's theory that

Drake landed at Whale Cove. Bawlf differed on a number of points, the most striking of which was his assertion that several important maps prove that Drake and his crew had sailed as far north as the Haida Gwaii archipelago, off the north coast of British Columbia.

18. Stan Allyn, *History of Whale Cove Inn* (Depoe Bay: Whale Cove Inn Booklet, n.d.).

19. Stan Allyn, *Top Deck Twenty! Best West Coast Sea Stories!* (Portland: Binford & Mort, 1989), 74–75.

20. Drake and Fletcher, "The Voyage about the World," transcribed in Vaux, *The World Encompassed*, 132.

21. Ronald, *The Pirate Queen*, 359. Dudley was the "base born" son of Her Majesty's great friend and favorite, the Earl of Leicester (Robert Dudley, Senior). Dudley was likely acquainted with Francis Drake, and his wife was the sister of Thomas Cavendish, the English circumnavigator who had followed in Drake's wake. He was the administrator of Cavindish's estate, and may have obtained his data on the west coast of America from either Drake himself, or Cavindish.

22. Dudley, manuscript charts of *Arcano del mare*, image 233. Dudley drew the fair bay in two additional pencil sketches, and these sketches repeat the shape of the bay illustrated in his main sketch of the coast.

23. Winsor, *Narrative and Critical History*, 77.

24. Dudley, *Arcano del Mare*, detail of image 238. The draft of the *Golden Hind* was about fourteen feet.

25. Dudley, *Arcano del Mare*, detail of image 239.

26. Ibid.

27. Robert Dudley, "Carta particolare dello stretto di Jezo fra l'America e l'Isola Jezo, XXXIII," *Dell'Arcano del mare*, (Florence: Francesco Onofri, 1647). Some of the geographic details seen in the manuscript charts are not included in the printed version (or they are in a different position). The point of land, the creek, and the cape are all depicted.

28. Juan Rodríguez Cabrillo may have ascended as far as 42° off the Oregon coast in 1542, and Martín de Aguilar ascended to perhaps 43° north in 1603. Harry Kelsey, *The First Circumnavigators: Unsung Heroes of the Age of Discovery* (New Haven: Yale University Press, 2016), 62.

29. Dudley, *Arcano del mare*, image 238; John Florio, *Queen Anna's New World of Words, Or Dictionaire of the Italian and English tongues* (London: Melch Bradwood, 1611), 613. Florio defines Zania as follows: "A kind of tree in America whereof they make their canoes or boats of one piece, and call that so by the name of the tree." In the Venetian dialect the (x) often represents the voiced sibilant (z) because the (x) was not part of the standard Italian alphabet.

30. These studies are: Melanie M. Diedrich, *Preliminary Site Stability Report: Whale Cove, Oregon* (Portland: Drake Anchorage Research Collaboration, 2010); and George R. Priest, Ingmar Saul, and Julie Diebenow, *Landslide and Erosion Hazards of the Depoe Bay Area, Lincoln County, Oregon* (Portland: Oregon State Department of Geology and Mineral Industries, 1994). The protection of the bay is due to the sea cliffs on the open coast, which are composed of two hard volcanic rock formations with well-consolidated sandstones sandwiched in between.

31. This reef can be seen in aerial photographs of the area, and is depicted on *Yaquina Head to Columbia River, Map 18520*, National Oceanic and Atmospheric Administration, National Ocean Survey (Washington D.C.: U.S. Department of Commerce, 1975).

Chapter 7: The Great Discoveries

1. Ross Parmenter, *Zelia Nuttall and the Recovery of Mexico's Past* (unpublished manuscript, ca. 1999), 748, MSS 2009/115, The Bancroft Library, University of California, Berkeley (hereafter Bancroft Library).

2. Corbett, *Drake and the Tudor Navy*, 1:101–19. Corbett devotes a chapter to this action.

3. Nuttall, *New Light on Drake*, xiv.

4. "Depositon by Nuno da Silva," transcribed in Nuttall, *New Light on Drake*, 301.

5. Parmenter, *Zelia Nuttall*, 115.

6. Ibid., 143.

7. Peter Diderich, "Assessing Ross Parmenter's unpublished biography about Zelia Nuttall and Recovery of Mexico's Past," *Newsletter of the SAA's History of Archaeology Interest Group*, 3, no. 3 & 4.

8. These are as follows: Zelia Nuttall, "The Fundamental Principles of Old and New World Civilizations: A Comparative Research Based on a Study of the Ancient Mexican Religious, Sociological and Calendrical Systems," in *Archaeological and Ethnological Papers of the Peabody Museum*, vol. 2 (Cambridge, MA: Peabody Museum of American Archaeology and Ethnology, Harvard University, 1901). Zelia Nuttall, "The Island of Sacrificios," *American Anthropologist* 12, no. 2 (1910). Zelia Nuttall, *Facsimile of an Ancient Mexican Codex Belonging to Lord Zouche of Harynworth, England* (Cambridge, MA: Peabody Museum of American Archaeology and Ethnology, Harvard University, 1902). For a full bibliography of her works, see Parameter's biography *Zelia Nuttall*.

9. Parmenter, *Zelia Nuttall*, 53. Her honors and positions did not pay the bills. When she died her beloved Casa Alvarado was confiscated by the

Mexican government in lieu of taxes, and her library of several thousand books was sold off to pay her debts.

10. Ibid., 109.
11. Ibid., 326–49.
12. Ibid., 495.
13. Zelia Nuttall, Correspondence, box 114, Records of the Department of Anthropology, CU-23, Bancroft Library.
14. Nuttall, *New Light on Drake*, 272–73.
15. Ibid., xviii.
16. Parmenter, *Zelia Nuttall*, 958.
17. Ibid., 885.
18. Nuttall, *New Light on Drake*, 5–6.
19. Ibid., xxx.
20. Ibid., xviii.
21. Ross Parmenter, *Zelia Nuttall and the Recovery of Mexico's Past*, ed. Kornelia Kurbjuhn (2014). This is from several unnumbered pages of an edited but unfinished version of Parmenter's biography of Nuttall provided to this writer by editor Kornelia Kurbjuhn. The unedited version is at the Bancroft Library.
22. Nuttall, *New Light on Drake*, xxi.
23. Nuttall, *New Light on Drake*, xxvi–xxvii. This is also called the Nicola van Sype French map, which has the title *La herdike enterprinse faict par le Signeur Draeck D'Avoir cirquit toute la Terre.*
24. Zelia Nuttall, "Captions for an Exhibit," circa 1914–1916, MSS Z-R 14, v.1, Bancroft Library.
25. "New Drake Documents Discovered by Mrs. Zelia Nuttall," *The Geographical Journal* 40, no. 6 (1912): 621–24.
26. C. R. M., "Drake's Voyage Round the World," *The Geographical Journal* 44, no. 6 (1914): 584–86.
27. Nuttall, *New Light on Drake*, xxvi–xxvii.
28. Ibid.
29. Ibid., lvi, xx, xxxiv.

Chapter 8: The California Juggernaut

1. Richard S. Kimball and Barney Noel, *Native Sons of the Golden West* (Charleston, SC, Chicago, IL, Portsmouth, NH, San Francisco, CA: Arcadia Publishing, 2005), 10. These men were known for placing plaques commemorating events in California history. In their annual flag ceremony they flew all the flags that had flown over California soil, including Drake's St. George's Cross, which was the standard of Elizabethan England.

2. Jim Newton, *Justice for All: Earl Warren and the Nation He Made* (New York: Riverhead Books, 2006), 74.

3. Ibid., 103–10.

4. "Thirty-Seventh Grand Parlor, N.S.G.W.," *The Grizzly Bear*, April 1914, supplement, 6.

5. Michael Kazin, *Barons of Labor: The San Francisco Building Trades and Union Power in the Progressive Era* (Urbana: University of Illinois Press, 1989), 86.

6. Gerald Woods, "A Penchant for Probity, California Progressives and the Disreputable Pleasures," *California Progressivism Revisited*, ed. William Deverall and Tom Sitton (Berkeley: University of California Press 1994), 102.

7. Kimball and Noel, *Native Sons of the Golden West*, 104.

8. Kazin, *Barons of Labor*, 86.

9. Map, Baumgartner, O'Brien & Reynolds/Britton & Rey, cartographers, *Birdseye View of the City of San Francisco, Showing The Pacific Ocean, The Golden Gate, and San Francisco Bay, The Great Inland Harbor, Golden Gate Park, in the Foreground, One of the Proposed Sites for the Panama-Pacific World's Fair of 1915*. San Francisco: Robert Behlow, 1910.

10. "Winston Churchill Wishes Portola Success," *San Francisco Call*, August 26, 1913, 9.

11. Albert L. Hurtado, *Herbert Eugene Bolton: Historian of the American Borderlands* (Berkeley: University of California Press, 2012), 98.

12. Ibid.

13. Ibid., 179. Bolton was a member and a frequent speaker at their gatherings. The organization also provided grant monies for his projects. For example, in 1913 the Native Sons offered two annual fellowships that had a stipend amount of $1500. These fellowships covered the maintenance expenses of students who were sent to find and bring back important new documents from the archives in Mexico and Spain that related to the history of California and the greater Southwest.

14. Ibid., 187.

15. Ibid., 158.

16. Ibid., 133.

17. Ibid., 190.

18. Ibid., 116.

19. Parmenter, *Zelia Nuttall*, 978.

20. Ibid.

21. Nuttall had become acquainted with Bolton and his wife during their year in Mexico City in 1906 when Bolton was conducting research in the Archivo General and the National Museum.

22. Nuttall to Bolton, March 11, 1915. Herbert Eugene Bolton Papers, 1870–1953, BANC MSS C-B 840, incoming correspondence, box 65, Bancroft Library (hereafter cited as Bolton papers).

23. Ibid.

24. Ibid.

25. Parmenter, *Zelia Nuttall*, 982.

26. Hurtado, *Herbert Eugene Bolton*, 145.

27. Ibid.

28. Parmenter, *Zelia Nuttall*, 990.

29. Henry R. Wagner, *Bullion to Books: Fifty Years of Business and Pleasure* (Los Angeles: The Zamorano Club, 1942).

30. "Mrs. Zelia Nuttall, World Famous Archaeologist, is Again at the Shattuck," *The Berkeley Daily Gazette*, October 16, 1916.

31. Albert L. Hurtado, "False Accusations: Herbert Bolton, Jews, and the Loyalty Oath at Berkeley, 1920–1950," *California History* 89, no. 2 (2012): 38.

32. Parmenter, *Zelia Nuttall*. Nuttall's biographer Parmenter discusses several of Nuttall's relationships with women.

33. Hurtado, *Herbert Eugene Bolton*, 106.

34. Ibid.

35. Ibid.

36. Ibid., 158.

37. Waterman to Nuttall, July 8, 1915, Correspondence, Zelia Nuttall, box 114, Records of the Department of Anthropology, CU-23, Bancroft Library.

38. Parmenter, *Zelia Nuttall*, 984.

39. Ibid., 990–92.

40. Ibid., 985.

41. "Lecture to Be Given on Sir Francis Drake," *San Francisco Examiner*, April 27, 1915.

42. Ibid.

43. "Madame Zelia Nuttall Heard at Exposition," *The San Francisco Chronicle*, April 28, 1915.

44. David B. Quinn, "Early Accounts of the Famous Voyage," in Thrower, *Sir Francis Drake and the Famous Voyage*, 33–48.

45. Parmenter, *Zelia Nuttall*, 775.

46. Ibid., 993.

47. *The Grizzly Bear*, July 1915.

48. Henry Morse Stephens and Herbert Eugene Bolton, eds., *The Pacific Ocean in History: Papers and Addresses Presented at the Panama-Pacific Historical Congress, Held at San Francisco, Berkeley and Palo Alto, California* (New York: Macmillan, 1917), 90.

49. John Franklin Jameson, "The Meeting of the American Historical Association in California," *The American Historical Review* 21, no.1 (October 1915): 96–97. The review is as follows:

> In a paper on the Northern Limits of Drake's Voyage, Mrs. Zelia Nuttall, whose recent Hakluyt Society volume of new Drake documents will be remembered, established careful comparisons between noteworthy maps covering his Pacific voyage—The Hakluyt copy of Drake's great map, made for Henry of Navarre, the Dutch-French map of 1586 in the New York Public Library, a second Dutch map corrected by Drake himself, and the Hondius's map and text of 1596, which Hakluyt took over from the Dutch into the 1598 edition of his Voyages, the only narrative he gives which tells the story of New Albion.

50. Zelia Nuttall, "Captions for an Exhibit," ca. 1914–1916, BANC MSS Z-R 14 v.1, Bancroft Library.
51. Ibid.
52. Ibid.
53. Ibid.
54. Ibid. Peter Carder listed a Dutchmen, Artyur, who was in a pinnace that was separated from Drake's ship in foul weather.
55. Nuttall, *New Light on Drake*, lv. This map is also known as the *French Drake Map* and has the title: *La herdike enterprinse faict par le Signeur Draeck D'Avoir cirquit toute la Terre.* See a digital copy online at The Kraus Collection of Sir Francis Drake, United States Library of Congress.
56. Zelia Nuttall, "Captions for an exhibit."
57. Hakluyt as quoted in Anna Maria Crinò and Helen Wallis, "New Researches on the Molyneux Globes," *Der Globusfreund* 35–37 (1987): 13. This was one of the famous globes made by Emery Molyneux in 1592, and Nuttall wrote that it is still preserved at the Middle Temple, in the City of London. They were the first printed English globes, and they are very large, over six feet in circumference. Molyneux presented his globe to Queen Elizabeth in 1592 at Greenwich. The information contained on the globe was considered too sensitive to display openly, and shortly after it was presented to the Queen, it was covered with a taffeta curtain encompassing it down to the ground, where an ornament secured it.
58. There are three pair of Molyneux globes known to have been produced, and two are pairs featuring both terrestrial and celestial depictions. A revised edition was printed in 1603. See Helen Wallis, "A Newly-Discovered Molyneux Globe," *Imago Mundi* 9 (1952): 78.

59. Ken MacMillan, *Sovereignty and Possession in the English New Word: The Legal Foundations of Empire, 1576–1640* (Cambridge: Cambridge University Press 2006), 161.
60. Parmenter, *Zelia Nuttall*, 992.
61. Ralph Falkiner-Nuttall affirmed that the family still treasures the arrow point made by Ishi, email message to author.
62. Nuttall to Stephens, July 16, 1915, and August 22, 1915. H. Morse Stephens Papers, BANC MSS 71/14c, box 1, Correspondence, Zelia Nuttall, Bancroft Library.
63. There are several letters from Nuttall to Bolton during this year. See Nuttall to Bolton, September 16, 1915, and October 26, 1915, box 65, folder 35, Bolton Papers.
64. Ibid., September 16, 1915.
65. Ibid., October 26, 1915.
66. Hurtado, *Herbert Eugene Bolton*, 98–99.
67. Zelia Nuttall to Herbert Bolton, March 2, 1916, Zelia Nuttall Materials Relating to Sir Francis Drake, BANC MSS Z-R 14, Bancroft Library.
68. Ibid.
69. Ibid.
70. Corbett, *Drake and the Tudor Navy*, 1:408.
71. Nuttall to Bolton, December 6, 1916, Zelia Nuttall Materials Relating to Sir Francis Drake, Bancroft Library.
72. Ibid.
73. Hurtado, *Herbert Eugene Bolton*, 108.
74. Parmenter, *Zelia Nuttall*, 1004. Parmenter is referencing a letter from Nuttall to Carl Ewald Grunsky, president of the California Academy of Sciences on March 2, 1916.
75. "Sausalito School Children Take Part in Monster Three Day Fete," *Sausalito News*, May 27, 1916.
76. "Kent Invites Government," *Sausalito News*, March 25, 1916.
77. Parmenter, *Zelia Nuttall*, 1009.
78. Ibid., 1010.
79. Ibid.
80. "News of the State," *The Grizzly Bear*, April 1916, 10.
81. "Sausalito School Children Take Part in Monster Three Day Fete," *Sausalito News*, May 27, 1916.
82. Ibid.
83. Parmenter, *Zelia Nuttall*, 1011.
84. Ibid., 1022.
85. Albert M. Tozzer, "Zelia Nuttall, Obituary," *American Anthropologist* 35, no.3 (1933): 475–82.
86. Parmenter, *Zelia Nuttall*, 1021.

87. Ibid., 1022.

88. Ibid.

89. "Miss Zelia Nuttall, Archaeologist, is Now in Islands Seeking Verification of Statements Made in Document Found among Spanish Archives," *Honolulu Star Bulletin*, January 24, 1917.

90. Parmenter, *Zelia Nuttall*, 1025.

91. Zelia Nuttall to Herbert Bolton, July 26, 1917, Zelia Nuttall Materials Relating to Sir Francis Drake, Bancroft Library.

92. Ibid.

93. Parmenter, *Zelia Nuttall*, 1536.

94. Parmenter manuscript, edited by Kornelia Kurbjuhn, chap. 26, sec 7, vol. 2, unnumbered page.

Chapter 9: Henry Wagner Huffs and Puffs and the British Blow Him Down

1. Wagner, *Bullion to Books*, 253.

2. Ibid., 266.

3. Ibid.

4. Ibid.

5. Ibid., 266–69.

6. Ibid., 294.

7. Nuttall, *New Light on Drake*, plate II, facsimile of a map "Seen and corrected by Francis Drake," facing lvi. This is called the French Drake Map, engraved by Nicola van Sype.

8. Parmenter, *Zelia Nuttall*, 1209.

9. Wagner, *Bullion to Books*, 267.

10. Henry Wagner, "Meetings of the Society," *California Historical Society Quarterly* 3 (1924): 206.

11. California Historical Society, Directors' Meetings Minutes, April 16, 1923, North Baker Research Library, San Francisco.

12. Zelia Nuttall, "Two Remarkable California Baskets," *California Historical Society Quarterly* 2, (January 1924): 341–43.

13. Parmenter, *Zelia Nuttall*, 1209, 1185.

14. Wagner, "Meetings of the Society," 206.

15. Parmenter, *Zelia Nuttall*, 1209.

16. Wagner, *Sir Francis Drake's Voyage*, 19.

17. Zelia Nuttall and H. R. Wagner "Communications," *The Hispanic American Historical Review* 8, no. 2 (1928): 256 (emphasis added).

18. Parmenter, *Zelia Nuttall*, 1356.

19. Zelia Nuttall, "Review of *Sir Francis Drake's Voyage around the World, Its Aims and Achievements*, by Henry R. Wagner," *The American Historical Review* 34, no. 2 (1928): 117 (emphasis added).

20. Parmenter, *Zelia Nuttall*, 1358.

21. Frederick Puller Sprent, *Sir Francis Drake's Voyage round the World, 1577–1580: Two Contemporary Maps*, (London: British Museum, 1927).

22. E. H., "Review of *Sir Francis Drake's Voyage round the World, 1577–1580: Two Contemporary Maps*, by F. P. Sprent" *The Geographical Journal* 70, no. 5 (1927): 479–81.

23. Helen Wallis, Officer of the Most Excellent Order of the British Empire, and Keeper of Maps, The British Library, accepts the date as 1583 or within a few years later, and noted it is one of the earliest maps. See Wallis, *The Voyage of Sir Francis Drake Mapped in Silver and Gold*.

24. John W. Robertson, *Francis Drake and Other Early Explorers along the Pacific Coast* (San Francisco: Grabhorn Press, 1927).

25. Joseph Schafer, "Review of *Francis Drake and Other Early Explorers along the Pacific Coast*, by John W. Robertson," *The American Historical Review* 33, no. 2 (1928): 411.

26. E. F. Benson, *Sir Francis Drake* (London: Harper & Brothers, 1927), 306.

27. Ibid., 102.

28. Ibid., 105.

29. Philip Ainsworth Means, "Zelia Nuttall: An Appreciation," *The Hispanic American Historical Review* 13, no. 4 (1933): 488.

30. Taylor, "The Missing Draft Project," 46.

31. BL Cotton MSS. Otho, E VIII, transcribed by Sugden in *Sir Francis Drake*, 97.

32. E. G. R. Taylor, "Early Empire Building Projects in the Pacific Ocean, 1565–1585," *The Hispanic American Historical Review*, 14, no. 3 (1934)" 298. Grenville intended to make the first English voyage through the Straits of Magellan, which would break the Spanish monopoly in the Pacific. Grenville was also to fortify the Strait of Magellan if it was deemed necessary.

33. Sugden, *Sir Francis Drake*, 97.

34. Taylor, "Early Empire Building Projects," 298. Also see Helen Wallis, "England's Search for the Northern Passages in the Sixteenth and Early Seventeenth Centuries," *Arctic* 37, no. 4 (1984): 453–72.

35. Wallis, "England's Search for the Northern Passages," 467.

36. Taylor, "More Light on Drake," 134.

37. Derek Wilson, *Sir Francis Walsingham: Courtier in an Age of Terror* (London: Constable, 2007), 145. See also Kelsey, *Sir Francis Drake: The Queen's Pirate*, 75–79, for a discussion of the plans of the voyage.

38. Taylor, "Francis Drake and the Pacific," 364. The Madox diary is at the British Library, London.

39. Taylor, "Early Empire Building Projects in the Pacific Ocean," 297.

40. Ibid. Also see the following by Taylor: *Late Tudor and Early Stuart Geography*; "Master John Dee, Drake and the Straits of Anian"; and *Tudor Geography, 1485–1583* (London, Methuen, 1930).

Chapter 10: The Historian on the Hill

1. Allen Chickering to Professor Sherman Kent, December 27, 1940. Allen Lawrence Chickering Papers, MS 371, California Historical Society.

2. "Replica Proposed to Mark Site Where Drake Brass Plate was Discovered," *Oakland Tribune*, April 7, 1937. In this article there is a photograph with Shinn pointing to the exact location of the find, which is a rock cairn. Aubrey Neasham, one of Bolton's PhD students, called it a rock pile, and thought that it may have been the base of the post that Drake nailed the plate to. Neasham and Heizer excavated an area twenty feet square around the rock pile, with negative results.

3. Herbert E. Bolton, "Francis Drake's Plate of Brass," *California Historical Society Quarterly* 16, no. 1 (1937): 1–16.

4. John Francis Bannon, *Herbert Eugene Bolton: The Historian and the Man, 1870–1953* (Tucson: University of Arizona Press, 1978), 199.

5. James Hart, Confidential Memorandum, August 10, 1977, Plate of Brass Administrative files, BANC MSS 2002/68 c, Bancroft Library (hereafter Plate of Brass Administrative files). The folder is marked "Confidential" and contains notes from an interview with Mrs. Harry Scoble. This is discussed in detail in subsequent chapters.

6. For a description of the lost mine, see Roderick B. Patten, "Miranda's Inspection of Los Almagres: His Journal, Report, and Petition," *The Southwestern Historical Quarterly* 74, no. 2 (1970): 223–54. Bolton's academic expertise was the history of the Spanish explorers, missionaries, and soldiers of the borderlands on the northern-most Spanish colonial territories. He did extensive research in archives in Mexico and the Southwest, and as a young man he had followed the trails of Spanish Conquistadors throughout the Southwest in order to get a sense of the experience of the explorers.

7. Hurtado, *Herbert Eugene Bolton*, 56. See also "Documents Concerning the Discovery of Silver in Arizona," box 17, folder 4–8, Bolton Papers.

8. "To Seek Old Spanish Treasure," *Los Angeles Times*, April 17, 1921.

9. "Buried Gold Documents Translated," *Oakland Tribune*, April 11, 1921.

10. "To Seek Old Spanish Treasure," *Los Angeles Times*.

11. "Buried Treasure will Be Found by Aid of Science," *Topeka Daily Capital*, May 1, 1921.

12. "Buried Gold Documents Translated," *Oakland Tribune*.

13. "To Seek Old Spanish Treasure," *Los Angeles Times*.

14. Agreement between John Mayeroff, Joseph R. Knowland and Herbert Bolton, box 57, folder 25, Mayeroff, Bolton Papers.

15. Mayeroff to Bolton, April 22, April 28, May 18, May 22, May 29, June 9, July 3, 1921, Incoming Correspondence, Bolton Papers.

16. Ibid., May 21, 1921.

17. George P. Hammond, *Agapito Rey, The Rediscovery of New Mexico, 1580–1594: The Explorations of Chamuscado, Espejo, Castaño de Sosa, Morlete, and Leyva de Bonilla and Humaña* (Albuquerque: University of New Mexico Press, 1966).
18. "18 Millions Spurned by U. C. Teacher," *Oakland Tribune*, July 8, 1921.
19. "Bolton Loses Share in Buried Treasure," *Berkeley Gazette*, July 8, 1921.
20. "Tells of Treasure Cave," *New York Times*, June 4, 1921.
21. "Professor in University of California Gains Fortune from Supposedly Abandoned Mines," *The Michigan Daily*, October 23, 1929.
22. "Historic Records Added to Archives," *New Castle News* (New Castle, PA), September 9, 1922.
23. Ibid.
24. "Kidd Loot Basis of Astor Wealth?," *Dubuque Telegraph-Herald*, May 15, 1923, 4.
25. Frederic Head, "Olmsted and Captains Kidd's Treasure," www.nps.gov /frla/learn/historyculture/capt-kidds-treasure.htm
26. H. H. Dunn, "Is Astor Fortune Founded on Captain Kidd's Gold?," *The Dearborn Independent*, March 20, 1926.
27. "Kidd's Buried Treasure Bobs Up in Tale of Sale by J. J. Astor," *East Liverpool Review Tribune* (OH), April 9, 1926.
28. J. Neilson Barry, Papers, MSS 1, box 10, folder 27, Special Collections, Boise State University Library.
29. Ibid.
30. David La Vere, *The Lost Rocks: The Dare Stones and the Unsolved Mystery of Sir Walter Raleigh's Lost Colony*, (Wilmington: Burnt Mill Press, 2010), 14.
31. Andrew Lawler, *The Secret Token: Myth, Obsession, and the Search for the Lost Colony of Roanoke* (New York: Doubleday, 2018), 347–48.
32. Haywood J. Pearce Jr., "New Light on the Roanoke Colony: A Preliminary Examination of a Stone Found in Chowan County, North Carolina," *Journal of Southern History* 4, no. 2 (1938): 148.
33. Ibid.
34. Pearce to Bolton, August 15, 1939, Incoming Correspondence, Brenau, Bolton Papers.
35. Ibid., September 28, 1940.
36. Lawler, *The Secret Token*, 246.
37. La Vere, *The Lost Rocks*, 199.
38. Ibid., 142.
39. Haywood J. Pearce Jr., "The Friars Come," *The Georgia Review* 1, no. 2 (1947): 218.
40. Ibid., 241.

41. La Vere, *The Lost Rocks*, 147.
42. Andrew Lawler, "Is This Inscribed Stone a Notorious Forgery—or the Answer to America's Oldest Mystery?" *National Geographic Magazine* (online article that was a follow up to a story in the June 2018 issue of *National Geographic* by Lawler), https://news.nationalgeographic.com /2018/05/lost-colony-roanoke-virginia-eleanor-dare-stone-mystery/.
43. Hurtado, *Herbert Eugene Bolton*, 225–26. The presence of these men in the region where petroglyph inscriptions allegedly made by Spanish explorers have been found may explain one or more of these that are now considered hoaxes.
44. Hammond to Bolton, June 28, 1935, box 38, folder 25, Incoming Correspondence, Bolton Papers. His work at that time included supervising the workers of the New Mexico Historical Records Survey for the Federal Writers Project. "53 Workers on the Historical Records Survey," *Santa Fe New Mexican*, June 24, 1936.
45. Handwriting and signature examples were drawn from the "Faculty Files, George Hammond," UNMA 152, box 12, Center for Southwest Research, University of New Mexico, Albuquerque. Supplementary material was found in the George P. Hammond Papers, BANC MSS 70/89, Bancroft Library, University of California, Berkeley (hereafter Hammond Papers). The L. E. Hammond signatures were from the "Dare Stones Collection 1937–1987" Series No. 71, Rose Library, Emory University, Atlanta.
46. Marcel B. Matley, *LE Hammond Signatures*, Document File Reference 180900-A, September 20, 2018. Brenda Petty Unlimited, LLC, *Questioned Document Examiner Letter and Report, George P. Hammond and L.E. Hammond Comparison*, September 25, 2018. Jacqueline Joseph, phone interview, September 27, 2018.
47. Petty, *Questioned Document Examiner Letter and Report*, 8.
48. Matley, *LE Hammond Signatures*, 1.
49. Joseph, verbal communication, email, September 27, 2018.
50. G. Matthew Throckmorton, *IFL-George P. Hammond Report*, September 21, 2018. Independent Forensic Laboratories, West Jordan, Utah.
51. Since the signatures were notarized on the contracts regarding the first Dare Stone (perhaps to lend credibility to the scheme), the present writer speculates that George Hammond used his real last name but slightly altered his first name or initials on one of his own identification cards.
52. Hammond to Bolton, October 14, 1937, box 38, folder 25, Incoming Correspondence, Bolton Papers.
53. Herbert E. Bolton, "The Free Negro in the South before the Civil War," (PhD diss., University of Pennsylvania, 1899), 13, 40.

54. See George H. Slappey, Haywood Pearce, and Pansy A. Slappey, *The South and the Nation* (New York: Stratford House, 1946), 301–4.
55. Ibid., 301.
56. Lawler, *The Secret Token*, 278.
57. Hammond to Norman J. Thrower, December 11, 1978, Hammond Papers.

Chapter 11: Behind the Scenes

1. Hurtado, *Herbert Eugene Bolton*, 207–8.
2. Ibid., 92.
3. Albert Shumate, "The Mysterious History of E Clampus Vitus," in *California Vignettes*, ed. Robert F. Schoeppner and Robert J. Chandler (San Francisco: San Francisco Corral of the Westerners, 1996), 44. Dane and Wheat had both attended Pomona College and received law degrees from Harvard, and were in practice for a while together.
4. Thomas Duncan, *E Clampus Vitus: Anthology of New Dispensation Lore* (Raleigh NC: Lulu Press, 2009). The date of the establishment of the revived group is given elsewhere as 1932, which is the date of their first general meeting. On Clampers letterhead at the Bancroft Library, the date is given as 1930.
5. George R. Stewart, "A Little of Myself," 1972, vii, transcript of an interview of Charles Camp, Professor of Paleontology, Regional Oral History Office, Bancroft Library.
6. James Hart, Memorandum to the Files, Visit to the Bancroft Library by Beryle Shinn, May 15, 1978. Plate of Brass Administrative files. Hart also noted that Beryle is the original spelling of his name but they changed it to Beryl.
7. Beryle Shinn to Albert E. Doerr, March 29, 1968, box 2, Plate of Brass Administrative files.
8. Allen Chickering to Professor Sherman Kent, December 27, 1940, Allen Lawrence Chickering Papers, MS 371, California Historical Society (hereafter Chickering Papers).
9. Drake Plate collection, box 131, folder 40, Bolton Papers.
10. Beryle Shinn to Albert E. Doerr, March 29, 1968, box 2, Plate of Brass Administrative files.
11. JHart, Memorandum to the files, 15 May 1978, Plate of Brass Administrative files.
12. George P. Hammond, "In Memoriam: Herbert Eugene Bolton, 1870–1953," *The Americas* 9, no. 4 (April 1953): 397.
13. Herbert Bolton to Colin G. Fink, October 13, 1938, Drake Correspondence, box 132, Bolton Papers.
14. Bolton, "Francis Drake's Plate of Brass," 1.

15. Ibid., 12. Bolton's typescript of the speech is slightly different and shows several equivocations.

16. W. J. Harte, "Historical Revision: LXXVI.1—Some Recent Views on Drake's Voyage round the World," *History* 20, no. 80 (1936): 348–53.

17. Taylor, "Francis Drake and the Pacific," 364.

18. Ibid.

19. Ibid.

20. Harte, "Historical Revision," 348–53.

21. Letter to William E. Lingelbach, quoted in Bannon, *Herbert Eugene Bolton*, 202.

22. *Time Magazine*, April 19, 1937.

23. "A Pirate Leaves His Calling Card," KGO San Francisco Broadcast, April 13, 1937.

24. Hurtado, *Herbert Eugene Bolton*, 190.

25. "U. C. Man Leaves on Lecture Tour," *Berkeley Daily Gazette*, March 13, 1941.

26. Bannon, *Herbert Eugene Bolton*, 203–4.

27. Hart, memorandum to the file regarding conversation with Bob Cowden, Walnut Creek, 1977, Plate of Brass Administrative files.

28. Herb Caen, "It's News to Me," *The San Francisco Chronicle*, July 9, 1938.

29. Ibid., July 20, 1938.

30. Bolton to Chickering, 20 July 1938, Chickering Papers.

Chapter 12: The Authentication of the Plate of Brass

1. O. Crawford to Bolton, August 5, 1937, box 132, 1, Bolton Papers.

2. Elizabeth Story Donno, *An Elizabethan in 1582: The Diary of Richard Madox, Fellow of All Souls* (London: Hakluyt Society, 1976), 177, and fig. 14, Sketch of the copper plate.

3. Haselden to Bolton, April 12, 1937, box 131, Drake Correspondence, Bolton Papers.

4. Ibid.

5. Vincent T. Harlow, quoted in a letter from Haselden to Robert Sproul, October 15, 1937, Haselden, Plate of Brass Collection, HIA 32.5.11.7., Henry E. Huntington Library, San Marino, California (hereafter Haselden Plate of Brass Collection).

6. Thomas A. Rickard to Bolton, October 8, 1937, Drake Correspondence, Bolton Papers.

7. Dr. Robin Flower to Haselden, September 1, 1937, Haselden Plate of Brass Collection. This is a copy of a letter Flower sent to Chickering and copied to Haselden.

8. Ibid.

9. Ibid.

10. Ibid., Dr. Vincent Harlow to Captain R. B. Haselden, July 22, 1937.

11. Ibid.

12. Robert Sproul to Bolton, May 3, 1937, box 13, Drake Correspondence, Bolton Papers.

13. R. B. Haselden, "Is the Drake Plate of Brass Genuine?," *California Historical Society Quarterly* 16 (1937): 272.

14. "Communications," *The American Historical Review* 42, no. 4 (1937): 863–65.

15. Haselden, "Is the Drake Plate of Brass Genuine?," 271–74.

16. Allen Chickering, "Some Notes with Regard to Drake's Plate of Brass," *California Historical Society Quarterly* 16 (1937): 275–81.

17. Chickering to Bolton, January 13, 1938, 15, box 13, Drake Correspondence, Bolton Papers.

18. Ibid., Bolton to Bartlett Brebner, May 20, 1937, box 131.

19. Ibid., Bolton to Sproul, October 6, 1937, box 132.

20. Ibid., Bolton to Kent, April 8, 1937, box 132.

21. Ibid., Chickering to Bolton, January 13, 1938, and January 18, 1938, box 13.

22. Hurtado, *Herbert Eugene Bolton*, 203.

23. Ibid.

24. Chickering to Bolton, March 16, 1938, box 13, Drake Correspondence, Bolton Papers.

25. Colin G. Fink et al., "The Report on the Plate of Brass," *California Historical Society Quarterly* 17 (1938): 10.

26. Ibid.

27. Bolton to Bartlett Brebur, May 20, 1937, box 131, Drake Correspondence, Bolton Papers.

28. Ibid., Bolton to Colin G. Fink, October 13, 1938, box 132.

29. James Hart, *The Plate of Brass Reexamined, Supplementary Report* (Berkeley: Bancroft Library, 1979), 6.

30. Earle R. Caley, *Confidential: Criticism of Professor Fink's Report*, Haselden Plate of Brass Collection. Caley was from the Frick Chemical Laboratory, Princeton University. The report was drafted for Dr. Robert G. Sproul and has no date.

31. Alan Chickering to Herbert Bolton, March 23, 1939, MSS 371, Allen Lawrence Chickering Papers, California Historical Society, San Francisco.

32. Ibid.

33. Jeff Greer, "$15 Million Treasure Buried in Marin?," *Independent Journal*, November 8, 1984.

34. Ibid.

35. Bolton to Parsons, December 11, 1939, box 132, Drake Correspondence, Bolton Papers.

36. Ibid.

37. Ibid., Bolton to Ellison, September 26, 1941.

38. Ibid.

39. Charles S. Dunning to H. R. Wagner, July 14, 1941, Drake's Plate of Brass Collection, Bancroft Library.

40. Robert Sproul to Bolton, May 3, 1937, Bolton Papers.

41. Dunning to Wagner, July 14, 1941.

42. Ibid.

Chapter 13: Investigations and Resolutions

1. Raymond Aker, V. Aubrey Neasham, and Robert H. Power, "The Debate: Point Reyes Peninsula/Drakes Estero; Bolinas Bay/Bolinas Lagoon; San Francisco Bay/San Quentin Cove," *California Historical Quarterly* 53, no. 3 (1974): 203–92.

2. Robert Heizer to Professor James Hart, December 19, 1974, Plate of Brass Administrative files.

3. Robert Heizer, "Speech upon Receiving the California Historical Society's Wagner Award," November 19, 1977, box 34, folder 11, Robert Fleming Heizer Papers, BANC MSS 78/17c, Bancroft Library.

4. Robert Heizer, "Robert F. Hiezer," in *There was Light: Autobiography of a University Berkeley, 1868–1968*, ed. Irving Stone (New York: Doubleday, 1970), 210.

5. Heizer, "Speech upon Receiving the California Historical Society's Wagner Award."

6. Heizer to Hart, December 19, 1974.

7. Ibid.

8. Raymond Aker to Norman Thrower, November 5, 1977, Sir Francis Drake Commission, subject files, Raymond Aker, R348.3, California State Archives.

9. James Hart, *The Plate of Brass Reexamined: A Report Issued by the Bancroft Library* (Berkeley: University of California, 1977), 8.

10. James Hart, *The Plate of Brass Reexamined: A Supplement* (Berkeley: University of California, 1979).

11. "Sir Francis Drake's Plate a Fake Tests Show," *The Argus* (Fremont, CA), July 28, 1977.

12. Testimony of Lorenz Noll to Herbert Hamlin, May 13, 1954, Plate of Brass Administrative files.

13. Ibid.

14. Ibid.

15. Ibid.

16. Ibid.

17. Phoebe Cutler, "Joaquin Miller and the Social Circle at the Heights," *California History* 90, no. 1 (2012): 40–69.

18. James Hart, Confidential Memorandum, August 10, 1977, box 2, Plate of Brass Administrative files. The folder is marked "Confidential, Mrs. Harry Scoble."

19. Ibid.

20. James Hart, Memoranda, Mrs. Harry Scoble née Dolores Barron second interview with James D. Hart, August 25, 1977, Plate of Brass Administrative files.

21. Hart, Memo to file, September 2, 1977, Plate of Brass Administrative files.

22. Hart, Memo to file, June 26, 1979, Plate of Brass Administrative files.

23. Ibid.

24. Hart, Memo to file, June 26, 1979, Plate of Brass Administrative files.

25. "Ray Taylor Joins Staff of the *Bulletin*," Newspaper clipping in Plate of Brass Administrative files. The day it was published is cut off in this clipping, but it can be discerned it was printed in November 1924.

26. Ibid.

27. James Hart, Confidential Memorandum, June 26, 1979, Plate of Brass Administrative files. Mrs. Clark berated Mr. Clark about the forgery. He said he signed it with a "GC."

28. James Hart, Memo to staff regarding Bolton correspondence, August 29, 1977, Plate of Brass Administrative files.

29. James Hart, Memo to file regarding conversation with Leon P. Adams about Bolton, February 25, 1980, Plate of Brass Administrative files.

30. James Hart, Memoranda, Mrs. Harry Scoble née Dolores Barron, August 25, 1977, Plate of Brass Administrative files.

31. 1920, *United States Federal Census, Berkeley, Alameda, California*; Roll: *T625_93*; Page: *6A*; Enumeration District: *193*.

32. "George Barron Wanted. Rita Arguello Swears Out a Warrant for His Arrest for Felony," *San Francisco Call*, June 13, 1895.

33. San Francisco, *Board of Park Commissioners Meeting Minutes*, San Francisco, April 12, 1917–May 3, 1917. Microfilm, San Francisco Public Library.

34. Ibid.

35. Ibid.

36. Newspaper clipping, April 13, 1917. This was a clipping in Hart's file, Plate of Brass Administrative files.

37. *Oakland, Berkeley, Alameda Directory*, (Oakland: Polk-Husted Directory, 1918), 184.

38. Undated newspaper clipping, box 2, Plate of Brass Administrative files.

39. *San Francisco City Directory* (San Francisco: Crocker-Langley, 1921), 289.

40. James Hart, Memoranda, Mrs. Harry Scoble née Dolores Barron, August 25, 1977, Plate of Brass Administrative files.

41. James Hart, Confidential Memorandum to the file, August 17, 1977, Plate of Brass Administrative files. Hart noted in this memo that he phoned Mrs. Scoble's daughter, Vicky Scoble Oldberg, and asked her questions about this troublesome early date of 1919 or 1920. Vicky indicated that her mother knew about the plate before she went to college at about age eighteen or twenty, and that she had told her daughter that the plate was a modern creation.

42. Ibid.

43. James Hart, Memorandum, August 16, 1977, Transcription of and interview with Thomas C. Howe, former Director of the Legion of Honor, Plate of Brass Administrative files.

44. James Hart, Memo to file, August 19, 1977, Plate of Brass Administrative files.

45. James Hart, Confidential Memorandum, January 4, 1979, Plate of Brass Administrative files.

46. James Hart, Confidential File, Memorandum, August 25, 1977, Plate of Brass Administrative files.

47. Charles Camp et al., *E Clampus Vitus, Ye Preposterous Booke of Brasse* (self-published, 1937). In 1935 Bolton contributed a chapter to a previous booklet, titled *Vituscan Voyages*, written under a pseudonym.

48. Edward Von der Porten et al., "Who Made Drake's Plate of Brass? Hint: It wasn't Francis Drake," *California History* 81, no. 2 (2002). Charles L. Camp was the primary author of *Ye Preposterous Booke of Brasse*. He was a long-standing member of the California Historical Society, and it is significant to note that he knew both Nuttall and the content of her Drake monograph. Camp had been the chairman of the publication committee for the *California Historical Quarterly* when Wagner was working on his book and making proclamations against Nuttall and the "English propaganda" she was promulgating.

49. Von der Porten et al., "Who Made Drake's of Plate of Brass."

50. James M. Spitze et al., *The Clampers and Their Hoaxes* (Berkeley: Friends of the Bancroft Library, 2018), 23.

51. *The Hew-Gag Brays*, undated announcement on the upcoming publication, *The Preposterous Booke of Brasse*. This was sent to Bolton by George Ezra Dane, Correspondence, box 28, folder 17, Bolton Papers.

52. Ibid., Eric Falconer to Bolton, January 25, 1949..

53. Ibid.

54. Ibid.

55. Leland Cutler to Bolton, April 7, 1937, box 13, Bolton Papers. This letter regarding display of the plate at the Golden Gate International Exposition, 1939.

56. "Exposition Program," *Berkeley Daily Gazette*, May 1, 1939.

57. Charles L. Camp and Fulmer Mood, "George Ezra Dane," *California Folklore Quarterly* 1, no. 1 (1942): 91–93.

58. Dane to Bolton, April 16, 1935, box 28, folder 17, Bolton Papers.

59. Franklin Walker and G. Ezra Dane, eds., *Mark Twain's Travels with Mr. Brown* (New York: Knopf, 1940).

60. Mark Twain, "The Petrified Man," in *Sketches, New and Old* (Chicago, IL: American Publishing, 1882), 239–42.

61. Ibid.

62. Ibid.

63. Stewart, "A Little of Myself," vii.

64. Ibid.

65. Ibid.

66. Von der Porten et al., "Who Made Drake's of Plate of Brass."

67. George Ezra Dane to Harry Peterson, April 11, 1937, series 11, box 2, E Clampus Vitus Archives, Mss 101, Holt-Atherton Department of Special Collections, University of the Pacific Library. Harry Peterson was the curator at Sutter's Fort. He announced that at the next Clamper meeting an important relic, thought to be lost, would be revealed. The meeting opened and he brought out a dusty old flag with a bear on it and said this was the original Bear Flag of the California rebellion of 1846 when a group of Americans took over the Mexican outpost in Sonoma and raised the flag as an act of defiance against Mexican rule of California. The real Bear Flag was lost in the fire after the 1906 earthquake in San Francisco. For a few minutes, the Clampers were taken in by an elaborate story he told about a man who saved the flag just before the museum was destroyed. Soon the men in the room realized it was a joke and they all had a good laugh.

68. Diana Dane Dajani, personal communication with author. Diana Dane Dajani graciously provided access to her father's papers for this project.

69. George Ezra Dane and Beatrice J. Dane, *Ghost Town* (New York: A.A. Knopf, 1941).

70. Ibid., 233.

71. "California Folklore," *Oakland Tribune*, October 19, 1941.

72. Dane family papers provided by Diana Dane Dajani. Special thanks to Elizabeth Baker, George Dane's niece.

73. Ibid.

74. Dane family papers, and personal communication with Diana Dane Dajani.

75. Herbert Eugene Bolton, "The Confessions of a Wayward Professor," *The Americas* 6, no. 3 (1950): 359–62.

76. There is no Bolton family connection to Bart and the Bowles family. Herbert Bolton was born in Wisconsin in 1870, five years before Bart

committed his first robbery and assumed the cover name of Charles Bolton. It is interesting that George Dane had almost finished a book on Black Bart, but stopped working on the manuscript some time before he died. His niece Laika Dajani edited the manuscript, and it was published posthumously in 1996.

77. Hurtado, *Herbert Eugene Bolton*, 165.

Chapter 14: The Commission and the Commemoration of Drake's Voyage

1. California State Archives, Administrative History on the Sir Francis Drake Commission Records, R348, California State Archives, Office of the Secretary of State, Sacramento, California (hereafter Drake Commission Records).
2. "Coin Fuels Debate on Where Drake Landed," *Los Angeles Times*, November 17, 1974.
3. "Coin Find Linked to Drake Landing," *Progress Bulletin* (Pomona, CA), November 10, 1974.
4. Ibid.
5. "Coin Fuels Debate," *The Los Angeles Times*.
6. Mike Moratto, email message to author, April 20, 2012.
7. Warren L. Hanna, *Lost Harbor: The Controversy over Drake's California Anchorage* (Berkeley: University of California Press, 1979), 236.
8. Fred Lew, *The Olompali Historic Tour: A Trek through Time*, California State Parks Video Transcript (California State Parks, 2004).
9. Edward Von der Porten to Col. William L. Shaw, June 19, 1975, OHS R348.3, Drake Commission Records.
10. Ibid., Thrower to Vaughan, April 18, 1977.
11. Garry David Gitzen, "Oregon's Stolen History," (unpublished manuscript, 2012), 56.
12. Ibid.
13. Thomas Vaughan to F. P. Heseltine, assistant private secretary, Buckingham Palace, May 16, 1977, quoted in Ibid., 66.
14. "Oregon's Drake Link," *The Sunday Oregonian*, editorial, July 17, 1977.
15. Raymond Aker, *Report of Finding Relating to Identification of Sir Francis Drake's Encampment at Point Reyes* (Palo Alto, CA: Drake Navigators Guild Report, 1970), 255–61.
16. Kenneth Holmes, Letter to Editor, *The Oregonian*, July 28, 1977.
17. Vernon Aubrey Neasham and William E. Pritchard, *Drake's California Landing: The Evidence for Bolinas Lagoon* (Sacramento, CA: Western Heritage, 1974).
18. "A Four-Hundredth Anniversary Commemoration," Drake Commission Records.
19. Ibid.

20. "NW Historians 'Reverse' Drake," *Oregon Journal*, August 6, 1977.
21. Aker to Thrower, January 24, 1978, Drake Commission Records.
22. Vaughan to Aker, October 12, 1977, quoted in Gitzen, "Oregon's Stolen History," 84–85.
23. "Short Abstract of the Present Voyage," transcribed in Vaux, *The World Encompassed*, 184.
24. Vaughan to Victor West, October 27, 1977, quoted in Gitzen, "Oregon's Stolen History," 86–87.
25. Parkinson to Thrower, October 12, 1977, Drake Commission Records.
26. Ibid., Aker to Thrower, January 24, 1978.
27. Ray Aker and Edward Von der Porten, *Discovering Portus Novae Albionis, Francis Drake's California Harbor* (Palo Alto: Drake Navigators Guild Publication, 1979), 30.
28. Alex Cumming to SFDC, March 20, 1979, Drake Commission Records.
29. "Discover Historic Bay Relics," *Berkeley Gazette*, December 16, 1941. Those from the late Ming period were specifically made for export to the European market. Late Ming is less exactly defined but the expert postulated that these were from the last century or so of the Ming period, ca. 1550–1644.
30. Russell, "Encounters at *Tamál-Húye*," 265.
31. Jessica Lally and Harvey Steele, *Oregon Coast Ceramics Roundtable*, discussion, Nehalem Valley Historical Society, October 2, 2010, Manzanita, Oregon.
32. *Drakes Bay Historic and Archaeological District, Appendix I: A Brief History of Scholarship Relating to Drake's Port of Nova Albion.* The National Park Service discussion of scholarship did not include the following: Taylor, "Early Empire Building Projects in the Pacific Ocean," 297; Taylor, "The Missing Draft Project of Drake's Voyage," 46–47, with plates showing two pages of the plan in facsimile; Taylor, "More Light on Drake," 134; E. F. Benson, *Sir Francis Drake* (London: The Bodley Head, 1928), 102; E. H., review of "Cartographical Records of Drake's Voyage," 479–81.
33. *Drakes Bay Historic and Archeological District Landmark Nomination*, redacted version, 2010.
34. The Drake Navigators Guild Press Release, October 17, 2012.
35. Erika Seibert, email message to Garry Gitzen, May 31, 2012, provided to author by Garry Gitzen.
36. Author Garry Gitzen protested to the NPS about the nomination. Gitzen has written several articles and two books about the theory that Drake landed at Nehalem Bay on the Oregon coast. The theory is based in part on the "Neahkahnie Stones." In the vicinity of Nehalem Bay is a prominent headland known as Neahkahnie Mountain where several boulders, single stones, and at least one portion of bedrock exhibit petroglyphs

(letters, numbers, arrows, lines) that are theorized to be survey stones that were used by Drake to determine longitude and that these stones marked distances and the incised lines indicated directions. However, no one so far has been able to explain how the survey was accomplished. In particular, what was the key calculation? Were they triangulating the azimuth of the moon with two points of known distance? Besides the stones with glyphs, there is a stone fence, and an undetermined number of rock cairns. The Neahkahnie Stones are a mystery, possibly one or more is a hoax, and the provenience information on some of the stones and features has been lost. A new comprehensive study of these features may be impossible. In addition to "Oregon's Stolen History," previously cited, Gitzen is the author of the following: *Francis Drake in Nehalem Bay: Setting the Historical Record Straight* (Wheeler, OR: Gitzen, 2013) and *The Plate of Brass Hoax White Paper* (unpublished manuscript, 2012).

Chapter 15: The People at the Landing

1. Clegg, *The Peaceable and Prosperous Regiment of Blessed Queen Elizabeth*, xiii.
2. Hakluyt, "Extracts from Hakluyt's Voyages: The Course [...]," transcribed by Vaux, Appendix V, 221.
3. Drake and Fletcher, "The Voyage about the World," transcribed in Vaux, *The World Encompassed*, 119–22.
4. Ibid., 119.
5. Ibid., 98. This attack occurred on November 26, 1578. Diego would die of his wound received at Isle Mocha in the Moluccas.
6. Vaux, *The World Encompassed*, v.
7. Drake and Fletcher, "The Voyage about the World," transcribed in Vaux, *The World Encompassed*, 120.
8. Ibid., 120–22. There is an archaeological site at the distance described.
9. Ibid., 122–23.
10. Ibid., 122–24.
11. Ibid., 124–25.
12. Ibid., 125.
13. Ibid.
14. Ibid.
15. Ibid., 128–30.
16. Ibid., 125.
17. Robert F. Heizer, *Elizabethan California: A Brief, and Sometimes Critical Review of Opinions on the Location of Francis Drake's Five Weeks' Visit with the Indians of Ships Land in 1579* (Ramona, CA: Ballena Press, 1974), 69.
18. Drake and Fletcher, "The Voyage about the World," transcribed in Vaux, *The World Encompassed*, 128–29.

19. Ibid., 129.
20. Ibid.
21. Ibid., 130.
22. Ibid., 129.
23. Ibid., 122–24.
24. Ibid., 130.
25. Ibid., 119.
26. Ibid., 132.

Chapter 16: An Ethnographic Assessment for an Oregon Landing

1. Lee R. Lyman, and Michael J. O'Brien, "The Direct Historical Approach, Analogical Reasoning, and Theory in Americanist Archaeology," *Journal of Archaeological Method and Theory* 8, no. 4 (2001). Lyman and O'Brian discuss two models of culture change. One is evolutionary, the other is checkered.

2. For this analysis, I draw on the ethnographic work of many anthropologists and ethnographers. For Oregon they include Melville and Elizabeth D. Jacobs, Leo Frachtenberg, Harry Hull St. Clair, John P. Harington, Willis Everette, James O. Dorsey, Albert Gatschet, Philip Drucker, John P. Harrington, and Homer Barnett. For California I include the work of Samuel Barrett, Isobel Kelly, E. W. Gifford, Robert Heizer, Alfred L. Kroeber, William Elmendorf, Edward Curtis, and Homer Barnett (who worked in both California and Oregon). The Native people who worked with the anthropologists who came in Oregon included Billy Metcalf and Tom McDonald, who were Chetco; Nettie West from Galice Creek; Oscar and Ellen Brown, and Lucy Smith who had traditional knowledge of the Coquille, Sixes River, and the inland mountain town of Power; Coquille Thompson who related his knowledge of the Coos and Upper Coquille; Hoxie and Bill Simmons, who contributed knowledge about the Takelma; Louis Fuller, who provided information about the Tilla-mook; Jim Bensell, who provided information about the Tututni material culture, and Spencer Scott, who provided information on the Siuslaw and lower Umpqua. Frank Drew from Yachats was both Melville Jacobs's and Leo Frachtenberg's ethnographic informant for the Coos. Jim Buchannan provided important information to Frachtenberg and St. Clair on Coos language, myth, and traditions. One of the most important of the informants was Annie Miner Peterson, a Coos woman whose Native role was as a guardian and keeper of culture. Her work with Melville Jacobs, in particular, provided important linguistic material for both Coos and Miluk people.

3. See Wayne Suttles, ed., *Northwest Coast*, vol. 7, *Handbook of North*

American Indians, series ed. William C. Sturtevant (Washington D.C.: Smithsonian, 1990). Authors include Michael Silverstein, "Chinookans of the Lower Columbia"; William R. Seaburg and Jay Miller, "Tillamook"; Henry B. Zenk, "Alseans" and "Siuslawans and Coosans"; Jay Miller and William R. Seaburg, "Athapaskans of Southwestern Oregon"; Daythal L. Kendall "Takelma."

4. Homer G. Barnett, "Culture Element Distributions: VII, Oregon Coast," *University of California Anthropological Records* 1, no. 3. (1937), 156.
5. Charles F. Wilkinson, *The People are Dancing Again: The History of the Siletz Tribe of Western Oregon* (Seattle: University of Washington Press, 2010), 363–74.
6. Melville Jacobs, series 10, box 100, folder 23, Miscellaneous, Melville Jacobs Papers, 1918–1978, Accession Number 1693, Manuscripts and University Archives, University of Washington, Seattle (hereafter Melville Jacobs Papers).
7. Jacobs, series 10, box 99 folder 21, Dance, Melville Jacobs Papers.
8. Barnett, "Culture Element Distributions: VII, Oregon Coast."
9. Leone Letson Kasner, *Siletz: Survival for an Artifact* (Dallas, OR: self-published, 1976), 9.
10. Mark Axel Tveskov, "The Coos and Coquille: A Northwest Coast Historical Anthropology" (PhD diss., University of Oregon, 2000), 16.
11. Barnett, "Culture Element Distributions: VII, Oregon Coast," 158. Alfred Kroeber pioneered the use of these trait lists in his efforts at salvage ethnography. See Lyman and O'Brien, "The Direct Historical Approach," 315. This approach is now considered reductive, ethnocentric, and from the colonizers point of view.
12. Barnett, "Culture Element Distributions: VII, Oregon Coast," 158.
13. Gordon W. Hewes, "California Flicker-Quill Headbands in the Light of an Ancient Colorado Cave Specimen," *American Antiquity* 18, no. 2 (1952): 150.
14. Isabel T. Kelly, "Yuki Basketry," *University of California Publications in American Archaeology and Ethnology* 24, no. 9 (1930): 432.
15. Richard Ross, "Prehistory of the Oregon Coast" in Suttles, *Northwest Coast,* 557.
16. Leland Gilsen, "Impacts of Earthquake Tsunamis on Oregon Coastal Populations," *Contributions to the Archaeology of Oregon,* Association of Oregon Archaeologists Occasional Papers, no. 7 (2002): 121–45. See also Loren R. Baker, *Cascadia Earthquake and Tsunami Events Reflected in Aboriginal Oral Tradition* (master's thesis, Evergreen State College, 2011).
17. John Draper, "A Proposed Model of Late Prehistoric Settlement Systems on the Southern Northwest Coast, Coos and Curry Counties, Oregon" (PhD diss., Washington State University, 1988).

18. Melville Jacobs, "Historic Perspectives in Indian Languages of Oregon and Washington," *Pacific Northwest Quarterly* 28, no. 1 (1937): 58. Linguist Joe Pierce disagreed with Jacobs.

19. Ibid., 64.

20. Elizabeth D. Jacobs, *Pitch Woman and Other Stories: The Oral Traditions of Coquelle Thompson*, ed. William R. Seaburg (Lincoln: University of Nebraska Press, 2007), 19.

21. Jacobs, series 10, box 99, folder 13, Ritual Oratory, Melville Jacobs Papers.

22. Jacobs, "Historic Perspectives in Indian Languages," 58.

23. Laurence C. Thompson, "Melville Jacobs, 1902–1971," *American Anthropologist* 80, no. 3 (1978): 640.

24. Alfred Louis Kroeber, "The Coast and Lake Miwok," in *Handbook of the Indians of California* (New York: Dover Publications, 1976), 278. Originally published in 1925 as Bulletin 78, Bureau of American Ethnology of the Smithsonian Institution.

25. Ibid., 277.

26. Dudley, manuscript charts of *Arcano del mare*, image 238.

27. Barnett, "Culture Element Distributions: VII, Oregon Coast," 172.

28. Homer Barnett, Notebook: Indian Tribes of the Oregon Coast, box 1, folder 9, 1934, Southwest Oregon Research Project (SWORP) Collection, Coll 268-1, Special Collections and University Archives, University of Oregon Libraries, Eugene, Oregon (hereafter SWORP Collection).

29. Wagner, "The Voyage to California of Sebastian Rodriguez Cermeño," 3–24.

30. Kroeber, "The Coast and Lake Miwok," 276.

31. Robert F. Heizer, "Francis Drake and the California Indians, 1579," *University of California Publications in American Archaeology and Ethnology* 42, no. 3 (1947): 251.

32. Heizer, "Francis Drake and the California Indians," 251.

33. Isobel Kelly, "Coast Miwok," *Handbook of North American Indians: California*, vol. 8, ed. Robert Heizer (Washington D.C.: Smithsonian Institution, 1978), 417.

34. Ibid.

35. Glenn J. Farris, "The Bodega Miwok as Seen by Mikhail Tikhonovich Tikhanov in 1818," *Journal of California and Great Basin Anthropology* 20, no. 1, (1998): 2–12.

36. Wagner, "The Voyage to California of Sebastian Rodriguez Cermeño," 3–24.

37. Ibid. Also see Henry R. Wagner, "The Last Spanish Exploration of the Northwest Coast and the Attempt to Colonize Bodega Bay," *California Historical Society Quarterly* 10, no. 4 (1931): 331.

38. Wagner, *Drake's Voyage around the World*, 154–56.

39. Jacobs, series 10, box 100, folder 21, Manufactures: Homes, Melville Jacobs Papers.

40. Elizabeth Jacobs, "Upper Coquille Athabaskan Ethnographic Notes," taken by Elizabeth Jacobs from Coquille Thompson in 1933–1934, Accession No. 6131-001, series 6, box 2/130. Elizabeth and Melville Jacobs Papers.

41. Barnett, "Culture Element Distributions: VII, Oregon Coast," 161–63. For specific ethnographic records on dwellings see SWORP Collection. Within this collection see Frachtenberg, 0330, Coos, box 5, folder 9. For a description of Rogue River houses see SWORP Collection, box 5, folder 3, Willis E. Everette's notes under Rogue River. According to Everette's unnamed Tututni informant, the inside of the houses were oval shaped, and used for the "double purpose of council lodge and sudatorie" (sweat-house).

42. Drake and Fletcher, "The Voyage about the World," transcribed in Vaux, *The World Encompassed*, 121.

43. S.A. Barrett, *The Ethno-Geography of the Pomo and Neighboring Indians* (Berkeley: University of California Press, 1908), 36–37.

44. Ray Aker and Edward Von der Porten, *Discovering Portus Novae Albionis, Francis Drake's California Harbor* (Palo Alto: Drake Navigators Guild publication, 1979).

45. Drake and Fletcher, "The Voyage bout the World," transcribed in Vaux, *The World Encompassed*, 126–27.

46. Coos History Museum, Coos Bay, Oregon. See collection catalog numbers as follows: 998D.69, 958.800, 958.798, 958.797, 958.799 and 958.794.

47. Kasner, *Siletz, Survival for an Artifact*, 40.

48. Ibid., 40. Kasner also lamented the loss of weaponry cases, war dance baskets, and fishing weirs (which disappeared long before the 1930s), and that women's hats, wedding baskets, and prayer baskets had become rarities.

49. Leo Frachtenberg, Notebook, Field notes from Kusan Place, box 5 folder 9, SWORP Collection. Frank Drew told Frachtenberg that only rich people wore ornaments of woodpecker on their hats. These hats were highly valued, $400–500. See also Alsea MS2516, William Smith, box 6, folder 15, 1910, SWORP Collection.

50. Jacobs, series 10, box 100, folder 19, Manufactures: Basketry, Melville Jacobs Papers.

51. Jacobs, series 10, box 100, folder 19, Supernatural, Melville Jacobs Papers.

52. Kasner, *Siletz, Survival for an Artifact*, 9

53. Heizer, "Francis Drake and the California Indians," 263.

54. For a good discussion and description see Travis Hudson et al., *Treasures from Native California: the Legacy of Russian Exploration* (Walnut Creek, CA: Left Coast Press, 2015), 126–28.

55. Leo Frachtenberg, Notebook, Field notes from Kusan Place, SWORP Collection.

56. Drake and Fletcher, "The Voyage about the World," transcribed in Vaux, *The World Encompassed*, 126.

57. Ibid.

58. Hanna, *Lost Harbor*, 201.

59. Heizer, *Francis Drake and the California Indians*, 269.

60. Patricia Whereat Phillips, *Ethnobotany of the Coos, Lower Umpqua, and Siuslaw Indians* (Corvallis: Oregon State University Press, 2016), 86. The fiber of the stem of fireweed was particularly important to the Coos, Lower Umpqua, and Siuslaw. The plant was harvested in early summer, and the outer stem fiber was peeled, dried, and made into a fine twine. The twine was then used to make a dress. It took so much fiber to make these dresses that only women in wealthy families wore them, and they wore them only for special occasions such as dances, feasts, or weddings. See also, Nancy J. Turner and Sandra Peacock, "Ethnobotanical Evidence for plant Resource Management on the Northwest Coast," in *Keeping it Living: Traditions of Plant Use and Cultivation on the Northwest Coast of North America*, ed. Douglas Deur and Nancy J. Turner (Seattle: University of Washington Press, 2005), 138. The plant had multiple uses. Besides the seed fluff, the leaves were used for tea, the roots for poultices, and the stems for fiber.

61. Drake and Fletcher, "The Voyage bout the World," transcribed in Vaux, *The World Encompassed*, 126.

62. C. Leo Hitchcock and Arthur Cronquist, *Flora of the Pacific Northwest: An Illustrated Manual* (Seattle: University of Washington Press, 1974).

63. Drake and Fletcher, "The Voyage about the World," transcribed in Vaux, *The World Encompassed*, 125.

64. Heizer, "Francis Drake and the California Indians," 268.

65. Mark A. Tveskov, "Social Identity and Culture Change on the Southern Northwest Coast," *American Anthropologist* 109, no. 3 (2007): 433.

66. Myron Eells, *The Indians of Puget Sound: The Notebooks of Myron Eells*, ed. George Pierre Castile (Seattle: University of Washington Press, 1976), 119–22. Myron Eells recorded that among the Northwest Makah people the use of this white yarn was reserved for the elites. Drake and Fletcher's account notes that the use of the plant fluff was restricted to "such persons as are about the king." Weavers on the Northwest coast spun fireweed fluff (sometimes combined with eagle or duck down) with mountain goat

wool or dog wool to make yarn, which was then made into textiles. The Salish peoples in particular made blankets, mantles, and caps from this yarn, and rattles and masks were often decorated with white strands of this yarn.

67. Robert Losey, *Archaeology of the Par Tee Site, Northern Oregon Coast*, https://sites.ualberta.ca/~rlosey/partee/tools.htm.

68. R. Lee Lyman developed a mountain goat dispersal model from documented historical occurrence, suspected historical occurrence, and documented archaeological occurrence of mountain goats in Washington, Oregon, and California. The data show that in early historical times *Oreamnos* sp. were present in suitable habitat around Mount Hood, Mount Jefferson, and the Three Sisters. Faunal remains of this species from archaeological contexts can be used to conjecture that mountain goats were present as far south as northern California. R. Lee Lyman, "Significance for Wildlife Management of the Late Quaternary Biogeography of Mountain Goats (Oreamnos Americanus) in the Pacific Northwest," *U.S.A. Arctic and Alpine Research* 20 (1988): 13–23.

69. Willis Everette, "Study of Indian Languages, Schedules," box 5, folder 3, SWORP Collection.

70. Ray T. Moe, *One Hundred Years in Lincoln County, Oregon, 1893–1993* (Newport, OR: Lincoln County Historical Society, 1993), 99, 101. Another example of the traditional use of wool may be evidenced in the photograph of well-known tribal leader Depoe Charlie posing with his regalia and crafts (see Figure 16.5). Next to him on a bench is a tall container decorated with long thick strands of white yarn hanging from the rim.

71. Depoe Charlie was born in a village at the mouth of the Rogue River. He was a well-known tribal leader on the Siletz Reservation. Bureau of Land Management records indicate that Depoe Charlie and his family's lands and allotments included several large parcels between Newport and Depoe Bay, including most of the land at Whale Cove.

72. For example, see Richard W. Rogers, "European Influences on Ancient Hawaii," *Maritime Symposium*, 2014 Northwest Anthropology Conference, Bellingham, Washington. In Hawaii carved effigies that predate the voyage of Captain James Cook in 1778 include several that depict an animal that resembles a stylized lion (theorized to be carvings inspired by a ship's figurehead or the stylized lion depicted on various European flags). There had been European visitors prior to Cook as evidenced by a metal knife he was shown.

73. Hakluyt, "Extracts from Hakluyt's Voyages: The Course [...]," transcribed by Vaux, *The World Encompassed*, Appendix V, 225.

74. *The Century Dictionary and Cyclopedia* (New York: Century, 1903): "The word is very frequent in early modern English in various deflected or allusive senses [derogative for mons Venus]. The name of the cony enters into a number of local names and surnames: A rabbit: a burrowing rodent quadruped of the genus Lepus: A daman or species of the family Hyracidoe used in the English bible."

75. Ibid., 132.

76. Drake and Fletcher, "The Voyage bout the World," transcribed in Vaux, *The World Encompassed*, 221.

77. J. D. B. Stillman, *Seeking the Golden Fleece* (San Francisco: A. Roman, 1877), 295–97.

78. Wagner, *Sir Francis Drake's Voyage*, 492n42.

79. Stillman, *Seeking the Golden Fleece*, 295–97. See also Hanna, *Lost Harbor*, 210–11.

80. Heizer, *Francis Drake and the California Indians*, 269.

81. Ibid., 269.

82. Hakluyt, *Divers Voyages Touching the Discovery of America and the Islands Adjacent*, 129. This was first published in 1582. Hakluyt suggested "blacke conie skinnes" could be sold in China because "wee abounde with the commoditie."

83. Laurier Turgeon, "French Fishers, Fur Traders, and Amerindians during the Sixteenth Century: History and Archaeology," *The William and Mary Quarterly* 55, no. 4 (October 1998): 595. See also Mancall, *Hakluyt's Promise*, 129–30.

84. Paul Kane, *Wanderings of an Artist among the Indians of North America* (London: Longman, Brown, Green, Longmans, and Roberts, 1859), 184.

85. Ibid. His painting showing a muskrat robe is in the Royal Ontario Museum, Toronto, and titled *Flat Head Woman and Child, Caw-wacham*, c. 1849–52.

86. Gary Moulton, ed., *The Journals of the Lewis and Clark Expedition* (Lincoln, NE: University of Nebraska Press, 2005), November 21, 1805.

87. Moulton, *The Journals of the Lewis and Clark Expedition*, November 17, 1805.

88. John Kirk Townsend, *Narrative of a Journey across the Rocky Mountains, to the Columbia River, and a Visit to the Sandwich Islands, Chili, &c.* (Philadelphia: Perkins & Marvin, 1839), 178.

89. Melissa Darby, "The Intensification of Wapato (*Sagittaria latifolia*) by the Chinookan People of the Lower Columbia River," in *Keeping It Living*. I model the use of wapato and muskrat based on the Chinookan use of these foodstuffs, and postulate this model would apply to other localities

in the Northwest, as well as in the extensive wetlands and lakes present in North America during the Pleistocene. See also Lee Lyman, Kenneth Ames, muskrat data sets in "Sampling to Redundancy in Zooarchaeology Lessons from the Portland Basin, Northwestern Oregon, and Southwestern Washington," *Journal of Ethnobiology* 24, no. 2 (2004).

Chapter 17: Linguistic Analysis

1. Drake and Fletcher, "The Voyage about the World," transcribed in Vaux, *The World Encompassed*, 124–38.
2. Taylor, *Francis Drake and the Pacific*. The diary belonged to Richard Madox, the chaplain of the follow-up voyage led by Fenton that only got as far as Brazil.
3. Barrett, "The Ethno-Geography of the Pomo and Neighboring Indians."
4. Ibid., 36n.
5. Kroeber, *Handbook of the Indians of California*, 277–78.
6. Ibid.
7. Drake and Fletcher, "The Voyage about the World," transcribed in Vaux, *The World Encompassed*, 97.
8. Taylor, *Francis Drake and the Pacific*.
9. E. G. R. Taylor to Alfred Kroeber, February 11, 1932, Collection CU-23, box 145, Department of Anthropology Records, University of California at Berkeley, Bancroft Library.
10. Ibid.
11. Ibid. The brackets indicate the rest of the sentence that Taylor did not include in her letter.
12. Taylor, "Francis Drake and the Pacific," 365.
13. G. Ezra Dane, "CLAMPROCLAMATION, Sixth Annual Pilgrimage." This was the announcement flyer for the Clampers unveiling of their "Plate of Brasse" and a Grand Pow-Wow. Mark Campion of Dallas, Oregon, provided a copy from his files. The text said that Olsen was in charge of general arrangements.
14. Heizer to Kroeber, January 27, 1941. Copy provided by researcher, historian, and Drake scholar Mark Campion from his archive.
15. Ibid.
16. Robert F. Heizer and William W. Elmendorf, "Francis Drake's California Anchorage in the Light of the Indian Language Spoken There," *The Pacific Historical Review* 11, no. 2 (June 1942).
17. Ibid., 216.
18. Heizer, *Elizabethan California*, 8–9.
19. Ibid., 6.

20. John Lyon, "Francis Drake's 1579 Voyage: Assessing Linguistic Evidence for an Oregon Landing," *Anthropological Linguistics* 58, no. 1 (2016). The Drake Anchorage Research Collaboration was a nonprofit organization that I established that provided support for his research.

21. Ibid.

22. Ibid., 2.

23. Ibid. For "wapato" see page 30, for "hiyu" and "caplil" and their variants see pages 42–43.

24. Ibid.

25. Ibid., 2.

26. R. James Holton, *Chinook Jargon, the Hidden Language of the Pacific Northwest* (San Leandro, CA: Wawa Press, 2004), 1.

27. F. W. Howay, "Origin of the Chinook Jargon on the North West Coast," *Oregon Historical Quarterly* 44, no. 1 (1943): 28.

28. N. A. Sloan, "Evidence of California-Area Abalone Shell in Haida Trade and Culture," *Canadian Journal of Archaeology* 27, no. 2 (2003): 273–86. Dentalium is an ocean mollusk that has a long narrow white shell that resembles an elephant tusk but is hollow and can be strung into necklaces or attached to clothing and regalia.

29. Leo Frachtenberg, Notebook: Field notes from Kusan Place, box 5 folder 9, SWORP Collection.

30. Barnett, "Culture Element Distributions: VII, Oregon Coast," 171.

31. Homer Barnett, Notebook: Indian Tribes of the Oregon Coast, 74, box 1 folder 9, SWORP Collection.

32. George Lang, *Making Wawa: The Genesis of Chinook Jargon* (Vancouver: UBC Press, 2008), 3. The origin of Chinook Jargon is contested by historians of the Northwest coast and concerns the existence of an intertribal jargon before the coming of French and English-speaking trappers and traders.

33. Sarah Grey Thomason, "Chinook Jargon in Areal and Historical Context," *Language* 59, no. 4 (1983): 867.

34. Drake and Fletcher, "The Voyage about the World," transcribed in Vaux, *The World Encompassed*, 126.

35. Lang, *Making Wawa*, 156, 158. For Sacagawea's quote see Moulton, *The Journals of the Lewis and Clark Expedition*, November 24, 1805.

36. Lang, *Making Wawa*, 156.

37. Kroeber, cited in Heizer, *Francis Drake and the California Indians*, 269.

38. Heizer, *Elizabethan California*, 71.

39. Melissa Darby, "Wapato for the People: An Ecological Approach to Understanding the Native American Use of Sagittaria Latifolia on the Lower Columbia River" (master's thesis, Portland State University, 1996).

40. A. G. Parker, "Iroquois Uses of Maize and other Food Plants," *New York State Museum Bulletin* 144 (1910): 105.

41. Martin Gorman, *Food Plants of the Indian Tribes of the Northwest*, unpublished manuscript, Martin W. Gorman Papers, Collection 169/3, Special Collections & University Archives, University of Oregon Libraries, Eugene, Oregon.

42. Lang, *Making Wawa*, 47–48, 53.

43. See various journal entries found in the online version of the journals at University of Nebraska Press/University of Nebraska-Lincoln Libraries-Electronic Text Center, https://lewisandclarkjournals.unl.edu/.

44. Moulton, *The Journals of the Lewis and Clark Expedition*, November 5, 1805.

45. Lyon, "Francis Drake's 1579 Voyage," 40–41.

46. T. C. Elliot, "The Journal of the Ship Ruby," *Oregon Historical Quarterly* 28, no. 3 (September 1927): 274. Captain Bishop wrote that he obtained a root he called "wappato" while trading with the Natives at the mouth of the Columbia River in 1795.

47. Henry B. Zenk and Tony A. Johnson, "Chinuk Wawa and its Roots in Chinookan," in *Chinookan Peoples of the Lower Columbia*, ed. Robert T. Boyd, Kenneth M. Ames, and Tony A. Johnson (Seattle: University of Washington Press, 2013), 281–82. Tony Johnson is a Chinook tribal leader.

48. Ibid.

49. Kroeber, *Handbook of the Indians of California*, 276–78.

50. Ibid., 215.

51. Heizer and Elmendorf "Francis Drake's California Anchorage," 269–70.

52. Lyon, "Francis Drake's 1579 Voyage," 5.

53. Cedar Media, *Tribal Journeys Handbook and Study Guide* (Seattle: American Friends Service Committee, 2011), 10.

54. Hakluyt, "Extracts from Hakluyt's Voyages: The Course [...]," transcribed by Vaux, Appendix V, 223.

55. Leo J. Frachtenberg, *Coos Texts* (New York: Columbia University Press, 1913), 196.

56. Drake and Fletcher, "The Voyage about the World," transcribed in Vaux, *The World Encompassed*, 127.

57. Ibid.

58. Ibid., 125.

59. Chinuk Wawa Dictionary Project, *Chinuk Wawa, As Our Elders Teach Us to Speak It* (Grand Ronde, OR: Confederated Tribes of the Grand Ronde Community, 2012.) The authors note that *hiyu* is frequently attached to any action verb to show the action in question is continuous or progressive, and that the word is often used as an adjective meaning "many" in

compound words. The authors also noted the syllables were variously stressed.

60. Earl Coe, *Indians of Washington* (Olympia: State of Washington Publication, 1950); Walter Shelley Phillips, *The Chinook Book: A Descriptive Analysis of the Chinook Jargon in Plain Words* (Seattle: R. L. Davis Printing, 1913), 33–34.

61. Ibid.

62. Lyon, "Francis Drake's 1579 Voyage," 13.

63. Phillips, *The Chinook Book*, 33–34. *Hiyu* is used also as a prefix meaning "much" or "a great amount."

64. Barnett, "Culture Element Distributions: VII, Oregon Coast," 175.

65. Lyon, "Francis Drake's 1579 Voyage," 27.

66. Ibid., 24–25. These are the two Coosan languages. Lyon notes that they share a great deal of vocabulary in identical or closely similar form, and their sound systems are nearly the same.

67. Heizer and Elmendorf, "Francis Drake's California Anchorage," 215.

68. Ibid.

69. Drake and Fletcher, "The Voyage about the World," transcribed in Vaux, *The World Encompassed*, 128.

70. Lyon, "Francis Drake's 1579 Voyage," 28.

71. Ibid., 389, 376.

72. Leo J. Frachtenberg, "Coos" in *Handbook of American Indian Languages*, Bureau of American Ethnology, Bulletin 40, part 2 (1922):410.

73. Ibid., 394

74. Lyon, "Francis Drake's 1579 Voyage," 28.

75. See the phonemes of Chinookan, in Michael Silverstein, "Chinookans of the Lower Columbia," *Handbook of North American Indians*, vol. 7 (Washington D.C.: Smithsonian Institution, 1990), 533.

76. Lyon, "Francis Drake's 1579 Voyage," 28.

77. Ibid., 47n23.

78. Ibid., 24.

79. Ibid.

80. Lang, *Making Wawa*, 46.

81. Edward Belcher, *Narrative of a Voyage Round the World, Performed in Her Majesty's Ship Sulphur, during the Years 1836–1842*, 2 vols. (London: Henry Colburn, 1843), 1:308.

82. Lyon, "Francis Drake's 1579 Voyage," 46n15. Frachtenberg's informant said that the Siletz spoke both Alsea and Tillamook, and originally they spoke Alsea only.

83. Jacobs, "Historic Perspectives in Indian Languages of Oregon and Washington," 58. Linguist Joe Pierce disagreed with Jacobs.

84. Draper, "A Proposed Model of Late Prehistoric Settlement Systems on the Southern Northwest Coast."

85. Gilsen, "Impacts of Earthquake Tsunamis on Oregon Coastal Populations," 121–45. See also Baker, *Cascadia Earthquake and Tsunami Events Reflected in Aboriginal Oral Tradition*; and Draper, "A Proposed Model of Late Prehistoric Settlement Systems on the Southern Northwest Coast.

Chapter 18: Thunder and Lightning: Cosmological Correspondences

1. Patricia J. O'Brien, "Prehistoric Evidence for Pawnee Cosmology," *American Anthropologist* 88, no. 4 (1986).

2. Kroeber, "The Coast and Lake Miwok," in *Handbook of the Indians of California*, 331.

3. Jacobs, series 10, box 99, folder 19, Cosmology, Melville Jacobs Papers.

4. Zelia Nuttall, "A Penitential Rite of the Ancient Mexicans," *Archaeological and Ethnological Papers of the Peabody Museum* 1, no. 7, (1904): 3. Writing about "Ancient Mexican" cultures, none other than Zelia Nuttall noted that, "The painful rite of drawing blood from one's body and offering it to the deity, commonly practiced by all persons, young and old, was a feature of everyday life."

5. Drake and Fletcher, "The Voyage about the World," transcribed in Vaux, *The World Encompassed*, 123.

6. Ibid., 129.

7. Hakluyt, "Extracts from Hakluyt's Voyages," transcribed by Vaux, 224.

8. Drake and Fletcher, "The Voyage about the World," transcribed in Vaux, *The World Encompassed*, 129–30.

9. Ibid., 130.

10. Jacobs, series 10, box 99, folder 21, Cosmology, Myths, Weltanschauung, Melville Jacobs Papers.

11. Drake and Fletcher, "The Voyage about the World," transcribed in Vaux, *The World Encompassed*, 133.

12. Ibid.

13. Ibid., 134.

14. Harold E. Driver, "Culture Element Distributions: X Northwest California," *Anthropological Records* 1, no. 6 (1939): 401.

15. Jacobs, series 10, box 99, folder 35, Fishing, Melville Jacobs Papers.

16. Jacobs, series 10, box 101, folder 2, Supernatural, Melville Jacobs Papers.

17. Jacobs, series 10, box 99, folder 19, Cosmology, Melville Jacobs Papers.

18. Ibid.

19. Melville Jacobs, *Coos Narrative and Ethnologic Texts*, University of Washington Publications in Anthropology 8, no. 1 (Seattle: University of Washington, 1939), 97.

20. Ibid.

21. Ibid.

22. Erminie W. Voegelin, "Culture Element Distributions: XX, Northeast California," *University of California Anthropological Records* 7, no. 2 (1942): 237.

23. Jacobs, series 10, box 99, folder 15, Class and Caste, Melville Jacobs Papers.

24. Leo J. Frachtenberg, *Alsea Texts and Myths*, Smithsonian Institution Bureau of American Ethnology (Washington D.C.: Government Printing Office, 1920), 231.

25. Ibid.

26. Jacobs, series 10, box 99, folder 19, Cosmology, Melville Jacobs Papers.

27. Curtis, *The North American Indian, Vol. 13*, 206.

28. Jacobs, series 10, box 99, folder 19, Cosmology, Melville Jacobs Papers.

Chapter 19: Epilogue

1. Taylor, "Early Empire Building Projects in the Pacific Ocean," 297.

Bibliography

Primary Sources
Manuscript Sources
Bancroft Library, Berkeley, California
Bolton, Herbert Eugene. Papers, 1870–1953. BANC MSS C-B 840.
Drake's Plate of Brass. Bancroft Library administrative files compiled by James
    Hart. BANC MSS 2002/68c.
Heizer, Robert Fleming. Papers. 78/17c.
Kroeber, Alfred Louis. Correspondence and Papers.
Nuttall, Zelia. Materials relating to Sir Francis Drake, circa 1914–1916. Z-R 14,
    Vol. 1.
Parmenter, Ross. "Zelia Nuttall and the Recovery of Mexico's Past."
    Unpublished manuscript. MSS 2009/115.
Records of the Department of Anthropology. CU-23.
Stephens, H. Morse. Papers. MSS 71/14c.

Boise State University Library
Barry, J. Neilson. Papers. MSS 1. Special Collections, Boise State University
    Library.

British Library, London
Harley Manuscript, 280—folios 80v–82r, Memoranda relating to the voyage.
    Folios 83v–90r. A Discourse of Sir Francis Drake's Journey by a Contem-
    porary Author.
Cotton Manuscripts. Otho E. VIII, Titus B. III. The Plan of the Voyage.

California State Archives, Sacramento
Drake, Sir Francis. Commission files. R348.3.

Elizabeth Baker and Diana Dane Dajani, Dallas, Oregon
Dane, George Ezra. Family Papers.

Huntington Library, San Marino, California
Haselden Plate of Brass Collection. HIA 32.5.11.7.

Library of Congress, Washington D.C.
Kraus, Hans P. Collection.

Museo Archeologico Nazionale di Venezia
Ven Globe of the World.

University of Oregon Special Collections
Southwest Oregon Research Project (SWORP) Collection, Coll 268. Special
    Collections and University Archives, University of Oregon Libraries,
    Eugene, Oregon.

University of Washington Special Collections
Jacobs, Elizabeth, and Melville. Papers. Upper Coquille Athabaskan Ethno-
    graphic Notes, taken by Elizabeth Jacobs from Coquille Thompson in
    1933–1934. Accession No. 6131-001, Series 6, box 2/130.
Jacobs, Melville. Papers, 1918–1978. Accession Number 1693.

Printed Sources
Aker, Raymond, V. Aubrey Neasham, and Robert H. Power. "The Debate:
    Point Reyes Peninsula/Drakes Estero; Bolinas Bay/Bolinas Lagoon; San
    Francisco Bay/San Quentin Cove." *California Historical Quarterly* 53, no. 3
    (1974): 203–92.
Bancroft, Hubert Howe. *History of California.* 7 vols. San Francisco: A. L.
    Bancroft, 1884.
Bannon, John Francis. *Herbert Eugene Bolton: The Historian and the Man,*
    1870–1953. Tucson: University of Arizona Press, 1978.
Barnett, Homer G. "Culture Element Distributions: VII, Oregon Coast." *Uni-*
    versity of California Anthropological Records 1, no. 3 (1937): 155–208.
Barrett, S.A. *The Ethno-Geography of the Pomo and Neighboring Indians.*
    Berkeley: University of California Press, 1908.
Barrow, John. *The Life, Voyages, and Exploits of Admiral Sir Francis Drake*
    […]. London: Jon. Murray, 1843.
Baumgartner, O'Brien & Reynolds, cartographers. "Birdseye View of the City
    of San Francisco, Showing the Pacific Ocean, the Golden Gate, and San
    Francisco Bay […]." San Francisco: Robert Behlow, 1910.
Bawlf, Samuel. *Sir Francis Drake's Secret Voyage to the Northwest Coast of*
    America, AD 1579. Salt Spring Island, B.C.: Sir Francis Drake Publications,
    2001.
Belcher, Edward. *Narrative of a Voyage Round the World, Performed in Her*
    Majesty's Ship Sulphur, during the Years 1836–1842 […]. Vol. 1. London:
    Henry Colburn, 1843.

Benson, E. F. *Sir Francis Drake*. London: Harper & Brothers, 1927.

Bolton, Herbert E. "Francis Drake's Plate of Brass." *California Historical Society Quarterly* 16, no. 1 (1937): 1–16.

Bolton, Herbert Eugene. "The Confessions of a Wayward Professor." *The Americas* 6, no. 3 (1950): 359–62.

Boyd, Robert T., Kenneth M. Ames, and Tony A. Johnson, eds. *Chinookan Peoples of the Lower Columbia*. Seattle: University of Washington Press, 2013.

California Historical Society. "Meetings of the Society." *California Historical Society Quarterly* 3, no. 2 (1924): 204–9.

Camden, William, *Annales Or, The History of the Most Renowned and Victorious Princesse Elizabeth, Late Queen of England: Containing All the Important and Remarkable Passages of State, Both at Home and Abroad, During Her Long and Prosperous Reigne* [...], 4 vols. (London: Benjamin Fisher, 1635).

Camp, Charles L., and Fulmer Mood. "George Ezra Dane." *California Folklore Quarterly* 1, no. 1 (1942): 91–93.

Chandler, Robert J., James M. Spitze, and Steven Zovickian. *An E Clampus Vitus Hoax Goes Awry: Sir Francis Drake's 1579 Plate of Brasse*. Berkeley: Friends of the Bancroft Library, 2017.

Chinuk Wawa Dictionary Project. *Chinuk Wawa, As Our Elders Teach Us to Speak It*. Grand Ronde, OR: Confederated Tribes of the Grand Ronde Community, 2012.

Clegg, Cyndia Susan. *The Peaceable and Prosperous Regiment of Blessed Queene Elisabeth: A Facsimile from Holinshed's Chronicles (1587)*. San Marino, CA: Huntington Library, 2005.

Clusius, Carolus (attributed). *Aliqvot Notae in Garciae Aromatum Historiam* [...]. Antwerp: Christopher Plantin, 1582.

Corbett, Julian Stafford. *Drake and the Tudor Navy: With a History of the Rise of England as a Maritime Power*. 2 vols. London: Longmans, Green, 1912.

Curtis, Edward S. *The North American Indian: Being a Series of Volumes Picturing and Describing the Indians of the United States, and Alaska*. Vol. 14. Norwood MA: The Plimpton Press, 1924.

Cutler, Phoebe. "Joaquin Miller and the Social Circle at the Heights." *California History* 90, no. 1 (2012): 40–69.

Dane, G. Ezra, and Beatrice J. Dane. *Ghost Town, Wherein Is Told Much That Is Wonderful, Laughable, and Tragic, and Some That Is Hard to Believe* [...]. New York: A.A. Knopf, 1941.

Darby, Melissa. "Wapato for the People: An Ecological Approach to Understanding the Native American Use of Sagittaria Latifolia on the Lower Columbia River." Master's thesis, Portland State University, 1996.

Davidson, George. "Francis Drake on the Northwest Coast of America in the Year 1579: The Golden Hind Did Not Anchor in the Bay of San Francisco." *Geographical Society of the Pacific Transactions and Proceedings* 5, no. 2, (1908): 1–114.

———. *Identification of Francis Drake's Anchorage on the Coast of California in the Year 1579.* California Historical Society Papers, Vol. 1, Pt. 3. San Francisco: Bacon, 1890.

———. *Voyages of Discovery and Exploration on the Northwest Coast of America from 1539 to 1603.* Washington, D.C.: U.S. Coast and Geodetic Survey, 1887.

Davies, Arthur. "The Golden Hind and the Tello on the Coasts of California." *The Geographical Journal* 148, no. 2 (1982): 219–24.

Davis, John. *The Worldes Hydrographical Discription. Wherein Is Proued Not Onely by Aucthoritie of Writers, but Also by Late Experience of Trauellers and Reasons of Substantiall Probabilitie [...].* London: Thomas Dawson, 1595.

Department of Anthropology. "Records of the Department of Anthropology." In *Records of the Department of Anthropology,* edited by University of California, Berkeley: The Bancroft Library, 1901–ongoing.

Deur, Douglas, and Nancy J. Turner. *Keeping It Living: Traditions of Plant Use and Cultivation on the Northwest Coast of North America.* Seattle: University of Washington Press, 2005.

Donno, Elizabeth Story. *An Elizabethan in 1582: The Diary of Richard Madox, Fellow of All Souls.* London: Hakluyt Society, 1976.

Drake, Francis, and Pierpont Morgan Library. *The Drake Manuscript in the Pierpont Morgan Library, Histoire Naturelle Des Indes.* London: Andre Deutsch Limited, 1996.

Drake, H. H. "Drake—the Arms of His Surname and Family." *Report and Transactions of the Devonshire Association for the Advancement of Science, Literature, and Art* 15 (1883): 487–89.

Draper, John. "A Proposed Model of Late Prehistoric Settlement Systems on the Southern Northwest Coast, Coos and Curry Counties, Oregon." PhD diss., Washington State University, 1988.

Driver, Harold E. "Culture Element Distributions: X, Northwest California." *University of California Anthropological Records* 1, no 6. (1939): 297–433.

Dudley, Robert. "Arcano del Mare." Ca. 1621. Manuscript at Bavarian State Library. http://daten.digitale-sammlungen.de/~db/0008/bsb00084103 /images/index.html?seite=238&fip=193.174.98.30.

———. "Dell'arcano Del Mare." Florence: Francesco Onofri, 1647.

Eells, Myron. *The Indians of Puget Sound: The Notebooks of Myron Eells.* Edited by George Pierre Castile. Seattle, WA: University of Washington Press, 1985.

Eliott-Drake, Lady Elizabeth Fuller. *The Family and Heirs of Sir Francis Drake*. 2 vols. London: Smith, Elder, 1911.

Elliott, T. C. "The Journal of the Ship Ruby." *Oregon Historical Quarterly* 28, no. 3 (September 1927): 258–80.

Farris, Glenn J. "The Bodega Miwok as Seen by Mikhail Tikhonovich Tikhanov in 1818." *Journal of California and Great Basin Anthropology* 20, no. 1 (1998): 2–12.

Fiske, John. "The Elizabethan Sea Kings." *The Atlantic Monthly* 76 (1895): 98–99.

Frachtenberg, Leo J., *Coos Texts*. New York: Columbia University Press, 1913.

——. "Coos". *Handbook of American Indian Languages*, Bureau of American Ethnology, Bulletin 40, part 2 (1922): 297–429.

Fuller, Mary C. "Writing the Long-Distance Voyage: Hakluyt's Circumnavigators." *Huntington Library Quarterly* 70, no. 1 (March 2007): 37–60.

Gilsen, Leland. "Impacts of Earthquake Tsunamis on Oregon Coastal Populations." *Contributions to the Archaeology of Oregon* 7 (2002): 121–45.

Gitzen, Garry David. *Francis Drake in Nehalem Bay 1579: Setting the Historical Record Straight*. Wheeler, OR: Isnik Publishing, 2013.

——. "Oregon's Stolen History, California's Sir Francis Drake Commission (1973–1980) and the Multiple Denials for Official Recognition by the California State Historical Resources Commission." Unpublished manuscript, 2012.

H. E., "Review of *Sir Francis Drake's Voyage round the World, 1577–1580: Two Contemporary Maps*, by F. P. Sprent." *The Geographical Journal* 70, no. 5 (1927): 479–81.

Hakluyt, Richard. *Divers Voyages Touching the Discovery of America and the Islands Adjacent*. Edited by John Winter Jones London: Hakluyt society, 1850.

——. *The Principall Navigations, Voiages and Discoveries of the English Nation, Made by Sea Over Land to the Most Remote and Farthest Distant Quarters of the Earth at Any Time within the Compasse of These 1500 Yeeres: Divided into Three Several Parts, According to the Positions of the Regions Whereunto They Were Directed*. London: George Bishop and Ralph Newberie, 1589.

——. *The Principal Navigations: Voiages, Traffiques and Discoveries of the English Nation, Made by Sea or Over-Land, to the Remote and Farthest Distant Quarters of the Earth, at Any Time within the Compasse of These 1500 Yeeres, Divided into Three Several Volumes, According to the Positions of the Regions, Whereunto They Were Directed. This First Volume Containing the Worthy Discoveries, &C. Of the English toward the North and Northeast by Sea… Together with Many Notable Monuments and Testimonies of the*

Ancient Forren Trades, and of the Warrelike and Other Shipping of This Realme of England in Former Ages. Whereunto Is Annexed Also a Briefe Commentarie of the True State of Island, and of the Orthern Seas and Lands Situate That Way. And Lastly, the Memorable Defeate of the Spanish Huge Armada, Anno 1588, and the Famous Victorie Atchieued at the Citie of Cadiz, 1596, Are Described. 3 vols. London: G. Bishop, R. Newberie, and R. Barker, 1598.

Haldane, Angus, "A Portrait of Drake? A Belief in the Possible," *The British Art Journal* 14, no. 3 (2013/2014): 42–44.

Hanna, Warren L. *Lost Harbor: The Controversy over Drake's California Anchorage.* Berkeley: University of California Press, 1979.

Harte, W. J. "Historical Revision: LXXVI.1—Some Recent Views on Drake's Voyage round the World." *History* 20, no. 80 (1936): 348–53.

Heizer, Robert F. *Elizabethan California: A Brief, and Sometimes Critical, Review of Opinions on the Location of Francis Drake's Five Weeks' Visit with the Indians of Ships Land in 1579* […]. Ramona, CA: Ballena Press, 1974.

———. "Francis Drake and the California Indians, 1579." *University of California Publications in American Archaeology and Ethnology* 42, no 3, (1947): 1–292.

Heizer, Robert F., and William W. Elmendorf. "Francis Drake's California Anchorage in the Light of the Indian Language Spoken There." *The Pacific Historical Review* 11, no. 2 (June 1942): 213–17.

Hewes, Gordon W. "California Flicker-Quill Headbands in the Light of an Ancient Colorado Cave Specimen." *American Antiquity* 18, no. 2 (1952): 147–54.

Hitchcock, C. Leo, and Arthur Cronquist. *Flora of the Pacific Northwest: An Illustrated Manual.* Seattle: University of Washington Press, 1974.

Hoffmann, Ann. *Lives of the Tudor Age, 1485–1603.* New York: Harper & Row, 1977.

Holmes, Kenneth L. "Francis Drake's Course in the North Pacific, 1579." *The Geographical Bulletin* 17 (1979): 5–41.

Holton, R. James. *Chinook Jargon, the Hidden Language of the Pacific Northwest.* San Leandro, CA: Wawa Press, 2004.

Hondius, Jodocus the Elder. *Vera Totius Expeditionis Nauticae Descriptio D. Franc* […]. [Amsterdam?], 1590.

Howay, F. W. "Origin of the Chinook Jargon on the North West Coast." *Oregon Historical Quarterly* 44, no. 1 (1943): 27–55.

Hudson, Travis, Craig D. Bates, Thomas C. Blackburn, John R. Johnson, Stephen D. Watrous, Glenn J. Farris, and Santa Barbara Museum of Natural

History. *Treasures from Native California: The Legacy of Russian Explora-tion.* Walnut Creek, CA: Left Coast Press, 2015.

Hulsius, Levinus. *kurtze, warhafftige Relation vnnd Beschreibung der wunderbarsten vier Schiffarhten, so jemals verricht worden.* : *Als nemlich: Ferdinandi Magellani, Portugalesers, mit Sebastiano de Cano. Francisci Draconis Engeländers. Thomae Candisch Engelländers. Oliuarii von Noort, Niederländers.* Frankfurt: Hartmannus Palthenius, 1626.

Hurtado, Albert L. "False Accusations: Herbert Bolton, Jews, and the Loyalty Oath at Berkeley, 1920–1950." *California History* 89, no. 2 (2012): 38–56.

——. *Herbert Eugene Bolton: Historian of the American Borderlands.* Berke-ley: University of California Press, 2012.

Jacobs, Melville. *Coos Narrative and Ethnologic Texts. University of Washing-ton Publications in Anthropology* 8, no. 1 (April 1939): 1–125.

——. "Historic Perspectives in Indian Languages of Oregon and Washington." *Pacific Northwest Quarterly* 28, no. 1 (1937): 55–74.

——. Kane, Paul. *Wanderings of an Artist among the Indians of North Amer-ica: From Canada to Vancouver's Island and Oregon, through the Hudson's Bay Company's Territory and Back Again.* London: Longman, Brown, Green, Longmans, and Roberts, 1859.

Kasner, Leone Letson. *Siletz: Survival for an Artifact.* Dallas, OR: self-published, 1976.

Kaufmann, Miranda. *Black Tudors: the Untold Story.* London: Oneworld Publications, 2017.

Kazin, Michael. *Barons of Labor: The San Francisco Building Trades and Union Power in the Progressive Era.* Urbana: University of Illinois Press, 1987.

Kelly, Isabel T. "Yuki Basketry." *University of California Publications in Ameri-can Archaeology and Ethnology* 24, no. 9 (1930): 421–44.

Kelsey, Harry. "Did Francis Drake Really Visit California?" *The Western His-torical Quarterly* 21, no. 4 (1990): 445–62.

——. *The First Circumnavigators: Unsung Heroes of the Age of Discovery.* New Haven: Yale University Press, 2016.

——. *Sir Francis Drake: The Queen's Pirate.* New Haven: Yale University Press, 1998.

Kimball, Richard S., and Barney Noel. *Native Sons of the Golden West.* Charleston, SC; Chicago, IL; Portsmouth, NH; San Francisco, CA: Arcadia Publishing, 2005.

Kohl, J. G. *A Descriptive Catalogue of Those Maps, Charts and Surveys Relat-ing to America, Which Are Mentioned in Vol. III of Hakluyt's Great Work.* Washington: Henry Polkinhorn, 1857.

Kroeber, Alfred Louis. "The Coast and Lake Miwok." In *Handbook of the Indians of California*, 272–78. New York: Dover Publications, 1976.

Kurbjuhn, Kornelia. Manuscript of an edited version of Ross Parmenter's "Zelia Nuttall and the Recovery of Mexico's Past." Provided by the author, unpaginated.

Lang, George. *Making Wawa: The Genesis of Chinook Jargon*. Vancouver: UBC Press, 2008.

La Vere, David. *The Lost Rocks: The Dare Stones and the Unsolved Mystery of Sir Walter Raleigh's Lost Colony*. Wilmington: Burnt Mill Press, 2010.

Lawler, Andrew. *The Secret Token: Myth, Obsession, and the Search for the Lost Colony of Roanoke*. New York: Doubleday, 2018.

Lyman, R. Lee, and Michael J. O'Brien. "The Direct Historical Approach, Analogical Reasoning, and Theory in Americanist Archaeology." *Journal of Archaeological Method and Theory* 8, no. 4 (2001): 303–42.

Lyon, John. "Francis Drake's 1579 Voyage: Assessing Linguistic Evidence for an Oregon Landing." *Anthropological Linguistics* 58, no. 1 (2016): 1–51.

Mancall, Peter C. *Hakluyt's Promise: An Elizabethan's Obsession for an English America*. New Haven: Yale University Press, 2007.

Moe, Ray, T. *One Hundred Years in Lincoln County, Oregon, 1893–1993*. Newport, OR: Lincoln County Historical Society, 1993.

Moulton, Gary, ed. "The Journals of the Lewis and Clark Expedition." Lincoln, NE: University of Nebraska Press, 2005.

National Oceanic and Atmospheric Administration. "Yaquina Head to Columbia River." In *National Ocean Survey*: U.S. Department of Commerce, 1975.

Neasham, Vernon Aubrey, and William E. Pritchard. *Drake's California Landing: The Evidence for Bolinas Lagoon*. Sacramento, CA: Western Heritage, 1974.

"New Drake Documents Discovered by Mrs. Zelia Nuttall." *The Geographical Journal* 40, no. 6 (1912): 621–24.

Newton, Jim. *Justice for All: Earl Warren and the Nation He Made*. New York: Riverhead Books, 2006.

Nuttall, Zelia. *New Light on Drake: A Collection of Documents Relating to His Voyage of Circumnavigation, 1577–1580*. London: Hakluyt Society, 1914.

———. "A Penitential Rite of the Ancient Mexicans." *Archaeological and Ethnological Papers of the Peabody Museum* 1, no. 7 (1904): 439–62.

———. "Review of *Sir Francis Drake's Voyage around the World, Its Aims and Achievements*, by Henry R. Wagner." *The American Historical Review* 34, no. 1 (1928): 114–17.

Nuttall, Zelia, and H. R. Wagner. "Communications." *The Hispanic American Historical Review* 8, no. 2 (1928): 253–60.

O'Brien, Patricia J. "Prehistoric Evidence for Pawnee Cosmology." *American Anthropologist* 88, no. 4 (1986): 939–46.

Oppenheim, M., ed. *The Naval Tracts of Sir William Monson*. London: Navy Records Society, 1913.

Parker, A. G. "Iroquois Uses of Maize and Other Food Plants." *New York State Museum Bulletin* 144 (1910): 1–113.

Patten, Roderick B. "Miranda's Inspection of Los Almagres: His Journal, Report, and Petition." *The Southwestern Historical Quarterly* 74, no. 2 (1970): 223–54.

Pearce, Haywood J., Jr. "New Light on the Roanoke Colony: A Preliminary Examination of a Stone Found in Chowan County, North Carolina." *Journal of Southern History* 4, no. 2 (1938): 148–64.

Phillips, Patricia Whereat. *Ethnobotany of the Coos, Lower Umpqua, and Siuslaw Indians*. Corvallis: Oregon State University Press, 2016.

Phillips, Walter Shelley. *The Chinook Book: A Descriptive Analysis of the Chinook Jargon in Plain Words* [...]. Seattle: R. L. Davis Printing, 1913.

Quinn, David Beers. *Explorers and Colonies: America, 1500–1625*. London: Hambledon Press, 1990.

———. *The Hakluyt Handbook*. 2 vols. London: Hakluyt Society, 1974.

———. *The Voyages and Colonizing Enterprises of Sir Humphrey Gilbert*. 2 vols. London: Hakluyt Society, 1940.

Rawlinson, H. G. *Narratives from Purchas His Pilgrimes*. Cambridge: University Press, 1931.

Robertson, John W. *Francis Drake and Other Early Explorers along the Pacific Coast*. San Francisco: Grabhorn Press, 1927.

Rogers, Richard W. "European Influences on Ancient Hawaii." Northwest Anthropology Conference. Bellingham, WA, 2014.

Ronald, Susan. *The Pirate Queen: Queen Elizabeth I, Her Pirate Adventurers, and the Dawn of Empire*. New York: HarperCollins, 2007.

Russell, Matthew A. "Encounters at *Tamál-Húye*: An Archaeology of Intercultural Engagement in Sixteenth-Century Northern California." PhD diss., University of California, Berkeley, 2011.

Schafer, Joseph. "Review of *Francis Drake and Other Early Explorers along the Pacific Coast*, by John W. Robertson." *The American Historical Review* 33, no. 2 (1928): 410–11.

Schoeppner, Robert F., and Robert J. Chandler, eds. *California Vignettes*. San Francisco, CA: San Francisco Corral of the Westerners, 2001.

Servín, Manuel P. "Symbolic Acts of Sovereignty in Spanish California." *Southern California Quarterly* 45, no. 2 (June 1963): 109–21.

Shangraw, Clarence F., and Edward P. Von der Porten. "The Drake and Cermeño Expeditions' Chinese Porcelains at Drakes Bay, California, 1579

and 1595." Unpublished manuscript, Santa Rosa Junior College and Drake
  Navigators Guild, 1981.

Sloan, N. A. "Evidence of California-Area Abalone Shell in Haida Trade and
  Culture." *Canadian Journal of Archaeology* 27, no. 2 (2003): 273–86.

Spate, Oscar. *The Spanish Lake*. Canberra: Australian National University
  E Press, 2004.

Spitze, James M., Robert Joseph Chandler, Edward P. Von der Porten, and
  Steven Zovickian. *The Clampers and Their Hoaxes*. Berkeley: University of
  California Press, 2018.

Stephens, Henry Morse, and Herbert Eugene Bolton, eds. *The Pacific Ocean in
  History: Papers and Addresses Presented at the Panama-Pacific Historical
  Congress, Held at San Francisco, Berkeley and Palo Alto, California, July
  19–23, 1915*. New York: Macmillan, 1917.

Stillman, J. D. B. "Did Drake Discover San Francisco Bay?." *Out West Magazine* 1, no. 4 (1868): 332–37.

———. *Seeking the Golden Fleece: A Record of Pioneer Life in California* […].
  San Francisco: A. Roman, 1877.

Sugden, John. *Sir Francis Drake*. London: Barrie & Jenkins, 1990.

Suttles, Wayne, ed. *Northwest Coast*. Vol. 7 of *Handbook of North American
  Indians*, edited by William C. Sturtevant. Washington, D.C.: Smithsonian,
  1990.

Taylor, E. G. R. "Early Empire Building Projects in the Pacific Ocean, 1565–
  1585." *The Hispanic American Historical Review* 14, no. 3 (1934): 296–306.

———. "Francis Drake and the Pacific: Two Fragments." *Pacific Historical
  Review* 1, no. 3 (1932): 360–69.

———. *Late Tudor and Early Stuart Geography, 1583–1650*. London: Methuen,
  1934.

———. "Master John Dee, Drake and the Straits of Anian." *Mariner's Mirror* 15,
  no. 2 (1929): 125–30.

———. "The Missing Draft Project of Drake's Voyage of 1577–80." *The Geographical Journal* 75, no. 1 (1930): 46–47.

———. "More Light on Drake." *Mariner's Mirror* 16, no. 2 (1930): 134–51.

———. *Tudor Geography, 1485–1583*. London: Methuen, 1930.

———. *Late Tudor and Early Stuart Geography, 1583–1650*. London: Methuen,
  1934.

Thomason, Sarah Grey. "Chinook Jargon in Areal and Historical Context."
  Language 59, no. 4 (1983): 820–70.

Thompson, Laurence C. "Melville Jacobs, 1902–1971." *American Anthropologist*
  80, no. 3 (1978): 640–49.

Thrower, Norman J. W. *Sir Francis Drake and the Famous Voyage, 1577–1580:*

Essays Commemorating the Quadricentennial of Drake's Circumnavigation of the Earth. Berkeley: University of California Press, 1984.

Townsend, John Kirk. *Narrative of a Journey across the Rocky Mountains, to the Columbia River, and a Visit to the Sandwich Islands, Chili, &C.* Philadelphia: Perkins & Marvin, 1839.

Turgeon, Laurier. "French Fishers, Fur Traders, and Amerindians during the Sixteenth Century: History and Archaeology." *The William and Mary Quarterly* 55, no. 4 (October 1998): 585–610.

Tveskov, Mark Axel. "The Coos and Coquille: A Northwest Coast Historical Anthropology." PhD diss., University of Oregon, 2000. Digital copy provided by the author.

———. "Social Identity and Culture Change on the Southern Northwest Coast." *American Anthropologist* 109, no. 3 (2007): 431–41.

Twain, Mark. *Sketches, New and Old.* Chicago: American Publishing, 1882.

Twiss, Travers. *The Oregon Question Examined, in Respect to Facts and the Law of Nations.* London: Longman, Brown, Green, 1846.

Van Sype, Nicola. *La Heroike Enterprinse Faict Par Le Signeur Draeck D'avoir Cirquit Toute La Terre […].* [Antwerp?], 1581.

Vancouver, George, and John Vancouver. *A Voyage of Discovery to the North Pacific Ocean, and Round the World: In Which the Coast of North-West America Has Been Carefully Examined and Accurately Surveyed.* 3 vols. London: G.G. and J. Robinson, 1798.

Vaux, W.S.W. *The World Encompassed by Sir Francis Drake Being His Next Voyage to That to Nombre De Dios.* New York: Burt Franklin, 1963. Originally published in London, 1854.

Von der Porten, Edward, Raymond Aker, Robert W. Allen, and James M. Spitze. "Who Made Drake's Plate of Brass? Hint: It Wasn't Francis Drake." *California History* 81, no. 2 (2002): 116–33.

Wagner, Henry R. *Bullion to Books: Fifty Years of Business and Pleasure.* Los Angeles: The Zamorano Club, 1942.

———. *Sir Francis Drake's Voyage around the World, Its Aims and Achievements.* San Francisco, CA: John Howell, 1926.

———. "The Voyage to California of Sebastian Rodriguez Cermeño in 1595." *California Historical Society Quarterly* 3, no. 1 (1924): 3–24.

Walker, Franklin, and G. Ezra Dane. *Mark Twain's Travels with Mr. Brown: Being Heretofore Uncollected Sketches.* New York: Alfred A. Knopf, 1940.

Wallis, Helen. "England's Search for the Northern Passages in the Sixteenth and Early Seventeenth Centuries." *Arctic* 37, no. 4 (1984): 453–72.

———. *The Voyage of Sir Francis Drake Mapped in Silver and Gold.* Number 27 in the Series of Keepsakes Issued by the Friends of the Bancroft Library for

Its Members. Berkeley: The Friends of the Bancroft Library, University of California, 1979.

Ward, Bob. *Lost Harbour Found! Where Sir Francis Drake Really Landed on the West Coast of America, and How He Also Discovered Canada.* Unpublished monograph, 1981.

Wathen, Bruce. *Sir Francis Drake: The Construction of a Hero.* Cambridge, UK; Rochester, NY: D.S. Brewer, 2009.

Wilkinson, Charles F. *The People Are Dancing Again: The History of the Siletz Tribe of Western Oregon.* Seattle: University of Washington Press, 2010.

Wilson, Derek. *Sir Francis Walsingham: A Courtier in an Age of Terror.* London: Constable, 2007.

Winsor, Justin. *Narrative and Critical History of America: English Explorations and Settlements in North America, 1497–1689.* Boston: Houghton Mifflin, 1884.

Woods, Gerald. "A Penchant for Probity, California Progressives and the Disreputable Pleasures." In *California Progressivism Revisited*, edited by William Deverall and Tom Sitton, 99–116. Berkeley: University of California Press, 1994.

Wright, Cyril Ernest. *Fontes Harleiani: A Study of the Sources of the Harleian Collection of Manuscripts Preserved in the Department of Manuscripts in the British Museum.* London: The Trustees of the British Museum, 1972.

Index

Page numbers in *italics* refer to images or tables.

Adams, Leon D., 156

Aguilar, Martín de, 258n28

Aker, Raymond, 149, 175, 176–77

Alsea: and cosmology, 235–36; and linguistic analysis, 229, 290n82

American Association for the Advancement of Science, 82

American Historical Association, 89, 129

American Historical Review, 95, 109, 142

animals: and archaeological evidence for mountain goats in Oregon, 285n68; and Chinookan use of wapato and muskrat, 286–87n89; and descriptions of Drake's landing site, 210–13; and elk in Willamette Valley (Oregon), 190

Anonymous Narrative, The. See Harley Ms.

anthropology: Nuttall's career in, 82; and research on Native American cultures of Oregon coast in early to mid-twentieth-century, 197

Anton, San Juan de, 53, 54–55

archaeology: and ethnographic record for Oregon, 192; and evidence for mountain goats in Oregon, 285n68; and evidence for textile manufacture on Oregon coast, 206–7, 284–85n66; and Heizer's excavations at Drakes Bay, 149. *See also* porcelain sherds

Archivo General de Indias, 51

Astor, John Jacob, 122

Athabascan languages, and differences among indigenous groups of coastal Oregon, 194

Bancroft, Hubert Howe, 14

Bancroft Library (University of California at Berkley), 99, 100, 138, 150

Barnett, Homer, *193*, 195, 197, 204, 221, 225

Barrett, Samuel, 201, 214, 215

Barron, George, 151, 155, 157–59, 160

Barrow, John, 58

Barry, James H., 101

Barry, J. Neilson, 123

basketry: and differences among indigenous groups of coastal Oregon, 194, 196; and Drake's descriptions of indigenous peoples, 201–4

Bawlf, Samuel, 64, 246n30, 257–58n17

Beechey, Frederick William, 13

Belcher, Edward, 228

Bensell, Jim, 280n2

Benson, E. F., 110–11

Berkeley Daily Gazette (newspaper), 120–21

Bishop, Charles, 223, 289n46

Blacks (Africans), status of in sixteenth century England, 249n12, 250n26. *See also* Cimarrons; Diego; Maria; slavery

blood-letting: and Drake's accounts of indigenous peoples of Northwest coast, 186, 188, 190, 231–32, 236; Nuttall on in ancient Mexican cultures, 291n4

Boas, Franz, 82

Bodega Bay (California), 13

Bolinas Bay (California), 170–71

Bolton, Herbert E.: early academic career of, 267n6; and Heizer's archaeological excavations at Drakes Bay, 149; and

Plate of Brass hoax, 8, 115–31, 132–39, 140, 143, 144, 146–47, 156–57, 160–61, 164–65, 167–68, 275n47; and Native Sons of the Golden West, 261n13; and response of California historians to Nuttall's research, 89–93, 99–100, 105

Bonilla, Francisco Leyva de, 118–20, 121

Book of Common Prayer, Drake's readings from, 57, 254n84. *See also* Prayer Book Cross

Brewer, John, 45, 48

British Museum, 141

Brown, Ellen, 280n2

Brown, Oscar, 198, 220–21, 280n2

Buchannan, Jim, 280n2

Burghley, Lord (William Cecil), 39–40, 111, 112

Butler, Henry, 50, 51, 54–55. *See also* Oxenham, John

Butler, John, 50, 51, 54–55, 84. *See also* Oxenham, John

Cabot, Sebastian, 70

Cabillo, Juan Rodríguez, 258n28

Caen, Herb, 138–39

Caley, Earle R., 145, 272n30

California: and commemoration of Drake's voyage, 169–81; origin of idea of Drake's landing on coast of, 10–17; Plate of Brass hoax and history in, 132–39; research on ethnography of Native peoples of, 280n2; response of historians to Nuttall's research on site of Drake's landing, 87–106; statement of historical problem of location of Drake's landing site, 5–7; Wagner and continuation of debate on site of Drake's landing, 107–14

California Academy of Sciences, 104–5

California Folklore Society, 165–66

California Historical Quarterly, 136, 142–43, 144, 148, 275n48

California Historical Society, 108–9, 136, 138, 139

California History (journal), 160

California State Historical Resources Commission, 177

Camden, William, 45

Camp, Charles L., 163–64, 275n48

Canada: and bootlegging trade during prohibition era, 73–75; estimates of distance between Newfoundland and west coast on early maps, 246n31. *See also* Frigid Zone; Haida Gwaii archipelago; Northwest Passage

canoes: lack of detail in Drake's descriptions of, 198; species of trees for making of and place names on Oregon coast, 77

Cape Arago (Oregon), 172, 173, 174

Cape Blanco (Oregon), 75

Cape Flattery (Washington), 5. *See also* Neah Bay

Cape of Good Hope, 68

Cape Horn, 47

Cape Verde Islands, 44–45

Carder, Peter, 48

Cecil, William. *See* Burghley, Lord

Cermeño, Sebastian Rodriguez, 11–12, 198, 200

Chester, John, 42

Chickering, Allen, 134, 136, 139, 141, 143, 144, 145, 149, 164–65

Chile, Drake on Spanish maps of, 12. *See also* Mocha, Island of; Valparaiso

Chinook, and use of wapato and muskrat, 212, 286–87n89. *See* Chinook Jargon

Chinookan language, and differences among indigenous groups of coastal Oregon, 194

Chinook Jargon (Chinook Wawa), and linguistic analysis of indigenous groups of coastal Oregon, 219–25, 228–29, 288n32

Christopher (ship), and Drake expedition, 42, 46

Churchill, Winston, 88–89

Cimarrons, Drake's alliance with in
    Panama, 37–38, 183
Clampers (association), 133, 134, 160–61,
    163, 165, 217, 270n4, 276n67
Clark, George, 151, 155
Clark, William, 212
Clatsop, and Chinookan language, 194
clothing: Drake's crew and sumptuary
    laws, 44; and historical portraits of
    indigenous people from Oregon coast,
    207–9; and processing of fireweed by
    Native peoples in Oregon, 284n60,
    284–85n66; and use of furs by indige-
    nous people on Oregon coast, 212–13.
    See also headwear
Coe, Earl, 225
colonialism. See England; Spain
Cook, James, 285n72
Cooke, John, 44, 46, 48
Coos: clothing of in historical portraits,
    209, 210; and cultural differences
    among indigenous groups of coastal
    Oregon, 195; and decoration of
    headwear, 205; and descriptions of
    housing, 200; linguistic analysis and
    use of words noted in Drake account,
    225–27, 229, 290n66; thunder in
    cosmology of, 234–35; and use of
    Chinook Jargon, 220
Coos Bay dune sheet (Oregon), 77
Coos History Museum, 203
Corbett, Julian, 13, 14–15, 25, 36, 100,
    245n21
cosmology, of Native peoples of Oregon
    coast, 230–38
Cotton, Richard, 251n6
Cotton MSS., Otho, E VIII, 40
Council of Learned Societies, Commit-
    tee on Research in American Indian
    Languages, 197
culture, and differences among indig-
    enous groups of coastal Oregon,
    194–97. See also cosmology; ethnogra-
    phy; linguistic analysis

Cumming, Alex, 177–78
Curtis, Edward, 237
Cutting, G. M., 102–3

Dajani, Diana Dane, 276n68
Dajani, Laika, 277n76
dancing: and cultural differences among
    indigenous groups of Oregon coast,
    194; of indigenous peoples encoun-
    tered by Drake, 188
Dane, Beatrice J., 165
Dane, George Ezra, 133, 161–63, 164–66,
    270n3, 276n68, 277n76
Dare Stone, as historic hoax, 8, 123–31,
    269n51
Davidson, George, 13–14, 15–17, 247n34
Davies, Arthur, 16
Davis, John, 15, 246n31
Davis, John F., 95
Dearborn Independent (newspaper), 122
Dee, John, 16, 40, 61
demographic shifts, among indigenous
    peoples of Oregon coast, 196, 229
Depoe Charlie, 207, 208, 209, 285n70–71
D'Ewes, Sir Simonds, 20, 25
Diaz Bravo, Benito, 53
Diego (Drake's crew), 37, 43, 49, 64, 67,
    250n26, 279n5
Discourse. See Harley Ms.
Domínguez-Escalante trail, 126–27
Dominican College (California), 171
Doughty, Thomas, 26, 44, 45
Drake, Edmund, 32–33
Drake, Sir Francis: and California
    commemorations of voyage, 169–81;
    cosmology of Native people of
    Oregon and, 230–38; early life of,
    32–38; encounters with Native people
    at "fair and good bay," 182–91; and
    ethnographic evidence for landing in
    Oregon, 192–213; Hakluyt's account
    of circumnavigation voyage, 18–31,
    241–42n6; introduction of histori-
    cal problem of specific location of

landing, 1–9; linguistic analysis and
evidence for site of landing, 214–29;
and maps of circumnavigation voyage,
70–78; Nuttall's archival research on,
79–86; origins of idea of landing on
California coast, 10–17; and plans
for circumnavigation voyage, 39–44;
response of California historians to
Nuttall's theory on site of landing in
Oregon, 87–106; proponents of landing at specific bays, 148–68; summary
of narratives on circumnavigation
voyage, 44–69, 239–40; Wagner and
debate among California historians on
site of landing, 107–14. See also Golden
Hind; Northwest Passage; Plate of
Brass; Prayer Book Cross
Drake, H. H., 32
Drake, John, 14–15, 21, 43, 49, 53, 64–65,
67, 242n6, 246n26, 247n8
Drake, Thomas, 31, 43, 45
Drake Anchorage Research Collaboration
(DARC), 218, 288n20
Drake Navigators Guild, 146, 149, 171–73,
177, 178–79, 202
Drake's Bay (California), 11, 14, 16, 17, 22,
95, 149, 170–71, 177, 244n3
Drakes Passage (Cape Horn), 47
Draper, John, 196
Drew, Frank, 205, 280n2, 283n49
Dubuque Telegraph-Herald (newspaper),
122
Dudley, Robert, 39, 73, 75–77, 113, 198,
258n21–22
Dunning, Charles, 147

l'Écluse, Charles de, 243n12
Eells, Myron, 284n66
Eliot, Lawrence, 44
Elizabeth, Queen: Drake's 1580 audience
with, 3–4; role of in plans for Drake's
voyage, 6, 40, 112–13; and secrecy concerning Drake's voyage, 31, 239

Elizabeth II, Queen, 173–74
Elizabeth (ship), and Drake expedition,
42, 46, 48
Elizabeth Island (south of Cape Horn),
85, 98
Elliott-Drake, Lady, 31, 32, 33
Ellison, Joseph, 146, 147
Elmendorf, William, 217, 223, 225, 226
England: Drake and land claims of in
New World, 23, 28–29, 30, 31, 39–40,
85, 97–98, 239; and Drake's role in
defeat of Spanish Armada, 24–25, 27;
narrative of events upon Drake's return to in 1580, 3–5; trade and English
motives for establishing colonies in
New World, 34–35; West Country and
family history of Drake, 32. See also
Elizabeth, Queen; Nova Albion
epidemic diseases, impact of on indigenous peoples of Oregon coast, 196,
229
ethnography: and evidence for Drake's
landing in Oregon, 192–213; research
on Native peoples of Oregon and
California, 280n2. See also cosmology;
linguistics
eugenics, and racism in California, 91
Everette, Willis, 207, 283n41
Evermann, Barton W., 101, 102

Fairchild, Baldwin, 207
Falconer, Eric, 161
Falkiner-Nuttall, Ralph, 264n61
"Famous Voyage, The." See Hakluyt,
Richard
Farrera, John, 246n31
fauna. See animals
Fenton, Edward, 23, 140, 246n26
Fink, Colin, 143–44, 145, 146
Fletcher, Alice, 81
Fletcher, Francis (chaplain on Golden
Hind), 10, 15, 18, 25–27, 29, 43, 49, 68,
94, 184, 187, 189

flora. *See* plants
Florio, John, 258n29
Flower, Robin, 141–42
Foxe, John, 41
Frachtenberg, Leo J., 224, 225, 235–36, 280n2
French Drake Map. *See* Van Syke, Nicola
Frigid Zone, and debate on latitudes of Drake's voyage, *28,* 30, 76
Frobisher, Martin, 16, 61
Fuller, Louis, 221, 280n2
Fuller, Mary, 23

Gass, Patrick, 212
Gates, William, 90
Geographical Journal (Royal Geographical Society), 85
gifts, and Drake's encounters with indigenous peoples of Northwest coast, 182, 183–84, 185, 188–89, 191
Gitzen, Garry, 278–79n36
gnaâh, and Native vocabulary words in accounts of Drake's landing, 214, 215, 217, 228, 237–38
Goelet, Peter Michael, 62–63
Golden Gate International Exposition (1939), 161
Golden Hind (ship), *42, 52:* and careening process, 62–63; description of at start of Drake expedition, 42–43; design of, 62, 255n108; and Doughty affair, 26; and Drake's return to England, 3; and narrative of events at "fair and good bay," 1; and navigability of Whale Cove (Oregon), 77–78; renaming of, 251n12; replica of, 169; and Strait of Magellan, 48
Golden Hind II (ship), 169, 255n108
Gomez, Alonso, 11
Gorman, Martin, 222
Gray's Harbor (Washington), 113
Green, Paul, 124
Grenville, Sir Richard, 39, 112, 266n32

Grunsky, Carl Ewald, 100–101
Guatulco (Mexico), Drake's raid on, 58–59
Guinea, Drake's landing in, 68

Haida Gwaii archipelago (British Columbia), 258n17
Hakluyt, Richard, 10, 12, 16, 22–25, 27, 28–29, 34, 54, 97, 98, 212, 214, 232, 241n6, 248n32, 286n82
Hakluyt Society, 79, 84, 86, 108
Haldane, Angus, 250n1
Hale, Horatio, 228
Hamlin, Herbert, 151
Hammond, George P., 120, 126–27, 128, 129, 131, 269n51
Hammond, L. E., 123, 125–26, 127–28
Handbook of North American Indians (Northwest Coast volume), 192–93
Hanna, Warren, 7, 29, 159, 171, 205
Harley Ms. 280, 15, 18, *19,* 20–22, 25–31, 56, 73, 242n6
Harlow, Vincent T., 141, 142
Hart, James, 117, 131, 145, 150–59, 162–63, 168, 270n6, 275n41
Harte, W. J., 137
Haselden, R. B., 140–41, 142–43
Hatton, Christopher, 39, 42, 113, 251n12
Hawaii, and European contact prior to Cook voyage, 285n72
Hawkins, John, 35–36, 79, 113
Hawkins, Richard, 48–49
Hawkins, William, 33, 43
headwear, and Drake's descriptions of indigenous peoples, 204–5, 206–7. *See also* clothing
Hearst, Phoebe Apperson, 82–83, 103, 104
Heizer, Robert F., 148–49, 188, 198–99, 204–5, 205–6, 211–12, 216–18, 222, 225, 226, 267n2
Henry R. Huntington Library (Pasadena, California), 140–41

Herrera, Antonio de, 36

hióh, and language of indigenous peoples encountered by Drake, 187, 214, 215, 217, 223–25

Hispanic American Historical Review, 111

historiography: and origins of idea of Drake's landing on California coast, 10–17; and Plate of Brass hoax, 132–39; and responses of California historians to Nuttall's research, 87–106; Wagner and debate on location of Drake's landing, 107–14

hoaxes, and Twain's writings, 162, 164. *See also* Dare Stone; Plate of Brass

Hobby, Theodore V., 178

Holinshed, Raphael, 4

Holmes, Kenneth, 173

Hondius, Jodocus, and map of Drake's voyage, 70–73, 97

housing, and Drake's descriptions of indigenous peoples, 193, 199–201

Howay, F. W., 219–20

Howe, Thomas, 158

Hulsius, Levinus, 52

Humaña, Antonio Guiterrez de, 118–20, 121

Huntington, Archer P., 97

Hurtado, Albert, 90, 92, 93, 132, 143, 168

Hymes, Dell, 221

Indian Ocean, and Drake's voyage, 68

Ishi (Yana), 98–99, 264n61

Jacobs, Elizabeth, 196–97

Jacobs, Melville, 194, 195, 196, 197, 229, 234–35, 236–37, 280n2, 290n83

Java: and Drake's voyage, 68; illustration of by Hondius, 71

Jesus of Lubeck (ship), and Hawkins affair, 35

Johnson, Hiram, 102, 103

Johnson, Tony A., 289n47

Joseph, Jacqueline, 127–28

Journal of Southern History, 124

Judith (ship), Drake as captain of, 35–36

Kane, Paul, 212

Kasner, Leone, 204, 283n48

Kate (Coos), 209, *210*

Kaufmann, Miranda, 35, 49, 57, 67

Kelly, Isobel, 199

Kelsey, Harry, 10, 35, 45, 241n4, 252n28

Kent, William, 101

Kidd, Captain William, 122–23

Knowland, Joseph R., 119, 121

Kohl, Johann George, 70

Kroeber, Alfred A., 82, 197–98, 215, 216, 222, 223, 226, 230, 281n11

Ku Klux Klan, 130

Kurbjuhn, Kornelia, 260n21

Lally, Jessica, 179, 244n3

Lambert, Cornieles, 55, 56, 59, 63

Lang, George, 222, 223

La Vere, David, 125

Lawler, Andrew, 126

Lawrence Berkeley Laboratory, 150

Legge, William, 21

Leicester, Earl of. *See* Dudley, Robert

Lew, Fred, 171

Lewis and Clark expedition, 221, 222

Lima (Peru), and Drake's raid on port of Callao, 50–51, 53

linguistic analysis, and languages: differences among indigenous groups of coast Oregon, 194–97, 289–90n59, 290n66; and evidence for Drake's landing in Oregon, 214–29. *See also* Chinook Jargon

Lizarza, Domingo de, 55

logbooks: Nuttall's discovery of Da Silva's, 83; suppression of Drake's original, 4–5

Los Angeles Times (newspaper), 118, 170–71

Lyman, R. Lee, 280n1, 285n68

Lyon, John, 218–20, 223, 224, 225, 226, 227–28, 290n66

MacMillan, Ken, 98
Madox, Richard, 113, 137, 140, 214, 215, 216, 221, 225, 226, 227
Magellan, Ferdinand, 2, 45
Maine, and Captain Kidd hoax, 122–23
Makah Tribe, Nuttall's visit to, 103, 104
Malony, Alice, 235
Mancall, Peter, 23
maps: and cartography of Drake's Famous Voyage, 70–78; Drake's original in Whitehall Palace, 4–5, 70, 85; Drake on Spanish maps of Chile, 12; estimates of distance between Newfoundland and west coast on early, 246n31; Mercator's of Northwest coast, 61, 114. See also Molyneaux globes; Van Sype, Nicola
Maria (Black woman on Golden Hind voyage), 1, 29, 57, 64, 67–68
Marigold (ship), and Drake expedition, 42, 46, 48
Matley, Marcel, 127
Mayerhoff, John, 118, 119
McDonald, Tom, 280n2
McGee, J. Sears, 20
Means, Philip Ainsworth, 111
Memoranda. See Harley Ms.
Mercator, Gerard, 4, 61, 114
Messa, Diego de, 55
Metcalf, Billy, 204, 280n2
Metropolitan Museum of Art, 144
Mexico: Drake's raids in, 58–59; and Mexican Revolution, 90; practice of blood-letting in ancient cultures of, 291n4. See also Vera Cruz
Michael, M. F., 108
Mille, Cecil B. de, 125
Minion (ship), and Drake's role in Hawkins affair, 36

Miwok: and descriptions of housing, 199; and Native vocabulary words in Drake's accounts, 214, 215; Olompali as village site of, 171
Mocha, Island of (Chile), 48–50, 183
Modoc, thunder in cosmology of, 235
Mogadore (Morocco), 44
Moluccas (Spice Islands), and Drake's voyage, 64, 65, 182
Molyneux Globes, 97, 98, 263n57–58
Monson, William, 27
Moon, Thomas, 21, 42
Moratto, Mike, 171
Mozambique, and Drake's voyage, 68

National Geographic, 126
National Landmarks, and Drakes Bay application, 177, 178–81, 244n3, 278n32, 278n36
National Museum of Anthropology (Mexico), 82
National Park Service, 180–81
Native American(s): accounts of Drake's encounters with at "fair and good bay," 182–91, 240; and Cermeño's landing at Drake's Bay, 11–12; and contemporary cultural revival movements, 240; cosmology of peoples of Oregon coast and Drake's visit to Nova Albion, 230–38; and ethnographic evidence for Drake's landing in Oregon, 192–213; Inuit and Frobisher's search for Northwest Passage, 61; linguistic analysis and evidence for Drake's landing in Oregon, 214–29
Native American Graves Protection and Repatriation Act, 192
Native Sons of the Golden West, 87–89, 95, 133, 138, 157, 260n1, 261n13
Navigation Manual (1577), 41
Neah Bay (Washington), 103–4, 257n16
Neasham, Aubrey, 173, 174–75, 176, 177, 267n2

Nehalem Bay, and Neahkahnie Stones (Oregon), 278–79n36
Nestucca, and Salish cultural group, 194
New York Times, 121
Nichols, William Ford, 16, 17, 107
Noll, Lorenz, 151
Nombre de Dios (Panama), 37, 38
Norgaard, Loring Christian, 255n108
North Pacific Gyre, 60–61
Northwest coast: and cultural complex of indigenous peoples, 193; Mercator's maps of, 61, 114; and theories on site Drake's landing, 5–9. *See also* Native American(s); Oregon; Washington
Northwest Passage: and California theory of Drake's landing, 15–16; Drake's voyage and search for, 8, 21–22, 40, 43, 61, 113, 239; and English colonies in North America, 34
Nova Albion: Drake and England's land claims in New World, 23, 85, 98, 239; Drake's choice of name, 2; Drake's plan to return to, 69; and Dudley on place names, 76; and John Drake's deposition to Spanish, 14
Nuestra Señora de la Concepción (Spanish ship), battle of *Golden Hind* with, 52, 53–55
Nuttall, Zelia: and archival research on Drake's voyage, 5–6, 51, 56, 59, 65, 69, 79–86, 242n6, 246n26; and Neah Bay as possible site of Drake's landing, 257n16; and Plate of Brass hoax, 159–60; on practice of blood-letting in Mexican cultures, 291n4; response of historians in California to theory on Drake's landing site in Oregon, 87–106, 107–10, 111, 132–33, 240

Oakland Tribune (newspaper), 103, 118, 120
O'Brien, Michael J., 280n1
O'Brien, Patricia J., 230

O'Brien, Patrick, 36
Olompali (Miwok village site), 171
Olson, Ronald Leroy, 216, 217
Oregon: cosmology of Native peoples and Drake's visit to Nova Albion, 230–38; and ethnographic evidence for site of Drake's landing, 192–213; and physical evidence for Drake's landing, 78; and proposed sites of Drake's "bad bay," *170*; research on ethnography of Native Peoples in, 280n2; topography of coast and lack of safe harbors, 75. *See also* Native Americans; Northwest coast; Whale Cove
Oregonian (newspaper), 172
Oregon Journal (newspaper), 174
Oxenham, John, 37–38, 50, 51, 54–55, 57–58, 84

Pacific Ocean: Drake's first sight of in Panama, 37–38; North Pacific Gyre and Drake's route northwest in, 60–61. *See also* Frigid Zone
painters and painting, and maritime expeditions in sixteenth century, 71. *See also* portrait
Panama, and Drake's alliance with Cimarrons, 37–38, 183
Panama-Pacific Historical Congress, 89, 94–106
Panama-Pacific International Exposition, 88–89
Parkinson, Robert W., 176
Park Memorial Museum (Golden Gate Park), 157
Parmenter, Ross, 84, 91, 94, 102, 103–4, 106, 108–9, 110, 260n21, 262n32, 264n74
Par Tee archaeological site (Oregon), 207
Peabody Museum for Ethnology and Archaeology, 81–82
Pearce, Haywood Jefferson, 123, 124–26, 129, 130

Pelican. See Golden Hind

Peru. *See* Lima

petâh, and Native vocabulary words in accounts of Drake's landing, 214, 215, 217, 221, 222, 223

Peterson, Annie Miner, 200, 204, 234–35, 237, 280n2

Peterson, Harry, 164, 276n67

Petty, Brenda, 127

Petty, Francis, 242n6

Phillips, Walter Shelley, 225

Pike, Donald, 7

Pinart, Alphonse, 92

Pinkerton National Detective Agency, 126, 128

pirates, and piracy: California landing theory and image of Drake as, 6, 14, 16, 87, 94, 95; Drake's return to England and accusations of, 3; and "letters of reprisal," 33–34

plants: and species of trees used for canoe construction, 77; and species of trees used for housing construction, 193; and use of fireweed (*Charmerion angustifolium*) by indigenous peoples, 206, 284n60, 284–85n66

Plate of Brass: Bolton's role in discovery and promotion of, 8, 115–31, 132–39, 140, 143, 144, 146–47, 156–57, 160–61, 164–65, 167–68, 275n47; Hart's investigation of, 148–68; as historical hoax, 5, 8, 115–31, 132–39, 140–47, 176; and support for California landing theory, 7

Polushkin, E. P., 144

Pomo, and Drake's descriptions of basketry, 201, 202, 203

porcelain sherds (Drakes Bay): and Heizer's excavations, 178–79; Kelsey's opinion of, 10–11; and late Ming period, 278n29; views on as evidence for Drake's landing in California, 5, 180–81, 244n2–3

Portola Festival, 88, 89

portrait, of Drake, 39, 250n1. *See also* painters and painting

Portus illustration, and Hondius map, 72–73, 75, 77, 78

Power, Robert, 177

Prayer Book Cross (Golden Gate Park), 16–17, 146, 166, *167*

Pretty, Francis, 248n32

Principall Navigations, The. See Hakluyt, Richard

Pritchard, William E., 173

Putnam, Frederic, 81

Quinn, David, 30, 242n6

racism: Bolton's hoaxes and ideology of white manifest destiny, 8, 130–31; and eugenics movement in California, 91

Raft River (Washington), 113

religion. *See* blood-letting; Book of Common Prayer; cosmology; Prayer Book Cross

Rickard, Thomas, 141

Roanoke, lost colony of, 8, 123, 130. *See also* Dare Stone

Robertson, John Wooster, 110

Rolph, James, 88–89

Ronald, Susan, 34, 38

Ross, Richard, 196

Roys, Ralph, 93

Russell, Matthew, 179

Sacagawea (Lewis & Clark expedition), 221

sacrifice. *See* blood-letting

St. Clair, Harry Hull, 280n2

Salazar, Ken, 180

Salish cultural group, and Tillamook, 194

San Agustín (ship), 11–12, 178, 179, 180

San Francisco Bay, 171

San Francisco Chronicle (newspaper), 94

San Francisco Examiner (newspaper), 94

San Francisco Park Commissioners, 16

San Quentin Cove (California), 170–71

San Saba silver mine (Texas), 117–18, 121

Sapir, Edward, 216

Saturday Evening Post, 125

Scoble, Dolores Barron, 116–17, 151–54, 156–57, 158, 160, 168

Scoble, Vicky, 158, 275n41

Scott, Spencer, 280n2

Sea Island (ship), 74–75

Seibert, Erika, 181

sexism, and response of California historians to Nuttall's research, 92

Shakespeare, William, 9

Shasta, thunder in cosmology of, 235, 237

shells, and trade of indigenous groups on Oregon coast, 195–96, 220, 288n28

Shinn, Beryle, 115, *116*, 117, 133, 134–35, 136

Siletz River drainage (Oregon), 194

Silva, Nuño da, 43, 45, 49, 59, 71, 80–81, 83

Silver Map of the World, 97

Simmons, Hoxie and Bill, 280n2

singing: and cosmology of Native peoples of Oregon, 238; and cultural differences among indigenous groups of coastal Oregon, 194–95; and indigenous peoples encountered by Drake, 187, 188

Sir Francis Drake Association, 17, 107

Sir Francis Drake Commission, 169–81

slavery, and Africans in Spanish colonies, 57, 249n12

Slaymaker, Charles, 171

Smith, Lucy, 280n2

Smith, Tom, 199

Smith, William, 235–36

smuggling, and Northwest coast during prohibition era, 73–75

South Cove (Oregon), 172

Spain: colonial policy of in 1570s, 33, 34–35; Drake and English land claims on west coast, 28; Drake's lifelong vendetta against, 36–38; and slavery, 57, 249n12; and Spanish Armada of 1585, 24–25, 27; and treasure hoaxes in U.S., 117–21. *See also* Chile; Mexico

Sparkes, Boyden, 125

Spate, Oskar H. K., 7, 45

Sprent, Frederick P., 110

Sproul, Robert, 142

Starkey, Ralph, 20

Steele, Harvey, 179, 244n3

Stephens, Henry Morse, 89, 99–100, 105

Stewart, George, 163–64

Stillman, J. D. B., 13, 211

Strait of Anian, 60, 61, 113

Strait of Magellan, 46–48, 266n32

Sugden, John, 48

Swan (ship), and Drake expedition, 42, 46

tabâh, and language of indigenous peoples encountered by Drake, 187, 214, 215, 217, 225–26

Taylor, E. G. R., 24, 27, 40–41, 111–14, 132, 137, 214, 215–16, 243n20

Taylor, Ray, 154–55

Taylor, Will, 154

Teggart, Frederick John, 92–93

Tello, Rodrigo, 55–56, 62, 63, 64

Tempest, The (Shakespeare), 9

textile manufacture, archaeological and ethnographic evidence for on Oregon coast, 206–7, 284–85n66. *See also* clothing

Thomas, John, 42

Thomason, Sarah Grey, 221

Thompson, Lawrence C., 197

Thompson, Coquille, 200–201, 280n2

three, cosmological significance of to Native peoples encountered by Drake, 232–33

Thrower, Norman, 172, 246n31

thunder, and cosmology of Native peoples of coastal Oregon, 231, 233–38

Tikhanov, Mikhail Tikhonovich, 199

Tillamook, and Salish cultural group, 194

Time Magazine, 138
Tordesillas, Treaty of (1494), 34
Townsend, John Kirk, 212–13
trade: and Chinook Jargon, 219, 220, 223;
    and Drake's interest in fur trade, 212;
    and English motives for establishing
    colonies in New World, 34–35; and
    indigenous groups of coastal Oregon,
    195–96
Tveskov, Mark, 195, 206
Twain, Mark, 162
Twiss, Travers, 24, 27, 248n17

University of California at Berkley. *See*
    Bancroft Library
University of California at Los Angeles
    (UCLA), 82, 169
University of California Press, 166
University of Michigan, 121
University of New Mexico, 127
University of Pennsylvania Museum, 82

Valparaiso (Chile), Drake's raid on, 50
Valverde, Licentiate, 58–59, 64
Vancouver, George, 12–13
Van Sype, Nicola, and French Drake map,
    96, 97, 98, 109, 110, 260n23
Vargas, Gaspar de, 41
Vaughan, Thomas, 171–73, 174, 175, 176, 177
Vaux, W. S. W., 13, 26, 45, 242n6, 247n2
Vera Cruz (Mexico), and Drake's role in
    Hawkins affair, 35–36

Wagner, Henry, 62, 92, 107–14, 147, 200
Wallis, Helen, 22, 70, 71, 72–73
Walsingham, Francis, 22, 39–40, 113

Ward, Bob, 73, 77, 257–58n17
Washington, and possible sites for Drake's
    landing, 113. *See also* Neah Bay
Waterman, Thomas Talbot, 93, 98–99
West, Nettie, 280n2
Whale Cove (Oregon), 73–75, 77–78, 229,
    257n17
Wheat, Carl, 133, 270n3
Wheeler, Benjamin Ide, 91
White, Mrs. Gordon, 154–55
White, John, 123, 124
Whitehall map, 4–5, 70, 85
Whitsell, Leon, 133
Willamette Valley (Oregon), 190
Wilson, Woodrow, 101
Winsor, Justin, 73
Winter, George, 113
Winter, John, 29, 41, 42, 44, 48
Winter, Sir William, 113
Wolfe, Heather, 247n3
women, and cultural differences among
    indigenous groups of coastal Oregon,
    195. *See also* blood-letting; Maria
*World Encompasses by Sir Francis Drake,
    The. See* Drake, Sir Francis; Fletcher,
    Francis
Wright, Edward, 242n7

Xerores, Thomas, 50, 51, 54–55, 84. *See
    also* Oxenham, John

Yurok, and Drake's descriptions of
    housing of indigenous peoples, 200

Zarate, Don Francisco de, 56–57, 71,
    254n80